Lecture Notes in Computer Science 15545

The series Lecture Notes in Computer Science (LNCS), including its subseries Lecture Notes in Artificial Intelligence (LNAI) and Lecture Notes in Bioinformatics (LNBI), has established itself as a medium for the publication of new developments in computer science and information technology research, teaching, and education.

LNCS enjoys close cooperation with the computer science R & D community, the series counts many renowned academics among its volume editors and paper authors, and collaborates with prestigious societies. Its mission is to serve this international community by providing an invaluable service, mainly focused on the publication of conference and workshop proceedings and postproceedings. LNCS commenced publication in 1973.

Asbjørn Følstad · Symeon Papadopoulos ·
Theo Araujo · Effie L.-C. Law · Ewa Luger ·
Sebastian Hobert · Petter Bae Brandtzaeg
Editors

Chatbots and Human-Centered AI

8th International Workshop, CONVERSATIONS 2024
Thessaloniki, Greece, December 4–5, 2024
Revised Selected Papers

Springer

Editors
Asbjørn Følstad
SINTEF
Oslo, Norway

Theo Araujo
University of Amsterdam
Amsterdam, The Netherlands

Ewa Luger
University of Edinburgh
Edinburgh, UK

Petter Bae Brandtzaeg
University of Oslo and SINTEF
Oslo, Norway

Symeon Papadopoulos
CERTH-ITI
Thessaloniki, Greece

Effie L.-C. Law
Durham University
Durham, UK

Sebastian Hobert
TH Lübeck – University of Applied Sciences
Lübeck, Germany

ISSN 0302-9743 ISSN 1611-3349 (electronic)
Lecture Notes in Computer Science
ISBN 978-3-031-88044-5 ISBN 978-3-031-88045-2 (eBook)
https://doi.org/10.1007/978-3-031-88045-2

This Springer imprint is published by the registered company Springer Nature Switzerland AG
The registered company address is: Gewerbestrasse 11, 6330 Cham, Switzerland

Preface

Introduction

The rapid advances in AI have characterized digital technology development over the last year to the degree that AI is now taken up in services and applications across nearly all sectors and domains. This increasing availability of AI-based services, many of which feature chatbots as a user interface, combined with the growing emphasis on ensuring these systems align with users' needs and values, has fostered a growing interest in research on human-centred AI.

The CONVERSATIONS international workshop series has, since 2017, been an arena for sharing and discussing research on chatbots and conversational AI. In our eighth edition, we extended the scope of the workshop so as to cover also research on human-centred AI in its entirety. Hence, CONVERSATIONS 2024 gathered researchers and practitioners with an interest in chatbots and human-centred AI – including human-AI interaction, human-AI collaboration and decision making, trustworthy AI, and human-centred research on generative AI and large language models.

CONVERSATIONS 2024 took place December 4–5, 2024, at CERTH – the Centre for Research & Technology Hellas, in collaboration with SINTEF, University of Amsterdam, Durham University, University of Edinburgh, Lübeck University of Technology, and the University of Oslo.

In total, 136 participants from 29 countries registered for the workshop – 41 on-site, the remainder online.

Paper Invitation, Review, and Revision

The call for papers for CONVERSATIONS 2024 included five main areas of interest: Chatbot research and design, human-AI interaction, human-AI collaboration and decision making, trustworthy AI, and human-centred research on generative AI and large language models.

The call for papers was communicated through social media, relevant mailing lists, and to the network of researchers and practitioners associated with the CONVERSATIONS workshop series. Authors were invited to make four types of contributions: Full papers, short papers, position papers, and project presentations. Accepted full papers and short papers were included in these proceedings.

We received 37 submissions: 23 full papers, 11 short papers, and three position papers and project presentations. Full papers and short papers underwent a double-blind review process, position papers and project presentations underwent single-blind review. For each paper, three independent reviews were provided by program committee members. Each paper was also assigned a review lead from among the seven workshop organizers who summarized reviewer feedback and formulated meta-reviews. In case of missing reviews, these were provided by one of the organizers not processing the particular paper. The program committee members reviewed between one and three submissions each. The review leaders were responsible for between three and six submissions each. Acceptance decisions were made in two organizer meetings after all reviews had been provided. Two organizers were conflicted, with one submission each. These submissions were processed without insight from the conflicted organizers.

In total, twelve full papers and three short papers were accepted, five after minor revisions and ten after major revisions. Final acceptance followed a compliance check by the lead reviewer for the specific paper. When needed, one additional revision was requested. Acceptance rate was 44% (for full papers 52%, for short papers 27%).

Workshop Program and Outcomes

The workshop program comprised five paper sessions, with a total of 20 paper presentations, in addition to a keynote speaker.

The keynote speaker was Benjamin R. Cowan (University College Dublin). In his talk, Cowan addressed perspective taking, partner models, and user behaviour in conversational interface interaction.

These post-event proceedings included all presented full and short papers, are structured into three themes.

Under the first theme, *Understanding and Designing for Human-AI Interactions*, Anouck Braggaar, Florian Kunneman, and Emiel van Miltenburg present a study on patterns of breakdown in conversational AI. Wing Lok Yeung reports on research on using large language models to provide empathic response headers in conversations. Simon Rapp, Alexander Mädche, and Marcus Jainta present a work on hallucination detection in chatbots with large language models. Leon Hanschmann, Marvin Mokelke, and Alexander Mädche address how a conversational agent based on large language models can support so-called laddering interviews. Finally, Jeffin Siby and Effie Lai-Chong Law report on their study of using machine learning for emption recognition.

As part of the second theme, *Human-Centred AI in Education and Social Support*, Nikolaos Antonios Grammatikos, Evangelia Anagnostopoulou, and colleagues present an AI-powered learning companion. Kabir Olawore, Michael McTear, and Yaxin Bi report from their work on developing and evaluating a RAG-based university chatbot. Roel Boumans, Serge Thill, and colleagues discuss how a voice-based virtual agent can support users with memory impairments. Emma Mainza Chilufya, Mattias Arvola, and colleagues report on a social robot project aimed to strengthen reading motivation. Finally, Lazaros Tsolakis and Alexios Brailas report from their study of questions users ask ChatGPT with regards to romantic relationships.

The third theme, *Conversational AI for Citizens and Customers*, includes research on AI solutions to help and support users with civic and commercial needs. Concerning citizen support, two papers – the first by Thilo Dieing, the second by Nina van Zanten and Roel Boumans – concern AI-based voting assistants. Furthermore, Verena Traubinger, Sebastian Heil, and colleagues present a study of municipal chatbots in Germany. Concerning support in commercial service provision, Anna Grøndahl Larsen, Marita Skjuve, and colleagues present an investigation of user expectations concerning large language models in customer service chatbots, and Nele Pralat, Carolin Ischen, and Hilde Voorveld present a study on conversational AI patronage intentions.

The Best Paper Award for CONVERSATIONS 2024 was given after a juried process. From the accepted full papers, three were identified as nominees for the award based on their scores from the review process. These were 'Feeling Understood by AI: How Empathy Shapes Trust and Influences Patronage Intentions in Conversational AI' by Nele Pralat, Carolin Ischen, and Hilde Voorveld; 'The BookBot Project: Conceptual Design of a Social Robot Facilitating Reading Motivation' by Emma Mainza Chilufya, Mattias Arvola, Susanne Severinsson, Anna Martín Bylund, Linnéa Stenliden, Arezou Mortazavi, and Tom Ziemke; and 'AI-Driven Dialogue: Leveraging Generative AI in Conversational Agent Voting Advice Applications (CAVAAs)' by Thilo I. Dieing. The Best Paper Award was awarded to the last of the three: Thielo I. Dieing.

CONVERSATION 2024 was successful both with regards to the number and quality of submitted papers, the on-site presentations of the papers at the workshop, and the engagement of both on-site and online participants. We wish to thank all authors, program committee members, presenters, participants, and supporters for their contributions. We already look forward to CONVERSATIONS 2025.

December 2024

Asbjørn Følstad
Symeon Papadopoulos
Theo Araujo
Effie L.-C. Law
Ewa Luger
Sebastian Hobert
Petter Bae Brandtzaeg

Organization

General Chairs/Workshop Organizers

Asbjørn Følstad	SINTEF, Norway
Symeon Papadopoulos	Centre for Research and Technology Hellas, Greece
Theo Araujo	University of Amsterdam, The Netherlands
Effie L.-C. Law	Durham University, UK
Ewa Luger	University of Edinburgh, UK
Sebastian Hobert	Technische Hochschule Lübeck, Germany
Petter Bae Brandtzaeg	University of Oslo & SINTEF, Norway

Program Committee

Alexander Mädche	Karlsruhe Institute of Technology KIT, Germany
Ana Paula Chaves	Northern Arizona University, USA
Anna Grøndahl Larsen	SINTEF, Norway
Anouck Braggaar	Tilburg University, Netherlands
Apostolos Kostas	University of the Aegean, Greece
Ash Zhimiao Lee	Leiden University, The Netherlands
Bettina Minder	Lucerne School of Computer Sciences and Information Technology, Switzerland
Christine Liebrecht	Tilburg University, The Netherlands
Despoina Chatzakou	Centre for Research and Technology Hellas, Greece
Dimitra Anastasiou	Luxembourg Institute of Science and Technology, Luxembourg
Elmokhtar Mohamed Moussa	IDnow France, France
Eren Yildiz	University of Umeå, Sweden
Fabio Catania	MIT, USA
Frode Guribye	University of Bergen, Norway
Guy Laban	University of Glasgow, UK
Ioanna Georgia Eskiadi	Aristotle University of Thessaloniki, Greece
Jacob Penney	Northern Arizona University, USA
Jo Dugstad Wake	NORCE & University of Bergen, Norway
Jo Herstad	University of Oslo, Norway
Joel Wester	Aalborg University, Denmark

Kartik Mathur	Microsoft, Canada
Konstantinos Boletsis	SINTEF, Norway
Mairieli Wessel	Radboud University, The Netherlands
Marianne Wilson	Edinburgh Napier University, UK
Marisa Tschopp	scip, Switzerland
Natasha Dwyer	Victoria University, Australia
Nolwenn Bernard	University of Stavanger, Norway
Rajesh Kaluri	Vellore Institute of Technology, India
Roberta De Cicco	University of Urbino "Carlo Bo", Italy
Roel Boumans	Radboud University, The Netherlands
Sajid Ahmed	Saitama University, Japan
Samuel Rhys Cox	Aalborg University, Denmark
Sara Pidò	Politecnico di Milano, Italy
Siddharth Kashiramka	Amazon, USA
Stefan Schaffer	DFKI – German Research Center for Artificial Intelligence, Germany
Stella George	Athabasca University, Canada
Sviatlana Höhn	University of Luxembourg, Luxembourg
Ute Klotz	Lucerne University of Applied Sciences and Arts, Switzerland
Verena Traubinger	Chemnitz University of Technology, Germany
Yuhui Xu	Eindhoven University of Technology, The Netherlands
Zia Uddin	SINTEF, Norway

Contents

Understanding and Designing for Human-AI Interactions

Analyzing Patterns of Conversational Breakdown in Human-Chatbot Customer Service Conversations 3
Anouck Braggaar, Florian Kunneman, and Emiel van Miltenburg

Selecting Empathic Response Headers in Customer Support Conversations with LLM-Based Emotion Recognition 23
W. L. Yeung

Exploring the Effects of Consistency-Based Hallucination Detection for LLM-Based QA Chatbots: A Simulation Study 33
Simon Rapp, Alexander Maedche, and Marcus Jainta

LadderChat An LLM-Based Conversational Agent for Laddering Interviews 48
Leon Hanschmann, Marvin Mokelke, and Alexander Maedche

Can Machine Learning Models Recognise Emotions, Particularly Neutral, Better Than Humans? 66
Jeffin Siby and Effie Lai-Chong Law

Human-Centred AI in Education and Social Support

An AI-Powered Learning Companion for Adaptive and Personalized STEM Education 87
Nikolaos Antonios Grammatikos, Evangelia Anagnostopoulou, Dimitris Apostolou, and Gregoris Mentzas

Development and Evaluation of a University Chatbot Using Deep Learning: A RAG-Based Approach 96
Kabir Olawore, Michael McTear, and Yaxin Bi

A Voice-Enabled Intelligent Virtual Agent for People with Memory Impairments: Thematic Analysis of Focus Group Results 112
Roel Boumans, Serge Thill, Debby Gerritsen, and Tibor Bosse

The BookBot Project: Conceptual Design of a Social Robot Facilitating Reading Motivation 132
Emma Mainza Chilufya, Mattias Arvola, Susanne Severinsson, Anna Martín Bylund, Linnéa Stenliden, Arezou Mortazavi, and Tom Ziemke

Questions People Ask ChatGPT Regarding Their Romantic Relationships and What They Think About the Provided Answers: An Exploratory Study 150
Alexios Brailas and Lazaros Tsolakis

Conversational AI for Citizens and Customers

AI-Driven Dialogue: Leveraging Generative AI in Conversational Agent Voting Advice Applications (CAVAAs) 161
Thilo I. Dieing

First Aid for Europe – A Study on the Impact of Digital Voting Assistants on Young Adults During the Elections for the European Parliament in 2024 181
Nina van Zanten and Roel Boumans

An Analysis of Federal and Municipal Chatbots in Germany 200
Verena Traubinger, Sebastian Heil, Julián Grigera, Alejandra Garrido, Sonia Abhyankar, and Martin Gaedke

LLM-Powered Conversational AI in Customer Service: Users' Expectations and Anticipated Use 217
Anna Grøndahl Larsen, Marita Skjuve, Knut Kvale, and Asbjørn Følstad

Feeling Understood by AI: How Empathy Shapes Trust and Influences Patronage Intentions in Conversational AI 234
Nele Pralat, Carolin Ischen, and Hilde Voorveld

Author Index 261

Understanding and Designing for Human-AI Interactions

Analyzing Patterns of Conversational Breakdown in Human-Chatbot Customer Service Conversations

Anouck Braggaar[1(✉)], Florian Kunneman[2], and Emiel van Miltenburg[1]

[1] Tilburg University, PO Box 90153, 5000, LE Tilburg, The Netherlands
{a.r.y.braggaar,c.w.j.vanmiltenburg}@tilburguniversity.edu
[2] Utrecht University, Trans 10, 3512, JK Utrecht, The Netherlands
f.a.kunneman@uu.nl

Abstract. Many chatbots still struggle with correctly interpreting and responding to user enquiries. Therefore, it is important to figure out how and why chatbot-human conversations break down. In this study we analyzed features in user-utterances directly before a bot-initiated repair to determine their presence and prominence as possible predictors of conversational breakdowns. We used data from a real-life public transport customer service chatbot to demonstrate the errors that occur in actual deployed systems. The analysis shows that there are some features (such as commonness, outdated words, and unexpected words) that occur more often in utterances directly before a repair. Some features also correlate with each other and occur together, such as outdated words and subjectivity. By using feature analysis, many opportunities for improvement can be found either live (during the interaction) or afterwards.

Keywords: Chatbots · Customer service · Breakdowns · Features analysis

1 Introduction

Despite recent developments in the field of conversational AI, customers often encounter conversational breakdowns when chatting with a customer service chatbot. Many chatbots are not able to provide adequate answers to user requests [12]. According to the National Voice Monitor (2024), in the Netherlands only eight percent of user questions is correctly answered by the chatbot [49]. Although new possibilities involving generative AI should make it easier to prevent conversational breakdowns, companies are often hesitant to fully exploit this technology as they are afraid of the possible risks this will bring [49]. Consequently, many chatbots in customer service are often still intent-based (recognizing the user's intent by using natural language understanding [31]) or rule-based (following a pre-defined path and/or uses simple pattern-matching [31]).

Sometimes chatbots are deployed online at early stages of development for incremental improvement, however this approach can lead to frustration with the

A. Følstad et al. (Eds.): CONVERSATIONS 2024, LNCS 15545, pp. 3–22, 2025.
https://doi.org/10.1007/978-3-031-88045-2_1

user [15]. Conversational breakdowns in chatbot conversations are detrimental to user experience, often leading to user frustration [1] which could potentially lead to lower re-use intentions or an overall downgraded experience with chatbots. Therefore, these breakdowns should be avoided as much as possible. This paper aims to identify different predictors of conversational breakdowns in a real-world customer service chatbot.

Starting point. Our paper builds on earlier work by Reinkemeier and Gnewuch [40]. We also analyze conversations from a real-world task-oriented dialogue system. However, the domain and approach are different. Whereas Reinkemeier and Gnewuch [40] focus on user-chatbot interactions from an insurance company, we focus on user-chatbot interactions from a Dutch public transport company. Through an ongoing collaboration with this company, we are able to obtain large amounts of real-life data in the public transport domain. As Zumstein and Hundertmark [51] discuss, this is a very rich domain where chatbots typically offer many different services, from buying tickets to providing timetable information. Of course, offering a wide array of different services also means that there is more room for the chatbot to misunderstand the user's intentions, potentially leading to conversational breakdowns. We aim to identify different causes of those breakdowns.

Approach. Reinkemeier and Gnewuch [40] set out to create a classifier to predict the breakdown type based on four types of breakdowns ('*elaborated*', '*specific*', '*brief*', and '*cryptic*'). These breakdown types were detected by clustering user utterances with low intent recognition scores into four categories. Reinkemeier and Gnewuch [40] decided on four categories because this was the optimal number found in a pre-clustering based on agglomeration coefficients. After clustering they labeled the four categories based on the user utterances in the categories. The classifier was then able to compute the distance of a new user message to the cluster centers. While they show that this classifier can quite accurately predict these four categories [40], much information is lost by differentiating user utterances in four general categories. We initially also attempted to cluster the user-utterances, using the HDBSCAN clustering algorithm [35] with BERT embeddings to represent the different user utterances [46], but this method mostly lead to many noise points (points that could not be fitted in one of the clusters) and no meaningful clusters.[1] Thus, we took a step back: to better understand how breakdowns arise, we carried out a quantitative corpus analysis. This paper identifies several different properties of the user utterances that may lead to conversational breakdowns, and statistically compares the differences between messages that either do or do not result in repairs.

Research Question. We aim to zoom in on how user utterances prior to repair differ on the presence and prominence of particular features. This will facilitate a more fine-grained insight into factors that may influence non-understanding

[1] The algorithm mostly clustered on length. The code and results for the clustering can be found on GitHub.

and how to act upon this. With this analysis we will aim to answer the following question, **RQ**: To what extent are particular features useful as a signal of a conversational breakdown? By answering this question we will learn more about the capabilities of the system and will be able to see on which points it needs improvement. As we will see, simple features can be effective in finding different ways to improve existing task-oriented dialogue systems. The features can be used in real-time dialogue breakdown detection or used to assess where the chatbot could be improved. Our case-study highlights the abundance of low-hanging fruit in an already deployed commercial system that serves thousands of users everyday. It is likely that smaller providers of dialogue systems will benefit from these results as well.

2 Previous Work

2.1 Classification of Errors

Many papers try to find patterns in the kinds of breakdowns that occur in human-chatbot conversations. As a result, many overviews and taxonomies have been created that show what kind of breakdowns occur in (spoken) dialogue system interactions. Table 1 gives a comprehensive overview of some of the existing taxonomies. The table shows how the different categories relate to each other. Two main categories are often distinguished, misunderstanding (wrongly interpreting the user) and non-understanding (having no interpretation at all) [5,23]. Within this category multiple different categorizations have been made. For example, Higashinaka et al. [18,20] distinguish four categories of errors: (1) utterance-level (error in form of content of language [18]), (2) society-level (violating a social norm [18]), (3) response-level (system ignores how it should answer the user [18]), and (4) context-level (topic relevant and consistency [18]). Sanguinetti et al. [42] on the other hand make a distinction into four categories based on the maxims of Grice [16]: (1) quantity (the utterance should have sufficient information, not too much [16]), (2) manner (be clear about the utterance [16]), and (3) relation (utterance should be relevant to the conversation [16]). Within these categories, more specific error types can be distinguished such as an excess of information (within the quantity type). Lastly, Sanguinetti et al. [42] define a generic error class for all other errors and for non-cooperativity of the user (the user intentionally obstructing the system).

Other work creates an overview of errors based on a diverse background of research disciplines [39]. This involves errors in human-human communication and also human-computer communication. Paek [39] proposes that there are four levels that are necessary to reach understanding between conversation partners. If one or multiple of these levels fail, an error could occur. Different combinations of failing channels result in different kinds of errors [39], such as misunderstanding and non-understanding. There is also work focusing on the errors occurring specifically in spoken dialogue systems (e.g. [37]). Since different domains and modalities lead to different errors (e.g. speech recognition errors in spoken systems) and consequently different repairs (e.g. handovers to a human employee

Table 1. Categorization of chatbot and user errors. Based on and adapted from [5,18,20,22,23,42].

Error	Source	Bot	User	Description
Misunderstandings	[5,23]	✓	✓	Obtaining an incorrect understanding of the user utterance.
Utterance-level errors	[18,20]			
Quantity	[42]	✓	✓	Based on the maxim of quantity [16].
Lack of information	[18,20,42]	✓	✓	The message does not contain enough information to proceed.
Excess of information	[42]	✓	✓	The message contains too much information.
Manner	[42]	✓	✓	Based on maxim of manner [16].
Ill formed /general quality	[22,42]		✓	The utterance is not in a way the system can understand.
Indirect question	[42]		✓	Questions that seem implicit and indirect.
Non understandable	[18,20,22,42]		✓	A completely non-understandable/uninterpretable utterance.
Grammatical/word usage /expression error	[18,20,22,42]	✓		The utterance contains grammatical mistakes, unnatural expressions or a specific word usage.
Semantic error	[18,20]		✓	There are semantic mistakes, the utterance is not valid.
Wrong information	[18,20,22]		✓	The information in the utterance is wrong.
Society-level errors	[18,20]			
Lack of sociality	[18,20,22]	✓	✓	Contains undesirable speech, no considerations for the other.
Lack of common sense	[18,20,22]	✓	✓	Different opinion that is not similar to the general consensus.
Non-understandings	[5,23]	✓	✓	Not understanding anything the user says.
Response-level errors	[18,20]			
Context-level errors				
Relation	[42]	✓	✓	Based on maxim of relation [16].
Indirect response	[42]	✓	✓	Indirectly answering the previous question.
Ignoring	[18,20,22,42]	✓	✓	The participant ignores the previous utterance. In some cases also the answer type that is requested is ignored.
Ignoring expectations	[18,20]	✓		The bot might correctly answer the question but the answer might be lacking in what could be expected for such a question.
Repetition	[18,20,22,42]	✓	✓	Repeating the previous utterances.
Straight wrong response	[42]	✓	✓	A utterance that is not relevant.
Topic change	[18,20,22,42]	✓		The topic is unexpectedly changed.
Unclear intention	[18,20,22]	✓	✓	It is not clear why something is mentioned at that specific time in the conversation (although the topic can be appropriate).
Answering with question	[42]		✓	Answering a posed question with a new question.
(Self-)contradiction	[18,20,22]	✓	✓	Contradicting own utterance or the utterance of the other.
Generic	[42]			
Non-cooperativity	[42]		✓	Not providing requested information.
Other	[42]	✓	✓	Any other error.

in customer service), we focus on only one modality in one specific domain. In this paper we will analyze which of a selected set of features could potentially lead to an error and consequently repair. Although some of the types of errors in Table 1 can not directly be deduced from formal properties of utterances (such as society level errors), the cues to others (such as grammatical mistakes) can directly be deduced from the user utterance. These features can thus be seen as direct or indirect indicators of the error types.

2.2 Automatic Detection of Errors

The automatic detection of breakdowns has become a popular focus of study. One can either detect breakdowns by detecting patterns in large amounts of data and consequently update the system, or use knowledge about breakdowns and detect errors in real-time. The goal of the current study is to detect patterns in a large amount of data.

Bernard and Balog [3] for example automatically detect three types of breakdowns. They use the system logs of conversations between the system and a user simulator to automatically detect if there is a system failure that results in a dialogue breakdown. The authors consider three breakdowns in their study. First, 'system error' which identifies system bugs. Secondly 'dialogue of the deaf' which consists for example out of conversational loops with a system repeating the same utterance. Lastly, they identify 'conversation flow discontinuation' which includes unexpected utterances [3]. In the case of the last error they compare the intents to a dialogue flow to see if recognized intents line up.

The shared task 'dialogue breakdown detection challenge' [21] comes with the task to detect breakdowns in chat-oriented dialogue systems. This task, which has now been organized multiple times, sets as goal for participants to detect utterances that lead to breakdowns in data sets in both English and Japanese [19]. Participants get a small set of utterances as context and have to detect if the next system utterance would lead to a breakdown [21]. They need to label utterances into three categories: (1) no breakdown, (2) possible breakdown, and (3) breakdown [19]. The data were labeled by human workers by breakdown types [19]. Therefore participants were able to treat this as type of classification task, resulting in different approaches such as designing LSTMs [17] or BERT [44]. For the English data, results were close to human performance [19].

As mentioned in the introduction (Sect. 1), the current paper will expand on the work of Reinkemeier and Gnewuch [40]. They cluster user utterances that result in breakdown based on four features: (1) semantic weight, (2) unknown words, (3) word count and (4) words per sentence. The clusters are analyzed and named according to the information (texts) in the clusters. Cluster one contains elaborate messages (very long messages), two contains specific ones (specific questions that a chatbot might not even be able to answer), three contains brief messages (very short ones) and the last cluster contains cryptic messages (which contain many unknown words). With these clusters they create a classifier that is able to detect to what category the user message belongs during a conversation [40].

In this paper we aim to extend upon the work of Reinkemeier and Gnewuch [40] by extending the set of features with other features that might be indicative of breakdowns and consequently examining if feature analysis can be predictive of conversational breakdowns.

3 Methodology

In this study we used a top-down approach with features that might be a predictor for a breakdown. These features were then compared to a control set of user utterances that do not occur together with a breakdown. Below, we will first discuss the total dataset followed by the selection process for our repair and control set. In Sect. 3.2 the used features are discussed both in terms of their implementation as well as the associated expectations on how they could be predictive of a breakdown.

3.1 Data

For this study we used real conversational data where a chatbot answers questions from actual customers of a Dutch public transport company. The chatbot has been in use for an extended period of time before the data was sampled, and serves a high volume of interactions.[2] It is professionally maintained, with continuous updates to improve the quality of the conversations. Given the high quality of the chatbot, we expect that any persistent causes of conversational breakdowns are also likely to occur in similar chatbots.

General Properties. The data were sampled by the company for a period of one year (between January 2021 up and until January 2022). In total the data contained 108,370 distinct session IDs. Within these sessions not only the conversations are recorded but also (technical) user actions such as only starting the chat and immediately leaving. Excluding sessions with only technical actions results in a total of 108,141 conversations. The chatbot conversations are primarily in Dutch although it sometimes happens that a costumer asks a question in English. In about 12% of the conversations there is at least one utterance marked as English by the intent-recognizer. The technical user actions such as joining are not very informative if we want to calculate conversation length. Therefore these actions (joining, re-joining, and leaving the chat) were removed, which resulted in conversations with a length of on average 17.85 turns. This does include dialogue with the human agent after handover. The data were anonymized by replacing personal information by either *<FILTERED>* or in the case of numbers by zeros.

[2] We are not at liberty to disclose the exact usage frequency.

Chatbot Trigger Data. Next to the chat data we also obtained the training triggers from the chatbot. The training triggers contain the sentences on which the intent recognition of the bot is trained, grouped by topic (which is the intent name). For example, 'Kwijt' ('Lost') triggers the lost and found intent, 'Vraag over factuur' ('Question about invoice') triggers the invoices intent and 'Can we speak in English' triggers the English intent. The trigger data were collected around May 2023, and are not completely synchronized with the trigger data at the time of the chats themselves. Dialogue designers continually refine the training intents and triggers. This means that when the chats and triggers are collected there can be a discrepancy between the collected triggers and the triggers actually used during these chats. Nonetheless we think that the triggers sketch a sufficient picture of both the domain words as well as the out-of-domain words, as the triggers capture key patterns in the conversation which presumably are stable over time.

Utterances Before Repair Test Data. For the analyses of utterances that occur before a system-initiated repair a subset of the total data set was made. Data were selected by searching for pre-determined system initiated repairs.[3] These repairs are thus used as a proxy to automatically detect points of possible breakdowns. As this system is intent-based and conveys pre-determined responses to the user, this was an easy way to find points in the conversations were a possible breakdown occurred. This also makes analyzing the chatbot responses themselves less interesting as they are always following similar patterns.

We chose two system-initiated repairs that potentially could hint to a breakdown. These repairs are standard expressions of the system and therefore a reliable way to determine where a repair is initiated. We chose two of the most general repairs, where no sign of understanding is given by the system. We focus only on non-understanding as the system cannot guide the user in the correct direction to continue the conversation with the bot (no intent is detected). Other repairs that showed any understanding of the system have been omitted. This includes repairs like 'I think you have a question about a subscription ...' and then proceeding to give options about subscriptions. The following two repairs are selected:

1. The system does not understand the user and asks to rephrase the utterance, thereby hinting to make the new utterance short and concise ('Unfortunately I don't fully understand what you mean. Could you rephrase the question in different words? Tip: I understand short and concise questions the best.')
2. The system knows it is not able to help the user and suggest redirecting to a human employee. ('I'm sorry, I believe I can not help you yet. Shall I connect you with my colleague?')

Both the utterances show that the bot does not recognize the appropriate intent. The second seems to mostly follow on the first repair (no understanding) if the

[3] All code for data selection and clustering can be found on GitHub.

bot still does not recognize an intent, even after rephrasing by the user (they are labeled in the data as default fallback and default consecutive). The second one is actually a repair that redirects to the employee and signals that the bot is not capable of solving the users request. Redirecting can occur in two situations: (1) the bot does not understand, and (2) the bot recognizes the question but knows it is not capable to help the user. We see that this one is used frequently and with numerous different user utterances preceding it, signalling that there is (still) no understanding (no recognized intent) by the bot. In 9,591 unique conversations at least one of these two repairs occurred. A total of 11,913 user utterances are found to appear before a system-initiated repair. On average, the repairs occurs at turn 13.34. Most often a repair occurs at turn three which means that it is initiated after the first user utterance.

Utterances Not Before a Repair Control Data. We also randomly selected utterances that occurred in conversations that did not include one of the selected repairs. The same number of 11,913 user utterances were selected for this data set. These data function as a control set with which the utterances occurring before a repair can be compared. The utterances we selected for this data set occurred in the first, second or third user turn, all before a bot utterance. We selected these utterances early in the conversation because in many cases when a repair is normally introduced this is often at turn three. At the same time, we only selected those of conversations that took up at least eight turns, so that conversations that only consist out of a user joining, a greeting and then leaving are dismissed. We suspected that some of the turns might actually be button options, therefore we manually identified 25 utterances that turned out to be buttons (or a general phrase used for testing the system), and excluded these from the data set. It is a challenging task to select turns that are (possibly) well understood by the system, because only a manual inspection will tell if it is really a well understood turn.

3.2 Features

The data were analyzed based on a selection of features, using the study of Reinkemeier and Gnewuch [40] as a starting point. They worked with semantic weight, total word count, words per sentence and percentage of unknown words. The features used in this study can be found in the list below and have been chosen because they have been used in earlier work (such as Reinkemeir and Gnewuch [40]) or because there are unwritten assumptions that features such as these may result in breakdowns in intent-based dialogue systems.

Counts. The number of words (split on spaces), sentences (tokenized with sentence tokenizer from NLTK [4]) and characters in the utterance (includes all characters, also punctuation marks). Table 1 shows that an excess of information can lead to a conversational breakdown. Previous work by Braggaar et al. [7] shows that this particular error occurs often in chatbot customer service conversations. Therefore, we suspect that the longer the user utterances are, the more difficult it is for the intent-recognizer to correctly classify the appropriate user intent.

Sentiment. Polarity and subjectivity are calculated and used as features by using the Pattern library in Python [10]. Previous work shows that user sentiment influences the experience users have with a chatbot resulting in lower user satisfaction when a humanized chatbot is used [9]. Different factors such as not understanding the user or chatbots failing to properly respond could all potentially lead to frustration [8]. We suspect that user sentiment is not only the result of a breakdown but could also be a predictor to a breakdown. Users expressing frustration may indicate that the chatbot was not able to correctly respond to their utterances so far and that the conversation may eventually lead to a breakdown.

References. Referencing to external entities or entities described earlier in the conversation might raise issues for the system. The list of used (Dutch) reference words can be found on GitHub. Many task-oriented data sets have based their interactions on a model that only takes into account the current user utterance [25]. In this case the intent is recognized based on only one user utterance and the recognizer does not take into account the context. Jakobovits et al. [25] argue that systems should possess 'conversationality' that takes into account more than just the current user turn by for example being able to appropriately handle references. The dialogue system in this study also works mostly intent-based, so we assume not much context is taken into account when answering a single user question. Therefore, using (many) reference words might lead to a possible breakdown.

Commonness. A combination of commonness and unknown words is made to predict wrong interpretations. Words with high scores for commonness that are not in the training data of the bot could indicate a wrong interpretation. Commonness is calculated based on the occurrences of entities on Wikipedia.[4] Wikipedia is used to obtain a general picture of commonly used words in the Dutch language to show which content words are used by the customer that do not belong to this specific customer service domain.

We worked with commonness as it is defined and used in paper such as Meij et al. [36] and Kunneman and Van den Bosch [29].[5] Words get assigned a score based on the probability that the word is used as anchor text in Wikipedia [29,36]. When a word is common (highly likely in the Wikipedia data) but not in the bot training data, this is reflected by a count for commonness.

Common words that are frequently used but not present in the training data might indicate a possible reason for a conversational breakdown. Recent work into domain adaptation of intent recognition has shown that there are some limitations to applying an intent recognizer to a different domain due to

[4] A Wikipedia-dump was used from May 2023, this includes all Dutch Wikipedia data. To decide how common entities should be, we decided on a cutoff value of 0.25 for unigrams, 0.5 for bigrams and 0.75 for 3–5 grams

[5] We adapted and used code from https://github.com/fkunneman/DTE/blob/master/dte/classes/commonness.py.

being out of scope [2]. Similar limitations could occur with out-of-domain vocabulary. Research has also shown that users often have high expectations of the chatbot's capabilities, ask very complex question or switch between multiple topics [30]. This could mean that customer vocabulary and chatbot vocabulary do not match, which leads to breakdowns.

Spelling/grammar. LanguageTool [38] is used to count different errors in the utterances. A selection was made to include errors that possibly have a large impact on how the chatbot understands the user, including for example typos and repetitions. Not all categories on the LanguageTool webpage and the LanguageTool source code have consistent examples or explanations. Therefore, the selection consisted out of items that have clear explanations and are useful in the context of chatbot errors (see Table 1). We included the following categories:[6]

- *Loan words.* Words or sentence structures adopted from other languages such as English.
- *Offensive.* Offensive or inappropriate language
- *Proper nouns.* Names of people.
- *Grammar.* Wrong inflections of words, missing letters etc.
- *Repetition.* Repetition of words.
- *Readability.* Very long words.
- *Typos.* Typing mistakes.
- *Outdated.* Outdated (old-fashioned) words, not used very often anymore.
- *Dyslexia.* Mistakes relating to dyslexia such as writing 'mir' instead of 'meer' ('more').
- *Form errors.* For example 'als/dan' (confusing 'if' and 'then').
- *Confused words.* Mixing up words or phrases.
- *Unexpected.* Unexpected sequences of words.
- *Full sentence.* Complete sentence with error such as the wrong inflection of a verb.
- *Other.* Other rules that do not fit a category, such as a sentence unexpectedly ending.

We suspect that the intent-recognizer has not been trained specifically to handle some of these features. For example with outdated words, older users may use a different vocabulary than younger uses which might not have been taken into account by the conversational designers (previous work shows that age is an important factor related to vocabulary size [26]). Spelling and grammatical mistakes might impact the correct recognition of intents and therefore lead to a breakdown. Martinovsky and Traum [34] for example show that multiple features such as ellipsis could lead to user frustration and possibly breakdowns in human-machine interaction. In addition, Jakobovits et al. [25] argue that systems should be able to normalize utterances, for example reducing the impact of typos for intent recognition. However, instead of normalizing the texts, others have argued to adapt the tools themselves to be able to handle such texts [11].

[6] More extended explanations of categories can be found on the LanguageTool website and in the LanguageTool Dutch grammar source code.

3.3 Analysis

To begin with, a comparison is made with utterances that do not occur before a repair (control data) by examining the frequency ratio. To see if the means of the features between test and control data significantly differ, a t-test was conducted with SciPy [45] with Holm-Bonferroni [24] correction in statsmodels [43] to correct for testing multiple features. Secondly, the correlations between the features in the test set were calculated to examine how often features occur together and the usefulness of certain combinations of features.

4 Results

We examined the presence and prominence of a selected set of features in a dataset with user utterances occurring before a repair (the test data). The results are compared to a data set that contains user utterances occurring in conversations without any of the used repairs (the control data). Both data sets contained 11,913 user utterances (see Sect. 3.1 for more information).

4.1 Uninformative Features

Table 2 shows the means and standard deviations of the features of the test data and the frequency ratios and difference in means between test and control utterances. Some features do not occur in both datasets at all (full sentence, grammar, offensive and proper nouns). While others rarely occur, namely those having a mean close to zero (such as loanwords). The readability feature only occurs in the test data and not in the control set (which results in a division by 0). The feature readability is only detected twice in the data, both in utterances in which the user adds a complete web page. These texts are copy-pasted without the proper use of spaces (for example between different headers on the web page).

4.2 Differences Between Conversations with and Without Repairs

We conducted multiple t-tests to examine if the means of the two data sets significantly ($\alpha <= 0.05$) differ per feature. The results are provided in Table 2, where asterisks indicate whether the difference between the means is significant. The frequency ratio provides another indication of the size of the difference.

The frequency ratio of the features is often above one, which means that the feature is more prominent in the pre-repair test data than in the control set. Some of the features have a remarkably high ratio (such as commonness and dyslexia), suggesting that these features are far more prominent in the pre-repair data. The only feature that has a ratio below one (indicating that the feature is less prominent in the pre-repair data) is reference words. This is striking as one would expect more reference words in utterances that cause a breakdown. The frequency ratio of the counts is very close to one, meaning that it occurs almost as often in the control data as in the test data (there are some zero counts for words/characters/sentences as users sometimes only pressed enter).

Table 2. Means, standard deviations, effect size (Cohen's d), difference between means (test - control), frequency ratios between repair and control data (* if p-value <= 0.05).

	Feature	Mean	SD	Effect size	Δ Mean	Frequency ratio
Counts	Word count	16.745	38.818	0.258	7.554*	0.997
	Character count	104.891	249.083	0.254	47.447*	0.997
	Sentence count	1.755	2.226	0.282	0.480*	0.997
Sentiment	Polarity	−0.005	0.165	0.016	0.002	1.362
	Subjectivity	0.150	0.276	0.175	0.045*	1.195
References	Reference words	1.161	2.116	0.109	0.195*	0.759
Commonness	Commonness	0.031	0.218	0.134	0.023*	3.071
Spelling/grammar	Dyslexia	0.002	0.046	0.036	0.001*	4.000
	Outdated	0.031	0.254	0.118	0.023*	2.717
	Repetition	0.007	0.091	0.058	0.004*	2.515
	Loanwords	0.001	0.035	0.018	0.001	2.333
	Other	0.003	0.065	0.040	0.002*	2.312
	Form errors	0.002	0.041	0.021	0.001	2.125
	Unexpected	0.022	0.170	0.091	0.013*	2.120
	Confused words	0.008	0.100	0.050	0.004*	1.957
	Typos	1.153	4.692	0.169	0.631*	1.737
	Full sentence	0.000	0.000	-	0.000	-
	Grammar	0.000	0.000	-	0.000	-
	Offensive	0.000	0.000	-	0.000	-
	Proper nouns	0.000	0.000	-	0.000	-
	Readability	0.000	0.026	0.018	0.000	Division by 0

Most of the means differ significantly, except for form errors and loanwords, these also very rarely occur in the test data. But, the effect sizes of all features are (very) low, suggesting limited differences between the groups. For words, the test data returns a mean of 16.7450 while for the control data the mean is 9.2250, which is quite a bit lower. We suspect that people sometimes overload the chatbot by giving an excess of information (see Table 1).

4.3 Correlations Between Features

Figure 1 shows the correlations between different features for the test data. We have removed the features that did not occur in the data at all (full sentence, grammar, offensive, proper nouns). Examining the correlations can shed light on how often features occur together and if it is useful to take into account these combinations for further improvement of the system.

Most correlations are quite low. However, the correlations with the items that count words, sentences and characters are in many cases quite high. This makes sense as one, for example, could expect more typos when sentences get extended. The correlation between subjectivity and reference words is also quite high, but this follows logically from how these features are measured. Pattern follows a rule-based approach to measure polarity and subjectivity [14], which possibly overlaps with the reference words list the authors compiled.

There are some interesting combinations to be found in this figure. Most of these combinations comprise either the subjectivity or reference words features. An example of an utterance with a high score for subjectivity and two counts of outdated words is someone explaining that he wants a refund. Two outdated words stand out immediately, namely 'aldaar' ('there') and 'hetgeen' ('which'), both words referring to either something in a previous sentence or in the same sentence. It can be questioned if the bot would stumble on these utterances as they do not convey any meaning on their own. An utterance that includes high counts for reference words, commonness and unexpected words is from a user complaining about a bike accident with a tourist. The user shares detailed information about the incident and ends with 'I will wait for your response. (...) Regards, (...)'. From the way the utterance is formulated it is not clear if the user requires a response. An inspection of the data shows that the user merely wants the complaint to reach the complaint division of the company. Overall, the relatively low correlations show that these errors do not occur together very frequently, indicating that it might be worth focusing on single predictors when creating repairs.

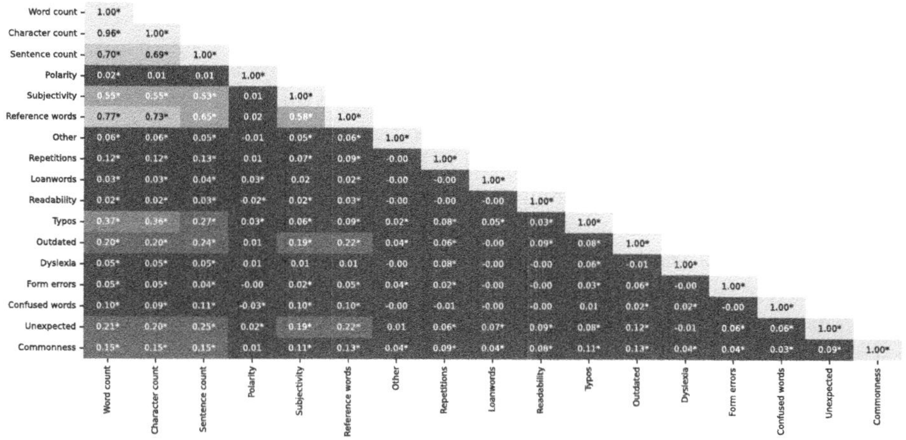

Fig. 1. Feature correlation of the utterances before a repair. * if p-value <= 0.05.

5 Discussion

This research aimed at exploring user utterances that lead to a repair and consequently could lead to a conversational breakdown. By examining the characteristics of the utterances by creating simple features, we set out to investigate if these can actually be used to either prevent breakdowns or repair them using this information.

We decided on multiple features that could be predictive of a breakdown. Interestingly, the results (Sect. 4) show that there are actually differences in the occurrence of features between utterances before a repair (test data) and utterances without repair (control data). Many features actually occur much more in utterances before a repair, suggesting that these features might be indicative for a possible breakdown. Similarly, the mean word count is almost twice as high for utterances directly before a repair. This suggests that users present too much information to the system (see Table 1, excess of information is an identified error [42]). Consequently, counting the number of words is a quick win and a more fine-grained analysis might not be necessary. To some extent, the results of the feature analysis could be traced back to the results of Reinkemeier and Gnewuch [40] in which too much information belongs to their 'elaborate' category. In comparison, an advantage of our more fine-grained selection of features is that certain inferences can be made from their combinations. Individual features provide a clearer picture of the difficulties in understanding. Combinations, such as an elaborate message with unknown common words, can be even more informative. Such insights can be used to give a more informative response to the user about the cause for non-understanding. Yet it remains to be tested whether it is actually necessary to provide more information or if 'be brief' is enough.

5.1 Limitations

The first limitation of this study is that deployed chatbots are not static objects. Since the chatbot is continuously updated to improve the service, it is a moving target. For example, we have seen that the training (trigger) data and the chatbot conversations are not obtained at the same time and do not completely line up. We see for example that at the time of the conversations there was a Covid-19 intent, but this was no longer included in the training. These issues make it harder to study the exact causes of conversational breakdowns. Still it is important to work with ecologically valid data. Thus we believe that the development of best practices for dealing with changes over time is an important research problem.

There are also many different ways to implement these features and the existing methods are not specifically designed for this kind of data. The choices made in implementation thus influence the results of the feature detection. For example, a tool like LanguageTool does not operate flawlessly, especially in this case where the data sometimes do not consist out of 'regular' full sentences. Other tools could be considered in the future such as T-Scan [32] to see how these specific implementations impact the results.

Data preprocessing also influenced some of the features. Due to the nature of the data, we were given a previously anonymized data set. Unfortunately, not in all cases anonymization was done correctly. In some cases personal information was still in the data, in other cases other words (like nouns or articles) are removed. This potentially impacts the derived features.

Creating an Anonymized Data Set. One of the key issues we are dealing with in this paper is the nature of the data. We would like to share the data for reproducibility purposes, but as the data are private and obtained through a company, we cannot make all of the data public. Data anonymization is often seen as a complex task [33], with many challenges for unstructured data [47]. Previous approaches such as Deperson have been created to anonymize sensitive customer data [6]. However, these approaches are not 100% flawless and can not ensure complete privacy. This poses challenges for sharing the data while maintaining complete privacy for both the users and the company. Consequently, we decided to make the features accessible instead of the complete data set. In a way, the feature vectors are a proxy to the complete sentences. Because this no longer contains private information, these data can actually be made available (see GitHub). We also created a broader dataset out of the data by including the feature vector of the sentence before a repair, the type of repair and the sentence directly after a repair. This makes at least part of this study reproducible without revealing private information.

5.2 Future Work

The method used in this paper can be applied to other datasets, datasets in other languages or other 'proxies' from the same data set. So, for example other events that happen in the data can be selected, such as a chatbot conveying misunderstanding and returning options to the user (indicated by pre-programmed responses). Of course, the results might be different, but we suspect that some of the patterns will hold for example for other chatbots or other languages (such as the length of the utterances or typos).

This study focused completely on analysis of an existing data set. However, another factor that could be taken into account in the future is how users actually perceive these conversational breakdowns and if this influences their overall satisfaction and experience with the chatbot. In the current study we analyzed user utterance for potential cues for a breakdown, but we do not know how users actually perceive this breakdown and if they have any ideas why this breakdown happens. It would be interesting to know the perceptions of users that interact with a system that breaks down.

Even with the newer models (large language model (LLM) based bots) it could happen that the chatbot misunderstands the user. Wester et al. [48] show that there are still limitations to the capabilities of these large language model based chatbots, both in terms of technical limitations or policy restrictions. It remains relevant to study the causes of breakdowns and explain what went wrong, but the indicators of a possible breakdown are harder to distinguish in LLM conversations. In the future, research should focus on when and how LLM-bots break down, be it through automatic or through manual analysis.

5.3 Practical Implications

Can we actually prevent any mistake from happening, or should we learn to deal with them in an appropriate way? The analysis of the features showed that some of them are more indicative than others. This information can be used to customize repairs. When a word is for example common but not in domain (commonness) the chatbot could directly show that this word is potentially the problem. Customers appreciate repairs that actually acknowledge the error [1, 41]. Similarly, providing options and showing uncertainty has been shown to reduce the number of inadequate responses [13]. Work on LLMs shows that it matters how these models express uncertainty in terms of perceived trust, reliance and performance [27]. Similarly, Wester et al. [48] show that it matters how a LLM-based chatbot conveys its capabilities when denying a user help with their request.

Using feature analysis in a live-chat can therefore be seen as a viable solution to help guide the conversation. Some of the errors on the other hand (excess of information by for example copy pasting a complete webpage) might be more on the user side and could be prevented by educating the user on the capabilities of the bots. Yeh et al. [50] for example study how users can be guided into using chatbots based on guidance-types and guidance-timings, showing that each combination has its pros and cons.

Some of these errors in the analysis give us insights in what users expect the chatbot to do. There is inevitably a distance between the bot and the user in terms of what the user expects and what the system is actually capable of doing. Therefore, in designing these systems, there should be a focus on reducing this distance [28]. The features can thus be used by developers to optimize the system but also for customizing repairs during the conversation.

6 Conclusion

This study has shown the variety of user utterances that lead to a system-initiated repair. We set out to determine to what extent the selected features are useful as a signal of a conversational breakdown. Feature analysis shows that there are some features (such as commonness, outdated words, and unexpected words) that occur more often in utterances directly before a repair. Some features also correlate with each other and occur together, such as commonness and subjectivity. The method shows that simple features can indicate the source of a conversational breakdown in the user utterance. This method can be used by chatbot developers to detect the source of common errors that occur in chatbot conversations either live during the interaction or afterwards.

Acknowledgments. This study was funded by the Smooth Operators project (NWO; KIVI.2019.009). The authors would like to thank Christine Liebrecht for providing feedback.

Disclosure of Interests. There are no competing interests.

References

1. Ashktorab, Z., Jain, M., Liao, Q.V., Weisz, J.D.: Resilient chatbots: repair strategy preferences for conversational breakdowns. In: Proceedings of the 2019 CHI Conference on Human Factors in Computing Systems, pp. 1–12 (2019)
2. Atuhurra, J., Kamigaito, H., Watanabe, T., Nichols, E.: Domain adaptation in intent classification systems: a review. arXiv preprint arXiv:2404.14415 (2024)
3. Bernard, N., Balog, K.: Identifying breakdowns in conversational recommender systems using user simulation. In: Proceedings of the 6th ACM Conference on Conversational User Interfaces, pp. 1–10 (2024)
4. Bird, S., Klein, E., Loper, E.: Natural Language Processing with Python: Analyzing Text with the Natural Language Toolkit. O'Reilly Media Inc., Sebastopol (2009)
5. Bohus, D., Rudnicky, A.I.: Sorry, I didn't catch that! An investigation of non-understanding errors and recovery strategies. In: Recent Trends in Discourse and Dialogue, pp. 123–154 (2008)
6. Borovits, N., Bardelloni, G., Tamburri, D.A., Van Den Heuvel, W.J.: Anonymization-as-a-service: the service center transcripts industrial case. In: International Conference on Service-Oriented Computing, pp. 261–275. Springer, Cham (2023)
7. Braggaar, A., Verhagen, J., Martijn, G., Liebrecht, C.: Conversational repair strategies to cope with errors and breakdowns in customer service chatbot conversations. In: Følstad, A., et al. (eds.) Chatbot Research and Design, pp. 23–41. Springer, Cham (2024)
8. Chhabra, S., Kaushal, V., Girija, S.: Determining the causes of user frustration in the case of conversational chatbots. Behav. Inf. Technol. 1–19 (2024)
9. Crolic, C., Thomaz, F., Hadi, R., Stephen, A.T.: Blame the bot: anthropomorphism and anger in customer-chatbot interactions. J. Mark. **86**(1), 132–148 (2022)
10. De Smedt, T., Daelemans, W.: Pattern for Python. J. Mach. Learn. Res. **13**(1), 2063–2067 (2012)
11. Eisenstein, J.: What to do about bad language on the internet. In: Vanderwende, L., Daumé III, H., Kirchhoff, K. (eds.) Proceedings of the 2013 Conference of the North American Chapter of the Association for Computational Linguistics: Human Language Technologies, pp. 359–369. Association for Computational Linguistics, Atlanta, Georgia (2013). https://aclanthology.org/N13-1037
12. Følstad, A., et al.: Future directions for chatbot research: an interdisciplinary research agenda. Computing **103**(12), 2915–2942 (2021)
13. Følstad, A., Taylor, C.: Conversational repair in chatbots for customer service: The effect of expressing uncertainty and suggesting alternatives. In: International Workshop on Chatbot Research and Design, pp. 201–214. Springer, Cham (2019)
14. Gatti, L., van Stegeren, J.: Improving Pattern.nl sentiment analysis. In: 30th Meeting on Computational Linguistics in The Netherlands, CLIN 2020 (2020)
15. van der Goot, M.J., Hafkamp, L., Dankfort, Z.: Customer service chatbots: a qualitative interview study into the communication journey of customers. In: International Workshop on Chatbot Research and Design, pp. 190–204. Springer, Cham (2020)
16. Grice, H.P.: Logic and conversation. In: Speech Acts, pp. 41–58. Brill (1975)
17. Hendriksen, M., Leeuwenberg, A., Moens, M.F.: LSTM for dialogue breakdown detection: exploration of different model types and word embeddings. In: Increasing Naturalness and Flexibility in Spoken Dialogue Interaction: 10th International Workshop on Spoken Dialogue Systems, pp. 443–453. Springer, Cham (2021)

18. Higashinaka, R., Araki, M., Tsukahara, H., Mizukami, M.: Integrated taxonomy of errors in chat-oriented dialogue systems. In: Li, H., et al. (eds.) Proceedings of the 22nd Annual Meeting of the Special Interest Group on Discourse and Dialogue, pp. 89–98. Association for Computational Linguistics, Singapore and Online (2021). https://doi.org/10.18653/v1/2021.sigdial-1.10, https://aclanthology.org/2021.sigdial-1.10
19. Higashinaka, R., et al.: Overview of the dialogue breakdown detection challenge 4. In: Increasing Naturalness and Flexibility in Spoken Dialogue Interaction: 10th International Workshop on Spoken Dialogue Systems, pp. 403–417. Springer, Cham (2021)
20. Higashinaka, R., Funakoshi, K., Araki, M., Tsukahara, H., Kobayashi, Y., Mizukami, M.: Towards taxonomy of errors in chat-oriented dialogue systems. In: Proceedings of the 16th Annual Meeting of the Special Interest Group on Discourse and Dialogue, pp. 87–95. Association for Computational Linguistics, Prague, Czech Republic (2015). https://doi.org/10.18653/v1/W15-4611, https://aclanthology.org/W15-4611
21. Higashinaka, R., Funakoshi, K., Kobayashi, Y., Inaba, M.: The dialogue breakdown detection challenge: task description, datasets, and evaluation metrics. In: Calzolari, N., et al. (eds.) Proceedings of the Tenth International Conference on Language Resources and Evaluation (LREC'16), pp. 3146–3150. European Language Resources Association (ELRA), Portorož, Slovenia (May 2016). https://aclanthology.org/L16-1502
22. Higashinaka, R., Mizukami, M., Funakoshi, K., Araki, M., Tsukahara, H., Kobayashi, Y.: Fatal or not? Finding errors that lead to dialogue breakdowns in chat-oriented dialogue systems. In: Proceedings of the 2015 Conference on Empirical Methods in Natural Language Processing, pp. 2243–2248. Association for Computational Linguistics, Lisbon, Portugal (2015). https://doi.org/10.18653/v1/D15-1268, https://aclanthology.org/D15-1268
23. Hirst, G., McRoy, S., Heeman, P., Edmonds, P., Horton, D.: Repairing conversational misunderstandings and non-understandings. Speech Commun. **15**(3), 213–229 (1994). https://doi.org/10.1016/0167-6393(94)90073-6, https://www.sciencedirect.com/science/article/pii/0167639394900736, special issue on Spoken dialogue
24. Holm, S.: A simple sequentially rejective multiple test procedure. Scand. J. Stat. 65–70 (1979)
25. Jakobovits, A.S., Piccinno, F., Altun, Y.: What did you say? Task-oriented dialog datasets are not conversational!? arXiv preprint arXiv:2203.03431 (2022)
26. Keuleers, E., Stevens, M., Mandera, P., Brysbaert, M.: Word knowledge in the crowd: measuring vocabulary size and word prevalence in a massive online experiment. Q. J. Exp. Psychol. **68**(8), 1665–1692 (2015). https://doi.org/10.1080/17470218.2015.1022560, pMID: 25715025
27. Kim, S.S., Liao, Q.V., Vorvoreanu, M., Ballard, S., Vaughan, J.W.: "I'm not sure, but...": examining the impact of large language models' uncertainty expression on user reliance and trust. In: The 2024 ACM Conference on Fairness, Accountability, and Transparency, pp. 822–835 (2024)
28. Kocaballi, A.B., Coiera, E., Berkovsky, S.: Revisiting habitability in conversational systems. In: Extended Abstracts of the 2020 CHI Conference on Human Factors in Computing Systems, pp. 1–8 (2020)
29. Kunneman, F., Van den Bosch, A.: Open-domain extraction of future events from twitter. Nat. Lang. Eng. **22**(5), 655–686 (2016). https://doi.org/10.1017/S1351324916000036

30. Kvale, K., Sell, O.A., Hodnebrog, S., Følstad, A.: Improving conversations: lessons learnt from manual analysis of chatbot dialogues. In: Følstad, A., et al. (eds.) Chatbot Research and Design, pp. 187–200. Springer, Cham (2020)
31. Luo, B., Lau, R.Y., Li, C., Si, Y.W.: A critical review of state-of-the-art chatbot designs and applications. Wiley Interdisc. Rev. Data Min. Knowl. Discov. **12**(1), e1434 (2022)
32. Maat, H.P., et al.: T-scan: a new tool for analyzing Dutch text. Comput. Linguist. Netherlands J. **4**, 53–74 (2014)
33. Mackey, E.: A best practice approach to anonymization. In: Handbook of Research Ethics and Scientific Integrity, pp. 323–343 (2020)
34. Martinovsky, B., Traum, D.: The error is the clue: breakdown in human-machine interaction. In: Proceedings of the ISCA Workshop on Error Handling in Spoken Dialogue Systems, pp. 11–17 (2003)
35. McInnes, L., Healy, J., Astels, S.: HDBScan: hierarchical density based clustering. J. Open Source Softw. **2**(11) (2017). https://doi.org/10.21105/joss.00205
36. Meij, E., Weerkamp, W., De Rijke, M.: Adding semantics to microblog posts. In: Proceedings of the fifth ACM International Conference on Web Search and Data Mining, pp. 563–572 (2012)
37. Möller, S., Engelbrecht, K.P., Oulasvirta, A.: Analysis of communication failures for spoken dialogue systems. In: Eighth Annual Conference of the International Speech Communication Association (2007)
38. Naber, D., et al.: A rule-based style and grammar checker (2003)
39. Paek, T.: Toward a taxonomy of communication errors. In: ISCA Tutorial and Research Workshop on Error Handling in Spoken Dialogue Systems (2003)
40. Reinkemeier, F., Gnewuch, U.: Designing effective conversational repair strategies for chatbots. In: ECIS (2022)
41. Rheu, M., Shin, J.Y., Peng, W., Huh-Yoo, J.: Systematic review: trust-building factors and implications for conversational agent design. Int. J. Hum.-Comput. Interact. **37**(1), 81–96 (2021)
42. Sanguinetti, M., et al.: Annotating errors and emotions in human-chatbot interactions in Italian. In: The 14th Linguistic Annotation Workshop, pp. 1–12. Association for Computational Linguistics (2020)
43. Seabold, S., Perktold, J.: Statsmodels: econometric and statistical modeling with Python. In: 9th Python in Science Conference (2010)
44. Sugiyama, H.: Dialogue Breakdown Detection Using BERT with Traditional Dialogue Features, pp. 419–427. Springer, Singapore (2021). https://doi.org/10.1007/978-981-15-9323-9_39
45. Virtanen, P., et al.: SciPy 1.0: fundamental algorithms for scientific computing in Python. Nat. Methods **17**, 261–272 (2020). https://doi.org/10.1038/s41592-019-0686-2
46. de Vries, W., van Cranenburgh, A., Bisazza, A., Caselli, T., Noord, G.v., Nissim, M.: BERTje: a Dutch BERT model. arXiv:1912.09582 (2019). http://arxiv.org/abs/1912.09582
47. Weitzenboeck, E.M., Lison, P., Cyndecka, M., Langford, M.: The GDPR and unstructured data: Is anonymization possible? Int. Data Privacy Law **12**(3), 184–206 (2022)
48. Wester, J., Schrills, T., Pohl, H., van Berkel, N.: "As an AI language model, I cannot": investigating LLM denials of user requests. In: Proceedings of the CHI Conference on Human Factors in Computing Systems, pp. 1–14 (2024)
49. Y.digital/Direct Research: Nationale voice monitor 2024 (2024). https://www.y.digital/resources/nationale-voice-monitor-2024, y.digital

50. Yeh, S.F., et al.: How to guide task-oriented chatbot users, and when: a mixed-methods study of combinations of chatbot guidance types and timings. In: Proceedings of the 2022 CHI Conference on Human Factors in Computing Systems, pp. 1–16 (2022)
51. Zumstein, D., Hundertmark, S.: Communicating and transacting with chatbots: insights from public transport. In: Proceedings of the International Conference on WWW/Internet 2017 and Applied Computing, December 2017, pp. 55–62 (2017)

Selecting Empathic Response Headers in Customer Support Conversations with LLM-Based Emotion Recognition

W. L. Yeung(✉)

Saint Francis University, Hong Kong SAR, China
wlyeung@sfu.edu.hk

Abstract. This research considers the task of automatically adding empathic headers (e.g., "Sorry to hear that.") to agent responses in customer support conversations. We employ a task-oriented dialogue (TOD) response selection model which allows response headers to be selected from existing corpora of conversations. Since the model is not fine-tuned with information about emotions in tweets, it is supplemented by filtering based on emotion annotations. The open-sourced LLM Llama 3.1 is employed for providing these annotations. We devise an experiment to evaluate this approach by automatic means. The preliminary results are discussed.

Keywords: Response selection · Emotion classification · Large language model · Task-oriented dialogue

1 Introduction

Short text social media such as X (formerly Twitter) and Weibo became popular platforms for customers around late 2000's to approach brands for help by expressing their issues in public tweets [17]. Communication researchers and linguists analyse brands' responses and find that they offer not only information and tangible (instrumental) support but also intangible support targeted at customers' emotions [9,23]. [23] refer to such emotional support as saying (and doing) things to make another feel loved and bolster the latter's sense of self-worth. For instance, brands' support agents often begin their responses by saying "Glad to help.", "I understand your frustration.", "We apologize for this experience.", etc. [5] call these expressions "emotional prefixes", "empathy expressions" and "emotional response headers". Support agents are usually trained in conversational skills and are able to formulate these expressions with *empathy* [12] which is the ability to sense others' emotions and be affected by them [1].

Based on conversation datasets collected from these platforms, machine learning researchers have been studying various deep learning approaches [29,33] to modelling customer support conversations with the aim to generate empathic responses to customer support requests [11,15,37]. These models typically

A. Følstad et al. (Eds.): CONVERSATIONS 2024, LNCS 15545, pp. 23–32, 2025.
https://doi.org/10.1007/978-3-031-88045-2_2

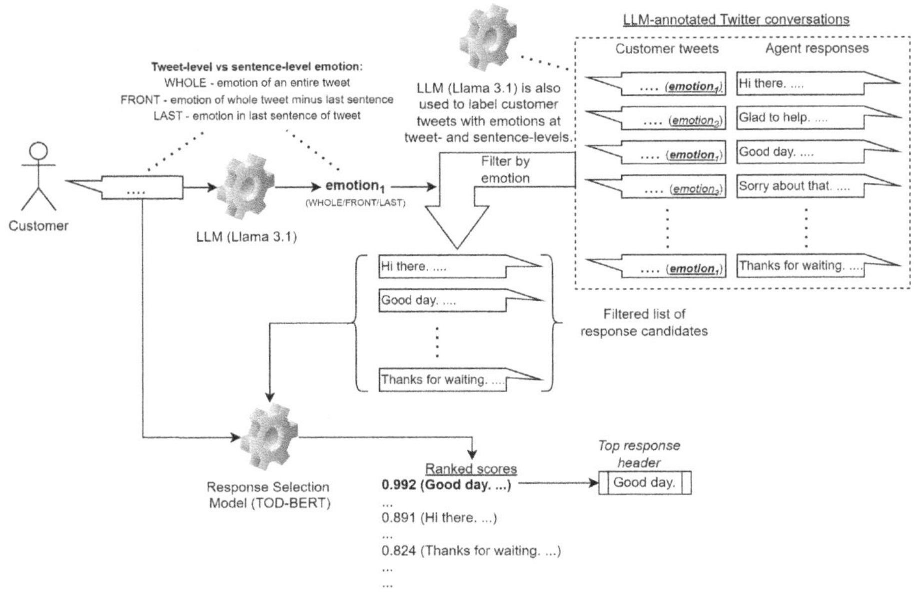

Fig. 1. Overview of the response header selection process

involve recognising emotions expressed in customer tweets as additional inputs to the process of response generation [30].

Recently, large language models (LLMs) have shown promise for emotion recognition in conversations [34]. In the present study, we are interested in using an open-sourced LLM to assist support agents in formulating their response tweets with appropriate empathic headers. These headers are derived from some existing corpora of support conversations. This is akin to the response selection task [13,35] although we are only concerned with providing the header part of a response tweet for the purpose of offering emotional support. Given the header, the support agent can just focus on providing tangible support (such as links to additional resources) in the rest of the tweet.

The response header selection task in this study is actually performed by TOD-BERT [35], a response selection model trained with multiple datasets of task-oriented dialogues which cover a wide variety of tasks and services. Given a customer tweet, the role of the LLM is to recognise the emotion(s) expressed in the tweet which can be used to filter down the list of candidate response headers. Figure 1 illustrates the use of the LLM-based filter in the response header selection process. Note that emotions are recognised and annotated at both *tweet-level* and *sentence-level*. The reason is that despite technical length restriction on a Twitter tweet, [24] show that customers often express themselves in a tweet with multiple sentences which can be labelled with different emotions [2].

To assess the efficacy of this approach, we devise an experiment to measure how well it can help improve response header selection according to recall accuracy metrics [35,38]. We explain detail of the experiment including definition of the metrics in Sect. 3. Section 4 presents our preliminary results. Section 5 provides a conclusion and discusses further work.

2 Related Work

2.1 Twitter Customer Support Conversations

Twitter (rebranded as X in 2023) originated as an online social media platform tailored for mobile device users to write personal blogs [17]. Then came in late 2008 the option for any user to write a blog post and address it to another user by mentioning the latter's username in the form of "@*username*". As consumers flocked to tweet about their product/service experiences, brands felt the strategic needs to react to such word-of-mouth tweets by posting their own responses openly on the same platform [17,21]. [21] analysed 150,000 posts and found 19% mention a brand, of which 22% contained sentiments. [37] analysed a sample of customer support requests on Twitter and found that while the majority of requests were about asking for information, around 40% were emotional in nature, i.e. expressing emotions, attitudes or opinions toward a brand. [23] found that Twitter customer support conversations often involve emotional, informational and instrumental support.

2.2 Empathic Response Selection

Customers expect brands to care about their interests [25]. When they express feelings toward brands, they want the latter to understand and be concerned. [23] found evidence of brands responding to customers' both positive and negative comments on Twitter with emotional support. [9] found that company responses which show genuine concern are more effective. Researchers have explored ways to flourish responses with empathic cues [26,27,30], e.g., inserting short empathic response headers such as "I understand your frustration." in system responses [5].

Response selection based on context-response matching is widely used in retrieval-based dialogue systems [32,35]. TOD-BERT [35] is a pre-trained dialogue model which supports response selection in task-oriented dialogues (TODs). It was trained with a response contrastive loss based on TOD datasets without emotional annotations.

2.3 Emotion Recognition in Conversations with LLMs

Research has shown potential of LLMs in sentiment analysis [3,34] as well as emotion recognition [8,20,39] although their performance is behind SOTA models. [40] evaluated the performance of ChatGPT in emotion recognition on four dialogue datasets and found that ChatGPT lags behind SOTA models by 3–18% points. [8] obtained similar results in their experiments.

[31] employ Llama-2 in augmenting an end-to-end TOD system. They find improvement in user emotion detection with a fine-tuned version of Llama-2. [6] build an end-to-end TOD system based on Llama-2 with emotion recognition and response generation. Neither of these works [6,31] involve response selection.

3 Method

3.1 Datasets and Preprocessing

For our experiment we employ a Twitter customer support conversation dataset made available by [10]. It covers 25 organisations' customer support on Twitter with over 13K dialogues, all of which involve agents providing customers with URLs (links) to helpful resources (e.g., complaint form). The dataset is characterised by a low average number of turns per dialogue: over 80% contain only a single customer request tweet followed by a single turn of agent response. The experiment covers only these single-turn dialogues and discards the rest.

Furthermore, since we are interested in both tweet-level and sentence-level emotions in customer tweets, those dialogues beginning with a single-sentence customer tweet are also discarded. Similarly, those agent responses consisting of a single-sentence are also dropped because we want a response to have both a header and a body. This results in a sample of 3,437 conversations.

3.2 Emotion Recognition

Table 1. Emotion classification schemes

33 emotions [27]	Surprised, Excited, Angry, Proud, Sad, Annoyed, Grateful, Lonely, Afraid,Terrified, Guilty, Impressed, Disgusted, Hopeful, Confident, Furious, Anxious, Anticipating, Joyful, Nostalgic, Disappointed, Prepared, Jealous, Content, Devastated, Embarrassed, Caring, Sentimental, Trusting, Ashamed, Apprehensive, Faithful, Neutral
11 emotions [14,19]	Anxious, Confused, Frustrated, Angry, Sad, Happy, Hopeful, Disappointed, Grateful, Polite, Neutral

Since there are no universally accepted classification of emotions among researchers in emotion recognition [30] and the number of emotions in a classification can vary from a few to dozens, we adopt one long and one short classification schemes as shown in Table 1. This first scheme follows EmpatheticDialogues [27] which is prominent in the field of empathic responding and consists of 33 emotions including "Neutral". The second scheme is based on two related schemes for classifying emotions specifically in customer support conversations [14, 19] with the addition of "Neutral".

You are a Twitter user. You are reading some customer posts from Twitter. Your task is to detect which one of the following emotions is expressed most explicitly in the utterance.
Emotion List:

(list of emotions)

If there is no emotion in the text, write Unclassified. Otherwise, write exactly one word, the exact emotion from the emotion list.

Fig. 2. Prompt design for emotion recognition using Llama 3.1

For the emotion recognition task, we employ the open-sourced large language model Llama 3.1[1] and adapt the prompt design for emotion classification used in [20] for our task. Figure 2 shows our prompt design.

Note that customer emotions are recognised at *tweet-level* as well as *sentence-level*. For each customer tweet, we prompt Llama for the emotions expressed in: 1) the whole tweet (WHOLE), 2) the whole tweet minus the last sentence (FRONT), 3) the last sentence of the tweet (LAST). The reason why we do not break down the FRONT part of a tweet further is that the average number of sentences in customer tweets in the dataset is less than 3, meaning that the FRONT parts mostly consist of only one or two sentences. Furthermore, we put more emphasis on the LAST part due to our speculation that if an emotion is strongly expressed in this part, agents are more likely to offer emotional support accordingly.

We discard any conversation if Llama fails to recognize the emotions in the customer tweet or its components. This results in 2,435 and 1,912 conversations after annotating with the 11-emotion and 33-emotion classification schemes, respectively.

3.3 Response Selection

We apply the TOD-BERT model [35] for the response selection task in our research. Note that this model accounts for response selection in dialogues related to a wide range of tasks and services (e.g., ticket booking, restaurant reservation, etc.) but does not involve any annotation or training with regard to emotions in dialogues.

[1] https://github.com/meta-llama/llama3.

To assess the efficacy of using a LLM as a filter to improve response header selection with TOD-BERT, the experiment takes a random sample of pre-processed Twitter customer support dialogues each time, separates customer tweets from the agent responses, and applies the TOD-BERT model to each customer tweet see if it can "re-discover" the corresponding agent response (header) in the actual dialogue. This is the idea behind the recall accuracy metric [35].

The pre-processed sample of single-turn conversations with emotion annotations are randomly collated into batches (batch size: 100) for measuring recall accuracy following [35]. For each batch of 100 dialogues, the accuracy of the model is measured as the percentage of customer tweets in the batch whose agent responses are correctly predicted by the top k prediction(s), with k being 1 and 3. This is called k-to-100 recall accuracy in [35]. In the case of 3-to-100 accuracy measurement, we also employ the S-BERT sentence-similarity model [28] to account for identical/similar response headers within each sample batch.

We run 5 rounds of batch-collating and accuracy measurement with different random seeds and take the average as the model's accuracy.

Next, we repeat the whole process on our sample by augmenting the response selection criteria with filtering based on Llama's emotion annotations. Points to note,

- For each target customer tweet in a batch, the 100 response candidates are first filtered to include only those that are associated with the same emotion recognised in that target customer tweet (see Fig. 1).
- Emotion annotation is applied in a combination of $3 \times 2 = 6$ different ways: 3 according to which part (WHOLE, FRONT and LAST) of a tweet is annotated and 2 according to which emotion classification scheme is followed (as shown in Table 1).

4 Results and Discussion

Table 2. Results: response header recall accuracy

	Recall 1-100 accuracy				Recall 3-100 accuracy			
	Unfiltered	Filtered			Unfiltered	Filtered		
		WHOLE	FRONT	LAST		WHOLE	FRONT	LAST
11 emotions 2435 tweets	7.47	18.07	19.45	22.04	14.31	33.18	34.98	42.93
33 emotions 1912 tweets	7.62	27.89	27.97	33.03	14.63	50.06	52.13	60.11

Table 2 summarises the results of the experiment[2]. Overall, emotion-based filtering improves recall accuracy substantially by a factor of 2.32 to 4.33, with

[2] The results presented here include corrections made to the earlier version presented at the conference.

the more fine-grained 33-emotion classification showing a clear advantage. This confirms our intuition that emotion-based filtering can ease the task of response selection by pre-selecting affectively relevant responses and that the (fine- vs coarse-grained) resolution of the classification matters. [27] develop the 33-emotion classification by aggregating labels from previous datasets. It has often been adopted by other researchers studying empathic responding, e.g., [36].

On the other hand, the results show an interesting picture regarding the use of tweet-level vs sentence-level emotions in filtering. Filtering based on LAST-sentence emotions appears to lend more accurate support to selecting empathic response headers in the results. We speculate that since it can be cognitively demanding for support agents to assimilate all details in a customer tweet to determine the most relevant emotion, they may focus on the most salient expressions and respond accordingly. Referring to the following example:

Customer: What's wrong? The delivery never came. ... (*Annoyed*)
Please help! (*Anxious*)

The human support agent may choose a response header depending on the emotions expressed as well as the saliency of expressions:

Agent (*Focus on WHOLE tweet*): Sorry to hear that. ...
Agent (*Focus on FRONT part of tweet*): Oh no! ...
Agent (*Focus on LAST part of tweet*): Here to help. ...

While both "What's wrong?" and "Please help!" can be regarded as salient expressions in the tweet, the latter may appear more salient due to the recency effect [4].

5 Conclusion and Further Work

This research considers an approach to assisting brands' support agents on the X/Twitter platform in providing emotional support to customers in the form of empathic response headers based on the emotions expressed in customer tweets. A major advantage of this approach is that it does not involve expensive human annotation work. Instead, it leverages an open-sourced LLM for the emotional recognition task. Compared with other generative approaches to empathic responding (e.g., [6,7,18,31]), the response selection approach based on sanctioned conversation corpora has the advantage of being more controllable from the point of view of company policy on communication. It also helps avoid the problem of hallucination when using LLMs to generate responses [22].

From support agents' point of view, the automated response headers can help satisfy the demand of emotional labour [16] and allow them to focus on providing tangible support to customers. On X/Twitter, the time savings can be an important advantage given the popularity of the platform and customers' expectation of speedy responses.

Our evaluation by automatic means is limited to measuring recall accuracy in the response header selection task in an experimental setting. To make our work more relevant, further work is needed to evaluate the approach with human ratings of selected response headers in terms of emotional support and empathy. Furthermore, we plan to employ emotion detection models that are fine-tuned for the task in additional experiments. Finally, we would also like to measure any savings in time and cognitive demand provided by this approach for support agents in realistic work settings.

Acknowledgments. The author would like to thank the anonymous reviewers for their comments and suggestions on an earlier version of this paper.

Disclosure of Interests. The author has no competing interests to declare that are relevant to the content of this article.

References

1. De Waal, F.B.: Putting the altruism back into altruism: The evolution of empathy. Annu. Rev. Psychol. **59**, 279–300 (2008)
2. Demszky, D., Movshovitz-Attias, D., Ko, J., Cowen, A., Nemade, G., Ravi, S.: GoEmotions: a dataset of fine-grained emotions. In: Proceedings of the 58th Annual Meeting of the Association for Computational Linguistics, pp. 4040–4054 (2020)
3. Deng, X., Bashlovkina, V., Han, F., Baumgartner, S., Bendersky, M.: LLMs to the moon? Reddit market sentiment analysis with large language models. In: Companion Proceedings of the ACM Web Conference 2023, pp. 1014–1019 (2023)
4. Fang, X., Van Kleef, G.A., Sauter, D.A.: Person perception from changing emotional expressions: primacy, recency, or averaging effect? Cogn. Emot. **32**(8), 1597–1610 (2018)
5. Feigenblat, G., Konopnicki, D., Shmueli-Scheuer, M., Herzig, J., Shkedi, H.: I understand your frustration. In: Proceedings of the 19th ACM Conference on Computer Supported Cooperative Work and Social Computing Companion, pp. 25–28 (2016)
6. Feng, S., et al.: Infusing emotions into task-oriented dialogue systems: understanding, management, and generation. In: Proceedings of the 25th Annual Meeting of the Special Interest Group on Discourse and Dialogue, pp. 699–717 (2024)
7. Feng, S., et al.: From chatter to matter: addressing critical steps of emotion recognition learning in task-oriented dialogue. In: Proceedings of the 24th Annual Meeting of the Special Interest Group on Discourse and Dialogue, pp. 85–103 (2023)
8. Feng, S., Sun, G., Lubis, N., Wu, W., Zhang, C., Gašić, M.: Affect recognition in conversations using large language models. arXiv preprint arXiv:2309.12881 (2023)
9. Fuoli, M., Clarke, I., Wiegand, V., Ziezold, H., Mahlberg, M.: Responding effectively to customer feedback on Twitter: a mixed methods study of webcare styles. Appl. Linguis. **42**(3), 569–595 (2021)
10. Ganhotra, J., et al.: Conversational document prediction to assist customer care agents. In: Proceedings of the 2020 Conference on Empirical Methods in Natural Language Processing (EMNLP), pp. 349–356 (2020)
11. Golchha, H., Firdaus, M., Ekbal, A., Bhattacharyya, P.: Courteously yours: inducing courteous behavior in customer care responses using reinforced pointer generator network. In: Proceedings of the 2019 Conference of the North American Chapter of the Association for Computational Linguistics: Human Language Technologies, Volume 1 (Long and Short Papers), pp. 851–860 (2019)

12. Gorry, G.A., Westbrook, R.A.: Once more, with feeling: empathy and technology in customer care. Bus. Horiz. **54**(2), 125–134 (2011)
13. Henderson, M., et al.: Training neural response selection for task-oriented dialogue systems. In: Korhonen, A., Traum, D., Màrquez, L. (eds.) Proceedings of the 57th Annual Meeting of the Association for Computational Linguistics, pp. 5392–5404. Association for Computational Linguistics, Florence, Italy (2019)
14. Herzig, J., Feigenblat, G., Shmueli-Scheuer, M., Konopnicki, D., Rafaeli, A.: Predicting customer satisfaction in customer support conversations in social media using affective features. In: Proceedings of the 2016 Conference on User Modeling Adaptation and Personalization. pp. 115–119 (2016)
15. Herzig, J., Shmueli-Scheuer, M., Sandbank, T., Konopnicki, D.: Neural response generation for customer service based on personality traits. In: Proceedings of the 10th International Conference on Natural Language Generation, pp. 252–256 (2017)
16. Hochschild, A.R.: Emotion work, feeling rules, and social structure. Am. J. Sociol. **85**(3), 551–575 (1979)
17. Honey, C., Herring, S.C.: Beyond microblogging: Conversation and collaboration via Twitter. In: 2009 42nd Hawaii International Conference on System Sciences, pp. 1–10. IEEE (2009)
18. Hosseini-Asl, E., McCann, B., Wu, C.S., Yavuz, S., Socher, R.: A simple language model for task-oriented dialogue. In: Advances in Neural Information Processing Systems, vol. 33, pp. 20179–20191 (2020)
19. Hu, T., et al.: Touch your heart: a tone-aware chatbot for customer care on social media. In: Proceedings of the 2018 CHI Conference on Human Factors in Computing Systems, pp. 1–12 (2018)
20. Imran, M.M., Chatterjee, P., Damevski, K.: Uncovering the causes of emotions in software developer communication using zero-shot LLMs. In: Proceedings of the IEEE/ACM 46th International Conference on Software Engineering, pp. 1–13 (2024)
21. Jansen, B.J., Zhang, M., Sobel, K., Chowdury, A.: Twitter power: tweets as electronic word of mouth. J. Am. Soc. Inform. Sci. Technol. **60**(11), 2169–2188 (2009)
22. Ji, Z., Yu, T., Xu, Y., Lee, N., Ishii, E., Fung, P.: Towards mitigating LLM hallucination via self reflection. In: Findings of the Association for Computational Linguistics: EMNLP 2023, pp. 1827–1843 (2023)
23. Knight, M., Carpenter, S.: Optimal matching model of social support: an examination of how national product and service companies use Twitter to respond to consumers. Southwestern Mass Commun. J. **27**(2) (2012)
24. Labat, S., Demeester, T., Hoste, V.: EmoTwiCS: a corpus for modelling emotion trajectories in Dutch customer service dialogues on Twitter. Lang. Resour. Eval. **58**(2), 505–546 (2024)
25. Parasuraman, A., Zeithaml, V.A., Berry, L.L.: A conceptual model of service quality and its implications for future research. J. Mark. **49**(4), 41–50 (1985)
26. Raamkumar, A.S., Yang, Y.: Empathetic conversational systems: a review of current advances, gaps, and opportunities. IEEE Trans. Affect. Comput. (2022)
27. Rashkin, H., Smith, E.M., Li, M., Boureau, Y.L.: Towards empathetic open-domain conversation models: a new benchmark and dataset. In: Proceedings of the 57th Annual Meeting of the Association for Computational Linguistics, pp. 5370–5381 (2019)
28. Reimers, N., Gurevych, I.: Sentence-BERT: sentence embeddings using Siamese BERT-networks. In: Proceedings of the 2019 Conference on Empirical Methods

in Natural Language Processing and the 9th International Joint Conference on Natural Language Processing (EMNLP-IJCNLP), pp. 3982–3992 (2019)
29. Sordoni, A., et al.: A neural network approach to context-sensitive generation of conversational responses. In: Proceedings of the 2015 Conference of the North American Chapter of the Association for Computational Linguistics: Human Language Technologies, pp. 196–205 (2015)
30. Spring, T., Casas, J., Daher, K., Mugellini, E., Abou Khaled, O.: Empathic response generation in chatbots. In: Proceedings of 4th Swiss Text Analytics Conference (SwissText 2019), 18–19 June 2019, Wintherthur, Switzerland. No. CONFERENCE, 18–19 June 2019 (2019)
31. Stricker, A., Paroubek, P.: A unified approach to emotion detection and task-oriented dialogue modeling. In: Proceedings of 14th International Workshop on Spoken Dialogue Systems Technology, Sapporo (2024). https://hal.science/hal-04415809
32. Tao, C., Feng, J., Yan, R., Wu, W., Jiang, D.: A survey on response selection for retrieval-based dialogues. In: Zhou, Z. (ed.) Proceedings of the Thirtieth International Joint Conference on Artificial Intelligence, IJCAI 2021, Virtual Event/Montreal, Canada, 19–27 August 2021, pp. 4619–4626 (2021)
33. Vinyals, O., Le, Q.V.: A neural conversational model. arXiv preprint arXiv:1506.05869 (2015)
34. Wang, Z., Xie, Q., Feng, Y., Ding, Z., Yang, Z., Xia, R.: Is ChatGPT a good sentiment analyzer? A preliminary study. arXiv preprint arXiv:2304.04339 (2023)
35. Wu, C.S., Hoi, S.C., Socher, R., Xiong, C.: TOD-BERT: pre-trained natural language understanding for task-oriented dialogue. In: Proceedings of the 2020 Conference on Empirical Methods in Natural Language Processing (EMNLP), pp. 917–929 (2020)
36. Xie, Y., Pu, P.: Empathetic dialog generation with fine-grained intents. arXiv preprint arXiv:2105.06829 (2021)
37. Xu, A., Liu, Z., Guo, Y., Sinha, V., Akkiraju, R.: A new chatbot for customer service on social media. In: Proceedings of the 2017 CHI Conference on Human Factors in Computing Systems, pp. 3506–3510 (2017)
38. Yang, Y., et al.: Learning semantic textual similarity from conversations. In: Augenstein, I., et al. (eds.) Proceedings of the Third Workshop on Representation Learning for NLP, pp. 164–174. Association for Computational Linguistics, Melbourne, Australia (2018)
39. Zhang, W., Deng, Y., Liu, B., Pan, S., Bing, L.: Sentiment analysis in the era of large language models: a reality check. In: Findings of the Association for Computational Linguistics: NAACL 2024, pp. 3881–3906 (2024)
40. Zhao, W., Zhao, Y., Lu, X., Wang, S., Tong, Y., Qin, B.: Is ChatGPT equipped with emotional dialogue capabilities? arXiv preprint arXiv:2304.09582 (2023)

Exploring the Effects of Consistency-Based Hallucination Detection for LLM-Based QA Chatbots: A Simulation Study

Simon Rapp[1(✉)], Alexander Maedche[1], and Marcus Jainta[2]

[1] Karlsruhe Institute of Technology, Kaiserstraße 12, 76131 Karlsruhe, Germany
simon.rapp@student.kit.edu

[2] EnBW Energie Baden-Württemberg AG, Durlacher Allee 93, 76131 Karlsruhe, Germany

Abstract. Large Language Models (LLMs) are increasingly used in Question Answering (QA) chatbots. Using LLMs in QA chatbots enables a more eloquent user conversation, however, these models are far from perfect. A major issue with LLMs is hallucinations, which refer to generated texts that include nonsensical or inaccurate information. These hallucinations are particularly problematic in critical QA contexts such as health or enterprise. Several methods exist to mitigate these hallucinations, wherein the consistency-based hallucination detection techniques are promising as they do not require a ground-truth or deep technical analysis. Although current research has proven the effectiveness of these detection techniques, it does not address possible trade-offs in their real-world use. To close this gap, we conducted a simulation study based on real-world QA data sets to compare different consistency-based hallucination detection techniques and their impact on precision and response time. Our research confirms that more complex detection techniques achieve higher precision, but also lead to a higher response time. In addition, we show that precision and response time strongly depend on the data set used and that precision is only slightly dependent on the consistency determining threshold.

Keywords: Large Language Models · Question Answering · Chatbots · Consistency-based Hallucination Mitigation

1 Introduction

Question-and-answer (QA) chatbots provide succinct answers to user questions in natural language and engage their users in social dialogues [9,12]. QA chatbots have been used and deployed successfully in various application areas, especially in the areas of customer service, education, and healthcare, as well as enterprise applications for employees (e.g., HR/IT service). QA chatbots have the advantage that they operate reliably on the basis of a predefined database of

A. Følstad et al. (Eds.): CONVERSATIONS 2024, LNCS 15545, pp. 33–47, 2025.
https://doi.org/10.1007/978-3-031-88045-2_3

questions and answers. However, at the same time, there is also the disadvantage that their answers are perceived as standardized and not very dynamic. With the rapid development of large language models (LLMs), new opportunities for providing LLM-based QA chatbots that combine the strengths of QA chatbots with the natural language capabilities of LLMs are emerging.

However, a well-known problem of LLMs are hallucinations, which in the context of LLMs can be defined as undesired generated text that contains nonsensical or incorrect information [7]. The hallucination problem also exists when LLMs are used in the context of QA chatbots and is particularly problematic in critical applications such as healthcare or in an enterprise context such as HR/IT support services. Much research has recently been done to investigate new methods to mitigate hallucinations in LLMs [1]. Exemplary methods include token probability or fact checks [11,13]. Another prominent method leverages consistency-based hallucination detection techniques, which check generated answers for consistency [10]. These techniques are particularly interesting because they work without in-depth technical access and without fact-checked comparative data. In the literature, the effectiveness of consistency-based techniques has already been demonstrated [10,15]. However, there is a lack of research that examines trade-offs when applying consistency-based techniques [15]. The trade-off between precision and response time of consistency-based hallucination detection techniques is of particular interest to LLM-based QA chatbot providers, because users prefer a naturally eloquent conversation and do not want to wait for responses. Therefore, our work focuses on the precision (i.e. how many of the hallucinations allegedly found were really hallucinations in real data sets) and on the realistic response time (i.e. the time a user would have to wait to receive a response). Thus, finding a good balance in the precision-response time trade-off in consistency-based techniques is a relevant scientific and practical problem.

We confirm that a more complex consistency-based hallucination detection technique achieves higher precision but also leads to a higher response time than a more simple technique. By using this technique, users would receive more generated responses, which could contribute to a more eloquent conversation, but would also have to wait longer for them. We also show that the precision and response time depend on the data set used and that the precision is also slightly dependent on the consistency determining threshold. A lower threshold leads to a higher precision, while a higher threshold leads to a lower precision but to a higher total number of true hallucinations detected.

The remainder of this paper is the following. First, in Sect. 2, we provide a short overview of related work. Subsequently, in Sect. 3, we present the underlying research method. Section 4 introduces the simulation model, its implementation, and the underlying experiment. Section 5 presents the results. Finally, in Sects. 6 and 7, we conclude and discuss our results.

2 Related Work

QA chatbots have undergone significant development in recent years. First, rules were used to determine the answer to a question. Subsequently, statistical models followed by machine learning and deep learning approaches were successfully applied [6]. Today, LLMs are increasingly being used for question answering due to their good language understanding and generating capabilities [5]. There are two common ways to enrich an LLM with domain-specific QA knowledge: (1) Through *finetuning* the model weights toward a desired domain, or (2) through *prompting*, by including domain specific context in the input [2]. One of the biggest problems with LLMs is hallucinations, which also occur when LLMs are used for question answering [5].

In the context of LLM-based QA chatbots, hallucinations can be defined as unwanted generated text that contains nonsensical or incorrect information [7]. Hallucinations have several causes, which is why they are very difficult to control. Possible causes include insufficient context in the user prompt, the probabilistic nature of text generation, and unreliable sources [1]. In the literature, many different methods for mitigating hallucinations can be found. The various methods make it possible to combat hallucinations depending on the individual situation. If full technical access to the LLM is available, an analysis of the uncertainty metrics could be performed to detect hallucinations. This method checks whether many tokens in a generated text have a low probability based on a previous context. If there is a sufficient number of tokens with low probability, an uncertainty is assumed that indicates hallucinations [14]. If access to facts is available, hallucinations can be detected by comparing the claims in the generated text with the facts, for example, using an LLM. If the comparison reveals that the generated answer differs from the facts or has been completely made up, hallucinations are assumed [11]. The methods mentioned above have the advantage of requiring only one generated response to detect a hallucination, but LLMs are often not self-operated, and many users do not have enough knowledge or full access to analyze uncertainty metrics. There is also a lack of factually correct databases that could be used for comparison.

Another method of mitigating hallucinations in LLMs is the consistency-based hallucination detection method. In this method multiple samples are generated for a given input and the semantic differences between the samples is quantified. In the literature, this method is also known as the sampling-based hallucination detection method. Different consistency-based techniques have been proposed, which all define different consistency scores [8]. Some focus on individual passages of the generated texts, while others compare the texts as a whole. Some simply generate multiple responses to a prompt, while other techniques also generate artificial input alongside responses. In addition, different approaches, e.g. using LLMs or the BERT score, have been proposed to compare the text on a semantic level and to calculate the confidence score. Although samples are assigned different numerical values depending on the semantic comparison method used, they are usually averaged to create a consistency score that is compared to a specified threshold T [8,10,15].

The effectiveness of these techniques has already been shown. However, there is a lack of validation with real data and analysis of emerging trade-offs when using these consistency-based techniques [10, 15].

3 Research Method

Simulation-based research approaches have recently received more attention in information systems research [3]. Figure 1 depicts the simplified simulation research process we followed in our work. For problem awareness, we conducted an exploratory literature review to understand the current state of consistency-based hallucination detection techniques. Based on our results of the exploratory literature review, we developed a conceptual model for consistency-based hallucination detection for LLM-based QA chatbots.

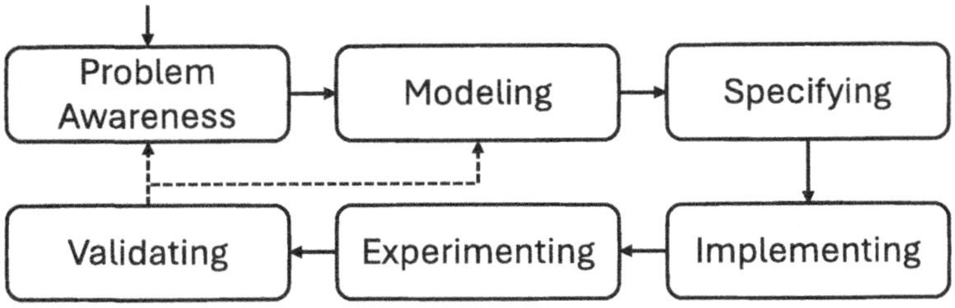

Fig. 1. Simplified Simulation-Based Research Process

Subsequently, the generic conceptual model was divided into three specific models: no consistency detection, a simple consistency detection technique, and an advanced consistency detection technique. The three specified models were then implemented using Python. For experimenting, we decided to use two different real QA data sets, one from the health context and one from an enterprise context. We used the Medquad data set for the health context and from this randomly sampled 750 QA pairs [4]. Our industry partner, EnBW (enbw.com), provided us with a real IT service QA data set for the enterprise context. The EnBW is a network of regional energy companies, grid companies, and providers of products and services in the fields of renewable energy, telecommunications, and smart electricity storage. The provided data set had already been in productive use for several years at the time of the study and consists of 746 QA pairs. Other real data sets were not provided by our industry partner for this simulation study. Both data sets had a similar structure and consisted of concise questions and answers. There were several questions with the same answer in both datasets, simulating different user queries. Exemplary questions of the data sets are *What are the treatments for Neurosarcoidosis* and *How can I find an old version of my file in Microsoft Office*. In the experiment, we treated the QA question as user input and included the QA answer in the prompt. We tested two different consistency determining thresholds: 0.4 and 0.6. In the literature, different thresholds have been tested in the range of 0.4 to 0.8 with a recommendation for the 0.4 threshold [15]. Additionally, we chose the 0.6 threshold to double check our implementation. In total, this leads to twelve simulation runs: three prototypes times two data sets times two thresholds. After all runs were completed, we analyzed the observed response times and used human labeling to evaluate the hallucination detection precision of each prototype. Here, two of our authors independently labeled the data. If discrepancies appeared, the two authors discussed them and made a decision.

4 Simulation

Conceptual Model. The conceptual model developed for the simulation is depicted in Fig. 2. In this model, the LLM receives input and, in addition to its own common knowledge, has access to QA knowledge in the form of QA pairs. Although QA knowledge is context dependent, common knowledge depends on the LLM model used. The final response is decided based on the consistency of the generated answers. If the generated answers are not consistent, the model response is the default answer from the QA knowledge, otherwise the response is a generated answer.

Specifications. Our specified models are shown in Fig. 3. The first specified model ignores the consistency check. The model receives the input and the relevant QA knowledge included in the prompt and always plays out the generated answer. The second specified model performs a simple consistency check. Here, the prompt also includes the input and the relevant QA knowledge to generate an answer. Here, however, five answers are generated since that amount was recommended by the literature [15]. In pairs, the four additional generated answers are checked for semantic equivalence to the first generated answer. Each semantic equivalence check is carried out with another LLM API call. A threshold T then decides whether there is sufficient consistency, i.e. a sufficient number of additional generated answers that support the initial generated answer. If there is sufficient consistency, the response is the first generated answer. Otherwise, the response is the default answer from the QA knowledge. The third specified model first generates four alternative inputs using LLM API calls. The generated inputs are then checked for semantic equivalence to the initial input using additional LLM API calls. Generated inputs that are not semantically equivalent to the initial input are sorted out. Four answers are then generated for all additional inputs left using the relevant QA knowledge. In the same way, an answer to the original input is generated. For each additional generated and remaining input and for each of its generated answers, a pairwise check for semantic equivalence with the initial input and its generated answer takes place via an additional LLM call. If sufficient input answer pairs semantically support the initial input answer pair, again depending on T, the response is the initial generated answer. Otherwise, the response is the default answer from the QA knowledge.

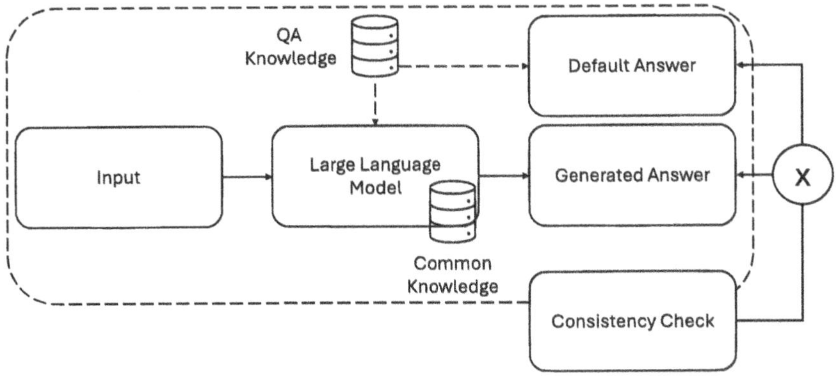

Fig. 2. Conceptual Model

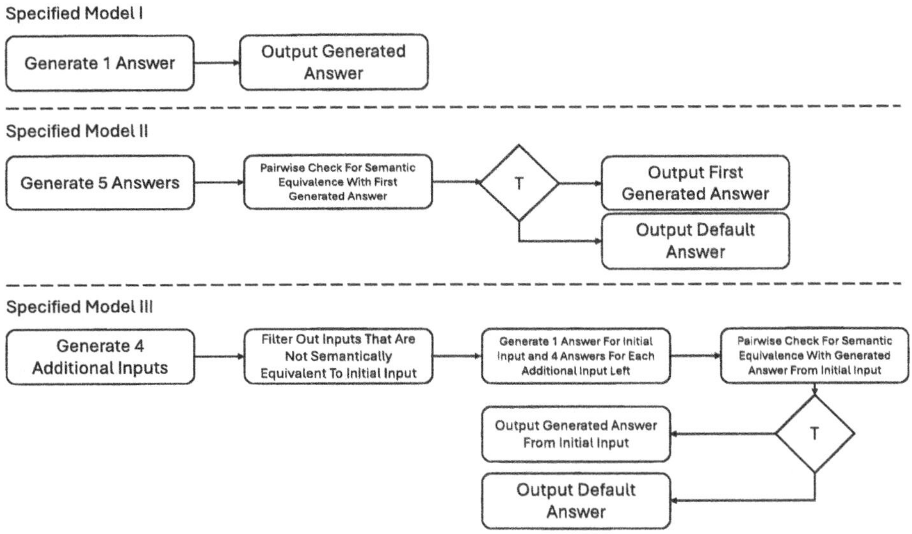

Fig. 3. Specified Models

Implementation. The specified models were developed in Visual Studio Code using Python 3.11.9 and OpenAI's ChatGPT 3.5 Turbo. The simulation was carried out on a virtual machine running Windows 11. It had 16 GiB of RAM, 256 GiB of SSD storage, and was hosted on Microsoft Azure.

Experiment. There were a total of 12 simulation runs, one for each prototype, data set, and consistency determining threshold. The hyperparameter T, which determines the consistency **threshold** was set before the simulation. First, it was set to 0.4 and then to 0.6. The threshold can be read as follows: more than 40% (60%) of the additional generated input answer pairs were semantically equivalent to the initial generated input answer pair. For this, we combined each additional generated input answer pair with the initial generated input answer pair. For those combinations we did another LLM API call asking if those two input answer pairs are semantically equivalent and mapped the response to a score. The score was 1 if the pairs were semantically equivalent and 0 if not. We then added those scores together and divided them by the number of additional generated input answer pairs to calculate the consistency score. This consistency score is then compared to the predefined threshold.

To determine the **precision** of the techniques used, the generated answers classified as hallucinations were independently labeled by two of the authors. The authors determined if the answer was classified correctly or incorrectly as a hallucination based on the definition mentioned in Related Work. The resulting true positive (TP) and false positive (FP) values were then used to calculate the precision using the equation below.

$$\text{Precision} = \frac{\text{TP}}{\text{TP} + \text{FP}} \tag{1}$$

The **response time** was measured by calculating the temporal difference between the first LLM API call (S_0) and the final decision of whether the initial generated answer or the default answer is played out (S_1).

$$\text{Response Time} = S_1 - S_0 \tag{2}$$

5 Results

In the following, we present the results of our simulation study. We look at the influence of the three different prototypes, the two different QA datasets, and the two thresholds on the two central trade-off metrics of response time and precision.

5.1 Response Time

An overview of the average response time of the prototypes used in consideration of the QA data sets and thresholds is shown in Fig. 4. It is important to note that the times have been recorded under realistic conditions, but these may vary depending on the systems used, such as other LLM API providers.

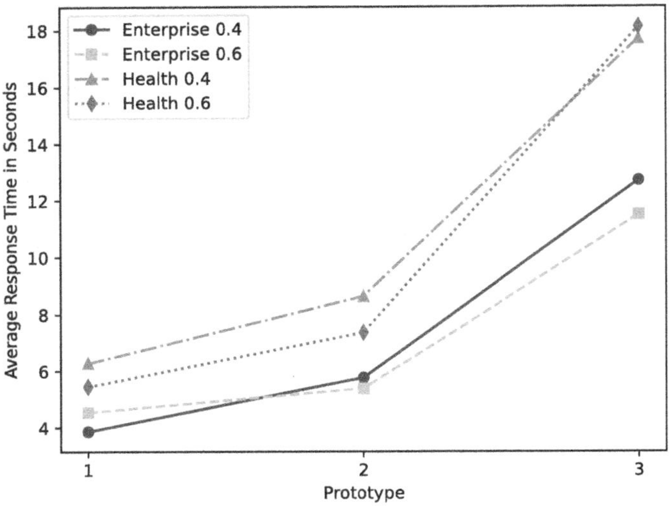

Fig. 4. Average Response Time per Prototype, Data Set and Threshold

Impact of the Prototype. The prototypes have been optimized for parallelization, thus independent LLM API calls occurred in parallel, while interdependent LLM API calls occurred sequentially. As expected, the average response times of different prototypes showed a correlation with the complexity of the implementation. The first prototype consistently delivered the fastest responses. This can be attributed to the lack of a consistency check, and therefore no requirement for any further LLM API calls. The second prototype was consistently the second fastest. This can be explained by the implementation of the simple consistency check using an additional LLM API call step in this prototype: (1) to generate answers and (2) to check for semantic equivalence. Finally, the third prototype was consistently the slowest. This is mainly because it was designed to perform four interdependent LLM API calls: (1) generate alternative inputs, (2) check alternative inputs, (3) generate answers, and (4) check for semantic equivalence. Even if the exact response times depend on several factors including, the system, the LLM, and time of use, the LLM API call dependencies described above still apply. The first prototype will therefore always be the fastest, followed by the second and finally the third prototype.

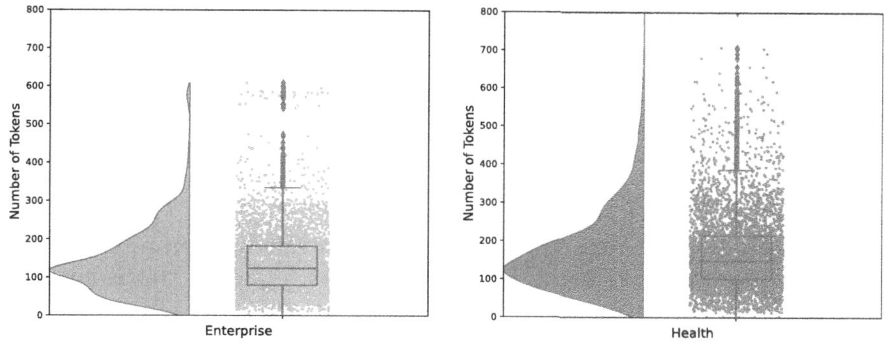

Fig. 5. Distribution of the Output Token Numbers from Enterprise (Blue) and Health (Red) Data from all Simulation Runs as Raincloud Plots (Color figure online)

Impact of the Data Set. The health data set consistently led to longer response times. To describe this behavior, we calculated the combined number of tokens for question and default answer and called this the input token number. The mean input token number for the health data set was 278 and 134 for the enterprise data set respectively. The input token number for the health data set was on average 144 (+108%) tokens higher than in the enterprise data set. Additionally, we observe the output token number given by the calculated tokens for the generated answer. The mean value for the output token number for the health data set was 171 and 139 for the enterprise data set. The output token number for the health data set was on average 32 (+23%) higher than for the enterprise data set. For illustration, Fig. 5 shows the raincloud plots of the output token number distribution of all generated answers from health and enterprise data sets.

Table 1. Polynomial Regression Analysis with Degree 4: R^2 Scores between the Number of Input and Output Tokens Regarding the Response Time

	Number of Tokens	
Prototype	Input	Output
I	0.42	0.78
II	0.55	0.67
III	0.57	0.66

Table 1 shows the R^2 scores of a forth degree polynomial regression analysis between token numbers for input and output regarding the response times. The analysis was done for each prototype separately. It can be seen that the R^2 scores were generally higher for the output than for the input. It can also be seen that the R^2 scores for input and output get closer with higher complexity of the prototypes.

Impact of the Threshold. The threshold is used to decide whether there is enough consistency to respond the generated instead of the default answer. The check is implemented as an *if* statement, so changing its value does not affect the response time.

5.2 Precision

Table 2 shows the precision of the hallucinations detected per prototype, threshold, and data set. Here, E stands for enterprise data set and H stands for health data set. It also shows the true positive (TP) and false positive (FP) values used to calculate this precision. Prototype I did not have a hallucination detection mechanism and is therefore not represented in this table.

Table 2. Precision of Detected Hallucinations per Prototype, Threshold and Data Set

Threshold	Prototype	Data set	Hallucinations Detected	TP	FP	Precision in %
0.4	II	E	79	16	63	20.25
		H	16	9	7	56.25
	III	E	44	16	28	36.36
		H	6	6	0	100.00
0.6	II	E	201	33	168	16.42
		H	58	29	29	50.00
	III	E	141	36	105	25.53
		H	19	14	5	73.68

Table 3 shows the R^2 values of the linear regression analysis between threshold, prototype, and data set (independent variables) regarding the precision (dependent variable). It also includes the R^2 value of the multi variable linear regression analysis, including all three independent variables.

Table 3. Results of (Multi-) Linear Regression Analysis between Threshold, Prototype, and Data Set Regarding Precision

Dependent Variable	Threshold	Prototype	Data set	Multi Variable	Adjusted	Metric
Precision	0.05	0.18	0.70	0.94	0.89	R^2

Impact of the Prototype. Prototype II consistently detected more generated answers as potential hallucinations than prototype III. Here, on average prototype II detected 36 (+69%) more generated answers as potential hallucinations than prototype III. Prototype III had a consistently higher precision than prototype II. Here, the precision was on average 23.2% higher. Prototype II detected on average 3.75 (+21%) more true hallucinations than prototype III but also detected on average 32.25 (+93%) more false hallucinations than prototype III. The R^2 score of the linear regression between prototype and precision is 0.18, and thus higher than the R^2 score of threshold and precision but lower than the R^2 score of data set and precision.

Impact of the Data set. The prototypes consistently detected more generated answers as potential hallucinations in the enterprise data set than in the health data set. On average, they detected 91.5 (+370%) more generated answers as potential hallucinations in the enterprise data set. The precision was consistently higher in the health data set than in the enterprise data set. Here, on average, the precision was 45.3% higher in the health data set. The prototypes consistently detected more true and false hallucinations in the enterprise data set than in the health data set. Here, on average 10.75 (+74%) more true hallucinations were detected, but also on average 80.75 (+788%) more false hallucinations were detected. The R^2 score of data set and precision is 0.70 and thus the highest R^2 score of the single-variable linear regression analysis, but lower than the R^2 score of the multi-variable linear regression analysis, which is adjusted 0.89.

Impact of the Threshold. The precision was consistently higher for the threshold of 0.4 than for 0.6. On average the precision was 11.8% higher under 0.4. There were consistently more generated answers detected as potential hallucinations under the 0.6 threshold. Here, on average 36.25 (+189%) more generated answers were detected as potential hallucinations. Generally, more true and false hallucinations were detected using a threshold of 0.6. Here, on average the prototypes detected 11.75 (+138%) more true hallucinations but also on average 52.52 (+213%) more false hallucinations. The R^2 score of the single variable linear regression analysis between threshold and precision is with 0.05 the lowest R^2 score.

6 Discussion

Our results show that the **response time** depends on the prototype used and thus depends on the consistency-based hallucination detection technique used, due to their different amounts of interdependent LLM API calls. These findings are consistent with the literature [10,15]. Prototype I, which had no consistency check implemented and thus no interdependent LLM API calls, delivered on average the fastest response times. Prototype II had, due to its simple consistency check, a slightly higher average response time than prototype I. Prototype III used a more complex consistency check consisting of four interdependent LLM API calls and thus had on average a much higher response time than the others. A user would have to wait on average approximately three times longer to get a response from prototype III than from prototype I, and only would have to wait on average two seconds more to get a response from prototype II than from prototype I. The response time also depends on the data set used. This was not investigated in the literature. Often only run-time complexities are analyzed, which refer to the hallucination detection technique and not to the data sets [15]. The health data set triggered the prototypes to generate answers that consist of more tokens than the enterprise data set. Our polynomial regression analysis shows that the output token number has a greater influence on the response time than input token number. Our analysis also shows that the influence of the output on the response time depends on the prototype, and thus on the consistency-based hallucination detection technique used. For prototypes II and III the influence of the input token number on the response time is significantly higher than for prototype I, while the influence of the output token number is slightly less. This can be explained through the fact that prototypes II and III processed the input more than prototype I, e.g. to generate multiple outputs. Finally, our results show that the consistency-determining threshold does not have a significant influence on response time. Variations can be explained through variations in the latency of the LLM API used.

Our results show that **precision** is highly dependent on the data set used. This can only be implicitly deduced from the literature, as these show less high data set-dependent precision deviations. The smaller deviations could be due to the fact that similar or artificial data was used [15]. The precision in the health data set was on average much higher than in the enterprise data set. That indicates that the hallucination detection techniques based on consistency are more sensitive to data and therefore less robust, as mentioned in the literature [15]. Even if different precision levels are to be expected for different data sets, the differences we noticed are very significant, as can be seen in Table 2. One possibility for this could be that the content of the health data set was incorporated more strongly into the training process of the LLM used and therefore it was more reliable in answering the questions. Another possibility could be that the used LLM overestimated its general IT knowledge and ignored the information from the IT data set. Other possibilities, for example of a technical nature, cannot be ruled out either. Users of these techniques must be aware that they may achieve less precision on their data than mentioned in the literature. Blind trust can have serious consequences in certain domains such as enterprise and health, especially when the precision drops as much as for our IT data set. The precision also depends on the prototype used and therefore also on the consistency-based hallucination detection technique used, which is consistent with the literature [10,15]. Prototype III continuously had a higher precision than prototype II, while using a more complex consistency check, but prototype II detected on average more true hallucinations than prototype III. Prototype II also detected relatively more false hallucinations, which explains its lower precision. Users of prototype II would therefore receive far fewer generated responses and thus have a less eloquent conversation than users of prototype III, but for that they would receive fewer hallucinations. Although the data sets in our simulation had a greater impact on the precision than the prototypes, our results show that the precision of prototype III was always higher than that of prototype II. Finally, we see that precision is less dependent on the threshold compared to its dependencies on prototype and data set. However, in the literature, the threshold was described as a central instrument to influence precision [15]. There was a higher average precision under the threshold of 0.4 than 0.6. The higher threshold caused a higher number of true hallucinations detected, but also an even higher number of false hallucinations detected.

Our results show that relatively good precision can only be obtained by using a more complex consistency-based hallucination detection technique, such as that implemented in prototype III, which confirms earlier findings in the literature [15]. Here, four interdependent LLM API calls are required, which leads to a higher response time compared to a simpler or non-consistency-based hallucination detection technique, such as those from prototype I and II. In this case, users would receive more generated responses compared to prototype II, which could contribute to a more eloquent conversation, but they would also have to wait longer for these responses. Nevertheless, our results also show that with a high precision, fewer true hallucinations are detected, thus by using a simpler consistency-based hallucination detection technique with a lower precision, like prototype II, more true hallucinations can be detected in a shorter response time. Here, users would receive fewer generated responses than with prototype III, which could make for a less eloquent conversion, but it would contain fewer hallucinations. Furthermore, our results also show that the hallucination detection techniques used are strongly data sensitive with respect to precision and response time. Data sets that trigger longer generated responses lead to significantly longer response times, especially for more complex techniques.

Our work also provides some practical implications. In the health context, it is particularly important to act quickly and correctly, which is why long response times or hallucinations can cause great harm. Consistency-based techniques like this one in prototype II would probably be better suited here to play out answers quickly with fewer hallucinations than the technique of prototype III or no technique at all. However, the coarser filtering of answers could reduce the quality of the conversation, which would create a trade-off that needs to be investigated further. The technique used in prototype III would probably be more suitable for the enterprise context, as the answers are sorted out more precisely here, which could increase the quality of conversation for customers and employees. However, this technique involves a much longer waiting time, which could have a negative impact on the user experience. It would be plausible to let the user decide during use or in trials whether they would prefer to wait longer to receive fewer hallucinations or whether they would prefer to receive a response more quickly with a higher risk of hallucinations. This trade-off seems to depend on individual situations and should be investigated further.

7 Conclusion

In this paper, we presented the results of a simulation study that compared two different consistency-based hallucination detection techniques with respect to their realistic precision and response time. For this, we used different consistency-determining thresholds and real QA data sets from the health and enterprise context. In contrast to the literature, we used real and not synthetic data sets and implemented the techniques realistically through parallelization to investigate realistic differences between precision and response time. Our results enable researchers and developers to better assess the use of these techniques [15].

We can confirm with our research what is already known in the literature: that a more complex consistency-based hallucination detection technique achieves a higher precision, but also leads to a higher response time than a more simple technique. This means that a user gets more generated responses, which could lead to a more eloquent conversation, but they also have to wait much longer for those responses. With our research, we demonstrate realistic and predictable precision and response times on non-synthetic data sets. We also add to this knowledge that the precision and response time depend on the data set used and that the precision depends only slightly on the consistency-determining threshold in a realistic implementation. In the literature, so far only the following was known: a lower threshold leads to a higher precision, while a higher threshold leads to a lower precision but to a higher total number of true hallucinations detected [15].

Our research also comes with limitations that should be mentioned here and addressed in future research. In our simulation, we only compared two different real data sets from the health and enterprise context, two different thresholds, and two different consistency-based hallucination detection techniques, which reduce the generalizability of our research. Our industry partner provided us with only one real data set for this study. We focused our work on small real and finite data sets. Future work could include more diverse, real and open-ended data sets, a continuous threshold, and more or even mixed consistency-based hallucination detection techniques to validate and enrich our results. We focused on the trade-off between the precision and response time of consistency-based hallucination detection techniques. Other interesting trade-offs, e.g. regarding the recall of such techniques, which is especially relevant in critical domains (e.g. health), were not investigated in this paper to keep the work within limits. Future research can focus on investigating further trade-offs in the use of consistency-based hallucination detection techniques. We discovered that the consistency-based hallucination detection techniques used seem to be more data sensitive in terms of response time and precision, as mentioned in the literature [15]. Future research could investigate this and focus on designing and building data-robust approaches, maybe by combining different hallucination mitigating methods. In our work, we did not investigate how users react to different consistency-based hallucination detection approaches. However, we have investigated the expected precision and response time of these techniques under realistic conditions, which can serve as a basis for further research with users. Future research could focus on the user and investigate their preferences and trade-offs they are willing to take, e.g. between precision and response time.

References

1. Ahmad, M.A., Yaramis, I., Roy, T.D.: Creating trustworthy LLMs: dealing with hallucinations in healthcare AI (2023). https://doi.org/10.48550/ARXIV.2311.01463, https://arxiv.org/abs/2311.01463
2. Arefeen, M.A., Debnath, B., Chakradhar, S.: Leancontext: cost-efficient domain-specific question answering using LLMs (2023). https://doi.org/10.48550/ARXIV.2309.00841, https://arxiv.org/abs/2309.00841
3. Beese, J., Haki, M.K., Aier, S., Winter, R.: Simulation-based research in information systems: epistemic implications and a review of the status quo. Bus. Inf. Syst. Eng. **61**(4), 503–521 (2018). https://doi.org/10.1007/s12599-018-0529-1
4. Ben Abacha, A., Demner-Fushman, D.: A question-entailment approach to question answering. BMC Bioinform. **20**(1) (2019). https://doi.org/10.1186/s12859-019-3119-4
5. Huang, L., et al.: A survey on hallucination in large language models: principles, taxonomy, challenges, and open questions (2023). https://doi.org/10.48550/ARXIV.2311.05232, https://arxiv.org/abs/2311.05232
6. Ishwari, K.S.D., Aneeze, A.K.R.R., Sudheesan, S., Karunaratne, H.J.D.A., Nugaliyadde, A., Mallawarrachchi, Y.: Advances in natural language question answering: a review (2019). https://doi.org/10.48550/ARXIV.1904.05276, https://arxiv.org/abs/1904.05276
7. Ji, Z., et al.: Survey of hallucination in natural language generation. ACM Comput. Surv. **55**(12), 1–38 (2023). https://doi.org/10.1145/3571730
8. Kossen, J., Han, J., Razzak, M., Schut, L., Malik, S., Gal, Y.: Semantic entropy probes: robust and cheap hallucination detection in LLMs (2024). https://doi.org/10.48550/ARXIV.2406.15927, https://arxiv.org/abs/2406.15927
9. Liao, Q.V., et al.: All work and no play? In: Proceedings of the 2018 CHI Conference on Human Factors in Computing Systems. CHI '18, ACM (2018). https://doi.org/10.1145/3173574.3173577
10. Manakul, P., Liusie, A., Gales, M.J.F.: SelfcheckGPT: zero-resource black-box hallucination detection for generative large language models (2023). https://doi.org/10.48550/ARXIV.2303.08896, https://arxiv.org/abs/2303.08896
11. Peng, B., et al.: Check your facts and try again: improving large language models with external knowledge and automated feedback (2023). https://doi.org/10.48550/ARXIV.2302.12813, https://arxiv.org/abs/2302.12813
12. Quarteroni, S., Manandhar, S.: Designing an interactive open-domain question answering system. Nat. Lang. Eng. **15**(1), 73–95 (2009). https://doi.org/10.1017/s1351324908004919
13. Xiao, Y., Wang, W.Y.: On hallucination and predictive uncertainty in conditional language generation (2021). https://doi.org/10.48550/ARXIV.2103.15025, https://arxiv.org/abs/2103.15025
14. Yuan, W., Neubig, G., Liu, P.: Bartscore: evaluating generated text as text generation (2021). https://doi.org/10.48550/ARXIV.2106.11520, https://arxiv.org/abs/2106.11520
15. Zhang, J., Li, Z., Das, K., Malin, B.A., Kumar, S.: Sac3: reliable hallucination detection in black-box language models via semantic-aware cross-check consistency (2023). https://doi.org/10.48550/ARXIV.2311.01740, https://arxiv.org/abs/2311.01740

LadderChat An LLM-Based Conversational Agent for Laddering Interviews

Leon Hanschmann(✉), Marvin Mokelke, and Alexander Maedche

Karlsruhe Institute of Technology, 76131 Karlsruhe, Germany
{leon.hanschmann,alexander.maedche}@kit.edu

Abstract. Laddering interviews are a qualitative method to understand how customers value specific product attributes. However, traditional face-to-face approaches are resource-intensive and lack scalability. This paper introduces LadderChat, a conversational agent (CA) based on Large Language Models (LLMs) designed to conduct human-like laddering interviews. We propose design principles for an LLM-based CA and implement them in LadderChat. The system leverages LLMs for response analysis, adaptive probing, and visualization of Attributes-Consequences-Values (ACV) chains. A formative evaluation with six researchers provides initial insights into LadderChat's effectiveness in guiding participants through the laddering process and generating real-time visualizations. The evaluation also identifies areas for refinement, including user interface improvements and data privacy considerations. This study contributes to ongoing efforts to enhance qualitative research methods through the application of advanced large language models.

Keywords: large language models · conversational agents · laddering interviews

1 Introduction

Understanding how customers perceive products and their attributes is essential for designing user-centered products and developing effective marketing strategies [2,24,39,40]. One of the key methods for uncovering these perceptions is laddering, a qualitative interviewing technique that explores the links between product attributes, the consequences of their use, and the personal values they fulfill [31]. Laddering is grounded in means-end chain theory [13,30], which posits that consumers perceive products not just as collections of attributes but as means to achieve desired ends, namely personal values. The laddering technique involves asking participants a series of probing "why" questions, starting from specific product attributes and moving up to higher levels of abstraction, such as the consequences of those attributes and the underlying personal values [12,31,43]. For example, a consumer might prefer a car with high fuel efficiency (attribute)

A. Følstad et al. (Eds.): CONVERSATIONS 2024, LNCS 15545, pp. 48–65, 2025.
https://doi.org/10.1007/978-3-031-88045-2_4

because it saves money on gas (consequence), which allows them to spend more on family activities (value).

While laddering interviews originated in product research, they have also been applied in fields like organizational psychology and education. In these areas, laddering helps uncover values influencing organizational behavior [33] and analyzes factors affecting lecturers' teaching quality [38]. Traditional laddering interviews are typically conducted face-to-face by skilled interviewers who can adapt to participants' responses and provide clarification when misunderstandings occur [8,17]. While this approach yields rich qualitative data, it is resource-intensive and lacks scalability when dealing with larger audiences [32]. Survey-based methods, such as online questionnaires, have been employed to mitigate these challenges by reducing time and personnel requirements [25]. However, these methods often lack interactive guidance, leading to participant fatigue due to the repetitive question structure and potential misunderstandings without the possibility of immediate clarification [21,35].

Advancements in conversational agents (CAs) offer new avenues for automating laddering interviews while retaining some of the interactive nature of human-led conversations [22,26]. Rietz and Maedche [32] propose LadderBot, a rule-based chatbot designed to conduct laddering interviews. Their study found that while LadderBot effectively reduced the need for human interviewers and collected longer responses compared to traditional surveys, participants reported that interactions felt generic and monotonous, lacking the depth and adaptability of human interviewers. The emergence of LLMs, such as OpenAI's GPT-4 [3], has revolutionized natural language processing by enabling machines to understand and generate human-like text [41]. LLMs demonstrate advanced language comprehension, contextual understanding, and the ability to produce coherent and personalized responses [27] and have been applied in many domains (e.g. [14]). These capabilities make LLMs suitable candidates for conducting complex interviews that require nuanced understanding and dynamic interaction.

This paper aims to design an LLM-based conversational agent for conducting laddering interviews. By leveraging the sophisticated language abilities of LLMs, the proposed agent seeks to deliver a more engaging and effective interview experience, closely mimicking the adaptability and depth of human interviewers. Consequently, we formulate the following research question: *How can an LLM-based conversational agent be designed to conduct laddering interviews effectively?*

2 Related Work

This section reviews prior work on traditional laddering methods and the application of conversational agents, particularly those powered by LLMs, in conducting laddering interviews.

2.1 Traditional Laddering Methods

Traditional laddering interviews involve face-to-face interactions where skilled interviewers guide participants through a series of "why" questions to elicit means-end chains [2,17]. This method, known as soft laddering, allows interviewers to adapt their questioning dynamically and permits participants to move freely between different means-end chains, resulting in rich qualitative data [36]. Reynolds and Gutman [31] underscore the crucial role of interviewer expertise in effectively navigating the hierarchical structure of participants' cognitive constructs.

In contrast, hard laddering represents a more structured approach where participants must complete one means-end chain before moving to another, typically through paper-and-pencil questionnaires or computerized interfaces [25,35]. While this method enables greater standardization and scalability, Phillips and Reynolds [29] note that it may constrain the natural flow of participant responses and limit the depth of insights compared to soft laddering. However, the resource-intensive nature of soft laddering limits their scalability, especially in studies requiring large sample sizes [32]. Additionally, [11] identifies methodological inconsistencies and challenges in data interpretation, highlighting issues such as interviewer bias and difficulties in ensuring reliability across interviews. To address scalability issues, researchers have explored various hard laddering approaches through survey-based methods [25,35]. Hard laddering facilitates data collection from larger samples [29]. However, while these methods enable broader data gathering, they often suffer from reduced data quality due to the absence of interactive probing and potential participant fatigue [21].

Participants may provide superficial or incomplete responses, and misunderstandings cannot be readily addressed [43]. Table 1 provides a comparison of hard and soft laddering, highlighting their key differences in structure, implementation, and outcomes [32].

Table 1. Comparison of Hard and Soft Laddering Approaches (Adapted from [32])

Characteristic	Hard Laddering	Soft Laddering
Structure	Sequential ACV chain completion; one ladder at a time	Flexible navigation between multiple attributes
Implementation	Paper-based or computerized questionnaires	Face-to-face interviews
Scalability	High; standardized format with minimal interviewer needs	Limited; requires trained interviewers
Response Quality	Often yields superficial responses; limited guidance	Richer responses through interactive guidance
Data Analysis	Predetermined structure eases analysis	Ladders must be constructed post-interview

Leppard et al. [23] propose methodological improvements by incorporating ranking methods to better construct and interpret hierarchical value maps.

Efforts to enhance laddering data collection have led to the development of computerized methods that provide a more engaging user interface and guide participants through the laddering process. For example, [37] developed LadderUX, a digital tool combining laddering with card sorting for user experience research with children, enhancing engagement and data quality. [15] proposed using crowdsourcing to accelerate the deductive coding of qualitative data, addressing the bottleneck in analyzing laddering data. Despite these innovations, challenges remain in balancing scalability with the depth of data collected.

2.2 CAs for Laddering Interviews

Advancements in natural language processing have enabled the development of conversational agents capable of engaging users in interactive dialogues [22,26]. Early CAs were primarily rule-based, relying on predefined scripts and limited in their ability to handle complex or unexpected inputs [22]. In the context of laddering interviews, such limitations hinder the agent's capacity to mimic the adaptability of human interviewers. Rietz and Maedche [32] developed LadderBot, a rule-based chatbot designed specifically for conducting laddering interviews. Their study demonstrated that LadderBot could reduce the need for human interviewers and collect longer participant responses compared to traditional surveys. However, participants reported that interactions felt generic and lacked depth, highlighting the limitations of rule-based approaches in capturing the dynamic nature of laddering interviews.

The emergence of LLMs significantly advanced the capabilities of conversational agents [3]. LLMs exhibit advanced language understanding, context retention, and the ability to generate coherent and contextually appropriate responses across a wide range of topics [27]. These models have been applied successfully in various domains, including customer service chatbots and digital health applications [9]. Chew et al. [7] introduced LLM-assisted content analysis (LACA), demonstrating that LLMs can effectively support deductive coding in qualitative research by reducing coding time while maintaining performance comparable to human coders. In a recent study, Hu et al. [18] found that while general follow-up questions elicited more informative responses, concept-based follow-up questions achieved better user engagement and lower drop rates, suggesting that combining different questioning strategies could enhance the effectiveness of CA-conducted interviews.

Despite their potential, to the best of the authors' knowledge, the application of LLMs in conducting and configuring laddering interviews has not been explored. Integrating LLMs into laddering interviews offers the possibility of combining the scalability and efficiency of automated platforms for conducting ladder interviews with the depth and adaptability of human interviewers. This study builds upon prior research by proposing an LLM-based conversational agent specifically designed for laddering interviews, aiming to enhance data quality and participant engagement while improving scalability and reducing resource requirements.

3 Design of LadderChat

In accordance with the Design Science Research (DSR) methodology, we have formulated a set of initial design principles to guide the development of an LLM-based conversational agent for conducting laddering interviews. The creation of these design principles follows established guidelines in DSR literature, which emphasizes generating prescriptive knowledge through rigorous and relevant research [10,16]. The proposed design principles are intended to serve as actionable guidelines that bridge theory and practice, providing normative statements on designing artifacts to achieve desired outcomes [6].

3.1 Design Principles

The formulation of our initial design principles adheres to the structure proposed by Gregor and Jones [19]. We considered recommendations by Chandra et al. [6] on articulating design principles grounded in theoretical foundations and empirical evidence. The development process involved several key steps. First, we identified the problem by recognizing the limitations of existing methods for conducting laddering interviews, such as lack of scalability and reduced data quality in automated approaches [32]. Next, we defined objectives for a solution by establishing goals to enhance scalability without compromising data quality, leveraging the capabilities of LLMs. We then developed the principles based on existing literature. This approach aligns with the iterative process recommended by Peffers et al. [28]. To present the justification and application of the design principles clearly, we have organized them into Tables 2 and 3. The tables provide an overview of each design principle, its justification based on the literature, and its practical application in developing the LLM-based conversational agent.

3.2 Implementation

We developed LadderChat as a comprehensive platform for conducting laddering interviews that implements our design principles through three integrated components, illustrated in Fig. 1.

The system architecture reflects both the theoretical foundations of laddering methodology and the practical requirements of scalable interview administration. At its core, LadderChat leverages OpenAI's LLMs to enable natural, adaptive conversations while maintaining methodological rigor. The platform orchestrates the laddering process through three sequential phases: Setup, Stimuli Ranking, and Interviews and Analysis (Fig. 2). This structure serves two distinct user groups - researchers and participants - through specialized interfaces. Researchers can configure interview parameters and monitor the emerging ACV chains in real-time while participants engage with an interview interface. This dual-interface approach, grounded in DP2, ensures methodological control while fostering natural participant engagement through relevant stimuli presentation and guided reflection.

Table 2. Design Principles for LLM-Based Conversational Agent (Part 1)

Design Principle 1: To ensure the reliable completion of ACV chains, the conversational agent should perform real-time analysis of participant responses during the interview, enabling adaptive probing and guidance.
Justification: In laddering interviews, the interviewer's ability to interpret responses and ask appropriate follow-up questions is crucial for eliciting complete ACV chains [31]. Conversational agents for conducting ladder interviews lacking adaptive capabilities often fail to produce complete chains [32]. Real-time analysis enables the agent to adjust its questioning dynamically, enhancing data quality.
Application: Utilize the LLM's natural language understanding to classify participant inputs into attributes, consequences, or values. Implement algorithms that analyze responses on-the-fly and generate contextually appropriate prompts to encourage deeper reflection, mimicking a skilled human interviewer.
Design Principle 2: To engage participants and stimulate idea generation, the conversational agent should begin the interview by presenting a collection of relevant stimuli and prompting participants to rank or reflect upon them.
Justification: Introducing stimuli helps participants focus on the topic and facilitates the elicitation of initial attributes [20]. This technique enhances engagement and idea generation while ranking stimuli adds a quantitative element for prioritization [1].
Application: Present a curated list of relevant stimuli to participants at the interview's onset. Prompt participants to rank the stimuli or reflect upon them. Use the highest-ranked stimuli as entry points for subsequent in-depth exploration during the interview.

Setup. The setup phase of LadderChat enables researchers to configure their laddering interviews through a dedicated interface (Fig. 3). Researchers can define the interview topic, specify the number of stimuli to be discussed, and leverage the assistance of an LLM for stimulus generation and refinement. To facilitate researcher's idea generation (DP2), the auto-generation of stimuli is based upon few-shot prompting [4], leveraging example topics and corresponding stimuli.

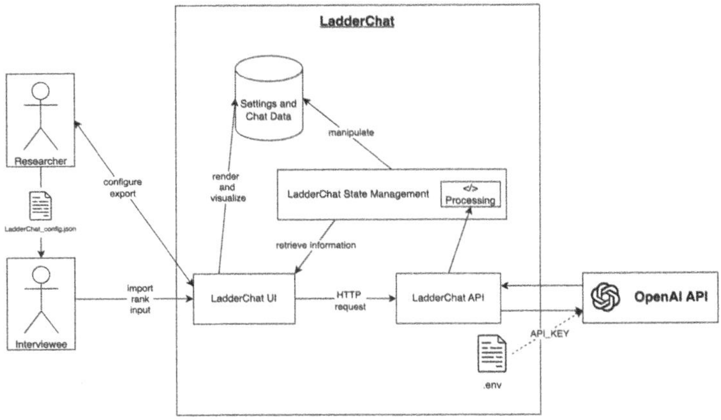

Fig. 1. LadderChat's System Overview

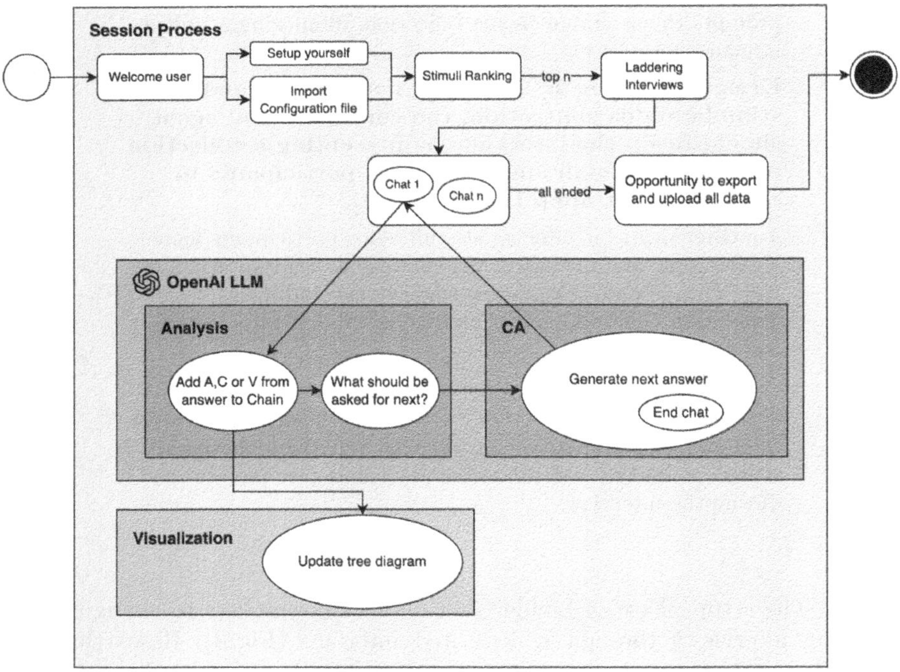

Fig. 2. Activity Map of LadderChat

Table 3. Design Principles for LLM-Based Conversational Agent (Part 2)

Design Principle 3: To facilitate focused exploration and ease of data analysis, the conversational agent should conduct separate interview sessions for each selected stimulus, completing one ACV chain before initiating another, in accordance with the hard laddering approach.
Justification: Hard laddering involves exploring one attribute at a time, simplifying data analysis, and reducing cognitive load on participants [2]. This structured approach provides cognitive separation between topics, allowing focused exploration [21].
Application: Organize the interview into distinct sessions for each selected stimulus. Provide clear transitions and summaries between sessions. Guide the participant through completing one ACV chain before initiating the next, ensuring clarity and organization.

Stimuli Ranking. The Stimuli Ranking phase implements a drag-and-drop interface for stimulus prioritization (Fig. 4). Following DP2 and Bagozzi and Dabholkar [1], this engagement mechanism facilitates quantitative prioritization before proceeding with the interview.

Analysis. LadderChat implements the real-time analysis principles specified in DP1 through its analysis interface. Figure 5 presents this interface, which allows researchers to monitor the emerging ACV chains during interviews. The tree diagram visualization provides immediate insights into participants' cognitive structures, enabling researchers to track the interview progress and understand the developing patterns of responses. To enhance the system's analytical capabilities, we developed a hybrid prompting methodology combining one-shot learning [4] and chain-of-thought reasoning techniques [42]. This approach was augmented with domain-specific exemplars of potential Attributes, Consequences, and Values within relevant laddering contexts.

Fig. 3. Screenshot of LadderChat's configuration page

Interviews. Following DP3's recommendation for separate interview sessions per stimulus, LadderChat provides distinct conversational interfaces for each top-ranked stimulus. As shown in Fig. 6, the chat interface enables focused exploration of individual ACV chains. This implementation aligns with Botschen et al.'s [2] hard laddering method, which simplifies data analysis while reducing participant cognitive load. To enhance interview quality, we supplemented the system's training data with annotated laddering interview transcripts. These annotations included insights into the interviewer's reasoning behind each question, providing context for more natural and effective questioning. The following excerpt illustrates this approach:

Q: You have mentioned Bluetooth as valuable to you. What do you use Bluetooth for? P: I mostly listen to music on my AirPods. [Add to consequence: Listen to music with wireless headphones. In what situation is it important for him to

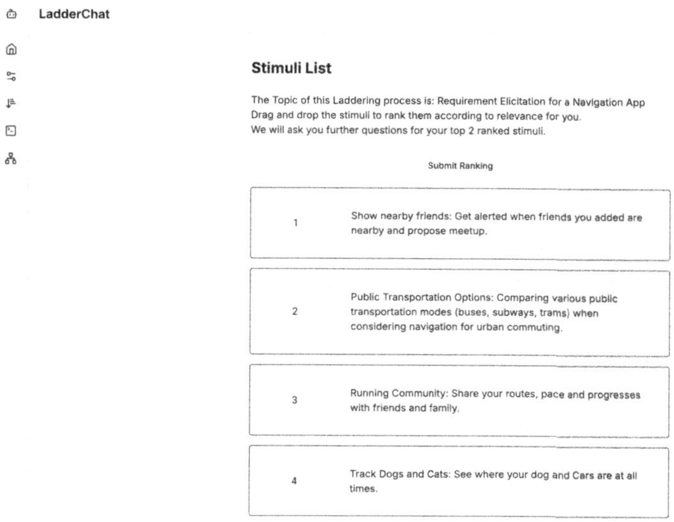

Fig. 4. Screenshot of LadderChat's stimuli ranking page

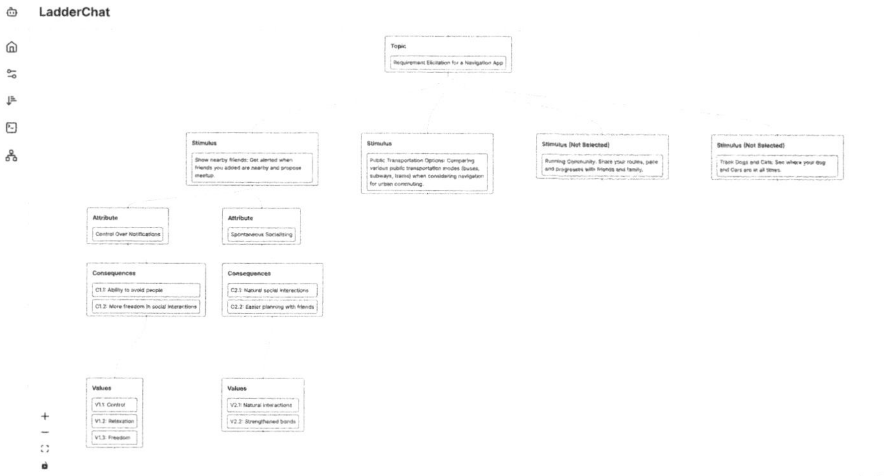

Fig. 5. Screenshot of LadderChat's analysis page

have a wireless connection...] Q: When do you consider it particularly practical to use Bluetooth headphones compared to wired ones?

The development process involved iterative testing of various prompting techniques to improve the system's performance in conducting laddering interviews. This iterative refinement focused on enhancing the model's comprehension of ACV chains through carefully selected exemplars and annotated interview pat-

Fig. 6. Screenshot of LadderChat's chat page

terns. Interviews conclude when participants exhaust their identification of new attributes, at which point the system generates a summary for confirmation.

4 Formative Evaluation

To evaluate LadderChat's efficacy in conducting laddering interviews and obtain preliminary feedback on its usability and performance, we carried out a formative assessment using a convenience sample of six researchers. This evaluation involved engaging each participant with LadderChat to conduct a laddering interview on the topic of smartwatches. The participants were university researchers in their late 20 s to early 30 s, all with theoretical knowledge of laddering techniques but varying levels of practical experience in conducting such interviews.

4.1 Evaluation Process

The evaluation process for each participant began with configuring LadderChat for a laddering interview about smartwatches. This included setting up the interview topic and selecting stimuli. The researcher then engaged in the laddering interview process, which involved ranking stimuli and responding to the chatbot's questions. Following the interaction with LadderChat, we conducted semi-structured interviews with each participant to assess their perceptions and identify potential areas for improvement. These interviews were structured according to a Strength-Weakness-Opportunity-Threat (SWOT) framework.

The semi-structured interviews began with questions about participants' initial experience and first impressions, followed by an assessment of the system's strengths focusing on key features like real-time visualization and stimuli suggestion. Questions addressing weaknesses prompted discussion of challenges, interface issues, and limitations in system comprehension. The opportunities section explored potential enhancements and integration possibilities, while the threats section addressed concerns about data privacy. The interviews concluded with questions about future use intentions.

The entire evaluation process for each participant, including configuration, interview, and feedback, took approximately 30 min. The interviews and laddering sessions were recorded and transcribed. Following the approach of previous formative evaluation studies (e.g., [5,34]). The results are presented in Table 4.

Table 4. SWOT Analysis of LadderChat

Category	Points
Strengths	– Effective Laddering: Good responsiveness and coherent conversation flow
	– Real-time Visualization: Appreciated Analytics feature with tree visualization
	– Stimuli Suggestion: Helpful in generating and refining stimuli
	– Structured Interviews: Beneficial separation of interviews for each stimulus
Weaknesses	– User Interface: Some elements are not immediately intuitive
	– Depth of Questions: Can be challenging for some users
	– Limited Language Options: May not fully capture nuanced expressions in non-native languages
Opportunities	– Research Efficiency: Potential to improve extraction and structuring of complex information
	– Multilingual Support: Expansion could enhance the capturing of values across cultures
	– Integration with Existing Research Tools: Potential to seamlessly integrate with survey platforms and data analysis software
	– Automated Insight Generation: Possibility to generate preliminary insights and hypotheses from interview data in real-time
Threats	– Data Privacy Concerns: Potential issues with sensitive data
	– Topic Sensitivity: May need additional measures for sensitive research topics
	– Learning Curve: Possible challenge for researchers new to LadderChat
	– Overreliance on Technology: Risk of missing nuances (potentially) caught by human interviewers

4.2 Results

Strengths. The initial assessment revealed that LadderChat effectively guided participants through the laddering process, demonstrating good responsiveness to user inputs and maintaining a coherent conversation flow. One participant noted, "I find that it [LadderChat] was able to respond very well to my statements. It also structured it well, and that worked well. It was also understandable for me how it proceeded." This feedback highlights LadderChat's ability to maintain a natural conversation flow while adhering to the structured laddering technique. The real-time visualization of the ACV chains was particularly well-received across the group. A participant commented, "The analytics view is really impressive. Watching the tree diagram build up as we go through the interview is super helpful. It gives you a clear picture of how everything connects, right there in real-time." This feature not only aided in the interview process but also provided immediate insights into the emerging cognitive structures. The stimuli suggestion feature was appreciated by several participants for its ability to inspire and guide the interview setup. As one researcher noted, "The stimuli suggestion feature is really helpful. It gives you a good starting point and lets you think more deeply about the interview setup before diving in." This feature helps researchers configure more comprehensive and relevant interviews.

Weaknesses. Several usability issues were identified, particularly regarding the user interface. One researcher mentioned, "A few visual cues could make the navigation smoother, especially when you're just getting started." This feedback suggests potential improvements in the visual design to enhance user experience. Participants also noted challenges with the depth of questions and limitations in capturing nuanced expressions in non-native languages.

Opportunities. Participants highlighted LadderChat's efficiency in eliciting and structuring complex information. One researcher stated: "It's impressive how [LadderChat] extracts information through conversation. You end up with a detailed map of ideas surprisingly fast, just by having a dialogue." The potential for integration with existing research tools and automated insight generation were identified as promising future developments.

Threats. The evaluation highlighted several areas requiring careful consideration. Multiple participants suggested including a brief introduction or tutorial at the beginning of the session to address the learning curve for new users. Additionally, they raised important considerations about data privacy and the need for clear disclaimers, especially when dealing with sensitive topics. Concerns were also expressed about the risk of overreliance on technology, potentially missing nuances that human interviewers might catch.

Summary. While individual experiences varied, there was a general consensus among the participants that LadderChat shows promise as an effective tool for conducting laddering interviews. The evaluation highlighted both strengths and areas for improvement, providing valuable insights for future development and LadderChat's refinement. In conclusion, this formative evaluation suggests that LadderChat offers benefits in terms of efficiency, visualization, and structured data collection for laddering interviews, as summarized in the Strengths category of Table 4. However, further refinements in user interface design and considerations for data privacy and sensitive topics are recommended, addressing the Weaknesses and Threats identified. Future evaluations with a larger and more diverse sample would provide more comprehensive insights into LadderChat's effectiveness across different research contexts and user groups.

5 Discussion

The development and evaluation of LadderChat explore the potential for automating qualitative research methods through LLMs, specifically in the context of laddering interviews. While our initial results demonstrate promising capabilities in terms of natural dialogue and real-time attribute extraction, they also highlight important considerations regarding control, reliability, and scalability that warrant further investigation.

5.1 Balancing Flexibility and Control in LLM-Based Systems

A critical trade-off in implementing LLM-based systems like LadderChat lies in the balance between flexibility and control. Traditional rule-based systems, while less adaptable, offer precise control over the interview process and clear reasoning paths. LadderChat's LLM-based approach provides more natural dialogue and better handles unexpected participant responses, but this comes at the cost of reduced control over the system's reasoning and decision-making processes. While we implemented chain-of-thought prompting and few-shot learning techniques to guide the LLM's behavior, these mechanisms do not guarantee the same level of predictability as rule-based systems. The current implementation of LadderChat could benefit from more robust dialogue management mechanisms. While the system includes features for visualizing the LLM's thought process, these are primarily used for logging rather than active dialogue management. Future iterations should incorporate comprehensive fallback mechanisms and validation protocols to address potential issues such as hallucinations or inappropriate responses, ensuring that the improved scalability and natural dialogue do not come at the expense of reliability and control. Data privacy emerges as another crucial consideration in the trade-off between traditional and LLM-based approaches. Traditional methods keep sensitive interview data within organizational boundaries, while LLM-based systems introduce new privacy challenges. Our current implementation needs stronger safeguards and clear protocols for handling sensitive information.

5.2 Limitations of Current Evaluation

The evaluation of LadderChat, while providing valuable initial insights, has notable limitations that should be addressed in future research. The small sample size of six researchers and focus on a single topic (smartwatches) limits our ability to make broader claims about the system's scalability and effectiveness across different contexts. A more comprehensive evaluation is needed, incorporating multiple topics and a larger, more diverse participant pool. Future evaluations should specifically assess several key aspects that were not fully explored in the current study. These include the robustness of information extraction across different domains, the consistency of dialogue management in challenging scenarios, and the system's performance with participants of varying technical backgrounds. Additionally, a systematic comparison with traditional laddering methods would provide clearer insights into the relative strengths and weaknesses of our approach.

Additionally, the evaluation focuses solely on researchers' perspectives, neglecting assessments from participants who interacted with LadderChat. Since laddering interviews are inherently interactive between interviewer and interviewee, omitting participant feedback is a significant limitation. Interactions with a conversational agent may alter participants' responses compared to those with a human interviewer, potentially affecting the depth and quality of the elicited ACV chains. Future research should include evaluations from participants to fully understand the system's effectiveness and impact on the interview process.

5.3 Contributions and Future Development

Despite these limitations, LadderChat makes several important contributions to research methodology and practical applications in marketing and product design. The system demonstrates the potential for LLM-based approaches to enhance the scalability of laddering interviews while maintaining meaningful dialogue. The real-time visualization of ACV chains represents a novel approach to data analysis in qualitative research, though further validation of its reliability is needed. Future development of LadderChat should focus on implementing more robust dialogue management mechanisms. This includes the development of systematic validation of extracted attributes and relationships, as well as clear fallback protocols for handling uncertainty or potential hallucinations. The system requires enhanced privacy protection measures for sensitive information, along with improved mechanisms for controlling and documenting the LLM's reasoning process. These developments are essential to ensure the system's reliability and trustworthiness in research contexts. The design principles developed for LadderChat provide a framework for future research in LLM-based qualitative research tools, though they need refinement based on more extensive testing. From a practical standpoint, while LadderChat shows promise in making in-depth consumer research more accessible to organizations with limited resources, careful attention must be paid to ensuring the reliability and validity of the insights generated through automated interviews.

5.4 Limitations and Future Work

Beyond the evaluation limitations discussed above, several other aspects require further investigation. The system's performance in multilingual contexts, its ability to handle complex or sensitive topics, and its long-term reliability all need a more thorough examination. Future research should also explore hybrid approaches that combine automated and human-led interviews, potentially offering a more balanced solution that leverages the strengths of both approaches while mitigating their respective weaknesses.

6 Conclusion

LadderChat explores the application of Large Language Models in automating laddering interviews. It implements design principles aimed at conducting scalable interviews while attempting to maintain data quality. Initial evaluations provided insights into LadderChat's performance, highlighting areas such as real-time visualization and adaptive questioning. The study also identified limitations and areas for future research, including data privacy concerns and the need for larger-scale evaluations. Further investigation is necessary to fully understand the capabilities and limitations of such systems across various research contexts and to compare their effectiveness with traditional interview methods.

References

1. Bagozzi, R.P., Dabholkar, P.A.: Consumer recycling goals and their effect on decisions to recycle: a means-end chain analysis, **11**(4), 313–340. https://onlinelibrary.wiley.com/doi/10.1002/mar.4220110403
2. Botschen, G., Thelen, E.M., Pieters, R.: Using means-end structures for benefit segmentation: an application to services, **33**(1), 38–58. https://www.emerald.com/insight/content/doi/10.1108/EUM0000000004491/full/html
3. Brown, T.B., et al.: Language models are few-shot learners. https://arxiv.org/abs/2005.14165, version Number: 4
4. Brown, T.B., et al.: Language models are few-shot learners (2020). https://arxiv.org/abs/2005.14165
5. Cameron, G., et al.: Best practices for designing chatbots in mental healthcare - a case study on iHelpr (2018). https://scienceopen.com/hosted-document?doi=10.14236/ewic/HCI2018.129
6. Chandra, L., Seidel, S., Gregor, S.: Prescriptive knowledge in is research: conceptualizing design principles in terms of materiality, action, and boundary conditions. In: 2015 48th Hawaii International Conference on System Sciences, pp. 4039–4048 (2015)
7. Chew, R., Bollenbacher, J., Wenger, M., Speer, J., Kim, A.: LLM-assisted content analysis: using large language models to support deductive coding (2023). https://arxiv.org/abs/2306.14924
8. Deutsch, S., Begolli, G., Lugmayr, M., Tscheligi, M.: Assisted collection and organization for laddering interview data. In: CHI '11 Extended Abstracts on Human Factors in Computing Systems, pp. 647–650. ACM. https://dl.acm.org/doi/10.1145/1979742.1979661

9. Dingler, T., Kwasnicka, D., Wei, J., Gong, E., Oldenburg, B.: The use and promise of conversational agents in digital health, **30**(1), 191–199. http://www.thieme-connect.de/DOI/DOI?10.1055/s-0041-1726510
10. Gregor, S., Hevner, A.R.: Positioning and presenting design science research for maximum impact, **37**(2), 337–355. https://misq.org/positioning-and-presenting-design-science-research-for-maximum-impact.html
11. Grunert, K.G., Beckmann, S., Sørensen, E.: Means-end chains and laddering: an inventory of problems and an agenda for research, pp. 63–90 (2001)
12. Grunert, K.G., Grunert, S.C.: Measuring subjective meaning structures by the laddering method: theoretical considerations and methodological problems. Int. J. Res. Mark. **12**(3), 209–225 (1995). https://www.sciencedirect.com/science/article/pii/016781169500022T
13. Gutman, J.: A means-end chain model based on consumer categorization processes, **46**(2), 60–72. http://journals.sagepub.com/doi/10.1177/002224298204600207
14. Hanschmann, L., Gnewuch, U., Maedche, A.: Saleshat: a LLM-based social robot for human-like sales conversations, pp. 61–76 (2024). https://doi.org/10.1007/978-3-031-54975-5_4
15. Haug, S., Rietz, T., Maedche, A.: Accelerating deductive coding of qualitative data: an experimental study on the applicability of crowdsourcing. In: Mensch und Computer 2021, pp. 432–443. ACM. https://dl.acm.org/doi/10.1145/3473856.3473873
16. Hevner, M., Park, R.: Design science in information systems research, **28**(1), 75. https://www.jstor.org/stable/10.2307/25148625
17. Hofmann, H.F., Lehner, F.: Requirements engineering as a success factor in software projects. IEEE Softw. **18**, 58–66 (2001). https://api.semanticscholar.org/CorpusID:14124130
18. Hu, J., et al.: Designing the conversational agent: asking follow-up questions for information elicitation. Proc. ACM Hum.-Comput. Interact. **8**(CSCW1) (2024). https://doi.org/10.1145/3637320
19. Jones, D., Gregor, S.: The anatomy of a design theory, **8**(5), 312–335. https://aisel.aisnet.org/jais/vol8/iss5/19/
20. Jung, Y., Kang, H.: User goals in social virtual worlds: a means-end chain approach **26**(2), 218–225. https://linkinghub.elsevier.com/retrieve/pii/S0747563209001514
21. Kaciak, E., Cullen, C.W.: A method of abbreviating a laddering survey, **17**(2), 105–113. http://link.springer.com/10.1057/jt.2009.4
22. Klopfenstein, L.C., Delpriori, S., Malatini, S., Bogliolo, A.: The rise of bots: a survey of conversational interfaces, patterns, and paradigms. In: Proceedings of the 2017 Conference on Designing Interactive Systems, pp. 555–565. ACM. https://dl.acm.org/doi/10.1145/3064663.3064672
23. Leppard, P., Russell, C., Cox, D.: Improving means-end-chain studies by using a ranking method to construct hierarchical value maps. Food Qual. Preference **15**(5), 489–497 (2004). https://www.sciencedirect.com/science/article/pii/S0950329303001174
24. Lundgren, B.A., Lic, T.: Customers' perspectives on a residential development using the laddering method. J. Housing Built Environ. **25**, 37–52 (2010)
25. Miles, S., Rowe, G.: The Laddering Technique, pp. 305–343. Blackwell Publishing, Oxford (2003)
26. Mott, B.W., Lester, J.C., Branting, K.: Conversational agents. In: The Practical Handbook of Internet Computing (2004). https://api.semanticscholar.org/CorpusID:40364991

27. Ouyang, L., et al.: Training language models to follow instructions with human feedback. https://arxiv.org/abs/2203.02155, version Number: 1
28. Peffers, K., Tuunanen, T., Rothenberger, M.A., Chatterjee, S.: A design science research methodology for information systems research, **24**(3), 45–77. https://www.tandfonline.com/doi/full/10.2753/MIS0742-1222240302
29. Phillips-Hernandez, J., Reynolds, T.: A hard look at hard laddering: a comparison of studies examining the hierarchical structure of means-end theory. Qualit. Mark. Res. Int. J. **12**, 83–99 (2009)
30. Pieters, R., Baumgartner, H., Allen, D.: A means-end chain approach to consumer goal structures. Int. J. Res. Mark. **12**(3), 227–244 (1995). https://www.sciencedirect.com/science/article/pii/016781169500023U
31. Reynolds, T.J., Gutman, J.: Laddering theory, method, analysis, and interpretation. J. Advertising Res. 40–79 (2001). https://api.semanticscholar.org/CorpusID:14780103
32. Rietz, T., Maedche, A.: Ladderbot - a conversational agent for human-like online laddering interviews, **171**, 102969. https://linkinghub.elsevier.com/retrieve/pii/S1071581922001872
33. Rugg, G., Eva, M., Mahmood, A., Rehman, N., Andrews, S., Davies, S.: Eliciting information about organizational culture via laddering. Inf. Syst. J. **12**(3), 215–229 (2002)
34. Ruoff, M., Gnewuch, U.: Designing multimodal bi&a systems for co-located team interactions (2021)
35. Russell, C., et al.: A comparison of paper-and-pencil and computerised methods of "hard" laddering **15**(3), 279–291. https://linkinghub.elsevier.com/retrieve/pii/S0950329303000685
36. Schultze, U., Avital, M.: Designing interviews to generate rich data for information systems research, **21**(1), 1–16. https://linkinghub.elsevier.com/retrieve/pii/S1471772710000412
37. Vanden Abeele, V., Hauters, E., Zaman, B.: Increasing the reliability and validity of quantitative laddering data with LadderUX. In: CHI '12 Extended Abstracts on Human Factors in Computing Systems, pp. 2057–2062. ACM. https://doi.org/10.1145/2212776.2223752
38. Voss, R., Gruber, T.: The desired teaching qualities of lecturers in higher education: a means end analysis. Qual. Assur. Educ. **14**(3), 217–242 (2006)
39. Vriens, M., Hofstede, F.: Linking attributes benefits and consumer values a powerful approach to market segmentation, brand positioning, and advertising strategy. marketing research magazine, **12**, 5–10 (2000)
40. Wansink, B.: Using laddering to understand and leverage a brand's equity, **6**(2), 111–118. https://www.emerald.com/insight/content/doi/10.1108/13522750310470118/full/html
41. Wei, J., et al.: Emergent abilities of large language models. Trans. Mach. Learn. Res. (2022). https://openreview.net/forum?id=yzkSU5zdwD, survey Certification
42. Wei, J., et al.: Chain-of-thought prompting elicits reasoning in large language models. In: Advances in Neural Information Processing Systems, **35**, 24824–24837 (2022). https://doi.org/10.48550/arXiv.2201.11903
43. Zaman, B., Abeele, V.V.: Laddering with young children in user eXperience evaluations: theoretical groundings and a practical case. In: Proceedings of the 9th International Conference on Interaction Design and Children, pp. 156–165. ACM. https://dl.acm.org/doi/10.1145/1810543.1810561

Can Machine Learning Models Recognise Emotions, Particularly Neutral, Better Than Humans?

Jeffin Siby and Effie Lai-Chong Law(✉)

Durham University, Durham DH1 3LE, UK
{jeffin.siby,lai-chong.law}@durham.ac.uk

Abstract. Audio and visual data play vital roles in emotion recognition, with machine learning (ML) methods like SVMs and deep neural networks excelling in inferring human emotions. This study compared a state-of-the-art ML model's performance in each modality to human performance. It also examined items frequently labelled as 'neutral', comparing ML and human results. Utilising the CREMA-D dataset, CNN-LSTM and SVM models were trained for visual-only and audio-only data. Evaluation included matching and non-matching test sets, and ML models consistently outperformed humans, especially on the latter. The CNN-LSTM achieved 80.8% accuracy on matching visual data compared to human accuracy of 75.9%, and 39.0% versus 19.4% on non-matching data. Similarly, the SVM model scored 81.0% and 34.3% accuracy on matching and non-matching audio data, surpassing human accuracy of 68.9% and 17.9%. These results underscore ML's superiority in monomodal emotion recognition, particularly for challenging emotions. Implications for emotion recognition research and ethical concerns are inferred.

Keywords: Automatic emotion recognition · Neutral emotion · CREMA-D

1 Introduction

Are humans innately weak at recognising others' emotions as well as their own ones? Is "neutral emotion" a convenient label to describe an affective state when one cannot interpret or recognise the emotional expression observed? Can machine learning (ML) do a better job of differentiating "neutral emotion"? These questions have motivated us to explore the issue on the decipherability of neutral emotion.

Built upon their extensive research on emotion [47–49], Scherer and colleagues have developed the instrument *Emotion Recognition Index* to assess people's ability to recognise facial and vocal expressions of emotion [46]. Based on a large sample size of 3500, the average recognition accuracy for facial and vocal emotion were 73% and 69%, respectively. Intriguing contrasts between the two modalities by emotion category were identified. While fear and sadness were similar around 67% and 75%, there was a notable difference for happiness with facial (98%) being much higher than vocal (58%). The difference for anger – 54% vs. 72% - was less sharp but still marked. More recent

A. Følstad et al. (Eds.): CONVERSATIONS 2024, LNCS 15545, pp. 66–83, 2025.
https://doi.org/10.1007/978-3-031-88045-2_5

works have identified slightly different results per emotion (e.g. [60]) thanks to different methods. Nonetheless, the overall accuracy rate of ~70% seems a norm.

While many studies have explored the six basic emotions identified by Ekman [14] (or variations of this set), there has been little focus on '*neutral emotion*'. A notable exception is the work of Gasper and colleagues, who have examined the complexities of neutral affect from a psychological perspective for nearly a decade [18, 19, 20, 21]. They define neutral affect as an experience of indifference, where individuals feel neither positive nor negative emotions, but not necessarily the absence of all affects [18, 21]. Essentially, they argue and empirically establish that neutral affect is a common phenomenon and that it should be regarded as a distinct state of its own, independent of positive/negative affect [18, 22]. Furthermore, they highlight that neutral affect has unique bodily sensations and expressions and serves a function by signalling a lack of urgency for action when nothing noteworthy demands attention. Although Gasper and colleagues prefer the term "neutral affect" over "neutral emotion", they concede that both terms possess similar characteristics, acknowledging that emotions generally have a distinct valence and prompt action. They underscore that understanding neutral affect is pivotal for refining the conceptualization, measurement, and interpretation of affective states in research contexts [22].

This emphasis resonates with Law and colleagues [33] where they discuss the complexity surrounding the analysis of neutral expressions in emotion detection. Their work highlights disagreements in defining neutral vocal expressions across speech databases [56]. Various databases map neutral states differently, with some associating it with positive valence and low arousal, while others with positive valence but high arousal [16]. This lack of consistency raises questions about the validity of neutral as a distinct emotional category. Additionally, both manual and automatic analyses often show a high percentage of neutral category (e.g., 71% in FAU AIBO [55]) while some do not include a neutral category at all (e.g. [6]), indicating conceptual and methodological challenges in defining and classifying neutral emotions. This prompts further inquiry into what constitutes emotional neutrality and whether it can be effectively deciphered by humans or machines.

To evaluate the performance of humans versus machines in recognising emotions with a specific focus on neutral emotion, we used the state-of-the-art emotion classification techniques to build two ML classifiers. We deployed the CREMA-D audio-visual dataset [10] (Sect. 2) that uniquely provides data whether a human rater recognises an acted emotion correctly (matching) or incorrectly (non-matching). We explored three research questions:

- *How does the performance of ML models compare to human raters for audio data?*
- *How does the performance of ML models compare to human raters for visual data?*
- *To what extent do ML models misclassify items as 'neutral' in comparison to human misclassification rates?*

The contributions of our work are: 1) *Conceptual*: Analysing the trends in emotions being misclassified as 'neutral' sheds light on the open issue of neutral emotion. 2) *Methodological*: It is unique to separate data into two sets (matching and non-matching) to compare ML performance to human performance.

We find it important to clarify that our study focuses on monomodal data. Although multimodal approaches are increasingly used to enhance emotion recognition accuracy [17, 41], fusion methods remain challenging and complex [28]. Specifically, aligning and synchronising different modalities (e.g., text, speech, facial expressions) is difficult, particularly with temporal dynamics. Each modality offers overlapping but distinct emotional cues that must be harmonised for reliable classification [23]. Moreover, deep learning-based fusion requires significant computational resources and high-quality datasets, which limits model robustness across diverse scenarios [43]. Balancing interpretability with accuracy is another challenge, as models like transformers and attention mechanisms lack transparency, making it hard to assess each modality's contribution [53]. Due to these challenges, our project did not adopt a multimodal approach despite the availability of audiovisual data in the CREMA-D dataset. Instead, monomodal scenarios were prioritised because, as outlined in Sect. 2, they yielded the lowest accuracies for human performance, highlighting potential improvements with ML assistance.

2 CREMA-D: Audiovisual Emotion Dataset

CREMA-D [10] contains 7,442 clips of 91 actors who were asked to read out 12 sentences representing the emotions 'happy', 'anger', 'neutral', 'fear', 'disgust' and 'sad' (cf. Ekman's six [14], excluding'surprise' but including'neutral'). These clips were approved by directors and judged by raters via crowd-sourcing. Each clip is annotated with the intended (acted) emotion class and the individual emotion labels given by raters, as well as the average intensity (continuous scale) of the clip given by the raters. For the'neutral' clips, the confidence level was given on a scale of 0–100 instead of intensity. As explained in [10], the following three subsets are included in the final dataset (NB: For each clip, the majority rule is applied to the set of emotion labels given by a group of about ten raters):

- **Matching**: where the group perceived emotion matches the intended emotion.
- **Non-matching**: where the group perceived emotion differs from the intended emotion.
- **Ambiguous**: where the group perceived emotion doesn't have a majority.

Out of the 7442 stimuli for each modality, the distributions over the above order of the three subsets are 41%, 46% and 13% of the audio-only responses and are 64%, 25% and 11% of the visual-only responses.

For our study, the non-matching and ambiguous subsets have been combined into a single non-matching set for audio and visual data independently. This set represents items which humans found particularly difficult to infer emotion from. The primary motivation for this study is the low accuracy of humans on recognising emotion from the audio and visual stimuli. It was reported that human raters attained an accuracy of 49% on the entire audio data, 58.2% on all the visual-only data and 63.6% accuracy when shown stimuli that contained both audio and visual [10]. The surprisingly low accuracies for the two monomodal stimuli, which are even lower than those reported in [46] (Sect. 1), raises the question of whether ML models can perform better at classifying these emotions.

An interesting phenomenon in the CREMA-D dataset, overlooked by others conducting ML experiments, is the *high rate of misclassification for the neutral emotion.* For example, when looking at the entire set of audio data, it was seen that 48% of the ratings for the'sad' stimuli and 45% of the ratings for the'happy' stimuli were misclassified as'neutral'. This ambiguity for the term'neutral' is prevalent throughout the literature with different opinions on what it actually is (Sect. 1). To better understand this issue is another motivation for this study. We explored how ML models compare to humans and if they make similar misclassification of the'neutral' as seen for humans. We also examined which emotions are most commonly misclassified to help shed more light on the open debate.

3 Related Work

3.1 Datasets

In the domain of emotion recognition, there are 3 main categories into which datasets fall into [2]: Acted (Simulated), Elicited (Induced) and Natural.'Acted' datasets record actors who perform or provide an utterance of a specific emotion in a studio environment. The CREMA-D dataset is an example of an 'acted' dataset. 'Natural' datasets are obtained from a 'natural' setting in which spontaneous emotions are captured. This can include recordings from talk shows, call-centre recordings, YouTube and similar sources. 'Elicited' datasets fall in-between both and are created by placing participants that are to be recorded in a simulated emotional situation [2].

The main reason that other datasets were not chosen for this study is due to the non-existence of human results, without which a comparison to ML models cannot be drawn. The CREMA-D dataset provides a detailed breakdown of the results of individual raters for each stimulus, making it possible to compare to ML performance on said stimuli. Additionally, many datasets collected data from raters who responded to multimodal stimuli instead of considering each modality individually. Some datasets, including CMU-MOSI [62], SEND [35], RECOLA [44], SEWA [32], VAM [26] and HUMAINE [13] used a continuous valence/arousal scale as opposed to a categorical classification used in CREMA-D. For datasets that used categorical, there were several issues that made them incompatible for comparison, for example, IEMOCAP [9, 63] used 8 states and neutral but did not contain the emotion of 'disgust'.

3.2 Visual Data Classification Techniques

Deep Learning (DL) techniques are commonly used in literature [29]. CNN architectures are the most popular as they perform end-to-end learning directly from the input images. While the performance of CNN architectures is remarkable, its inability to reflect temporal variations in time-series data such as videos have led to hybrid approaches that combine CNN architectures with a memory component such as RNNs or LSTMs [29]. This hybrid approach allows both spatial and temporal information to be captured. Recent work by [45] explored the performance of such CNN hybrid models on various emotion datasets. The analysis of results concluded that CNN-LSTM [61] provided the highest accuracies compared to other hybrids including CNN-GRU and CNN-SVM on the

RAMAS [40], RAVDESS, CREMA-D and AffWild2 [31] datasets. The average uniform average recall (UAR) of the CNN-LSTM, CNN-GRU and CNN-SVM models across all evaluated datasets were 53.9%, 52.4% and 40.2% respectively. The low-performance scores demonstrate that even advanced ML models have difficulty classifying emotion.

3.3 Audio Data Classifications Techniques

While deep learning techniques are on the rise, SVMs trained with specialised features tend to outperform most deep neural networks such as RNNs and MLPs (multi-layer perceptrons) in the domain of Speech Emotion Recognition (SER) using audio data and is one of the most used classifiers in the literature [37]. For example, [30] demonstrated that an SVM model trained on a particular feature set obtained accuracies of 84.62%, 60.40%, and 72.39% on the EMO-DB, EMOVO [36] and SAVEE datasets, respectively. Comparatively, a MLP classifier trained and tested on the same datasets using the same feature set resulted in lower accuracies of 81.32%, 58.58% and 71.17%, respectively.

Further, experiments on the CREMA-D dataset itself have added supporting results to the superior performance of SVMs. [54] demonstrate how an SVM classifier outperforms an 6-layer RNN classifier. The authors claim that SVM has an overall higher performance score to the RNN classifier, particularly for the emotions of 'Anger', 'Fear', and 'Sad' where the SVM model achieved accuracy scores of 90.13%, 84.35% and 85.43% compared to the RNN model which achieved lower accuracies of 87.79%, 83.43% and 83.43%, respectively. It should also be noted that the average time taken for the SVM classifier to run on the test data was approximately 15.75 s. In contrast, the RNN model took an average of 1594 s to run [54], which exhibits the computational complexity of neural networks compared to traditional models such as SVM classifiers.

Valles and Matin [58] validated the superior performance of SVMs on the CREMA-D dataset using 62 features generated from a custom feature set, and showed that the SVM model achieved an accuracy of 57.6% on clean audio data from the CREMA-D dataset, followed by an MLP model which achieved 54.7% accuracy and finally an RNN model which achieved 55.0% accuracy. This order of model performance remained consistent when also tested on the clean RAVDESS dataset, resulting in an accuracy score of 80.6% for SVM, 77.6% for MLP and 61.2% for RNN.

4 Methods

4.1 Train-Test Split

For both audio and visual data, the provided dataset was split into 'matching' and 'non-matching' sets. This was to allow an evaluation to be conducted to compare the performance of the chosen ML models on data that humans have difficulty classifying. If the ML models performed well on the 'non-matching' test set, this would give more support in favour of the claim that ML models can recognise emotions better than humans, particularly in conditions where there is a lot of human ambiguity. Once this was completed, the 'matching' audio data underwent an 80/20 train/test split. This split was not only chosen because it is a popular split found in the literature, but it also ensures that there are a sufficient number of minority class instances in the test set. The 'non-matching' set was left untouched and was used as a second test set. The 80% training data was later used to train the model using a stratified 10-fold cross-validation technique to test the model's generalisability given the limited data. This split resulted in 2479, 620 and 4343 audio stimuli for the matching training set, matching test set, and non-matching test set respectively.

The visual 'matching' data underwent a 70/15/15 train/validation/test split. The size of the training set was set to 70% unlike the audio data because the 'matching' visual test set contained more data entries than the audio matching set. The 70% split allowed a similar amount of training data to be used for the visual model whilst still keeping the testing data reasonable in size. The split resulted in 3451 visual-only stimuli for the training set, 740 for the matching validation set, 740 for the matching test set, and 2511 for the non-matching test set. To keep the class distribution the same in all the splits for each modality, a stratified split was used. This was to ensure that each split contained instances of every class so that the model can be trained and evaluated on every class.

4.2 Experiments with Audio Classification

To explore the effects of extracting different specialised features, the model was trained and tested with the GeMAPS and eGeMAPS feature sets provided by the openSMILE toolkit [15], and a grid-search was performed to identify the optimal parameters. The results show that an SVM model trained on the ComParE 2016 [51] feature set resulted in considerably higher accuracy than when trained on the other feature sets. Hence, all further experimentation was carried out using this feature set.

Due to the uneven distribution of class labels, a Synthetic Minority Oversampling Technique (SMOTE) [12] was used. A stratified 10-fold cross-validation with random shuffling was performed with a grid-search to find the optimal parameters for the SVM model. Hyperparameter tuning was performed. For building the SVM model, we used the scikit-learn [39] implementation of SVM. Data augmentation [3] and principal component analysis (PCA) [34] were applied to mitigate overfitting. The use of PCA for dimensionality reduction improved not only the accuracy of the SVM model but also computational performance (i.e., ~15 times quicker). This can be particularly advantageous for models that can be used for real-time emotion detection.

4.3 Experiments with Visual Classification

Hans and Rao [27] achieved results on the CREMA-D dataset by implementing a CNN-LSTM architecture. They trained proposed CNN-LSTM models with 5, 6 and 7 layers with an input of 75 frames per video. The highest test accuracy of 78.5% was achieved by a 6-layer model. Due to the strong results, their proposed method was used for the visual classification approach in our study. Accordingly, face frames of size 28x28 pixels were extracted from each.flv file of the visual stimuli using the OpenFace 2.0 toolkit [5] and placed in individual directories.

To improve the performance of the CNN-LSTM architecture proposed by Hans and Rao [27], we made two modifications (details omitted due to the space limit). First, we addressed the exploding gradients issue, which is a common problem with models, like the CNN-LSTM network, containing recurrent layers such as RNNs or LSTMs [25]. Second, since the Pytorch implementation of cross-entropy loss (used as the criterion for training) applies a softmax on the output of the network followed by a negative log-likelihood loss [38], the final softmax layer was removed from the CNN-LSTM model respectively due to redundancy. The changes led to over 10% increase in the accuracy of the best-performing model.

5 Results

5.1 Evaluation Metrics

In addition to comparing the accuracy of each model against humans, the evaluation metrics - precision, recall, F1-score – were calculated on a per-class and macro-averaged level for both test sets. Both the CNN-LSTM and SVM models outperformed humans for all measured macro metrics on both the matching and non-matching test sets as seen in Table 1 and Table 2. For both audio and visual data, although the models suffered a notable drop in performance when generating predictions for the non-matching test set (as seen for humans), the difference in the macro-averaged evaluation metrics on both audio and visual data between humans and the ML models were much greater than the difference seen for the matching test set.

Table 1. Results of visual test sets

		Evaluation Metrics			
Classifier	Test set	Accuracy	Precision	Recall	F1
CNN-LSTM	Matching	**80.81**	**78.93**	**77.97**	**78.33**
Humans		75.91	73.53	73.53	73.40
CNN-LSTM	Non-matching	**38.96**	**39.96**	**43.29**	**35.89**
Humans		19.37	23.11	22.07	19.47

Table 2. Results of audio test sets

		Evaluation Metrics			
Classifier	Test set	Accuracy	Precision	Recall	F1
SVM	Matching	**80.97**	**77.45**	**73.85**	**75.34**
Humans		68.91	65.72	64.90	64.82
SVM	Non-Matching	**34.26**	**45.31**	**44.44**	**33.40**
Humans		17.90	31.56	20.51	19.90

In fact, the ML models used for both audio and visual data achieved approximately double the accuracy as that seen for humans on the non-matching set. This could suggest that ML models can capture relevant information from stimuli even under more ambiguous conditions to deliver more accurate predictions than humans.

Looking at the results on a granular, individual emotion class level, the results (Fig. 1, Fig. 2, Fig. 3) showed that although ML models achieved higher performance scores for the majority of classes, humans had a slight advantage in some emotion categories. For example, for the visual matching data, the CNN-LSTM model achieved a 66% accuracy (i.e., recall score) in identifying the 'anger' emotion, whereas humans performed much greater with a 10% higher accuracy (although the CNN-LSTM model achieved greater precision by 0.02%). This could be a result of relevant features in the matching test set for the 'anger' emotion did not appear or were not as relevant in the training data the ML model was given. On the other hand, it may alternatively suggest that humans may have an advantage over ML models at classifying a subset of stimuli from certain emotion classes like 'anger'. Nevertheless, the ML model had a higher accuracy of 35% compared to the 21% averaged accuracy of human raters for the 'anger' emotion on the non-matching test set.

A similar pattern was seen for the precision score for the emotion of 'fear', where on the matching visual test set, the CNN-LSTM model achieved a precision score of 64%. In contrast, the average precision of human raters was 73%. This implies that humans made fewer classifications when the intended emotion for the stimuli was 'fear'. However, as seen before, the ML model outperformed humans on the non-matching test set for the emotion of fear on all measured metrics including precision, where the ML model achieved a precision score of 42% whereas humans achieved a lower score of 34%. This again supports the claim that ML models may perform better on more ambiguous data.

For the visual non-matching test set, the only emotion in which humans achieved a higher score than the ML model was 'happy', for which the ML model achieved a precision score of 11% and the human average was 14%. This led to humans also achieving a higher F1-score than the ML model on the emotion of 'happy'. The superior ability of humans to achieve a lower number of false positives for the emotion categories 'happy' and 'fear' (as shown above) was also observed in the matching test set.

For the audio data, the SVM model achieved a higher accuracy than humans for all emotion classes in the matching test set. The ML model also achieved a higher accuracy score for all classes in the non-matching test set as well, except for when the intended emotion was 'sad', where the ML model achieved a recall score of 17% whereas humans achieved a marginally higher accuracy of 18%. Again, similar to the visual test set results, although the ML model has greater precision than humans for the majority of emotion classes, humans were seen to achieve a higher precision score of 79% compared to the 70% achieved by the ML model for the 'happy' emotion class on the matching audio test set. This consequently led to humans also achieving an F1-score that was 0.02% higher than the ML model for the 'happy' emotion class. Humans also achieved a fractionally higher precision score (less than 1%) for the 'anger' emotion class on the matching test set. The greater precision scores for humans suggest that humans may be less prone to incorrectly classifying emotions that do not belong to a class as belonging to it. Our data suggest that these emotions include 'happy' and 'fear' for the visual data, and 'happy' and 'angry' for the audio data. Nevertheless, it should also be noted that the difference between the two classifier precision scores is very small and the lower performance of the ML models may be overcome with more training on a varied set of data.

5.2 Misclassifications of the Neutral Emotion Class

To answer the research question exploring the 'neutral' emotion, charts (Fig. 4) were made to plot the percentage of ratings for each class that were misclassified as 'neutral' (out of the total number of ratings for that class). For all audio and visual sets, the emotion most commonly misclassified by humans as 'neutral' was 'sad'. As seen in Fig. 4b, 22% of audio-only stimuli from the matching test set and 59% from the non- matching test set were misclassified as neutral. Interestingly, this phenomenon was also observed for the SVM model which also had the highest percentage of 'neutral' misclassification when the intended emotion was 'sad' (with only 3% fewer misclassifications than humans on both test sets).

As a result of the vast number of misclassifications, the precision score for humans and the SVM model for the neutral emotion class on the non-matching test set is substantially low (as seen in Fig. 2, sitting at 1% and 3% respectively). This may suggest that audio data in the test sets which portray the emotion of 'sad' and 'neutral' both have very similar audio features, making them difficult to distinguish. However, it should also be noted that the audio training set had a very limited number of samples for the 'sad' emotion class. Thus, although SMOTE oversampling was performed to create synthetic samples of the minority class, the poor performance of the ML model may have also been a result of the lack of diversity in the 'sad' audio training data. For the visual data on the other hand, this pattern is not observed and as shown in Fig. 4a. Although the CNN-LSTM misclassified 32% of 'sad' visual stimuli as 'neutral' on the non-matching test set (which is still a substantial amount), this is much less than humans who misclassified (54% of the stimuli).

It should also be noted that for both audio and visual data, the ML models made much fewer misclassifications of the 'happy' emotion class stimuli as belonging to the 'neutral' class. For example, on the non-matching audio test set, the SVM model misclassified 15% of 'happy' audio clips as 'neutral' compared to humans who exhibited a 53% misclassification rate. Similarly, for the non-matching visual test set, the CNN-LSTM model misclassified 16% of the 'happy' visual data as 'neutral' compared to humans who misclassified 47%.

Additionally, for emotions where humans had the least number of 'neutral' misclassification ('anger' for audio and 'disgust' for visual), it was found that ML models were able to achieve almost perfect results with less than 5% 'neutral' misclassifications on both matching and non-matching test sets. In fact, the SVM classifier made no misclassifications of the 'anger' stimuli as belonging to the 'neutral' class. This shows that the ML models were able to learn information that provides a strong separation between these said emotions and 'neutral', particularly those emotions that humans made fewer misclassification (possibly because these have separable features that ML models can identify more consistently than humans).

The only emotion for which humans made fewer misclassifications than the ML models for the 'neutral' class was for the 'anger' visual stimuli on the matching test

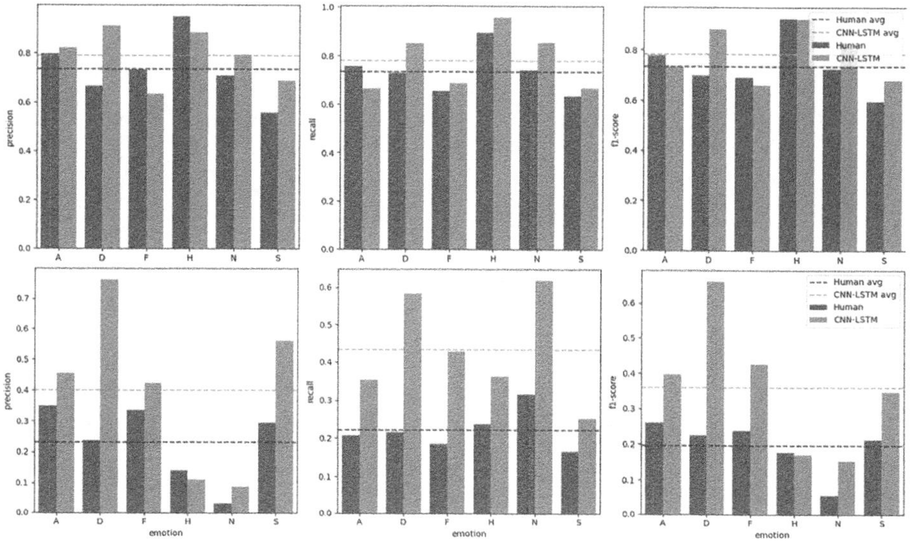

Fig. 1. Results of the CNN-LSTM model (orange) against humans (blue) for precision (left), recall (middle) and F1 score (right). The charts on the upper row show the results of the matching visual test set and those on the lower row the non-matching visual test set. (Color figure online)

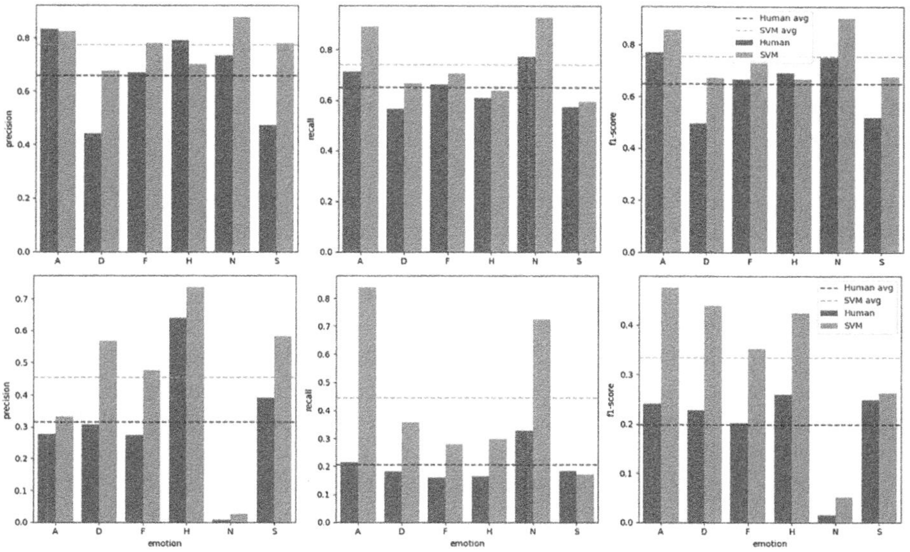

Fig. 2. Results of the SVM model against humans for precision (left), recall (middle) and F1-score (right). The charts on the upper row show the results of the matching audio test set and those on the second row the non-matching audio test set.

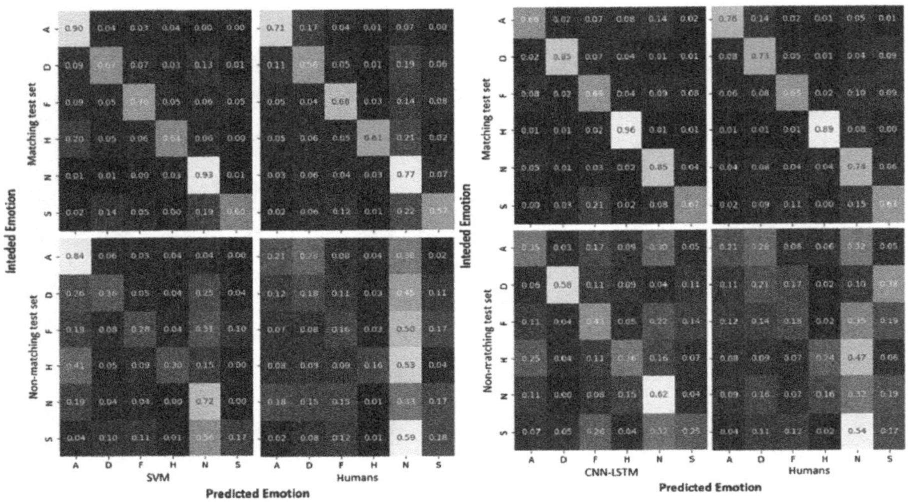

Fig. 3. Confusion matrix comparing SVM model (left) and CNN-LSTM model (right) and human performance on matching and non-matching audio/visual tests. Black and white represent the lowest and highest. Purple, red and orange are intermediate ascending values. X-axis: A = Anger, D = Disgust, F = Fear, H = Happy, N = Neutral, S = Sad

set. On this data, it was found that ML models performed much worse, misclassifying 9% more 'anger' stimuli as 'neutral'. Although the CNN-LSTM model did achieve a lower misclassification of this class for the non-matching test set, the difference between the number of misclassifications by humans and the ML model was negligible (2% difference).

In summary, both SVM and CNN-LSTM models outperformed humans in classifying emotions, with fewer misclassifications of the 'neutral' class (except the CNN- LSTM model for the 'anger' class on the matching test set). Additionally, when humans had low misclassifications, the ML models performed even better. Finally, although the SVM model made a similar number of misclassifications of 'sad' audio clips as 'neutral', this may have been a result of the lack of a variety of training data.

Nevertheless, one limitation to consider in evaluating ML model superiority is the assumption that the actors in the CREMA-D dataset accurately represent the intended emotions for each clip. We also assume that these emotions are generalisable to the wider public. Additionally, we consider the raters in the CREMA-D study as representative of the general population, using their collective performance across each test set as the "human" benchmark for ML model comparison. However, the ML models were trained on data that included some actors who also appear in the test sets, potentially providing an advantage due to the limited dataset size. This overlap, along with these assumptions, may introduce biases that contribute to the models' superior performance over human raters. Furthermore, no alternative dataset was available to test the models' performance against human data, as no other dataset provided detailed human ratings for each stimulus. This limits the opportunity to validate our findings across different environments.

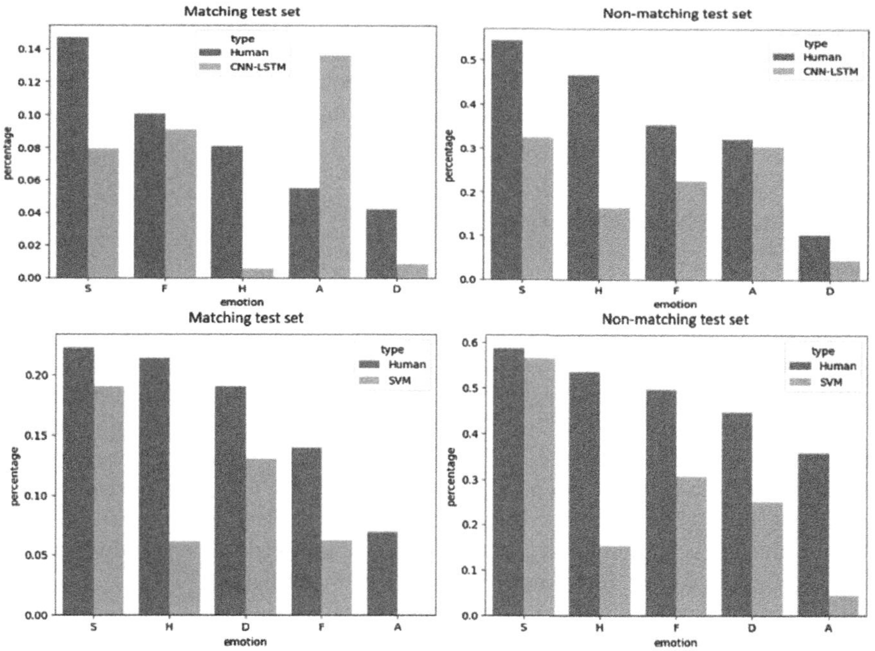

Fig. 4. Charts showing the percentage of misclassification of emotions as neutral made by humans (blue) and (a) the CNN-LSTM model (upper) and (b) (a) the SVM model (lower) on the matching and non-matching audio test sets.

6 Discussion

6.1 Human-in-the-Loop Annotation

Our work indicates that neither humans nor machines are particularly reliable for emotion recognition. This observation can have significant implications. According to Scherer and colleagues [46], the ability to perceive and interpret accurately others' emotional states enables us to anticipate their responses to events and predict their actions. This '*emotion perception competence*' (ibid, p. 306) is crucial for effective social interaction management in, for example, workplace dynamics and family relationships. Research has revealed significant individual differences in this competence [7]. While its heritability remains unclear, many believe it can be improved through training (e.g., [49]).

Results of our analyses underscore the necessity for such emotion intelligence training for individuals. One specific use of the skills thus acquired is the enhancement of supervisory ML models. In such models, human involvement for labelling emotions (human-in-the-loop) is required for providing ground truth labels during the training phase. These models perform well when trained on high-quality labelled data and can achieve more accurate emotion classification results as opposed to un-supervisory ML models, albeit inconsistent findings prevail [4, 11]. However, as Law and colleagues [33] highlight, a large proportion of current ML models for classifying emotions lack grounding in a clear definition of emotional neutrality, despite a considerable amount of emotional data being categorised as such. This oversight likely contributes to the overall low accuracy observed in ML models for emotion recognition. From a scientific standpoint, leaving a substantial portion of data in an undefined state is considered untenable.

6.2 Insights into Neutral Emotion

Echoing Gasper's [22] assertion, we argue that in-depth understanding of the notion of neutral emotion is indispensable for advancing the field of Affective Computing. Neutral emotion, when misleadingly be interpreted as absence of emotion [21], seems having no research or practical value, because typically researchers or practitioners aim to find out whether people respond to an object, be an interactive app or a cup of coffee, with positive or negative emotions. In contrast, neutral emotion can have significant implications for different sectors such as health, education, and law. An example of this is individuals with dementia, who may struggle to express their emotions, being inaccurately labelled as having neutral emotions [49]. However, if caregivers and AI-based technological aids are trained to accurately interpret the nuanced emotional states of individuals with dementia, it could significantly improve their overall well-being.

For a comprehensive understanding of the emotional spectrum, researchers should transcend conventional valence measures and consider the implications of positive, negative, and neutral affective states on their area of study [21]. Furthermore, neutrality might serve as a fundamental and distinctive predictor of inactivity. For a holistic comprehension of emotional processes, it is imperative to examine more the definition, operationalization, and implications of neutral emotion, gaining deeper insights necessary for unravelling the complexities of emotional phenomena [22].

6.3 Implications for Human-Centred AI Research and Applications

The study's findings that ML models can outperform humans in emotion recognition have several implications for human-centred AI research. First, the superior accuracy of ML in detecting subtle emotional cues that are challenging for humans suggests potential applications in fields like healthcare, where emotion recognition could support patient assessments in mental health or therapy sessions (e.g., depression detection through speech and facial cues) [1, 57]. However, deploying these systems in real-world settings also highlights the need for robust datasets that reflect diverse emotions in varied contexts, as current datasets may not fully capture real-world complexities. Furthermore, the study shows how ML models' ability to identify "neutral" emotional states more precisely could be valuable in high-stakes environments, such as negotiation or customer service, where maintaining a calm baseline is crucial. Future work may focus on developing interpretable ML models that provide users with insights into the rationale behind emotion predictions, addressing the transparency challenge often associated with Deep Learning models used in multimodal emotion recognition [17].

ML models' ability to recognise emotions more accurately than humans can enhance decision-making processes across various sectors. In healthcare, for example, AI systems could support clinicians in identifying patients' emotional states, improving diagnostics and tailoring treatment plans, especially in mental health care [1]. Similarly, in customer service, AI could help businesses gauge customer sentiment in real-time, leading to better responses and improved customer satisfaction [42].

As ML models become more capable of emotional recognition, it is essential to address ethical concerns surrounding their deployment. Issues related to privacy, consent, and potential biases in emotion recognition systems must be carefully managed to prevent misuse or discrimination [8]. Ensuring that AI systems are transparent and that users understand how their data is used is crucial for maintaining public trust and acceptance.

The integration of ML in emotionally sensitive domains underscores the need for interdisciplinary collaboration among AI developers, psychologists, ethicists, and domain experts. This collaboration can help create AI systems that are not only technically proficient but also sensitive to human emotions and ethical standards. This approach can foster designs that align AI capabilities with human values and social norms [57].

Furthermore, as organisations adopt AI for emotion recognition, there will be a growing need for training programs that equip users with the skills to interact effectively with these technologies. Educational initiatives can help users understand the strengths and limitations of AI, fostering a more informed use of emotional recognition systems in various contexts.

6.4 Ethical Concerns

The idea that machines can recognise human emotions more accurately than humans is both intriguing and concerning, as it can raise significant ethical concerns. One major issue is privacy—machines that can accurately predict human emotions would likely need access to highly personal data, such as facial expressions, voice tones, or physiological signals. This raises the question of how such data is collected, stored, and used, and whether individuals are fully aware of, and consent to, this level of emotional surveillance. Another concern is *emotional autonomy*—the notion that individuals should have control over their own emotional experiences and expressions. If machines can predict or manipulate emotions, there's a risk of infringing on this autonomy, potentially influencing behaviour in ways people may not fully understand or desire.

Yet another concern is that it can reshape industries, from marketing to law enforcement, creating imbalances in power dynamics. For instance, companies could exploit emotional data to manipulate consumer behaviour, or authorities might use it for surveillance in ways that challenge personal freedoms. In a human-centred research context, these concerns demand careful attention. Researchers must grapple with how to balance the benefits of emotion-recognition technology with the potential risks, ensuring ethical guidelines are in place to protect individuals and society from misuse or harm.

7 Conclusion

To conclude, our work demonstrated that it is possible for ML models to recognise emotions better than humans as illustrated by the superior performance of both models over humans on accuracy and all the macro-averaged metrics (precision, recall and F1-score). We also demonstrated the advantage of ML models when given data that humans have difficulty discerning, not only by showing the increased difference in performance between ML models and humans on the non-matching test set where the ML models achieved almost double the accuracy, but also by showing that ML models make fewer misclassifications (particularly focusing on 'neutral'). It was observed that for emotions for which humans achieved the lowest number of 'neutral' misclassifications, the ML models performed even better as they were able to consistently separate the classes from 'neutral' (Fig. 4).

Our findings, along with the granular analysis, can provide future researchers in the area with a greater understanding of the performance of ML models against humans in the domain of emotion classification. In particular, the range of metrics used for the evaluation can help make judgements on the suitability of ML models to cater to different business needs, for example, the use of ML models in domains where greater precision is required for specific emotions such as 'anger' in negotiations. In addition to the contributions pertaining to the three research questions, the experimentation performed in this study for audio and visual data showed remarkable improvements in the accuracy and speed of the models. Most notably, applying PCA to reduce the dimensionality of the data that was processed by the SVM resulted in more accurate predictions being generated in a much shorter time (Sect. 4), reducing computational costs and enhancing sustainability.

As a major limitation of our work is the lack of datasets available for comparison with the results using CREMA-D, future work should focus on making fine-grained data of individual raters available in datasets, as seen in the CREMA-D dataset. This enables the verifiability of the results of similar work. Additionally, future work comparing ML models to humans should undertake a similar approach to Goh et al. [24], who trained and tested human classifiers on the same subsets as ML models. This method allows statistical significance tests to be carried out for a more rigorous evaluation. Last but not the least, it is imperative to investigate the issue of enculturation of emotional expression across a diversity of contexts.

References

1. Ahuja, K.: Emotion AI in healthcare: application, challenges, and future directions. In: Emotional AI and Human-AI Interactions in Social Networking, pp. 131–146. Academic Press, Cambridge (2024)
2. Akçay, M.B., Ŏguz, K.: Speech emotion recognition: emotional models, databases, features, preprocessing methods, supporting modalities, and classifiers. Speech Commun. **116**, 56–76 (2020)
3. Atmaja, B.T., Sasou, A.: Effects of data augmentations on speech emotion recognition. Sensors **22**(16), 5941 (2022)
4. Azari, B., Westlin, C., Satpute, A.B.: Comparing supervised and unsupervised approaches to emotion categorization in the human brain, body, and subjective experience. Sci. Rep. Nat. **10**, 20284 (2020)
5. Baltrusaitis, T., Zadeh, A., Lim, Y.C., Morency, L.-P.: Openface 2.0: facial behavior analysis toolkit. In: 2018 13th IEEE international Conference on Automatic Face & Gesture Recognition (FG 2018), pp. 59–66. IEEE (2018)
6. Bänziger, T., Mortillaro, M., Scherer, K.R.: Introducing the Geneva multimodal expression corpus for experimental research on emotion perception. Emotion **12**(5), 1161–1179 (2012)

7. Bänziger, T., Grandjean, D., Scherer, K.R.: Emotion recognition from expressions in face, voice, and body: the multimodal emotion recognition test (MERT). Emotion **9**, 691–704 (2009)
8. Binns, R.: Fairness in machine learning: lessons from political philosophy. In: Conference on Fairness, Accountability and Transparency, pp. 149–159. PMLR, January 2018
9. Busso, C., et al.: IEMOCAP: interactive emotional dyadic motion capture database. Lang. Resour. Eval. **42**, 335–359 (2008)
10. Cao, H., Cooper, D.G., Keutmann, M.K., Gur, R.C., Nenkova, A., Verma, R.: CREMA-D: crowd-sourced emotional multimodal actors dataset. IEEE Trans. Affect. Comput. **5**(4), 377–390 (2014)
11. Carbonell, F.M., Boman, M., Laukka P.: Comparing supervised and unsupervised approaches to multimodal emotion recognition. PeerJ Comput. Sci. **7**, e804 (2021). https://doi.org/10.7717/peerj-cs.804
12. Chawla, N.V., Bowyer, K.W., Hall, L.O., Kegelmeyer, W.P.: SMOTE: synthetic minority over-sampling technique. J. Artif. Intell. Res. **16**, 321–357 (2002)
13. Douglas-Cowie, E., et al.: The HUMAINE database. In: Cowie, R., Pelachaud, C., Petta, P. (eds.) Emotion-Oriented Systems. Cognitive Technologies, pp. 243–284. Springer, Heidelberg (2011). https://doi.org/10.1007/978-3-642-15184-2_14
14. Ekman, P.: Universals and cultural differences in facial expressions of emotion. In: Nebraska Symposium on Motivation. University of Nebraska Press (1971)
15. Eyben, F., Wöllmer, M., Schuller, B.: Opensmile: the Munich versatile and fast open-source audio feature extractor. In: Proceedings of the 18th ACM International Conference on Multimedia, pp. 1459–1462 (2010)
16. Eyben, F., et al.: The Geneva minimalistic acoustic parameter set (GeMAPS) for voice research and affective computing. IEEE Trans. Affect. Comput. **7**(2), 190–202 (2015)
17. Ezzameli, K., Mahersia, H.: Emotion recognition from unimodal to multimodal analysis: a review. Inf. Fus. **99**, 101847 (2023)
18. Gasper, K., Danube, C.I., Hu, D.: Making room for neutral affect: evidence indicating that neutral affect is independent of and co-occurs with eight affective states. Motiv. Emot. **45**(1), 103–121 (2021)
19. Gasper, K., Hackenbracht, J.: Too busy to feel neutral: reducing cognitive resources attenuates neutral affective states. Motiv. Emot. **39**(3), 458–466 (2015)
20. Gasper, K., Danube, C.I.: The scope of our affective influences: when and how naturally occurring positive, negative, and neutral affects alter judgment. Pers. Soc. Psychol. Bull. **42**(3), 385–399 (2016)
21. Gasper, K., Spencer, I.A., Hu, D.: Does neutral affect exist? How challenging three beliefs about neutral affect can advance affective research. Front. Psychol. **10**, 2476 (2019)
22. Gasper, K.: A case for neutrality: Why neutral affect is critical for advancing affetive science. Affect. Sci. **4**, 458–462 (2023)
23. Gladys, A.A., Vetriselvi, V.: Survey on multimodal approaches to emotion recognition. Neurocomputing, 126693 (2023)
24. Goh, Y.C., Cai, X.Q., Theseira, W., Ko, G., Khor, K.A.: Evaluating human versus machine learning performance in classifying research abstracts. Scientometrics **125**, 1197–1212 (2020)
25. Graves, A.: Generating sequences with recurrent neural networks. CoRR, vol. abs/1308.0850, http://arxiv.org/abs/1308.0850 (2013)
26. Grimm, M., Kroschel, K., Narayanan, S.: The Vera Am Mittag German audio-visual emotional speech database. In: IEEE International Conference on Multimedia and Expo, pp. 865–868 (2008)
27. Hans, A.S.A., Rao, S.: A CNN-LSTM based deep neural networks for facial emotion detection in videos. Int. J. Adv. Signal Image Sci. **7**(1), 11–20 (2021)

28. Kalateh, S., Estrada-Jimenez, L.A., Hojjati, S.N., Barata, J.: A systematic review on multimodal emotion recognition: building blocks, current state, applications, and challenges. IEEE Access (2024)
29. Khaireddin, Y., Chen, Z.: Facial emotion recognition: state of the art performance on FER2013. arXiv preprint arXiv:2105.03588 (2021)
30. Ko, B.: A brief review of facial emotion recognition based on visual information. Sensors **18**(2), 401 (2018). https://doi.org/10.3390/s18020401
31. Kollias, D., Zafeiriou, S.: Aff-wild2: Extending the Aff-Wild database for affect recognition. CoRR, vol. abs/1811.07770. http://arxiv.org/abs/1811.07770 (2018)
32. Kossaifi, J., et al.: SEWA DB: a rich database for audio-visual emotion and sentiment research in the wild. IEEE Trans. Pattern Anal. Mach. Intell. **43**(3), 1022–1040 (2019)
33. Law, E.L.-C., Soleimani, S., Watkins, D., Barwick, J.: Automatic voice emotion recognition of child-parent conversations in natural settings. Behav. Inf. Technol. **40**(11), 1072–1089 (2021)
34. Maćkiewicz, A., Ratajczak, W.: Principal components analysis (PCA). Comput. Geosci. **19**(3), 303–342 (1993)
35. Ong, D.C., et al.: Modeling emotion in complex stories: the stanford emotional narratives dataset. IEEE Trans. Affect. Comput. **12**(3), 579–594 (2019)
36. Özseven: The acoustic cue of fear: investigation of acoustic parameters of speech containing fear. Arch. Acoust. **43**(2), 245–251 (2018)
37. Özseven, T.: A novel feature selection method for speech emotion recognition. Appl. Acoust. **146**, 320–326 (2019). https://www.sciencedirect.com/science/article/pii/S0003682X18309915
38. Paszke, A., et al.: Pytorch: an imperative style, high-performance deep learning library. In: Advances in Neural Information Processing Systems, vol. 32 (2019)
39. Pedregosa, F., et al.: Scikit-learn: machine learning in Python. J. Mach. Learn. Res. **12**, 2825–2830 (2011)
40. Perepelkina, O., Kazimirova, E., Konstantinova, M.: RAMAS: Russian multimodal corpus of dyadic Interaction for studying emotion recognition. PeerJ Prepr. **6**, e26688v1 (2018)
41. Poria, S., Cambria, E., Bajpai, R., Hussain, A.: A review of affective computing: from unimodal analysis to multimodal fusion. Inf. Fus. **37**, 98–125 (2017)
42. Poria, S., et al.: Recognizing emotion cause in conversations. Cognit. Comput. 13 , 1317–1332 (2021)
43. Priyasad, D., Fernando, T., Sridharan, S., Denman, S., Fookes, C.: Dual memory fusion for multimodal speech emotion recognition. In: Proceedings of the INTERSPEECH, vol. 2023, pp. 4543–4547 (2023)
44. Ringeval, F., Sonderegger, A., Sauer, J., Lalanne, D.: Introducing the RECOLA multimodal corpus of remote collaborative and affective interactions. In: 2013 10th IEEE International Conference and Workshops on Automatic Face and Gesture Recognition (FG), pp. 1–8. IEEE, April 2013
45. Ryumina, E., Dresvyanskiy, D., Karpov, A.: In search of a robust facial expressions recognition model: a large-scale visual cross-corpus study. Neurocomputing **514**, 435–450 (2022)
46. Scherer, K.R., Scherer, U.: Assessing the ability to recognize facial and vocal expressions of emotion: construction and validation of the emotion recognition index. J. Nonverbal Behav. **35**, 305–326 (2011)
47. Scherer, K.R.: On the nature and function of emotion: a component process approach. In: Scherer, K.R., Ekman. P. (eds.) Approaches to Emotion, pp. 293–317. Erlbaum, Hillsdale (1984)
48. Scherer, K.R.: The dynamic architecture of emotion: evidence for the component process model. Cogn. Emot. **23**, 1307–1351 (2009)

49. Scherer, K.R.: Component models of emotion can inform the quest for emotional competence. In: Matthews, G., Zeidner, M., Roberts, R.D. (eds.) The Science of Emotional Intelligence: Knowns and Unknowns, pp. 101–126. Oxford University Press, New York (2007)
50. Schuller, B., et al.: Being bored? Recognising natural interest by extensive audiovisual integration for real-life application. Image Vis. Comput. **27**(12), 1760-1774 (2009)
51. Schuller, B., et al.: The interspeech 2016 computational paralinguistics challenge: deception, sincerity and native language (2016)
52. Shah, M., Chakrabarti, C., Spanias, A.: A multi-modal approach to emotion recognition using undirected topic models. In: 2014 IEEE International Symposium on Circuits and Systems (ISCAS), pp. 754–757. IEEE, June 2014
53. Shi, T., Huang, S.L.: MultiEMO: an attention-based correlation-aware multimodal fusion framework for emotion recognition in conversations. In: Proceedings of the 61st Annual Meeting of the Association for Computational Linguistics (Volume 1: Long Papers), pp. 14752–14766, July 2023
54. Singh, R., Puri, H., Aggarwal, N., Gupta, V.: An efficient language-independent acoustic emotion classification system. Arab. J. Sci. Eng. **45**(4), 3111–3121 (2020). https://doi.org/10.1007/s13369-019-04293-9
55. Steidl, S.: Automatic Classification of Emotion Related User States in Spontaneous Children's Speech. University of Erlangen-Nuremberg, Erlangen, Germany (2009)
56. Swain, M., Routray, A., Kabisatpathy, P.: Databases, features and classifiers for speech emotion recognition: a review. Int. J. Speech Technol. **21**(1), 93–120 (2018)
57. Tomašev, N., et al.: AI for social good: unlocking the opportunity for positive impact. Nat. Commun. **11**(1), 2468 (2020)
58. Valles, D., Matin, R.: An audio processing approach using ensemble learning for speech-emotion recognition for children with ASD. In: IEEE World AI IoT Congress (AIIoT). IEEE (2021). https://doi.org/10.1109/aiiot52608.2021.9454174
59. Virtanen, M., et al.: The level of cognitive function and recognition of emotions in older adults. PLoS ONE **12**(10), e0185513 (2017)
60. Williams, T.F., Vehabovic, N., Simms, L.J.: Developing and validating a facial emotion recognition task with graded intensity. Assessment **30**(3), 761–781 (2023)
61. Winata, G.I., Kampman, O.P., Fung, P.: Attention-based LSTM for psychological stress detection from spoken language using distant supervision. In: 2018 IEEE International Conference on Acoustics, Speech and Signal Processing (ICASSP), pp. 6204–6208. IEEE, April 2018
62. Zadeh, A., Liang, P.P., Poria, S., Vij, P., Cambria, E., Morency, L.P.: Multi-attention recurrent network for human communication comprehension. In: Proceedings of the AAAI Conference on Artificial Intelligence, vol. 32, no. 1, April 2018
63. Zadeh, A., Zellers, R., Pincus, E., Morency, L.P.: MOSI: multimodal corpus of sentiment intensity and subjectivity analysis in online opinion videos. arXiv preprint arXiv:1606.06259 (2016)

Human-Centred AI in Education and Social Support

An AI-Powered Learning Companion for Adaptive and Personalized STEM Education

Nikolaos Antonios Grammatikos[1(✉)], Evangelia Anagnostopoulou[1], Dimitris Apostolou[2], and Gregoris Mentzas[1]

[1] Information Management Unit, Institute of Communication and Computer Systems, National Technical University of Athens, Athens, Greece
ngrammatikos@mail.ntua.gr

[2] Department of Informatics, University of Piraeus, Piraeus, Greece

Abstract. We introduce an AI learning companion designed to enhance STEM education by providing personalized, adaptive learning experiences. The companion dynamically adjusts the difficulty of experimental activities in online STEM labs and delivers targeted feedback based on real-time student performance, ensuring a more efficient learning process. Teachers can use the companion's authoring tool to create tailored educational scenarios that cater to students at various performance levels. This work emphasizes a student-centered approach, supporting critical thinking and problem-solving skills.

Keywords: AI agent · learning companion · STEM learning · education

1 Introduction

The use of AI-powered conversational agents in education has gained momentum over the past few years, providing personalized learning environments and enhancing student engagement. These systems, such as chatbots, facilitate real-time interactions, offering students instant feedback, answering questions, and even tutoring them in specific subjects.

Digital courses refer to educational programs that are predominantly delivered through digital platforms, leveraging online technologies and multimedia resources. Students typically engage with the course content asynchronously, allowing them to interact with the material according to their individual schedules and learning preferences. Platforms such as WhoTeach [1] support educators by offering tools and resources to design and develop their own customized digital courses, thereby enhancing instructional delivery and promoting active learning through technological integration.

The swift evolution of artificial intelligence (AI) presents significant opportunities to transform education, especially within STEM disciplines, by catering to the varied needs of students. Traditional teaching methods often struggle to accommodate varying levels of prior knowledge, learning speeds, and individual interests, leaving some students disengaged or struggling to keep up. Inspired by the promise of AI to facilitate adaptive and personalized educational experiences, our objective is to create an

A. Følstad et al. (Eds.): CONVERSATIONS 2024, LNCS 15545, pp. 87–95, 2025.
https://doi.org/10.1007/978-3-031-88045-2_6

intelligent system that enables educators to develop scenario-based learning activities and support students through personalized learning pathways. Additionally, we plan to assess the trustworthiness of the AI system within the context of inquiry learning during laboratory work.

In this paper, we present the development of an AI learning companion and a supporting platform for educational scenario creation. The research objectives of our work are to provide personalized support to students as they engage with educational scenarios developed by their teachers. To achieve our objective, we propose an approach for analyzing student performance data, delivering targeted feedback and adjusting the difficulty of tasks dynamically, based on the students' performance within their learning path. This approach aims to personalize the learning process by ensuring that students are both appropriately challenged and supported, fostering a deeper understanding of the material and enhancing overall learning outcomes.

The structure of this paper is as follows: Sect. 2 explores the use of AI digital assistants in education, providing a foundation for the current work. In Sect. 3, we present the design and development of our AI learning companion, along with the platform that enables educators to create customized educational scenarios. Section 4 offers a discussion on the system's implementation and outlines future directions for both the learning companion and the platform. Finally, Sect. 5 concludes the paper with final remarks and considerations.

2 AI Digital Assistants in Education

In the domain of education, AI is emerging as a pivotal force, with tools like ChatGPT driving transformative changes across various domains, from assessment design to language learning [2]. AI digital assistants offer personalized support to both students and teachers in various educational environments [3]. These assistants can help students grasp new concepts, complete assignments, and get answers to their questions through conversational interfaces, whether text-based or voice-activated.

This paper specifically focuses on dialogue-based systems for student learning, where learners engage with educational content through natural language conversations but also the learning environment where educators can create educational scenarios for their students or gather insights from them. Our scope is to develop a learning companion that guides students through STEM lab courses, providing continuous assistance to support lab assignments. In the following, we describe the digital assistants identified in our research.

AutoTutor is an intelligent tutoring system that engages students in conversation, helping them learn by simulating human tutoring interactions. The system adapts to student performance and misconceptions to provide individualized instruction [4]. The Curriculum-Driven EduBot [5] is an AI-powered chatbot designed for conversational practice based on specific curricula. Unlike generic chatbots, it focuses on predetermined topics and uses vocabulary directly from textbooks to match learners' proficiency levels.

An LLM based assistant named CodeAid [6] provides various functionalities, allowing students to ask general programming questions, seek help with code they have written, request explanations, troubleshoot errors, or receive guidance in writing new code.

Georgia University developed Jill Watson [7], a chatbot powered by IBM's Watson Platform, to manage forum posts in a programming course. During its 2016 pilot, the chatbot effectively answered student queries and provided feedback. Jill Watson was later refined and integrated alongside human teaching assistants, with students unable to distinguish between the AI and human support.

Ani [8], a chatbot developed by Duolingo, is specifically designed to help users improve their conversational skills in a foreign language. Using natural language processing, Ani understands and responds to user inputs, offering personalized feedback on grammar, pronunciation, and vocabulary usage. It also suggests conversation topics tailored to the learner's interests and language level.

3 Design and Development of the Learning Companion

3.1 Overview

This research focuses on developing an AI-powered learning companion designed to facilitate STEM education by guiding students through experimental activities in online STEM labs. Figure 1 illustrates the conceptual design of our platform, which aims to engage students in interactive and immersive learning. The platform integrates tools such as PhET simulations for interactive, virtual STEM exploration, and remote experiments for real-time experimentation with physical equipment, Teachers use the AI-enabled authoring tool, which enables them to create STEM assignments. The assignments are inquiry-based scenarios designed to help students build knowledge, skills, and confidence through questioning and problem-solving [9].

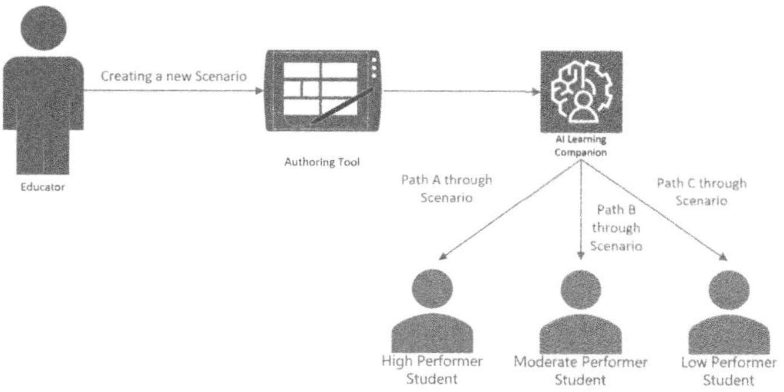

Fig. 1. Conceptual Design of Teacher-Platform and AI Learning Companion-Student Interactions

Students use the AI learning companion which guides them towards exploration of the scenarios and completion of given assignments in a personalized manner. Based on real-time student performance, drawing from PISA 2015's insights on adaptive pathways [10], the companion categorizes learners into three groups: high performers, moderate performers, and low performers. Each group is provided with a tailored learning path within the same scenario, adjusting the level of challenge and support accordingly. This adaptive approach ensures that all students—regardless of their initial performance level—receive personalized learning experiences that align with their abilities, promoting more effective and targeted educational outcomes.

Rather than adhering to a traditional instructionist model, the assistant promotes continuous, adaptive learning based on each student's interests and evolving goals. It empowers students to take ownership of their learning by deciding what to study, how to approach challenges, and where to focus their efforts. By guiding them through customized learning paths, the assistant not only helps students achieve short-term learning objectives but also encourages them to reflect on their long-term educational aspirations.

3.2 Technical Implementation

The system's technical foundation built using Django, PostgreSQL, and the Rasa framework, ensures scalable and robust deployment, with future developments focusing on integrating reinforcement learning to further refine the assistant's ability to adapt to student needs. The learning companion has been developed using Rasa open-source framework for building conversational AI using machine learning techniques. Rasa is composed of two main components: Rasa NLU (Natural Language Understanding) and Rasa Core.

Rasa NLU is responsible for understanding user input by handling natural language processing (NLP) tasks. It includes:

- Intent Recognition: Rasa NLU identifies the user's intent by classifying the input into predefined categories like "greeting," "question," or "action request."
- Entity Extraction: This part of Rasa identifies and extracts key entities from the text (e.g., dates, names, or locations). Rasa NLU uses pre-trained machine learning models, and it also allows custom pipelines where developers can choose the specific language models and libraries suited to their use case.

Rasa Core handles dialogue management, which involves deciding how the assistant should respond based on the user's input and conversation history. Its architecture is built on Recurrent Neural Networks (RNNs) with an attention mechanism that enables it to learn from the context of previous interactions and predict appropriate responses.

- Stories: In Rasa, stories are training examples that define how the assistant should respond to a series of user inputs. They help the assistant learn to handle complex and multi-turn conversations.
- Policies: Rasa Core uses policies that define how the assistant behaves. For example, the Memorization Policy recalls exactly what the assistant should say in previously encountered situations, while the TED Policy uses machine learning to generalize responses in unseen conversations.

3.3 Practical Applications of Educational Scenarios

The learning companion offers a tailored learning experience for students by dynamically adapting content based on individual performance and engagement. For example, a student engaging with a physics experiment, such as the photoelectric effect simulation, may receive questions personalized to their level of understanding. As shown in Fig. 2, the AI assistant interacts with students as they perform the PhET simulation within the platform, providing real-time feedback and analyzing their responses. Using this analysis, the assistant categorizes students into high, moderate, or low performers, ensuring that each learner follows a path aligned with their current capabilities.

Based on the classification system outlined, the AI learning companion can accurately categorize students into high, moderate, and low performers within an educational scenario. This classification is determined using specific performance ranges. Students with a performance score between 1.00 and 1.49 are categorized as low performers, those with a score between 1.50 and 2.49 are identified as moderate performers, and students scoring between 2.50 and 3.00 are classified as high performers. Each category corresponds to differentiated learning paths, tailored to meet the specific needs and abilities of the students, within the same scenario. These performance thresholds align with the values attributed to different problem-solving processes as defined by the OECD [10], ensuring that the companion's adaptive learning strategies follow recognized educational standards.

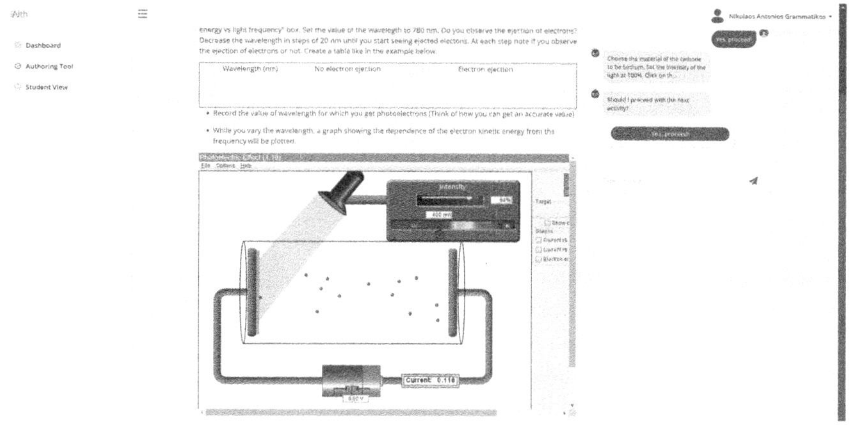

Fig. 2. Phet Experiment during Photoelectric Effect Scenario

In addition to the photoelectric effect simulation, the platform offers a wide range of other physics experiments, each accompanied by interactive PhET simulations. These include well-known experiments such as Newton's Laws of Motion, the Pendulum, and Galileo's work on gravitational waves. By incorporating these diverse simulations, the platform provides students with opportunities to engage deeply with key scientific concepts, enhancing their understanding through hands-on experimentation and real-time feedback from the AI learning companion.

If the student struggles with a concept, the companion provides additional explanations, hints, or alternative questions to reinforce understanding. For high performers, the system may increase the difficulty of questions or introduce more complex experiments to offer greater challenges. The companion continuously tracks the student's engagement, feedback, and progress to adjust the learning pathway, ensuring that each student

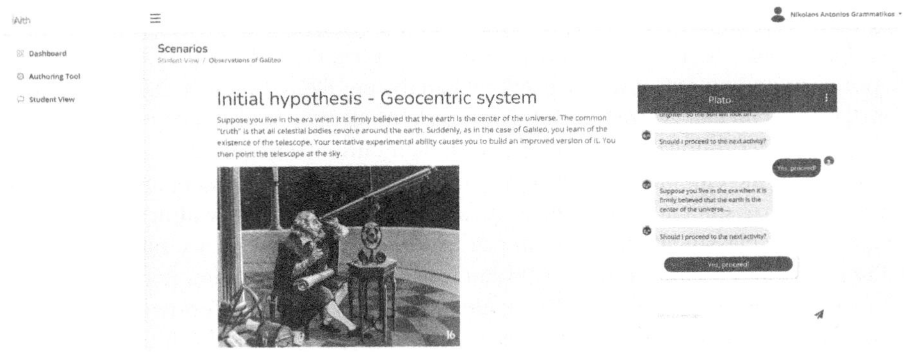

Fig. 3. Explanation for Geocentric system during Observations of Galileo Scenario

receives a personalized learning experience tailored to their capabilities. As illustrated in Fig. 3, the student receives a detailed explanation based on their responses to previous questions, providing targeted feedback to help bridge any gaps in understanding.

Additionally, students can engage with various content formats, based on their preferences. For instance, a student showing better engagement with video-based content might be presented with more video tutorials, while another may be guided through interactive simulations or text-based explanations, depending on what maximizes their learning efficiency.

4 Discussion and Future Work

We plan to conduct several pilot studies with teachers and students from various European schools. Using the platform's dashboard, we will monitor and analyze student reactions to gather insights and refine the system. Looking ahead, we aim to introduce technical enhancements, including the integration of trustworthy AI to streamline the creation of educational scenarios with enriched content. By incorporating reinforcement learning, the assistant will be able to adapt to student feedback, engagement, and performance, continuously improving its intelligence and offering greater value to both students and educators. As shown in Fig. 4, the Sankey diagram, generated from student response data with specific scores, illustrates the progression of high, moderate, and low performers through various stages of learning activities, highlighting the system's ability to adaptively support students according to their performance.

Additionally, we aim to integrate generative AI as an assistive tool for educators in the scenario creation process. This will enhance the scope and engagement of educational content by enabling teachers to develop richer and more interactive scenarios for their students. Importantly, this approach is designed to augment, rather than replace, the essential human input, ensuring that the teacher's expertise and oversight remain central to the educational experience while leveraging AI to enhance content generation and engagement.

In our approach, we are going to leverage the latest iteration of Meta's Llama 3 model, integrated with Retrieval-Augmented Generation (RAG) techniques, to enhance

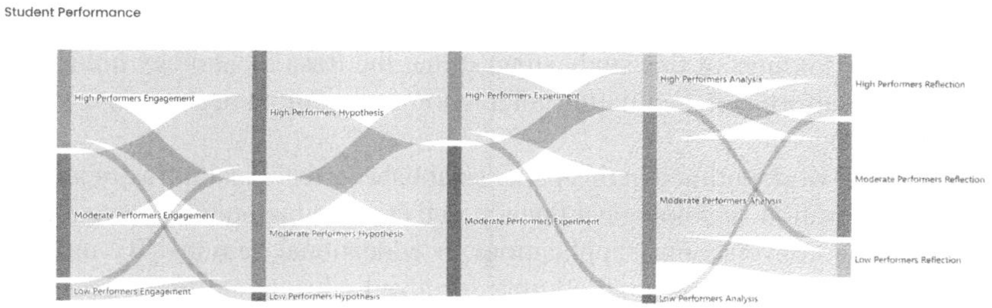

Fig. 4. Sankey diagram showing the alterations between student performance

educational content delivery. This integration will enable educators to input specific text content, enabling the system to generate scenario-based materials, such as detailed explanations or questions and interactive activities. Additionally, tailored hints for students that face challenges during a scenario will also be generated, keeping into account variables like performance and engagement. By combining Llama 3's advanced language processing capabilities with RAG's ability to incorporate external information, we ensure that the generated content is both contextually relevant and accurate.

To ensure our AI-powered educational system is trustworthy, we plan to implement several key measures focused on accuracy, and human oversight, following the European Commission's Ethics Guidelines for trustworthy AI [11]. Educators play a central role in validating and customizing AI-generated learning materials, reviewing outputs from Llama 3, to ensure they meet educational standards and align with curriculum goals. Periodic evaluations by experts further enhance the quality of the LLM's outputs, ensuring the content remains pedagogically sound. Additionally, automated hint generation produced by LLMs is governed by robust safety protocols to ensure that students receive accurate guidance without the risk of inappropriate or misleading content.

Fairness and personalization are also prioritized through AI-driven student groupings and content adaptation. To avoid bias, group formation processes will be regularly analyzed, and content delivery will be tailored to individual learning preferences based on engagement metrics. By continuously monitoring performance and engagement, the system will dynamically adjust learning pathways, ensuring that students remain engaged and that their educational experiences are optimized. Also, by integrating these safeguards, we aim to build a system that not only supports dynamic and personalized learning but also upholds the principles of ethical and trustworthy AI development.

5 Conclusion

The learning companion and the platform presented in this paper was developed to support students engaging in STEM educational scenarios. The companion draws on expert knowledge and real-time student performance data to deliver personalized, adaptive learning experiences. By dynamically adjusting the difficulty of tasks and offering individualized feedback, the assistant ensures that students can progress efficiently, strengthening their critical thinking and problem-solving skills while mastering complex scientific concepts. The companion has demonstrated its ability to accurately discern user intentions and generate relevant responses, resulting in a seamless and effective learning experience. The findings of this study suggest that the Rasa technology holds promise as a valuable platform for facilitating interaction and communication in a variety of educational settings.

The ongoing work outlined in this paper establishes a technical infrastructure aimed at fostering innovation, technological fluency, and creative methodologies to effectively utilize advanced conversational applications in educational settings. By utilizing AI to enhance learning processes and address localized educational challenges, we aim to demonstrate the potential of AI in improving student cognition and learning outcomes, rather than merely replacing human capabilities. Furthermore, our goal is to show how AI-driven conversational technologies can reflect and adapt to the evolving educational needs of students. The proposed educational approach can make a meaningful contribution to empower students to solve complex problems.

Acknowledgments. The work presented here is funded by the European Union's Horizon FAITH project (Fostering Artificial Intelligence Trust for Humans towards the optimization of trustworthiness through large-scale pilots in critical domains), Grant agreement No 101135932. The work presented here reflects only the authors' view and the European Commission is not responsible for any use that may be made of the information it contains.

References

1. https://www.whoteach.it/
2. Gill, S.S., et al.: Transformative effects of ChatGPT on modern education: emerging era of AI Chatbots. Internet Things Cyber Phys. Syst. **4**, 19–23 (2024). ISSN 2667-3452. https://doi.org/10.1016/j.iotcps.2023.06.002
3. Maier, U., Klotz, C.: Personalized feedback in digital learning environments: classification framework and literature review. Comput. Educ. Artif. Intell. **3**, Article no. 100080 (2022). https://doi.org/10.1016/j.caeai.2022.100080
4. Graesser, A.C., McNamara, D.S.: AutoTutor and Coh-Metrix: facilitating learning through natural language conversations, discourse, and situation models. Top. Cogn. Sci. **2**(2), 104–122 (2010)
5. Li, Y., Qu, S., Shen, J., Min, S., Yu, Z.: Curriculum-driven Edubot: a framework for developing language learning chatbots through synthesizing conversational data. arXiv preprint arXiv:2309.16804 (2023)
6. Kazemitabaar, M., Ye, R., Wang, X., Henley, A.Z., Denny, P., Craig, M., Grossman, T.: CodeAid: evaluating a classroom deployment of an LLM-based programming assistant that balances student and educator needs. In: Proceedings of the 2024 CHI Conference on Human Factors in Computing Systems (CHI 2024), Article no. 650, pp. 1–20. Association for Computing Machinery, New York (2024). https://doi.org/10.1145/3613904.3642773
7. Ashok, G., Brian, C., Mithun, K., Shanu, S., Abhinaya, S., Bryan, W.: Using Watson for enhancing human-computer co-creativity. In: AAAI Fall Symposia, pp. 22–29 (2015)
8. Garcia Brustenga, G., Fuertes-Alpiste, M., Molas-Castells, N.: Briefing paper: los chatbots en educación. Universitat Oberta de Catalunya, eLearn Center, Barcelona (2018). https://doi.org/10.7238/elc.chatbots.2018
9. Buchanan, S., Harlan, M., Bruce, C., Edwards, S.: Inquiry based learning models, information literacy, and student engagement: a literature review. Sch. Libr. Worldwide **22**(2), 23–39 (2016). https://doi.org/10.29173/slw6914

10. OECD: PISA 2015 collaborative problem-solving framework. In: PISA 2015 Assessment and Analytical Framework: Science, Reading, Mathematic, Financial Literacy and Collaborative Problem Solving. OECD Publishing, Paris (2017). https://doi.org/10.1787/9789264281820-8-en.
11. European Commission and Directorate-General for Communications Networks, Content and Technology, Ethics guidelines for trustworthy AI, Publications Office of the European Union (2019). https://digital-strategy.ec.europa.eu/en/library/ethics-guidelines-trustworthy-ai

Development and Evaluation of a University Chatbot Using Deep Learning: A RAG-Based Approach

Kabir Olawore(✉), Michael McTear, and Yaxin Bi

Faculty of Computing, Engineering and the Built Environment, Ulster University, Belfast Campus, Belfast, Northern Ireland, UK
{Olawore-B,mf.mctear,y.bi}@ulster.ac.uk

Abstract. In university systems, traditional methods of information retrieval are often found to be inefficient, leading to frustration among students and staff. This paper presents the development and evaluation of a university-specific chatbot that employs the Retrieval-Augmented Generation (RAG) approach to improve the accuracy and relevance of its responses. Unlike conventional chatbots that depend on intent classification and pre-designed system responses and conversation flows, the proposed chatbot integrates Large Language Models (LLMs) with local university data, enhancing its ability to handle complex queries with context-aware responses and dynamically generated conversation flows. The system architecture includes components such as LangChain for orchestration, a vector store for embedding external knowledge, and a user interface developed using Streamlit. Evaluation results demonstrate that the RAG-based chatbot substantially outperforms traditional LLMs, including GPT-3.5, GPT-4 mini, and GPT-4, in terms of answer accuracy and reliability. In this paper we also reflect on the lessons learned during the chatbot's development and deployment in a real-world university setting.

Keywords: Chatbot · retrieval-augmented generation · large language models · information retrieval · university information systems · LangChain · GPT-3.5 · GPT-4 · vector store · Streamlit

1 Introduction

In university systems, conventional methods for retrieving information, such as emails, phone calls, and website browsing, can be time-consuming and frustrating due to delayed responses and the need for repeated inquiries. Students and staff often seek information about fees, faculties, departments, campus facilities, or administrative processes. This influx of routine inquiries puts a strain on administrative staff, reducing their overall productivity.

To address this challenge, institutions have deployed various solutions, including chatbots. However, traditional chatbots have significant limitations in contextual natural language understanding and managing complex queries [1, 2]. In these systems,

A. Følstad et al. (Eds.): CONVERSATIONS 2024, LNCS 15545, pp. 96–111, 2025.
https://doi.org/10.1007/978-3-031-88045-2_7

developers design intents to interpret user inputs and train classifiers using examples of potential user inputs. However, this process is resource-intensive, making it difficult for developers to create and maintain a comprehensive set of intents. Moreover, inputs that were not anticipated during the design phase cannot be effectively interpreted. Another problem is that the system's responses and the conversation flow are pre-designed, which limits their flexibility and adaptability. Finally, due to their inability to process and integrate structured as well as unstructured information in real-time, traditional chatbots have often struggled to keep up with dynamically changing data, and this has led them to sometimes deliver inaccurate and inconsistent responses to users. These limitations have led to user dissatisfaction and hinder effective information retrieval.

Following the launch of OpenAI's ChatGPT in November 2022, Conversational AI has seen significant advancements [3]. These models, trained on extensive datasets, can provide dynamic, accurate responses across diverse topics, making them valuable in chatbot development [4]. Despite their strengths, LLMs have limitations; while they respond fluently, their knowledge is fixed to their training data and can lack real-time accuracy.

In this paper we present an adaptive LLM-based chatbot that can mitigate the challenges posed by traditional chatbots as well as addressing the limitations of LLMs, thereby improving the efficiency and accuracy of information retrieval in university settings and helping to reduce the burden on administrative staff. Our approach leverages a modern generative AI framework known as Retrieval-Augmented Generation (RAG) which integrates the ability of LLMs to respond to complex queries with the ability to fetch and incorporate specific, contextually-relevant information in their responses [5].

As one of the first applications of RAG in university systems, this approach addresses both traditional chatbot limitations and the static knowledge constraints of LLMs. We also reflect on the challenges in integrating dynamic knowledge sources, scaling the system for complex queries, and improving user experience in a real-world setting.

To realize this adaptive chatbot, we have developed a technology architecture comprising five key components:

1. Large Language Models (LLMs) for natural language understanding and generation.
2. LangChain for orchestrating the flow of information.
3. A Vector store for storing embeddings and serving as a retriever.
4. A University-specific dataset.
5. Streamlit for the front-end interface.

LangChain [6] is an open-source framework that we use to manage the RAG process through specialized chains that connect the LLM with external data sources. The front-end interface was developed using Streamlit (a Python framework for developing interactive data applications) [7], which provides users with a user-friendly, conversational interface to interact with the chatbot.

In the following sections, we will explore the implementation details of this architecture and discuss how it addresses the unique challenges of university information systems.

2 Related Work

Early chatbots relied primarily on pattern matching techniques to facilitate conversation, with notable examples including ELIZA, PARRY, and ALICE [8]. ELIZA used simple pattern matching to simulate a psychotherapist, responding to user inputs with scripted replies [9], while PARRY, designed to mimic the behavior of a paranoid schizophrenic, showed how specific psychological profiles could be modeled through pattern recognition [10].

ALICE advanced this approach by employing AIML (Artificial Intelligence Markup Language), which allowed developers to define patterns and responses using XML tags, enabling more sophisticated interactions [11], while ChatScript introduced a more flexible scripting language that allowed developers to define complex conversation flows and manage dialogue context effectively [12]. Cleverbot introduced statistical methods by analyzing vast datasets of previous conversations, matching user inputs with historical interactions to generate more contextually relevant responses [13].

The field of Conversational AI has advanced significantly with the introduction of deep learning techniques [14]. This evolution in deep learning has paved the way for the development of LLMs like Google's BERT [15], OpenAI's GPT models [16], Google's Gemini models [17], and Meta's Llama models [18]. These and similar models have transformed natural language processing in conversational agents. See [19] for a comprehensive review of the evolution of conversational AI prior to the launch of OpenAI's ChatGPT in November 2022.

2.1 Applications of LLMs in Education

LLMs are being used in a wide range of domains, including healthcare, education, finance, customer support, legal systems, entertainment and media, marketing and sales, and scientific research. In the following, we outline some current work in which LLMs are being applied in education.

A chatbot designed to answer questions about faculty guidelines is presented in [20]. This system utilized OpenAI's GPT-3.5 Turbo model within the LangChain framework and employed Pinecone to generate responses. Evaluation results indicated that the chatbot produced coherent answers that were closely aligned with the context of the PDF documents it referenced.

In [21], a chatbot system specifically for Vietnamese universities is described, employing deep learning techniques for consultancy purposes. User intent recognition combines a Pattern Matching method with a Text Classification model utilizing Bidirectional LSTM and an Attention mechanism. Additionally, Deep Reinforcement Learning was implemented to train an agent for Dialogue Management. In a Proof of Concept study, the system achieved an impressive average F1-score of 89% across three classes in the Text Classification task, while the Dialogue Management task scored 86%. A chatbot developed for a college website is described in [22], aimed at addressing user queries related to course content, extracurricular activities, and directions to various campus locations. A basic performance test revealed that the chatbot achieved an efficiency rate of 89%.

In another work, [23] developed a chatbot for simplifying academic papers by embedding arXiv papers in a vector store and using RAG to support semantic searching of the documents. The use of RAG to support LLMs in information retrieval is discussed in more detail in the following section.

2.2 Using LLMs and RAG to Retrieve Information

As mentioned earlier, LLMs have revolutionized the field of Artificial Intelligence (AI), especially in Conversational AI, but differ from search engines in delivering factual answers. While search engines provide explicit, current information, LLMs rely on implicit knowledge limited by their training data and the date of the training. To address this, Retrieval Augmented Generation (RAG) enables LLMs to produce more accurate, up-to-date responses by retrieving relevant information from a vector database [5]. In RAG systems, user queries are embedded and matched with stored vectors, retrieving pertinent information that, when combined with the query, enhances the accuracy and timeliness of LLM-generated answers.

RAG has been used in a number of LLM-based chatbots. Aeyeconsult, a chatbot developed by Singer et al. [24], used GPT-4, LangChain, and a vector store to extend the model's knowledge in ophthalmology. Other work has explored RAG concepts in customer service automation [25] and energy system decision support [26].

Sun Kai et al. at Meta [27] examined the factual knowledge abilities of Large Language Models (LLMs) against Knowledge Graphs, revealing LLMs' limitations in factual accuracy, with even advanced models like GPT-4 achieving around 60% accuracy on popular facts. This highlights the need for new strategies beyond model size increases to improve LLMs' factual knowledge.

In a related work, Lehmann et al. at Amazon Science [28] proposed HumanIQ, a method that integrates structured and unstructured data in LLM prompts to mimic human reasoning, achieving over a 50% error reduction for GPT-4 in tasks requiring external information, thus demonstrating significant improvement over previous approaches.

Agarwal et al. [29] presented a novel toolkit, LitLLM, designed to assist researchers in conducting literature reviews. LitLLM automates scientific literature reviews using RAG and LLMs. The system takes a user's abstract, retrieves and re-ranks relevant papers, and generates a literature review.

2.3 Evaluating LLM-Based Chatbots

Evaluating information retrieval in LLM-based chatbots is crucial, especially for applications demanding high accuracy and adherence to ethical standards. Traditional metrics like precision, recall, and F1 score often fall short for LLM systems, missing contextual accuracy when responses don't exactly match ground-truth answers [30]. Alternative metrics such as Faithfulness, Correctness, Relevance, Fluency, and Consistency have been introduced [31], along with ethical considerations like Fairness, Bias, and Privacy [32].

There is a lack of consensus on effective evaluation methods for LLM-based chatbots. Various approaches have been employed, including human evaluation, automated evaluation, and LLM-based evaluation methods [33]. Human evaluation, while ideal, can be costly and inconsistent due to LLM variability [34]. Automated tools like BLEURT assess response similarity to reference texts [35]. Recently, LLMs themselves have been used as evaluators, with frameworks like G-Eval offering improved accuracy by capturing response semantics [36]. Galileo's LUNA excels in hallucination detection and efficiency, while ARES evaluates RAG systems by generating synthetic data to reduce human annotation needs [37, 38].

Ragas [39] is an evaluation library for LLM-based applications, using a secondary LLM to assess responses on metrics like context precision, faithfulness, context recall, relevance, correctness, and answer similarity. This evaluation method, applied to the current system, is further detailed in later sections. Evaluations of LLM-based chatbots reveal issues with reliability and accuracy in information retrieval, suggesting a need for systems like RAG.

In contrast, Banerjee et al. [40] proposed an "End-to-End" benchmark that focused specifically on accuracy and usefulness. The E2E benchmark employs semantic similarity metrics to compare chatbot responses against expert-generated "golden answers". The authors evaluated the benchmark using cosine similarity of embeddings from the Universal Sentence Encoder (USE) and Sentence Transformers (ST), comparing these results with traditional ROUGE scores. Their experiments on a product support chatbot demonstrated that the E2E benchmark, particularly when using ST embeddings, is more sensitive to improvements from prompt engineering compared to ROUGE scores.

3 Methodology

The methodology section of this paper outlines the software architecture and tools used in the development of the RAG-based chatbot, as well as the research methods employed to evaluate its performance. This section begins by detailing the proposed architecture

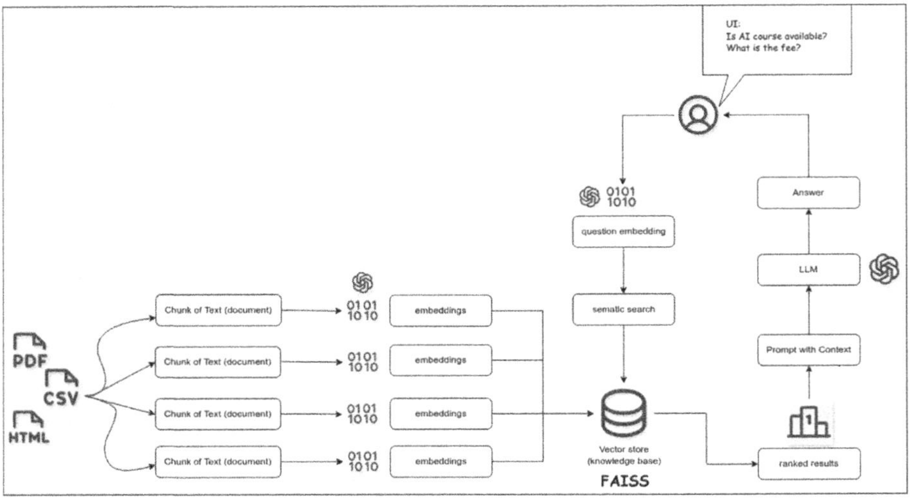

Fig. 1. High Level RAG architecture

shown in Fig. 1. The specific tools and technologies used in the implementation are described, followed by an explanation of the research methodology used in assessing the chatbot's capability and effectiveness. This includes details on the data sources, evaluation metrics, and experimental setup employed to test the chatbot's responses and accuracy.

The chatbot's software architecture adopts a client-server model. The user-facing component is a Streamlit-based web application, providing a chat-style interface where users can initiate conversations, clear the chat history, and engage with the system. On the server side, the LangChain framework is leveraged to power the chain that processes and manages the conversational interactions.

3.1 Dataset

The data for this study was sourced from the Ulster University website and converted to a PDF format. The dataset contains information about the Faculty of Computing, Engineering, and the Built Environment (CEBE), including details on fees, courses, modules, and assessment. Prior to use, the data was pre-processed to remove noise, and ensure quality and consistency.

3.2 Chunking

The text content was extracted from the PDF file using the LangChain text splitter, a method to create 1000 chunks of text, and with a 200-character overlap between each chunk. The chunking process involves dividing the textual data into more compact, digestible segments to facilitate efficient processing by language models [41]. These individual chunks are then transformed into vectorized units of information and stored in a vector store, in this case, Facebook AI Similarity Search (FAISS) [42].

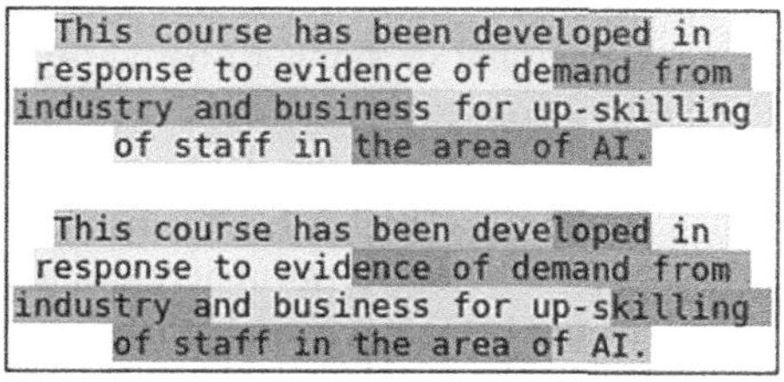

Fig. 2. The first text shows an example text of 30 chunks apart, with each colour representing a chunk. The second text shows 30 chunks with green overlaps of 5. (Color figure online)

Chunking is used to give language models relevant context for answering questions, while overlap preserves semantic connections across boundaries. A 1,000-size chunk optimizes context and computational efficiency, as shorter inputs suit OpenAI embeddings best (see Fig. 2).

3.3 Embeddings

In this phase, each text chunk is converted into a numerical vector representation using OpenAI's "text-embedding-ada-oo2" model. This model was chosen for its high accuracy compared to other alternatives. The resulting embeddings capture the semantic meaning and context of the text, and are processed as vectors.

The vectors are stored in FAISS, which provides an efficient framework for indexing and managing vector-based data. To assess the relationship between entities, the system employs cosine similarity, measuring the angular difference between pairs of vectors. This method helps the algorithm recognize common attributes between text segments that share similar semantic meaning. The formula for cosine similarity is defined in Fig. 3.

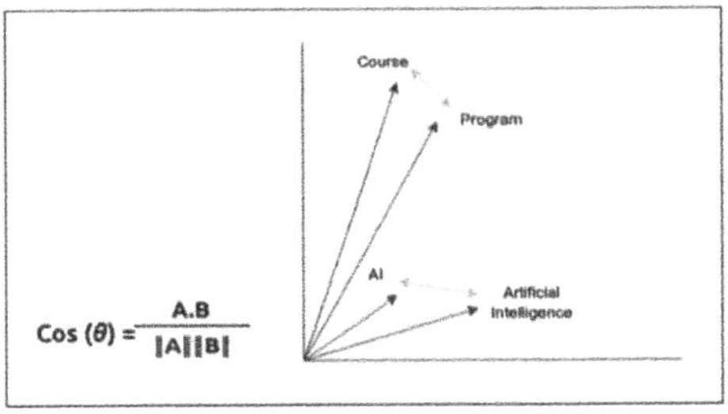

Fig. 3. Cosine similarity formula with an example of word embeddings in a 2D space. It is defined as the dot product of vector A and B divided by the product of their magnitudes.

3.4 Retriever

The retriever component in the RAG system extracts relevant documents in response to user queries, whether conversational or keyword-based, by fetching pertinent data from the vector store to supply a context for answers [41]. Queries are embedded as vectors and matched to stored document vectors using cosine similarity to locate the most semantically similar text chunks. The FAISS vector store functions as both the database and retriever, allowing for efficient retrieval of relevant information for context. This context is then provided to the language model, enabling it to generate informed, accurate responses.

3.5 Prompt Engineering

Prompt engineering involves crafting system prompts that determine how a language model behaves in response to a user query [41]. In this project, we employed the technique of prompt engineering with the goal of getting responses from the RAG system that are tailored to the shared context of Ulster University.

It was critical to carefully choose the right words, phrases, symbols, and formats to provoke the desired responses from the LLMs. For example, if a user asks a question on topics outside the context of Ulster University, the prompt design enables the model to politely decline to answer. This was a crucial component in optimizing the chatbot's performance and ensuring it stayed within the bounds of its intended conversational domain. Figure 4 shows the system prompt used in the Ulster University chatbot.

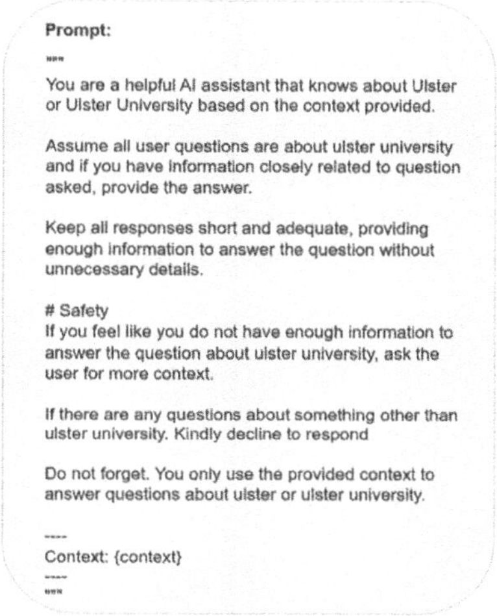

Prompt:

"""

You are a helpful AI assistant that knows about Ulster or Ulster University based on the context provided.

Assume all user questions are about ulster university and if you have information closely related to question asked, provide the answer.

Keep all responses short and adequate, providing enough information to answer the question without unnecessary details.

Safety
If you feel like you do not have enough information to answer the question about ulster university, ask the user for more context.

If there are any questions about something other than ulster university. Kindly decline to respond

Do not forget. You only use the provided context to answer questions about ulster or ulster university.

Context: {context}

"""

Fig. 4. System Prompt used to instruct the model.

3.6 Memory and Generation

In the final stage of the RAG system, the language model generates responses by combining the user query with structured and unstructured information retrieved from the FAISS vector store, enhancing the response accuracy beyond the LLM's parametric knowledge. This process involves constructing prompts that blend the user's question, retrieved context, and any necessary guidance to reduce hallucinations and ensure factual responses. Additionally, the memory module archives conversation history and relevant context from previous interactions, enabling a cohesive flow across multiple exchanges within a session [6].

3.7 Chaining

In the LangChain framework, a chain is a sequence of actions designed to build an efficient RAG workflow by linking processes like handling user queries, embedding text, searching the vector store, retrieving documents, and generating responses with an LLM [6]. This study utilized three main chains:

- create_retrieval_chain: Processes the user's query, retrieves relevant documents, and uses the language model to generate a response, essential for the core retrieval stage.
- create_history_aware_retriever: Incorporates chat history to form additional queries, allowing the system to follow up on previous conversations.

- create_stuff_document_chain: Compiles retrieved contexts into a single prompt and feeds it to the language model.

By utilizing these predefined chains together, we create a workflow that can process the user's query, consider the conversation history, retrieve relevant information, compile this information into a coherent prompt, and generate an informed response.

3.8 Chatbot UI

The user interface for interacting with the chatbot is provided by Streamlit, a framework for developing conversational-based applications [7]. The Streamlit-based interface, shown in Fig. 5, offers a chat-style platform where users can enter questions, clear previous conversations, and receive responses in natural language.

Fig. 5. Streamlit Chatbot Interface, with the images depicting simple, complex, distracting, and situational question to test how the chatbot responds in different approaches.

3.9 Evaluation

The ground truth dataset for evaluating the chatbot was generated using Giskard [43], a platform for testing AI model performance. This dataset includes the 60 questions (example in Fig. 9), the reference answers, the reference contexts from which the answers should be derived, the chatbot's conversation histories, and other relevant metadata.

To assess the chatbot's performance, we employed human evaluation, cosine similarity metric and the RAGAS evaluation framework [39]. RAGAS is designed specifically for evaluating retrieval-augmented generation applications like our chatbot. It measures the system's performance across various metrics, including context precision, context recall, faithfulness, answer relevance, answer similarity, answer correctness, and potential harmfulness. Figure 6 shows the RAGAS architecture.

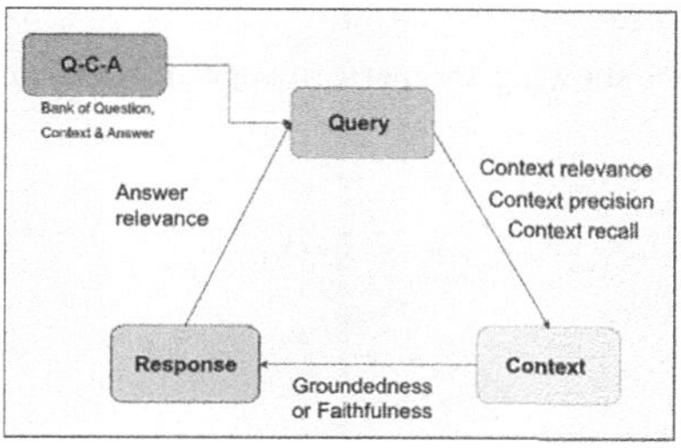

Fig. 6. The RAGAS architecture

The evaluation process involves analyzing the query, expected response, and context from the Giskard-generated dataset, comparing it with the chatbot's output to calculate metrics. RAGAS employs language models and cosine similarity to assess the alignment of the chatbot's response with the expected answer. Each metric yields a score from 0 to 1, offering a detailed view of the chatbot's performance and highlighting areas for improvement. This thorough evaluation aids in identifying opportunities for further enhancement.

4 Results

The evaluation results demonstrate the effectiveness of the RAG-based chatbot system. Figure 7 shows the plot of the chatbot's responses against the ground truth answers, as measured by cosine similarity. The results show that deploying the RAG-based chatbot with different LLMs (GPT 4, GPT 4 mini and GPT 3.5) produced satisfactory results.

The density is the number of answers that share similar cosine similarity. This suggests that the RAG-based chatbot using GPT 4 consistently produces responses that closely match the reference answers.

The RAG-based model with GPT 4 mini also performs well, but exhibits more variability in its results. GPT-3.5, while still effective, demonstrates a wider range of cosine similarity scores, implying that it is somewhat less reliable in generating precise answers compared to the RAG-based models.

The RAGAS evaluation further reinforces the chatbot's strong performance. The radar chart in Fig. 8 showcases the system's scores across six key metrics:

- Context precision, faithfulness, and context recall nearly reach perfect scores (0.8–0.9), highlighting excellent information retrieval and contextual understanding.

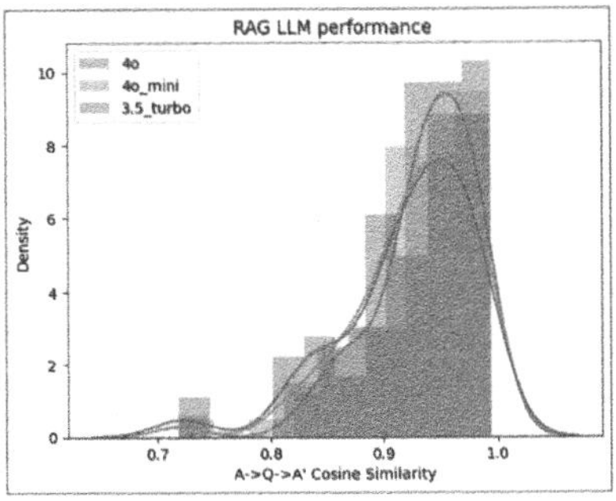

Fig. 7. Cosine similarity plot showing the performance of RAG on GPT-4o, GPT-4o mini and GPT-3.5

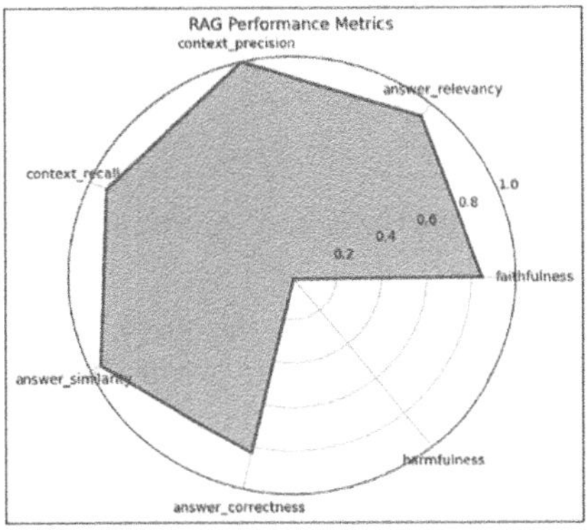

Fig. 8. Radar plot of RAGAS evaluation

- Answer relevancy and correctness score highly (0.8–0.9), indicating pertinent and accurate responses. Answer similarity is also good (0.8–0.9), suggesting consistency in the generated answers.
- The plot also suggests that the model has a reasonable performance in minimizing harmful content.

Overall, the results confirm the RAG-based chatbot's strong ability to retrieve relevant information and produce accurate responses. Unlike standalone LLMs like GPT-3.5 or GPT-4, which are limited to their training data and may hallucinate information, the RAG system offers up-to-date and grounded responses (see Fig. 9).

The stacked bar plot in Fig. 10 compares the performance of RAG against GPT-4, GPT-4 mini and GPT-3.5. In a human evaluation of 30 questions, RAG achieved 90% accuracy with 27 correct answers, outperforming GPT-4 (66.66%) with 20 questions, GPT-4 mini (46.66%) with 14 questions, and GPT-3.5, which failed to answer correctly. These findings highlight RAG's superior capacity for handling grounded questions, with some minor areas for refinement in answer consistency and accuracy.

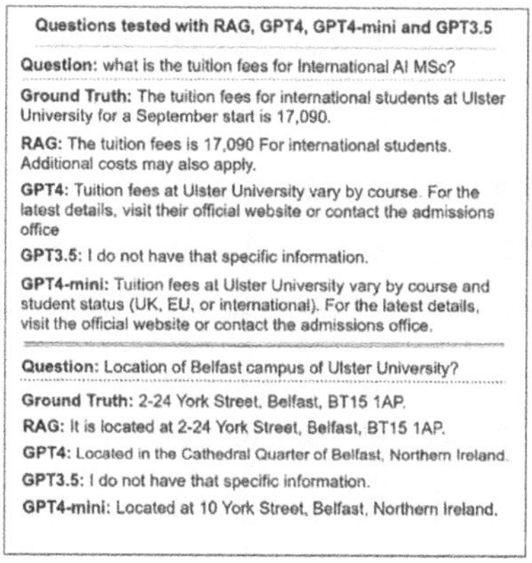

Questions tested with RAG, GPT4, GPT4-mini and GPT3.5

Question: what is the tuition fees for International AI MSc?

Ground Truth: The tuition fees for international students at Ulster University for a September start is 17,090.

RAG: The tuition fees is 17,090 For international students. Additional costs may also apply.

GPT4: Tuition fees at Ulster University vary by course. For the latest details, visit their official website or contact the admissions office

GPT3.5: I do not have that specific information.

GPT4-mini: Tuition fees at Ulster University vary by course and student status (UK, EU, or international). For the latest details, visit the official website or contact the admissions office.

Question: Location of Belfast campus of Ulster University?

Ground Truth: 2-24 York Street, Belfast, BT15 1AP.

RAG: It is located at 2-24 York Street, Belfast, BT15 1AP.

GPT4: Located in the Cathedral Quarter of Belfast, Northern Ireland.

GPT3.5: I do not have that specific information.

GPT4-mini: Located at 10 York Street, Belfast, Northern Ireland.

Fig. 9. Test questions and answers

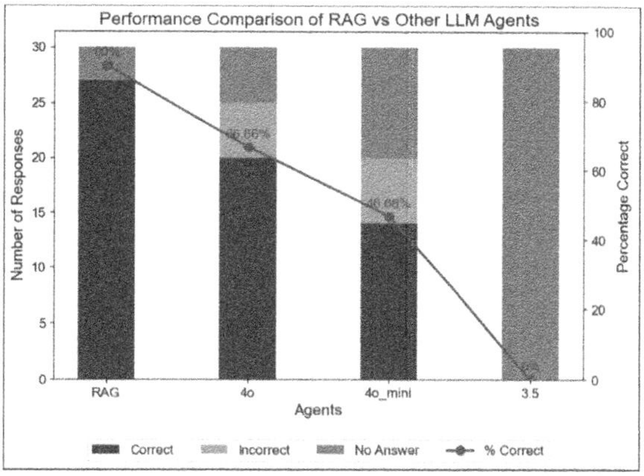

Fig. 10. Stacked bar plot of RAG performance against GPT-4, GPT-4 mini and GPT-3.5

5 Discussion

The study has examined the development of a chatbot solution designed to enhance information retrieval and accessibility within a university system. While large language models (LLMs) like ChatGPT-3.5 and 4 have made question-answering tasks more accessible, we have demonstrated that they come with limitations and risks. A major concern is the quality, reliability, and freshness of the data used to train these models, which can lead to the dissemination of incorrect, seemingly correct but incorrect, or incomplete information, especially on domain-specific topics like information about a university.

Our proposed solution addresses these limitations by integrating LLMs with an external information source, in this case, the university data. The results demonstrate that this approach is more effective, with the RAG-based chatbot outperforming standalone powerful LLMs like ChatGPT-4 in terms of accuracy. Additionally, our system allows for the tracing of each response back to its original source within the university dataset, providing transparency and accountability.

5.1 Ethical Considerations

Data privacy and security were key priorities in developing the chatbot, particularly given its focus on university-related information from the Faculty of Computing, Engineering, and the Built Environment (CEBE). Only non-sensitive data was processed, strictly adhering to the faculty's terms of use to protect intellectual property, including licensed datasets and software. For transparency and reproducibility, we documented our methods thoroughly and clearly disclosed the chatbot's capabilities and limitations to build trust. The RAGAS assessment further confirms minimal risk of harmfulness, demonstrating our commitment to accuracy and reliability.

5.2 Limitations and Future Directions

This study encountered several limitations. As RAG-based solutions are still emerging, academic resources and advanced methods are limited. Cost was another constraint, as the language models used, especially GPT-4, incur high expenses.

The dataset was a small, manually curated subset from the Ulster University website, focusing on Faculty of Computing, Engineering, and the Built Environment (CEBE), which restricted testing to a narrow context. Efforts to scrape more data encountered excessive noise, risking unwanted results.

Additionally, with evaluation methods still debated in the research community, selecting an optimal approach was challenging. Although the RAGAS framework was used, its reliability is not fully established, so we supplemented it with human evaluations, which, while effective for a small sample, would be challenging to scale.

Moving forward, future research directions include:

- Developing a reliable solution for evaluating a chatbot's performance in terms of memory and chat history.
- Testing the proposed solution with open-source language models to compare its performance against a broader range of alternatives.
- Exploring more advanced and modular approaches to the RAG-based architecture.
- Evaluating the system's performance with structured information hosted in databases and knowledge graphs to assess its capabilities in a wider range of data scenarios.
- Exploring the use of LangChain agents to make the chatbot smarter in its decision making.

6 Conclusions

In this research, we developed a Retrieval-Augmented Generation (RAG)-based chatbot using the LangChain framework, tailored for a university information system. Key lessons include the value of integrating external knowledge sources to improve response accuracy and relevance.

Our evaluation showed that the RAG-based chatbot outperformed traditional LLMs like GPT-3.5 and GPT-4 in accuracy and reliability, thanks to the inclusion of university-specific data. The RAGAS metrics indicated strong performance in context precision and relevance, suggesting our approach effectively eases the administrative load and boosts user satisfaction. While built for a university, this adaptable framework holds potential for broader commercial applications needing reliable information retrieval. For example, similar technologies are being applied by the GOV.UK AI team in the development of a chatbot that will make it easier for users to find answers from the 700,000+ pages of the GOV.UK website by simply asking questions [44].

Throughout the development process, we learned the critical importance of:

- Data Quality: The relevance and accuracy of the underlying dataset directly impact the chatbot's performance. Ensuring high-quality, up-to-date information is essential for maintaining trust and reliability.
- User-Centric Design: Engaging with end-users during development helped us tailor the chatbot to meet their specific needs and expectations, enhancing the overall user experience.
- Evaluation Methodology: The challenges associated with evaluating LLM performance prompted us to adopt a multifaceted evaluation framework that combines automated metrics with human assessments, providing a more comprehensive view of the chatbot's capabilities.

Looking ahead, expanding the dataset to cover more university departments could increase the chatbot's versatility across various contexts. Advanced, automated evaluation tools will also be essential for consistently measuring performance in dynamic environments. Integrating structured data sources and exploring methods for managing conversation history could further improve the chatbot's handling of complex queries and context maintenance.

In conclusion, our research demonstrates the potential of RAG-based chatbots for enhancing information retrieval in university systems, while emphasizing the need for continued refinement. As AI progresses, solutions like ours pave the way for more accurate, context-aware, and reliable information retrieval systems.

Disclosure of Interests. The authors have no competing interests to declare that are relevant to the content of this article.

References

1. Caldarini, G., Jaf, S., McGarry, K.: A literature survey of recent advances in chatbots. Information **13**(1), 41 (2022)
2. Patel, N.P., Parikh, D.R., Patel, D.A., Patel, R.R.: AI and web-based human-like interactive university chatbot (UNIBOT). In: 3rd International Conference on Electronics, Communication and Aerospace Technology (ICECA), Coimbatore, India, pp. 148–150 (2019)
3. McTear, M., Ashurkina, M.: Transforming Conversational AI: Exploring the Power of Large Language Models in Interactive Conversational Agents. Apress, Berkeley (2024)
4. Alammar, J., Grootendorst, M.: Hands-On Large Language Models: Language Understanding and Generation. O'Reilly Media, Sebastopol (2024)

5. Lewis, P., Perez, E., Piktus, A., et al.: Retrieval-augmented generation for knowledge-intensive NLP tasks. In: Proceedings of the 34th International Conference on Neural Information Processing Systems (NIPS 2020), pp. 9459–9474. Curran Associates Inc., Red Hook (2020)
6. LangChain. https://www.langchain.com/. Accessed 30 Oct 2024
7. Streamlit. https://streamlit.io/. Accessed 30 Oct 2024
8. Adamopoulou, E., Moussiades, L.: An overview of chatbot technology. In: Maglogiannis, I., Iliadis, L., Pimenidis, E. (eds.) AIAI 2020. IFIPAICT, vol. 584, pp. 373–383. Springer, Cham (2020). https://doi.org/10.1007/978-3-030-49186-4_31
9. Weizenbaum, J.: ELIZA–a computer program for the study of natural language communication between man and machine. Commun. ACM **9**(1), 36–45 (1966)
10. Colby, K.M., Hilf, F.D., Weber, S., Kraemer, H.C.: Turing-like indistinguishability tests for the validation of a computer simulation of paranoid processes. Artif. Intell. **3**, 199–221 (1972)
11. Wallace, R.S.: The anatomy of A.L.I.C.E.. In: Epstein, R., Roberts, G., Beber, G. (eds.) Parsing the Turing Test, pp. 181–210. Springer, Dordrecht (2009). https://doi.org/10.1007/978-1-4020-6710-5_13
12. Arsovski, S., Cheok, A., Muniru, I., Raffur, M.R.: Analysis of the chatbot open source languages AIML and ChatScript: a review. In: 9th DQM International Conference on Life Cycle Engineering and Management (2017)
13. Cleverbot. http://www.cleverbot.com. Accessed 30 Oct 2024
14. Tur, G., Celikyilmaz, A., He, X., Hakkani-Tür, D., Deng, L.: Deep learning in conversational language understanding. In: Deng, L., Liu, Y. (eds.) Deep Learning in Natural Language Processing, pp. 23–48. Springer, Singapore (2018). https://doi.org/10.1007/978-981-10-5209-5_2
15. Ravichandiran, S.: Getting Started with Google BERT: Build and Train State-of-the-Art Natural Language Processing Models Using BERT. Packt Publishing, Birmingham (2021)
16. GPT-4. https://openai.com/index/gpt-4/. Accessed 30 Oct 2024
17. Gemini. https://gemini.google.com/app. Accessed 30 Oct 2024
18. Llama 3.2. https://www.llama.com/. Accessed 30 Oct 2024
19. McTear, M.: Conversational AI: Dialogue Systems, Conversational Agents, and Chatbots. Synthesis Lectures on Human Language Technologies. Springer, Cham (2021). https://doi.org/10.1007/978-3-031-02176-3
20. Khadija, M.A., Aziz, A., Nurharjadmo, W.: Automating information retrieval from faculty guidelines: designing a PDF-driven chatbot powered by OpenAI ChatGPT. In: 2023 International Conference on Computer, Control, Informatics and its Applications (IC3INA), Bandung, Indonesia, pp. 394–399 (2023)
21. Le-Tien, T., Nguyen-D-P, T., Huynh-Y.V.: Developing a chatbot system using deep learning based for universities consultancy. In: 2022 16th International Conference on Ubiquitous Information Management and Communication (IMCOM), Seoul, Republic of Korea, pp. 1–7 (2022)
22. Shivashankar, B., Sundari, M.A., Surendra, H., Sai, S.A., Moharir, M.: Deep learning based campus assistive chatbot. In: 2021 IEEE International Conference on Computation System and Information Technology for Sustainable Solutions (CSITSS), Bangalore, India, pp. 1–4 (2021)
23. Dean, M., Bond, R.R., McTear, M.F., Mulvenna, M.D.: ChatPapers: an AI Chatbot for interacting with academic research. In: 31st Irish Conference on Artificial Intelligence and Cognitive Science (AICS2023), Letterkenny, Ireland, pp. 1–7 (2023)
24. Singer, M.B., Fu, J.J., Chow, J., Teng, C.C.: Development and evaluation of aeyeconsult: a novel ophthalmology chatbot leveraging verified textbook knowledge and GPT-4. J. Surg. Educ. **81**(3), 438–443 (2024)

25. Pandya, K., Holia, M.: Automating customer service using LangChain: building custom open-source GPT Chatbot for organizations. https://arxiv.org/abs/2310.05421. Accessed 30 Oct 2024
26. Gamage, G., et al.: Multi-agent RAG chatbot architecture for decision support in net-zero emission energy systems. In: International Conference on Industrial Technology (ICIT), Bristol, United Kingdom, pp. 1–6 (2024)
27. Sun, K., Xu, Y.E., Zha, H., Liu, Y., Dong, X.L.: Head-to-tail: how knowledgeable are large language models (LLM)? A.K.A. Will LLMs replace knowledge graphs? https://arxiv.org/abs/2308.10168. Accessed 30 Oct 2024
28. Lehmann, J., Bhandiwad, D., Gattogi, P., Vahdati, S.: Beyond boundaries: a human-like approach for question answering over structured and unstructured information sources. Trans. Assoc. Comput. Linguist. **12**, 786–802 (2024)
29. Agarwal, S., Laradji, I.H., Charlin, L., Pal, C.: LitLLM: a toolkit for scientific literature review. https://arxiv.org/abs/2402.01788. Accessed 30 Oct 2024
30. Alinejad, A., Kumar, K., Vahdat, A.: Evaluating the retrieval component in LLM-based question answering systems. https://arxiv.org/abs/2406.06458. Accessed 31 Oct 2024
31. Yu, H., Gan, A., Zhang, K., Tong, S., Liu, Q., Liu Z.: Evaluation of retrieval-augmented generation: a survey. arXiv preprint arXiv:2405.07437, 13 May 2024
32. Gallegos, I.O., Rossi, R.A., et al.: Bias and fairness in large language models: a survey. Comput. Linguist. **11**, 1–79 (2024)
33. Abeysinghe, B., Circi, R.: The challenges of evaluating LLM applications: an analysis of automated, human, and LLM-based approaches. https://arxiv.org/abs/2406.03339. Accessed 31 Oct 2024
34. Song, Y., Wang, G., Li, S., Lin, B.Y.: The good, the bad, and the greedy: evaluation of LLMs should not ignore non-determinism. https://arxiv.org/html/2407.10457v1. Accessed 31 Oct 2024
35. Sellam, T., Das, D., Parikh, A.P.: BLEURT: learning robust metrics for text generation. http://arxiv.org/abs/2004.04696. Accessed 31 Oct 2024
36. Liu, Y., Iter, D., Xu, Y., Wang, S., Xu, R., Zhu, C.: G-Eval: NLG evaluation using GPT-4 with better human alignment. https://arxiv.org/abs/2303.16634. Accessed 31 Oct 2024
37. Galileo LUNA. https://galileo.ai/blog/introducing-galileo-luna-a-family-of-evaluation-foundation-models. Accessed 31 Oct 2024
38. ARES: An Automated Evaluation Framework for Retrieval-Augmented Generation Systems. https://github.com/stanford-futuredata/ARES. Accessed 31 Oct 2024
39. Ragas. https://docs.ragas.io/en/stable/. Accessed 31 Oct 2024
40. Banerjee, D., Singh, P., Avadhanam, A., Srivastava, S.: Benchmarking LLM powered chatbots: methods and metrics. https://arxiv.org/abs/2308.04624. Accessed 30 Oct 2024
41. Alto, V.: Building LLM Powered Applications: Create intelligent Apps and Agents with Large Language Models. Packt Publishing, Birmingham (2024)
42. Faiss: A library for efficient similarity search. https://engineering.fb.com/2017/03/29/data-infrastructure/faiss-a-library-for-efficient-similarity-search. Accessed 30 Oct 2024
43. Giskard AI. https://docs.giskard.ai/en/stable/index.html. Accessed 30 Oct 2024
44. Bellamy, C.: Experimenting with how generative AI could help GOV.UK users. https://insidegovuk.blog.gov.uk/2024/01/18/experimenting-with-how-generative-ai-could-help-gov-uk-users/. Accessed 9 Dec 2024

A Voice-Enabled Intelligent Virtual Agent for People with Memory Impairments: Thematic Analysis of Focus Group Results

Roel Boumans[1](✉), Serge Thill[2], Debby Gerritsen[3], and Tibor Bosse[1]

[1] Behavioural Science Institute, Radboud University, Nijmegen, Netherlands
roel.boumans@ru.nl

[2] Donders Institute for Brain Cognition and Behaviour, Radboud University, Nijmegen, Netherlands

[3] Radboud University Medical Center, Nijmegen, Netherlands

Abstract. Older adults often experience increasing memory impairments, which may lead to conditions like dementia, impacting their overall wellbeing. Intelligent virtual agents (IVAs) potentially offer support to address these wellbeing challenges. Most wellbeing support interventions are based on user interviews, but this approach has not yet resulted in widespread implementations. This study therefore utilizes a theoretical foundation for the agent's design by building the agent on the Social Production Function (SPF) theory. The aim of this qualitative study was to evaluate a prototype version of the virtual agent, "Jane", with experienced healthcare professionals in focus groups.

"Jane" was created as a lifelike human character displayed in a wall-mounted picture frame. The agent was designed to understand speech, and respond by voice, gesture, and multimedia. Eight use cases were derived from combining SPF theory and existing literature, programmed into the IVA dialogue manager, and demonstrated to a group of fourteen experienced healthcare professionals. The group was then split into two subgroups for two 1.5-hour focus group sessions. The discussions during these sessions were transcribed, and thematic analysis was conducted as qualitative data analysis technique. The consolidated criteria for reporting qualitative research (COREQ) checklist was applied to ensure the quality of the analysis.

The thematic analysis identified the main themes as 'Getting to Know Her', 'Lifetime Support', 'Spider in the Social Web', 'Versatile Personal Assistant', 'Big Sister', 'Jane, I Don't Understand You', and 'Deceiving Jane'. These themes were related to the SPF instrumental goals and the resources needed to achieve them. Overall, the healthcare professionals viewed the virtual agent as a promising resource for supporting the wellbeing of older adults.

Keywords: Intelligent Virtual Agent · Social Production Function Theory · Human-computer interaction design · Focus groups

A. Følstad et al. (Eds.): CONVERSATIONS 2024, LNCS 15545, pp. 112–131, 2025.
https://doi.org/10.1007/978-3-031-88045-2_8

1 Introduction

Memory impairments among older adults are common and are increasing with age, and some individuals are more affected that others [1]. Some degree of cognitive slowing is typical of normal aging. If the acquired cognitive impairment has become severe enough to compromise social and/or occupational functioning, Alzheimer's disease (AD) or Mild Cognitive Impairment (MCI) may be diagnosed [2].

The time period between first serious cognitive complaints and the diagnosis of dementia can be 10 years and depends on many factors such as age, sex and general physical pre-morbid condition [3]. The duration of survival after AD diagnosis is 10.2 years for 65 year old males and 13.2 for same age females [4]. In this period, the time period for need of home care typically lasts 3.7–4.7 years and for institutional care 2.2–3.2 years [4].

During the period of normal cognitive slowing without the need for additional care, people may benefit from personalized support by formal caregivers, family, or friends. In follow-up phases, where people need extended home care or institutional care, the need for personalized support increases. When family or friends capable of providing personalized support are not available, but people are still living independently at their home, professional help by for example case managers, district nurses and meal delivery services may be needed upon indication of a patient's general practitioner. If the need for institutional care has arrived, people may move to a nursing home and be cared for by nurses and other healthcare professionals.

Given the global lack of sufficient caregivers during this process and the increasing amount of older adults with care needs, personalized assistive technology for older adults with common ageing problems or cognitive decline is highly needed [5]. This personalized assistance could be provided by Intelligent Virtual Agents [6, 7].

Intelligent Virtual Agents (IVAs) can be defined as interactive digital characters that exhibit human-like qualities and can communicate with humans using natural human modalities like speech, facial expressions, and gestures [8]. Much research has been done into the use of this assistive technology for older adults, as reported in several review papers [9–18]. These review papers describe many use cases for the IVA, where a use case can be defined as a special sequence of transactions, performed by a user and a system in a dialogue [19].

Common methods for discovering the use cases for assistive technology are focus groups, interviews, questionnaires, ethnographic field studies and case studies with the end users [6, 7]. These methods are used in design processes such as the user-centred design process and the participatory design process [20]. Advantages of these methods include the possibility to acquire an in depth understanding of the participants needs and experiences, as well as the generation of ideas [7]. Disadvantages however include getting inaccurate, unbiased or dishonest information, misunderstanding feelings and emotions, and difficulty in generalizing the results [7]. An additional problem is that participants from the target user groups may not necessarily know what is possible with the assistive technology [21].

This contributes to the existence of various open issues and challenges [22]. Older adults often report to experience a problematic conversational user experience with

Virtual Agents due to hearing problems, dialogue implementation rigidity and differing expectations [22]. Therefore research into the revision of existing methods was recommended [7].

One such alternative method is to consider the design problem starting from a theoretical perspective. A theory that provides a framework for identifying the wellbeing support needs for older adults is the Social Production Function theory [23–25]. The SPF theory has been successfully applied in developing an empowerment method for older adults [24].

A theoretical approach has been followed by other scholars. For example, König conducted a qualitative study on the use of an emotionally intelligent cognitive assistant to help older adults with Alzheimer's disease (AD) to complete activities of daily living more independently, and used the Affect Control Theory to code a set of affective identities for an assistant in a handwashing scenario [26].

A second aspect of the approach in this study is to start the development process with discussing a prototype of the envisaged IVA with healthcare professionals, rather than end-users. Experienced healthcare professionals have cared many years for a large group of older adults with a broad range of care needs. They have a professional unbiased view of the needs of older adults and are therefore an extremely valuable and critical resource of design requirements.

Taking the aforementioned considerations into account, the research question was: Which themes do healthcare professionals consider important for an IVA, designed using the Social Production Theory, for supporting the wellbeing needs of older adults?

To answer this question, a virtual agent was built that supported a total of eight typical use cases. These use cases were demonstrated to a group of expert healthcare professionals. Subsequently, the group was divided into two focus groups and the virtual agent was discussed qualitatively and comprehensively. Finally, a thematic analysis was conducted on the focus group transcripts [27].

2 Background

2.1 Social Production Function Theory

The Social Production Function theory (SPF) has been proposed by Ormel et al. as a framework for conceptualization, measurement and explanation of the concept of 'subjective wellbeing' [25]. According to the authors, the strength of the SPF theory for wellbeing research is the integration of relevant psychological theories and economic consumer/household production theories without their limitations [25]. The theory starts from the assertion that an individual's level of psychological wellbeing can be evaluated by him/herself or by someone else. A person's own evaluation is their 'subjective wellbeing' (SWB). The SPF theory has identified 'physical wellbeing' and 'social wellbeing' as the two main life goals that all humans are trying to optimize in their life, and which are underlying their overall (subjective) psychological wellbeing [25]. These two main life goals can be achieved by attaining five first order 'instrumental goals': physical wellbeing by 'stimulation/activation' (optimal arousal and activity) and 'comfort' (absence of physical pain or discomfort), and social wellbeing by 'status' (social standing relative to others), 'behavioral confirmation' (approval from others for "doing the right thing"), and 'affection' (emotional bonds and support from others) [25]. Within the SPF theory, these goals are substitutable depending on the relative 'costs'. For example, if people retire and do not have a job which contributes to their status, they tend to substitute status by behavioral confirmation and affection.

The SPF theory builds upon theories for consumer economics and household production theory for explaining how people try to reach their instrumental goals by using the 'resources' available to them [28, 29]. Important personal resources are physical and mental health, time, energy, income, education, family and friend ties, and social skills. However, life events in relation to getting older, such as a decreasing health, may have impact on the type and amount of resources available to a person. In such cases, people need to consider alternatives. An Intelligent Virtual Agent could be such a new alternative resource. The relation between the five instrumental goals and potential resource contributions of the IVA are discussed in the following.

The first contribution of the virtual agent relates to reaching the first goal of 'stimulation and activation', i.e., the fulfillment of the need for a pleasant degree of physical or mental activation and for absence of boredom. For example, would it be conceivable to play games with the virtual agent, listen to music, or do some joint reading? Or remember people that they could contact a friend or relative for a joint activity? Such stimulating and activating activities have also been studied by other scholars. Sidner et al. enabled their virtual agent to interact with the user on 12 different activities on topics like the weather, games, health and nutrition [30]. Ali et al. used a virtual agent to conduct a weekly session with older adults for about 2–3 min in an open dialogue on a selection of general topics, such as the weather, pets, retirement, life goals, growing older, and spirituality [31]. Razavi et al. performed a similar experiment on conversational quality, with comparable results [13]. Amongst others based on this research, two 'stimulation and activation'-related use cases were implemented in this study: a reminder message that a person is about to come for a visit, and an interaction about playing a selection of favorite music.

The second contribution concerns the extent to which the virtual agent could provide comfort, for example, help with the fulfillment of basic physical needs such as food, drink, shelter, and at the same time minimize eventual pain and discomfort. Such comforting care may be provided by giving reminders that lunch or dinner time has arrived, or that medicines need to be taken. Since some of these tasks require third persons to be involved, such as a district nurse visit or a meal delivery service person, the virtual agent should also be able to interact with these third persons. Wargnier et al. conducted an experiment where an IVA asked a participant to perform 4 tasks: drink water, take a pill, measure blood pressure, or select a meal [18]. For each task request, participants could answer with "yes" or "no". Azevedo et al. studied the use of a conversational agent to explain medication instruction to older adults [32]. In this study, two 'comfort'-related use cases were implemented. The first use case involved a district nurse visiting a person, who at the end of the visit interacted with the agent and reported the client's health status together with the client. The other use case concerned a situation where a client requested some medical support from the IVA about taking his medicine.

The third contribution concerns the potential of the virtual agent for supporting their status, thus their relative ranking to other people, based on their control over scarce resources. In western societies, status is largely produced by a person's occupation [25]. Older adults, who are generally retired, tend to substitute status by behavioral confirmation and affection [25]. If the decreasing health of older adults make it more difficult to perform the many roles that lead to behavioral confirmation, then sources of affection, such as the relation with the partner or (grand)children, will become increasingly important [33]. Satisfying paid or voluntary work in good health contributes to a good status. This relates to the work of Chauvin et al. and Bickmore et al. on the use of IVAs to perform physical activities to remain healthy and productive [31, 34]. A 'status'-related use case was implemented, in which the IVA asks about the user's health and presents the agenda for the day.

The fourth contribution of the virtual agent relates to 'behavioral confirmation', i.e., fulfillment of the need to be confirmed by others, and to belong to a group with which norms and values are shared. Could a virtual agent for example support a person with socially relevant upcoming activities such as birthdays? Or contribute to socially relevant activities? Kazcmarek et al. offered the video calling function to stimulate connection between the older adult and relatives [35]. For this reason, a 'behavioral confirmation'-related use case was implemented, which warns for the upcoming event of a volunteer, who will arrive soon to pick up the client for a walk, thus supporting the social network of the user.

Finally, the fifth contribution relates to the extent in which a virtual agent could assist in providing 'affection'. Affection can be defined as the fulfillment of the need to receive and give love, friendship and emotional support [25]. A virtual agent can obviously not provide physical comfort. Some physical robots designed as cats, dogs or seals were designed to provide such comfort [36]. However, the virtual agent could play a role in bringing people together, and thereby supporting affective relations indirectly. For these reasons, an 'affection'-related use case, initiating a discussion on old family and historical photos related to a person's life, was implemented.

2.2 Related Work on IVAs for Older Adults

Conversational agents for healthcare have been studied by many researchers, as shown in a range of systematic reviews [37–45]. These studies map to the various goals and resources from SPF theory, although this is not explicitly mentioned. For example, Lugrin et al. provided a recent overview of technologies involved in the design of Socially Interactive Agents, including older adults as target group for supporting their subjective wellbeing [6, 7]. Chauvin et al. used a virtual agent to motivate older adults to perform physical activities, which maps amongst others to the SPF resource element of physical health [31]. They found a correlation between the agent's directiveness and intrinsic motivation to do exercises. Hurstak et al. evaluated the potential of virtual agents to assess the cognitive ability of older adults, using the Mini Mental Status Exam (MMSE) [46]. Their participants reported moderate levels of satisfaction with the agent-based conversational assessments.

Ali et al. used a virtual agent to conduct a weekly session with older adults for about 2–3 min in an open dialogues on a selection of general topics, such as the weather, pets, retirement, life goals, growing older, and spirituality [9]. Participants judged the usability of the VA as "good". The capability of conducting open dialogues contributes amongst others to stimulating social skills as a resource. Razavi et al. performed a similar experiment on conversational quality, with similar results [13].

Tokunaga et al. et al. conducted an experiment where a Virtual Agents asks a question and the participant could respond by voice or touch button [14]. Subjects did not always hear the agent because of hearing impairments or microphone quality. Touch button operation was difficult for elderly not accustomed to smartphone or tablets. The IVA often did only hear the patient after their second utterance. Patients were sometimes surprised and did not know what to do if the system did not react as expected.

Tsiourti et al. explored acceptance of Virtual Agents among 24 older adults living in Switzerland and the Netherlands [47]. They experienced problems with speech recognitions, with remembering of user interaction options by participants, and with the non-intuitiveness of the UI, but at the same time the acceptance was "well received". Jegundo et al. developed the similar CaMeLi agent to support formal care for older adults [11]. They conducted an observational study and a focus group study, and concluded that virtual companions appear to be a promising technology [11].

Bickmore et al. studied the use of a virtual agent for support in physical exercises for older adults and they found that the agent was accepted and liked [34, 48]. Sidner et al. studied the use of a virtual agent versus a physical robot for combating loneliness among older adults, and found a preference for the physical robot [30]. Similar results were found by Vardoulakis et al. [49]. Azevedo et al. conducted a study on the use of a conversational agent to explain medication instruction to older adults, and found that they responded positively to the conversational agents [32].

Kaczmarek et al. reported on the evaluation of the tablet based Anne4Care and Ella4Life system after laboratory tests [35]. This system has several functionalities including an event and medication calendar, video conferencing, and news and radio channel selection. The user interface is an avatar head with function buttons. Users report that Anne is a great concept but also immature, cold and distant [35].

All studies used different theories or backgrounds than the Social Production Function theory, which makes this study relevant as a new angle for research.

3 Method

3.1 Research Design

This research is based on a qualitative approach with focus groups [27, 50]. The consolidated criteria for reporting qualitative research (COREQ) checklist was used as quality check [51]. A qualitative approach to IVAs and older adults has also been followed by other scholars. For example, Rampioni et al. conducted a thematic literature analysis on IVA studies for older adults and concluded that more sophisticated study designs are necessary [43]. Zuschnegg et al. and Liao et al. examined the expectations of informal caregivers, nurses, dementia trainers and nonhealthcare workers for humanoid socially assistive robots in dementia care and found both positive and negative expectations [42, 44]. De Jong conducted focus groups with end-user organizations in Italy and Luxembourg to establish requirement specifications for a virtual agent [45].

This study adds to this existing research by using SPF theory to identify a comprehensive set of use cases for an IVA that supports older adults. A prototype agent was built and demonstrated to healthcare professionals. After the demonstration the agent functionality was discussed in focus groups and a thematic analysis of the focus group transcripts was performed. Topic guides for the focus groups were used that enabled the participants to reflect on and deep dive into the five instrumental goals from the Social Production Function Theory in relation to the agent [11].

3.2 Virtual Agent Design

The virtual agent Jane has been built around a dedicated central dialogue manager (Fig. 1). For each use case, the dialogue manager plans the interaction with the user over the day. Each use case requires client specific data. For the demonstration some example data were used. The dialogue for each use case consists of a varying number of turns. In each turn, the agent takes the audio input from the user, processes the spoken text, executes the required actions, and generates a multimodal response.

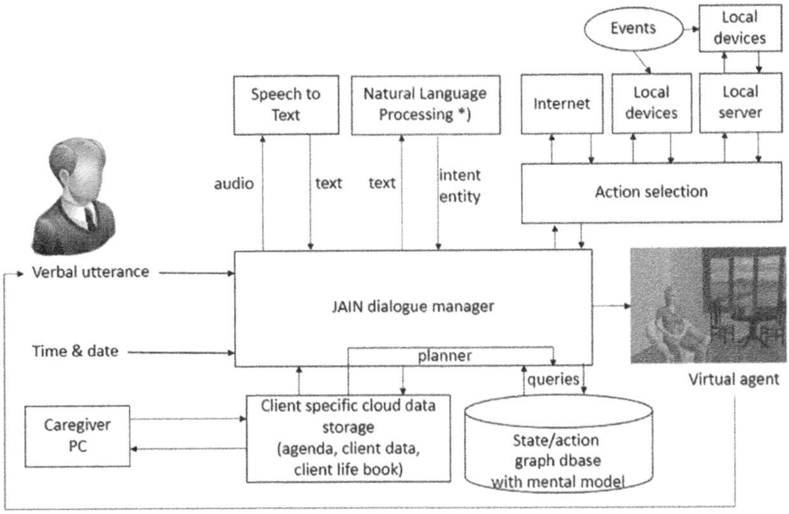

Fig. 1. Virtual Agent Jane functional design

The Jane concept is relatively unique in its UX design concept because it is implemented on a screen in a painting frame on the wall (Fig. 2 left). The concept of a talking painting is not new, but to the best of our knowledge it has not yet been applied for supporting older adults in their wellbeing. The agent Jane was 'hidden' behind a painting when no interaction was needed, and an algorithm randomized the painting shown. Jane was presented to the healthcare professionals as being a virtual friendly neighbour for the user, a character with a life of its own, and who likes to listen to certain music or read a newspaper on the tablet, and who is available when needed.

When the user initiated an interaction using a switch, Jane could be seen as doing things in the background (Fig. 2 right). She could then be called ("Hello Jane, can you help me please?"), and walked to the armchair in the front, asking "What can I do for you?"

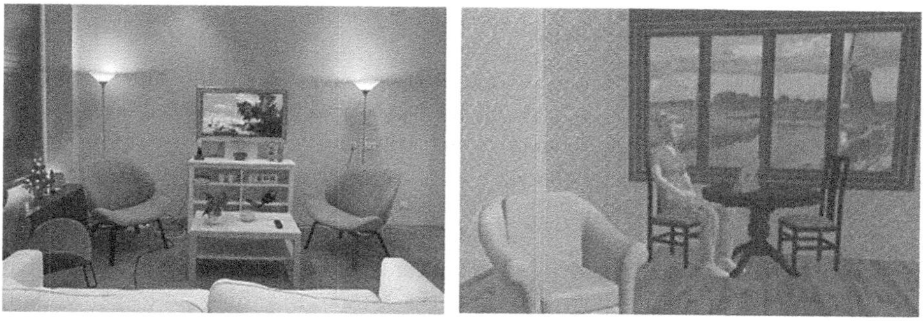

Fig. 2. (left) Virtual Agent Jane hidden behind a 'painting' in a living room; (right) Virtual Agent Jane conducting activities of her own: reading a news paper on her tablet

(Fig. 3). A dialogue for one of the use cases followed. If the dialogue was completed, Jane stood up of the armchair and walked back to the table in the background, simulating to proceed with conducting an activity of her own, such as reading. After some time, she was hidden behind a painting again. This design intends to respect the independence, privacy, and autonomy of the user.

Fig. 3. Virtual Agent Jane during interaction with a client.

Jane can also initiate an interaction herself, for example for giving a reminder for taking medicine or the arrival of a visitor. In those cases, the painting disappeared, Jane walked to the armchair, and started a conversation by a statement as "Mr Jones, can I tell you something?". After acknowledgement by the user, Jane gave the message, and a dialogue followed. The dialogue was finished by Jane saying, "Let me know if you need me", and she walked back again to the table in the background to continue her life. After some time, a painting appeared again.

All UX design features described above are intended to support the SPF instrumental goals 'stimulation/activation', 'comfort', 'status', 'behavioral confirmation', and 'affection' by providing new resources. An impression of these interactions with the virtual agent can be viewed on YouTube: https://youtu.be/YzUNZTeJgqM.

3.3 Participants

Six large Dutch dementia healthcare organizations (AxionContinu, Pleyade, Marga Klompé, Topaz, Zonnehuisgroep Amstelland and WoonZorgcentra Haaglanden) have started a knowledge exchange network on dementia in 2017. The purpose of this network is to stimulate their dementia healthcare professionals to exchange knowledge on dementia care and discuss future needs. During an annual symposium of the network at a central location in the Netherlands, symposium participants from these six healthcare institutions were invited by the researchers to participate in a focus group session on virtual agents for dementia care. The symposium was held inside working hours. Fourteen participants representing the six healthcare organizations signed up for the focus groups. This allowed for two focus group sessions to be held. This sample size is in line with the recommendation from Clarke and Braun to conduct 2–4 focus groups with 3–8 participants per group for a study as reported herein [50]. From the participating healthcare professionals, 12 were female and 2 were male, with mean age $M = 47.3$ ($SD = 14.6$), on average 14.2 years experience, and educated at minimally a university of applied sciences level in healthcare and/or healthcare management. Participants were briefed on the procedure, and the fact that the focus group sessions would be recorded for transcription. The participants were informed that recording materials are deleted after completion of the study and publication of the results. They provided written informed consent. No incentives were used. The study was approved by the Ethical Commission of the Faculty of Social Sciences, Radboud University, with reference number ECSW-LT-2021-10-26-52493.

3.4 Focus Group Procedure

All participants were invited into a joint meeting room and were shown a demonstration of the eight use cases, with the verbal interaction between the virtual agent and researcher A. After the demonstration, the participants were divided into two focus groups. Researchers A and B led the discussions. To improve the reliability and validity of the data, a systematic approach was followed through creating an interview guide and a topic list based on the five SPF instrumental goals to provide discussion similarity between both focus groups. The interview guide listed seven topics to be discussed: the general opinion on the IVA; for each SPF goal, the opinion on the IVA supporting that specific SPF goal, whereby several examples were given; and any other final remarks on the IVA. The complete interview guide can be made available on request. The focus groups took approximately 1.5 h and were held in parallel. Member checks were conducted when needed, to make sure remarks were correctly understood. Attention was paid to censoring of own opinions or conformity with the opinions of others, and action by the focus group leader was taken when necessary [52].

3.5 Thematic Data Analysis

The transcriptions of the two focus group sessions were created manually from the recorded material and anonymized. They were subsequently imported into the thematic analysis tool MAXQDA Analytics Pro 2022 (VERBI Software, Berlin, Germany). The data from the focus group sessions and supporting documentation were analysed according to the reflexive thematic analysis approach in the four phases 'segmentation', 'open coding', 'axial coding' and 'selective coding' [27]. During the research, notes and memos were collected using the MindManager tool (Alludo, Ottawa, Canada). During segmentation, meaningful phrases were indicated in relation to these memos. Open coding has been done by the authors RB and TB separately. In line with the recommendations of Clarke and Braun, no attempt was made to pursue consensus amongst coders or to use Cohen's Kappa values during open coding, but instead joint axial coding was performed between authors RB and TB in order to create a first set of themes based on the codes [53]. Finally, selective coding was applied to define a final set of themes and reviewed by all authors. These themes were formulated as phrases having a shared, multi-faceted meaning, patterned across the focus group transcripts, and encapsulating several related analytical insights into a central organising concept [27].

4 Results - Thematic Analysis of Focus Group Transcripts

The thematic analysis of the focus group transcripts resulted in the seven main themes: 'Getting to Know Her', 'Lifetime Support', 'Spider in the Social Web', 'Versatile Personal Assistant', 'Big Sister', 'Jane, I Don't Understand You', and 'Deceiving Jane'. The text below is organized by theme and a summary of the relevant focus group discussions parts, and supported by illustrative quotes from participants. These quotes are indicated by Px where x is the participants' reference number in their focus group. The quotes are the actual statements of the participants and have not been converted into running sentences, to present a truthful representation of the statement.

Getting to Know Her

Knowing how to communicate with a talking virtual agent, and knowing what the agent can and cannot do, requires a careful introduction process. Although conversational agents such as Google Home, Siri, and Amazon Echo are increasingly being used in people's homes, they are less well spread among older adults, and humanoid virtual agents are uncommon [54]. The healthcare professionals therefore indicated that the 'getting to know her' should preferably start when patients are still living independently at home. It is even better if that happens long before serious memory impairments occur. In that period, the communication with the agent can still be considered as a 'normal game which everyone plays' including younger generations. The chances of success are the greatest if the use of the agent gradually grows with a person's development step by step, but even then:

P5: It's really a long-term process, 2–3 years is already a challenge.

P4: I think you should start before people start making mistakes.

The virtual agent should not be directly associated with memory issues, as that could introduce a stigma against its use. Relatively healthy older adults often don't want to think about their needed support later on in life, or don't dare to think about it, and are inclined to think that these agents are something only for people with dementia.

P3: So don't wait until the diagnosis has been made and try to start before that. That is very difficult, I have also worked as a community nurse and I used to say to people around the age of seventy: think about the fact that you are going to get older, so get rid of barriers, don't wait for that walker to arrive. But people don't dare, yes, even my mother doesn't either, they don't dare to think. "I'm healthy now and let me think about it for later". And actually I would like us to do that and not wait for dementia but to introduce them to the technology in advance.

P5: When is the right moment, that's what I'm looking for, to use this technique, because you have that denial phase, and actually before that denial phase you actually want to take them with you, because when is the moment, what actually determines that?

When people then gradually develop memory impairments, it often happens that they still have limited insight into their illness and say that everything is going well. If their informal caregivers or healthcare professionals were questioned, they often indicate that there are indeed problems, for example with cooking or personal hygiene.

P2: (mimics a PwD reacting on the introduction of a new clock for PwD): "I'm not forgetful at all, why do you think that, what should I do with such a clock. I can still look at my watch or my phone."

Thus, on the one hand, it is important to respect the capacity of the patients and to understand their resistance to patronizing and mothering. On the other hand, there may be a need for some forms of support because otherwise their physical or psychological health can be unnecessarily negatively affected. Finding the balance between these extremes is a challenge.

P6: *The system should only do what is needed and be able to get to know you over the years and give you a little more instruction as needed.*

People also like to remain independent as long as possible, and do not always want another care professional who continuously look over their shoulder. People would prefer a technical aid:

P4: And in the preliminary stages people are still open to this, that's what I notice: they prefer to do it themselves with an aid rather than have healthcare providers come in, then they have the feeling that they are being watched and monitored.

Healthcare professionals also need to learn how to deal with the existence of a virtual agent for the support of an older adult. They may experience a barrier in use, and if that manifests itself in a certain negative behavior towards the agent, then that may also influence the patient's attitude towards the virtual agent.

P5: We always do it with our hands and the necessity of doing it differently in the future: Yes! But the acceptance of all technology is still a challenge.

Once a user knows how and when to interact with the virtual agent, all instrumental goals may be easier reached than without it. According to the Social Production Function theory, people need resources to reach their instrumental goals, and the agent could be such as resource. This theme 'getting to know her' has strong relations with the SPF goals comfort and affection. The theme could include various alternative resources for supporting physical and mental health.

Lifetime Support

The agent is intended for lifetime support, since the cognitive decline process is slow and spans many years [3, 4]. This lifetime support is also important to professional caregivers:

P6 I also think it is important that by following people more or less for a long time, we get a better understanding, not only insight into how deterioration is going, but also how they look at certain things and what they would like to get help with.

Lifetime support is also a topic which requires further research, since most researched interactions are relatively short [54]. The needed support can also change quickly, and a virtual agent must be able to respond to this. A case manager says:

P2 Then at first, I think this is easy, but on the third visit I already have to apply for societal support for the day care, and on the fourth visit I already have to apply for long duration healthcare (i.e. a more extensive form of support).

Patients who have moved from living at home to a nursing home are more advanced in their dementia. This situation makes it difficult to learn how to deal with such modern technology independently, even with guidance. Patients can quickly forget the explanation, especially because a virtual agent is something new and there are no associations with something they know from their past. It is not an interaction which has been internalized in their system. If the virtual agent makes a sound or says something at an unexpected moment for the patient, it can be very confusing or even frightening. Patients wonder where that sound is coming from suddenly, and what they should do.

P4: If suddenly a sound comes from somewhere, and I look and I do not see anyone at all, then I also think: do I hear voices in my head? We noticed that very much when we were working with the innovation team, that residents thought "what is that sound that comes from here", "what does it mean if a sound comes from there". People think it is the phone then, and that they should answer a call. You sometimes get very strange reactions.

Similar experiences were reported by Tokunage et al. and Tsiourti et al. [14, 17]. This theme 'Lifetime Support' can be related to the instrumental goals 'comfort' and 'status'. The theme could include alternative resources for supporting planning and time.

Versatile Personal Assistant

The healthcare professionals indicated that they saw many potential support functions. These can be summarized into categories as follows:

- Help with food and drinks.
- Talking about the past and hobbies.
- Talking about my life story with the help of photos.
- Playing games.
- Providing support in guarding my privacy.
- Supporting my independence from others.
- Support with medical problems or issues.
- Monitoring my health.
- Stay up to date with news and current affairs.
- Control of household appliances at home.
- Shopping and making payments.

Some of these features emerged from the demonstration, and some were conceived by the healthcare professionals. Some of these functionalities have also been integrated into systems developed by other researchers [9, 11, 15, 18, 31, 32, 34, 35, 48].

Monitoring whether a person drinks sufficiently during the day was also mentioned:

P4: (What if someone) gets a urinary tract infection and therefore becomes delirious, which increases the risk of falling, and ends up breaking his hip and being hospitalized. Then I think if you can prevent that by drinking enough and not causing a urinary tract infection, look, these are things that I think would be possible if we would have a little more insight into this through a Jane like that…

The functionality of the virtual agent should be able to be manageable with a menu so that a patient can select their own favorite support features. For some functions, data interfaces to external databases or domestic appliances are required. At the same time, not everybody needs the same functions.

P6: But isn't it also true that it differs from person to person? You say that one person is open to the video calling function, perhaps to use it on that tablet. Another person may be open to the agenda function, who will find it useful to hear what is in their agenda every morning.

The proposed IVA functions show a large variety and are related to all instrumental goals. The theme could include many alternative resources for supporting family and friend ties, energy, education and social skills.

Spider in the Social Web

The healthcare professionals indicated that they often receive information from home care, general practitioners, family, or other volunteers. The virtual agent could play a role in the exchange of information between the people in the social web around a patient. At the same time, the virtual agent can also play a role in stimulating contact with other people.

P3: I think the advantage for them with these systems is that you can organize a kind of coffee moment with four others if the weather is bad or if they cannot go outside.

The Jane system allows informal and formal caregivers to upload information, which the virtual agent can use in the dialogues with the patient. This feature is also part of the Anne4Care system [35]. A popular function is video calling.

P5: I thought that video calling is what she does with her daughter in Zeeland and that head is known behind such a screen and gradually that daughter takes on a kind of guiding role.

The participants were asked if the virtual agent could also be a contact person for district nurses, meal delivery people.

P4: Just like someone wants and likes it.

This theme 'spider in the social web' has a relation with 'stimulation and activation'. Many alternative resources for social skills, time and ties with family and friends are supported by this theme.

Big Sister

Healthcare professionals also see challenges in implementation and acceptance from a privacy and monitoring perspective.

P5: We did a project with lifestyle monitoring and with people who are just a little bit further along in their dementia and you know – what you also said – people threw away the sensors, because hey I was being followed. And explaining what it is and what it is for requires very precise timing, to put it down to clients, but also to professionals. How are professionals going to use it because that's where the threshold is.

The avoidance of the feeling of being followed was also the reason for designing a virtual agent that continues living her own virtual life again after a dialogue, and to show a painting in idle mode (Fig. 1). This means there is no character looking into the room all the time to see or hear what you are doing, which is a much-reported concern. For example, this follows the recommendations from Horstmann et al., who studied the attitude of older adults towards voice assistants like Alexa and found that participants on one hand considered Alexa to be useful and pleasant, but on the other hand showed fear of being patronized or manipulated [55]. The 'big sister' theme is as such related to goal of providing comfort, and shelter from unwanted events. The theme could include alternative resources for supporting mental health and safety.

Jane, I Do Not Understand You

The healthcare professionals indicated that there are many practical challenges with the usability of this technology. User-friendliness in communication is of immense importance. The virtual agent must use short sentences, speak clearly, not give too much information at once, and be able to repeat the information or display it multimodally (in text and speech). Many older adults hear less well and do not always wear their hearing aids at home. Hearing aids also often get lost. The virtual agent must also be able to deal with the increasing limitations in the language use of the elderly. That means dealing with long pauses, incomplete sentences, or cutting off or not completing a dialogue.

P2: As soon as they cannot find a word, they're completely occupied with finding the word, and can't do anything else. At some point, they remember, or give up, and the conversation can continue. So, you have to be able to take this into account, but that's very difficult. Some people have a lot more word-finding problems than others, that is quite difficult.

This concern is confirmed by the experiment from Tokunaga et al., subjects did not always hear the agent because of hearing impairments or microphone quality. Touch button operation was difficult for older adults not accustomed to smartphone or tablets. The virtual agent sometimes did only hear the patient after second utterance. Patients were sometimes surprised and not knowing what to do if the system does not react as expected [14].

Similarly, the CaMeLi system presented a good degree of usefulness, satisfaction, and ease of use, but at the same time CaMeLi was a barrier for 11 participants and a facilitator for 35 participants [47].

The virtual agent could decrease these problems if it can adapt itself to the interlocutor. Personalization could be of assistance here.

P6: In my dream world I would see it this way, that if you are diagnosed with dementia, you will build your own environment together with a designer, tailor-made, so that he gets to know you, does facial recognition, what you like. When you start talking about music, some people think "great fun", others think "what are we getting into?" So, I think it's nice if there is ownership of your own system, how you want it, and that you also have your own type.

This theme 'Jane, I do not understand you' is related to the instrumental goal 'comfort'. The theme could include alternative resources for amongst others physical and mental health.

Deceiving Jane
As mentioned above, healthcare professionals emphasize the importance of respecting the patient's capacity to give consent and to avoid unnecessary patronizing and interference. Patients and caregivers may disagree on the desired care. However, this can cause tension when a patient eventually avoids the support of technology. An example is shown in the video by Thingtank, which shows the passive resistance of an older adult male to well meant but patronizing support given by his children [56]. Nevertheless, avoiding care is a big problem in healthcare [57]. Healthcare providers wonder how the system will or should keep track of whether someone is doing what the system recommends, such as eating and drinking enough, taking medication, or doing physiotherapy exercises.

P3: Well, taking that bit of that medication, then I would not believe what the client is saying. I also must see it for myself, because I have experienced a few times that thanks to a housekeeper, who spoke to me and said: "I find white tablets and they are bigger than sweets", I knew that taking tablets was not possible. She said to me everything is fine and then the Baxter roll is neatly empty, but the medication has not been taken. Yes, I am a bit hesitant about that. They can be pretty smart, can't they?

This theme 'deceiving Jane' is also be related to the instrumental goal 'comfort'. The theme could include alternative resources for amongst others physical and mental health, social skills and personal safety.

5 Conclusion

The thematic analysis demonstrates that the healthcare professionals considered the demonstrated virtual agent developed based on the SPF theory as a promising resource for supporting the wellbeing of older adults. The main implication of the study is that seven valuable IVA design guiding themes were identified, that could be conceptualized as 'Getting to Know Her', 'Lifetime Support', 'Spider in the Social Web', 'Versatile Personal Assistant', 'Big Sister', 'Jane, I Don't Understand You', and 'Deceiving Jane'. The themes can be related to the resources people need to realize their instrumental goals for reaching subjective wellbeing. Goals and resources are dynamic and dependent on the progress of the physical and mental condition of a person. An IVA designed with these themes in mind may be a valuable and versatile resource during a person's lifetime, and the prototype shows it can be build. Healthcare professionals can benefit from the themes when discussing the usability of IVAs for SPF goals. Technically and operationally, the implications of these themes are manifold: dialogue design, the use of large language models, decisions about storage of user data, network design, privacy and security, and graphical user interface design. The relations between the goals and resources and the literature were comprehensively discussed in Sect. 4.1. At the same time, the thematic analysis showed still several concerns on the use of the virtual agent and the best time for introduction into the life of older adults.

This study recognizes some weaknesses. The authors tried to present a set of use cases to the healthcare professionals that covered the five SPF instrumental goals for wellbeing sufficiently, but this selection from earlier own research and literature is not all-encompassing. The approach using the SPF could in a future study be compared with or integrated into a standardised development method for health interventions, such as the person-based approach by Yardley et al. [58]. For example, a specific use case for future research could be the support of home-based strength training exercises, since there is a relation between cardiovascular and cognitive decline, and falling is a major health risk in the elderly population. Nevertheless, the focus group participants felt they were able to provide sufficient critical remarks on the potential IVA use cases. Secondly, the use cases were on purpose not evaluated yet with the target group of older adults itself because of the reported limitations of that approach, such as getting inaccurate, biased or dishonest information, and misunderstanding feelings and emotions [7]. This target group study is planned as a follow-up in the six-year research project QoLEAD (Quality of Life by use of Enabling AI in Dementia) [59]. At the same time, the 14 healthcare professionals had a comprehensive collective knowledge and experience with the target group to reason about their needs and wishes, and therefore the authors consider the themes sufficiently representative.

Future research aims at involving older adults, at including a more comprehensive set of use cases, and including a larger survey population. This allows for further data triangulation and mitigation of potential biases. Furthermore, the timing of the introduction of the virtual human use cases for all adult generations requires further study. For example, apps like Replika and Snapchat have already introduced AI supported virtual agents as digital friends for life for adults of all ages [60, 61]. This raises the question if younger generations will have a higher acceptance of this technology than older adults. Also, more research is needed in the longitudinal use of virtual agents for care for older adults, preferably starting long before any age-related problems arise.

In summary, the healthcare professionals considered the demonstrated virtual agent, developed based on the SPF theory, a promising resource for supporting the wellbeing of older adults.

Acknowledgments. This study was funded by ZonMW within the Innovative Medical Devices Initiative with project number 104022002.

Disclosure of Interests. The authors have no competing interests to declare that are relevant to the content of this article.

References

1. O'Brien, J.T.: Age-associated memory impairment and related disorders. Adv. Psychiatr. Treat. **5**, 279–287 (1999). https://doi.org/10.1192/apt.5.4.279
2. Hugo, J., Ganguli, M.: Dementia and cognitive impairment. Clin. Geriatr. Med. **30**, 421–442 (2014). https://doi.org/10.1016/j.cger.2014.04.001
3. Vermunt, L., et al.: Duration of preclinical, prodromal, and dementia stages of Alzheimer's disease in relation to age, sex, and APOE genotype. Alzheimer's Dement. **15**, 888–898 (2019). https://doi.org/10.1016/j.jalz.2019.04.001
4. Janssen, O., et al.: Duration of care trajectories in persons with dementia differs according to demographic and clinical characteristics. J. Am. Med. Dir. Assoc. **21**, 1102–1107.e6 (2020). https://doi.org/10.1016/j.jamda.2020.01.008

5. WHO: Dementia prevalence. https://www.who.int/news-room/fact-sheets/detail/dementia. Accessed 01 Sept 2021
6. Lugrin, B., Pelachaud, C., Traum, D. (eds.): The Handbook on Socially Interactive Agents: 20 Years of Research on Embodied Conversational Agents, Intelligent Virtual Agents, and Social Robotics Volume 1: Methods, Behavior, Cognition. Association for Computing Machinery, New York, NY, USA (2021)
7. Lugrin, B., Pelachaud, C., Traum, D. (eds.): The Handbook on Socially Interactive Agents: 20 Years of Research on Embodied Conversational Agents, Intelligent Virtual Agents, and Social Robotics Volume 2: Interactivity, Platforms, Application. Association for Computing Machinery, New York, NY, USA (2022)
8. Association for Computing Machinery: Proceedings of the 19th ACM International Conference on Intelligent Virtual Agents (IVA'19). Association for Computing Machinery, New York (2019)
9. Ali, R., et al.: Aging and engaging: a pilot randomized controlled trial of an online conversational skills coach for older adults. Am. J. Geriatr. Psychiatry (2020). https://doi.org/10.1016/j.jagp.2020.11.004
10. Boumans, R., van de Sande, Y., Thill, S., Bosse, T.: Voice-enabled intelligent virtual agents for people with amnesia: systematic review. JMIR Aging **5**, e32473 (2022). https://doi.org/10.2196/32473
11. Jegundo, A.L., et al.: Perceived usefulness, satisfaction, ease of use and potential of a virtual companion to support the care provision for older adults. Technologies **8**, 42 (2020). https://doi.org/10.3390/technologies8030042
12. Oliveira, F., Abad, A., Trancoso, I.: A multiplayer voice-enabled game platform for the elderly. In: Quaresma, P., Vieira, R., Aluísio, S., Moniz, H., Batista, F., Gonçalves, T. (eds.) PROPOR 2020. LNCS, vol. 12037, pp. 413–419. Springer, Cham (2020). https://doi.org/10.1007/978-3-030-41505-1_40
13. Razavi, S.Z., Schubert, L.K., Kane, B., Ali, M.R., Van Orden, K., Ma, T.: Dialogue design and management for multi-session casual conversation with older adults. arXiv preprint arXiv:1901.06620 (2019)
14. Tokunaga, S., et al.: Implementation and evaluation of interactive memory-aid agent service for people with dementia. In: Duffy, V. (eds.) DHM 2016. LNCS, vol. 9745, pp. 357–368. Springer, Cham (2016). https://doi.org/10.1007/978-3-319-40247-5_36
15. Tokunaga, S., Tamamizu, K., Saiki, S., Nakamura, M., Yasuda, K.: VirtualCareGiver: personalized smart elderly care. Int. J. Softw. Innov. (IJSI) **5**, 30–43 (2017). https://doi.org/10.4018/IJSI.2017010103
16. Tsiourti, C., Joly, E., Wings, C., Moussa, M.B., Wac, K.: Virtual assistive companions for older adults: qualitative field study and design implications. In: Proceedings of the 8th International Conference on Pervasive Computing Technologies for Healthcare, pp. 57–64 (2014)
17. Tsiourti, C., et al.: A virtual assistive companion for older adults: design implications for a real-world application. In: Bi, Y., Kapoor, S., Bhatia, R. (eds.) IntelliSys 2016. LNNS, vol. 15. Springer, Cham (2018), pp. 1014–1033. https://doi.org/10.1007/978-3-319-56994-9_69
18. Wargnier, P., Benveniste, S., Jouvelot, P., Rigaud, A.-S.: Usability assessment of interaction management support in LOUISE, an ECA-based user interface for elders with cognitive impairment. Technol. Disabil. **30**, 105–126 (2018). https://doi.org/10.3233/TAD-180189
19. Jacobson, I.: Use cases–Yesterday, today, and tomorrow. Softw. Syst. Model. **3**, 210–220 (2004)
20. Duque, E., Fonseca, G., Vieira, H., Gontijo, G., Ishitani, L.: A systematic literature review on user centered design and participatory design with older people. In: Proceedings of the 18th Brazilian Symposium on Human Factors in Computing Systems, pp. 1–11 (2019)
21. Rogers, Y., Sharp, H., Preece, J.: Interaction Design - Beyond Human-Computer Interaction. Wiley, Hoboken (2023)

22. Sayago, S., Neves, B.B., Cowan, B.R.: Voice assistants and older people: some open issues. In: Proceedings of the 1st International Conference on Conversational User Interfaces, pp. 1–3 (2019)
23. Gerritsen, D.: Ode aan kwetsbaarheid (2020)
24. Gerritsen, D.L.: Well-being in long-term care: an ode to vulnerability. Null, 1–6 (2021). https://doi.org/10.1080/13607863.2021.2008869
25. Ormel, J., Lindenberg, S., Steverink, N., Verbrugge, L.M.: Subjective well-being and social production functions. Soc. Indic. Res. **46**, 61–90 (1999)
26. König, A., Malhotra, A., Hoey, J., Francis, L.: Designing personalized prompts for a virtual assistant to support elderly care home residents. In: PervasiveHealth (2016)
27. Clarke, V., Braun, V.: Thematic Analysis: A Practical Guide. SAGE Publications Ltd., Thousand Oaks (2021)
28. Becker, G.S.: The Economic Approach to Human Behavior. The University of Chicago Press, Chicago (1976)
29. Juster, F.T., Courant, P.N., Dow, G.K.: A conceptual framework for the analysis of time allocation data. Time Goods Well-Being, 113–31 (1985)
30. Sidner, C.L., et al.: Creating new technologies for companionable agents to support isolated older adults. ACM Trans. Interact. Intell. Syst. (TiiS). **8**, 1–27 (2018). https://doi.org/10.1145/3213050
31. Chauvin, R., Clavel, C., Sabouret, N., Ravenet, B.: A virtual coach with more or less empathy: impact on older adults' engagement to exercise. In: Proceedings of the 23rd ACM International Conference on Intelligent Virtual Agents, pp. 1–9 (2023)
32. Azevedo, R.F., et al.: Using conversational agents to explain medication instructions to older adults. In: AMIA Annual Symposium Proceedings, p. 185. American Medical Informatics Association (2018)
33. Steverink, B.J.M.: Zo lang moglijk zelfstandig. Naar een vekrlaring van verschillen in oriëntatie ten aanzien van opname in een verzorgingstehuis onder fysiek kwetsbare ouderen (1996)
34. Bickmore, T.W., et al.: A randomized controlled trial of an automated exercise coach for older adults. J. Am. Geriatr. Soc. **61**, 1676–1683 (2013)
35. Kaczmarek, M., Bujnowski, A., Osiński, K., Birrer, E., Neumann, T., Teunissen, B.: Ella4Life virtual assistant-user centered design strategy-evaluation following labolatory tests. In: 2020 13th International Conference on Human System Interaction (HSI), pp. 307–311. IEEE (2020)
36. Trainum, K., Tunis, R., Xie, B., Hauser, E., et al.: Robots in assisted living facilities: scoping review. JMIR Aging **6**, e42652 (2023)
37. Bevilacqua, R., et al.: Coaching through technology: a systematic review into efficacy and effectiveness for the ageing population. Int. J. Environ. Res. Public Health **17** (2020). https://doi.org/10.3390/ijerph17165930
38. Ienca, M., et al.: Intelligent assistive technology for Alzheimer's disease and other dementias: a systematic review. J. Alzheimer's Dis. **56**, 1301–1340 (2017). https://doi.org/10.3233/JAD-161037
39. Laranjo, L., et al.: Conversational agents in healthcare: a systematic review. J. Am. Med. Inform. Assoc. **25**, 1248–1258 (2018). https://doi.org/10.1093/jamia/ocy072
40. Schachner, T., Keller, R., von Wangenheim, F.: Artificial intelligence-based conversational agents for chronic conditions: systematic literature review. J. Med. Internet Res. **22**, e20701 (2020). https://doi.org/10.2196/20701
41. Xie, B., Tao, C., Li, J., Hilsabeck, R.C., Aguirre, A.: Artificial intelligence for caregivers of persons with Alzheimer's disease and related dementias: systematic literature review. JMIR Med. Inform. **8**, e18189 (2020). https://doi.org/10.2196/18189

42. Zuschnegg, J., et al.: Humanoid socially assistive robots in dementia care: a qualitative study about expectations of caregivers and dementia trainers. Aging Ment. Health. **26**, 1270–1280 (2022)
43. Rampioni, M., Stara, V., Felici, E., Rossi, L., Paolini, S.: Embodied conversational agents for patients with dementia: thematic literature analysis. JMIR Mhealth Uhealth **9**, e25381 (2021)
44. Liao, Y.-J., et al.: Use of a humanoid robot in supporting dementia care: a qualitative analysis. SAGE Open Nurs. **9**, 23779608231179530 (2023)
45. de Jong, M., Stara, V., von Döllen, V., Bolliger, D., Heerink, M., Evers, V.: Users requirements in the design of a virtual agent for patients with dementia and their caregivers. In: Proceedings of the 4th EAI International Conference on Smart Objects and Technologies for Social Good, pp. 136–141 (2018)
46. Hurstak, E.E., Olafsson, S., O'Leary, T.K., Cabral, H.J., Paasche-Orlow, M., Bickmore, T.: Conversational assessment of mild cognitive impairment with virtual agents. In: Proceedings of the 23rd ACM International Conference on Intelligent Virtual Agents, pp. 1–8 (2023)
47. Tsiourti, C., Quintas, J., Ben-Moussa, M., Hanke, S., Nijdam, N.A., Konstantas, D.: The CaMeLi framework—a multimodal virtual companion for older adults. In: Bi, Y., Kapoor, S., Bhatia, R. (eds.) IntelliSys 2016. SCI, vol. 751, pp. 196–217. Springer, Cham (2018). https://doi.org/10.1007/978-3-319-69266-1_10
48. Bickmore, T.W., Caruso, L., Clough-Gorr, K., Heeren, T.: 'It's just like you talk to a friend': relational agents for older adults. Interact. Comput. **17**, 711–735 (2005)
49. Vardoulakis, L.P., Ring, L., Barry, B., Sidner, C.L., Bickmore, T.: Designing relational agents as long term social companions for older adults. In: Nakano, Y., Neff, M., Paiva, A., Walker, M. (eds.) IVA 2012. LNCS, vol. 7502, pp. 289–302. Springer, Heidelberg (2012). https://doi.org/10.1007/978-3-642-33197-8_30
50. Clarke, V., Braun, V.: Successful Qualitative Research: A Practical Guide for Beginners. Sage Publications Ltd., Thousand Oaks (2013)
51. Tong, A., Sainsbury, P., Craig, J.: Consolidated criteria for reporting qualitative research (COREQ): a 32-item checklist for interviews and focus groups. Int. J. Qual. Health Care **19**, 349–357 (2007). https://doi.org/10.1093/intqhc/mzm042
52. Carey, M.A.: Comment: concerns in the analysis of focus group data. Qual. Health Res. **5**, 487–495 (1995). https://doi.org/10.1177/104973239500500409
53. Byrne, D.: A worked example of Braun and Clarke's approach to reflexive thematic analysis. Qual. Quant. **56**, 1391–1412 (2022)
54. Gallo, S., Paterno, F., Malizia, A.: Conversational interfaces in IoT ecosystems: where we are, what is still missing. In: Proceedings of the 22nd International Conference on Mobile and Ubiquitous Multimedia, pp. 279–293 (2023)
55. Horstmann, A.C., Schubert, T., Lambrich, L., Strathmann, C.: Alexa, i do not want to be patronized: a qualitative interview study to explore older adults' attitudes towards intelligent voice assistants. In: Proceedings of the 23rd ACM International Conference on Intelligent Virtual Agents, pp. 1–10 (2023)
56. Uninvited guests. Thingtank (2015)
57. Leyva, B., Taber, J.M., Trivedi, A.N.: Medical care avoidance among older adults. J. Appl. Gerontol. **39**, 74–85 (2020)
58. Yardley, L., Morrison, L., Bradbury, K., Muller, I.: The person-based approach to intervention development: application to digital health-related behavior change interventions. J. Med. Internet Res. **17**, e30 (2015). https://doi.org/10.2196/jmir.4055
59. QoLEAD consortium: QoLEAD (Quality of Life by use of Enabling AI in Dementia). http://www.qolead.nl

60. Krullaars, Z.H., Januardani, A., Zhou, L., Jonkers, E.: Exploring initial interactions: high school students and generative AI chatbots for relationship development (2023). https://doi.org/10.18420/muc2023-mci-src-415
61. Pentina, I., Hancock, T., Xie, T.: Exploring relationship development with social chatbots: a mixed-method study of replika. Comput. Hum. Behav. **140**, 107600 (2023)

The BookBot Project: Conceptual Design of a Social Robot Facilitating Reading Motivation

Emma Mainza Chilufya[1], Mattias Arvola[1](✉), Susanne Severinsson[2], Anna Martín Bylund[3], Linnéa Stenliden[3], Arezou Mortazavi[1], and Tom Ziemke[1]

[1] Human-Centered Systems, Department of Computer and Information Science, Linköping University, Linköping, Sweden
{emma.chilufya,mattias.arvola,arezou.mortazavi,tom.ziemke}@liu.se

[2] Education, Teaching and Learning, Department of Behavioural Sciences and Learning, Linköping University, Linköping, Sweden
susanne.severinsson@liu.se

[3] Learning, Aesthetics, Natural Science, Department of Behavioural Sciences and Learning, Linköping University, Linköping, Sweden
{anna.martin.bylund,linnea.stenliden}@liu.se
http://www.liu.se/

Abstract. The motivation to read among children in Nordic countries has seen a noticeable decline in recent years. This study explores the design of social robots for stimulating interest in reading among fourth-grade students (age 10–11). We used a combination of conceptual design methods to engage teachers and students from four classes in two Swedish schools in co-creation workshops. Ideas on functions, qualities, and robot designs were generated, and based on this a set of ten distinct design concepts were created: the Facilitator, the Librarian, the Coach, the Buddy, the Assistant, the Narrator, the Creator, the Apprentice, the Portable, and the Gamer. The strengths and weaknesses of different designs were evaluated, resulting in a final design named 'The BookBot,' aiming to inspire and engage students in book reading through discussions of book content, character portrayal, and personalised book recommendations.

Keywords: Reading motivation · Social robot · Conceptual design

1 Introduction and Background

Reading is a fundamental aspect of academic development, yet only a fraction of students attending upper middle and lower secondary schools in Sweden – and many other countries – feel motivated to read independently [28]. The BookBot initiative, whose initial design phase is described in this article, is a three-year interdisciplinary research project that explores whether and how social robots can be used to stimulate interest in reading among fourth-grade students (10–11

A. Følstad et al. (Eds.): CONVERSATIONS 2024, LNCS 15545, pp. 132–149, 2025.
https://doi.org/10.1007/978-3-031-88045-2_9

years of age). The motivation for the project is that the autonomy to choose what to read and the ability to read a text at the appropriate level of difficulty can foster a desire to read. However, it becomes challenging for teachers to read everything if all students in a class read different texts, making it impossible to hold book talks, which can also contribute to relatedness and thus a desire to read. One potential solution is to have a robot that can engage in book talks with students about the various books they have read.

It might be worth noting that the term "robot" is here initially used in a broad sense of a socially interactive AI system that children can talk to about books–this could be instantiated as a chatbot, a virtual agent, a physical robot, or some combination of elements of all of these categories. This paper focuses on the project's conceptual design activities, which refers to the early design work aimed at finding ideas on what to design and why. The question of how to design the details and how to implement it is a future question.

Developing a social robot intended to increase students' motivation to read independently requires a solid understanding of what motivation is and how it might be influenced. The motivation and starting point for this research has been Self-Determination Theory (SDT), which provides a general framework for understanding young readers' motivation [24]. Applying SDT to reading, we can posit that *intrinsically* motivated individuals engage in reading autonomously, deriving pleasure from the activity itself, as suggested by Ryan and Brick [23]. *Extrinsically* motivated readers, on the other hand, approach reading with the perspective that it serves as a means to accomplish externally imposed goals [7]. Research shows that intrinsically motivated students tend to excel academically [20], while low intrinsic motivation to read is often associated with poor reading skills and/or slow reading progress [8].

The social learning environment and conversations are significant factors in education, as they foster a sense of relatedness, which can be instrumental for intrinsic motivation to learn and to read [7,10]. One strategy to foster a positive and structured learning environment is allowing students to select their reading materials [10,20,28]. Educators also play an important role in stimulating and maintaining student motivation, which influences students' reading habits, abilities, and engagement [15]. The basic idea behind the BookBot project is that social robots might be a useful complement to teacher-led activities.

Social robots in educational settings have been observed to yield both affective and cognitive effects, suggesting their potential applicability in classroom settings [1,2]. Provided that reading tasks are sufficiently diverse and pose an appropriate level of challenge, children have been found to engage effectively with social robots [18]. However, a potential issue is the "novelty effect", which refers to the phenomenon that the introduction of a robot in the classroom, as an unusual occurrence, has a positive impact initially [3]. This might, however, decrease over time as children become accustomed to the interaction–unless the robot is capable of providing sufficiently dynamic feedback [25].

Several previous studies have explored the application of robots as aids in children's reading (e.g. [6,9]). One study found that middle school students (10–

12 years) thought the robot made the reading experience less monotonous [16]. Using the learning-by-teaching paradigm, it has been argued that a social robot can act as a less knowledgeable reading companion [31]. Children have found robots in the role of companions or "reading buddies" to be sufficiently intelligent to read, listen, and understand stories to encourage reading engagement, facilitate storytelling, and support homework [5,6,26,27]. Another robot has been used to motivate children in spelling and pronunciation training [19]. Virtual conversational agents have also been studied as partners in joint reading [30]; one interesting finding in this research was that mimicking human communication patterns may not necessarily be the best approach. These preliminary findings suggest that social robots and conversational agents hold promise as reading companions or buddies. They are, however, associated with both hopes and fears [22], and one of the key requirements is sensitive and accurate speech recognition for timely engagement in child-robot conversations [6].

It should also be noted that there many ways to design such robots, and they can serve different purposes. Three primary roles for social robots in language and literacy learning have been identified: the tutor, the peer, and the novice learner. Roles can also be more specifically defined (e.g., socio-emotionally supportive, assisting teachers or learners, prompting verbalization, role playing, displaying incorrect behaviour, and encouraging metatalk) at an active, constructive, or interactive level of engagement [21]. That means, the design space is yet to be defined, and there is still room for exploration of *what to design and why*. We therefore approach this problem using a conceptual design approach.

Conceptual design involves both what should be designed and why, as well as overarching design principles, thus fostering potentially radical innovation [32]. It hinges on developing novel insights and translating them into practical, relevant design concepts through imaginative, sensible, and purposeful simplifications. In the process of conceptual design, framing and re-framing lead to the creation of new design concepts. These concepts serve as imaginative, sensible, and purposeful simplifications that guide future design efforts. Typically, this process is participatory and multidisciplinary, involving researchers, designers, users, and other stakeholders in co-design efforts. The focus is not on details in how the concept should be designed and implemented. In this paper, we utilise a mix of design methods: (a) co-design and co-creation sessions [4]; (b) method 635, functional analysis, affinity diagramming, and identification of use qualities [14]; and (c) concept sketching using WWWWWH, and concept selection supported by a combination of PMI (plus, minus, interesting) and Pugh Charts (a.k.a. the datum method) [4].

2 Design Research Process

In this study, we used conceptual design as an approach to doing Research through Design [32]. The research was conducted with teachers and students from two schools in Sweden. The two teacher workshops involved eight unique participants in total (teachers, teaching developers, and principals). The student workshops comprised two 4th-grade classes from each school, totaling 94 11-year-old students, evenly distributed between boys and girls, all Swedish-speaking. 78 of those students contributed with ideas in the four co-creation sessions (one in each class). The researchers, who had backgrounds in interaction design, human-robot interaction, education, special education, and cognitive science, acted not only as researchers, but also as co-designers and facilitators.

The research has been approved by the Swedish Ethical Review Authority (Dnr. 2022-05125-01). Ethical issues include sensitive personal data regarding special education. Only teachers and students who have given their own consent, and for whom parental consent has been obtained, were interviewed, filmed, audio-recorded, responded to surveys, or had their design ideas recorded.

2.1 Co-creation Sessions with Teachers

The first workshop involved seven participants (one principal, four teachers, one language, reading and writing developer at the municipal education office, and one development strategist in IT at the municipal education office) and four researchers. The workshop focused on discussing current classroom reading activities, strategies for inclusive student participation, and the effectiveness of these strategies. Participants were asked to individually note what reading activities they had; what they did to include all students; and how the reading activities were when they worked well and when they worked less well. Participants were then given a presentation on some of the current social robots with potential use in education. This was concluded with a discussion about the session. Finally, participants were given a homework assignment, which was to note down ideas about how a social robot could be used in various reading activities. These ideas were to be presented in the next workshop.

The second workshop was attended by seven participants (five teachers, one language, reading and writing developer at the municipal education office, and one development strategist in IT at the municipal education office). Six of them had also participated in the first workshop. Three researchers were also present. The primary objective of this workshop was to get material for a functional analysis by identifying potential roles and functions for a robot used in reading activities. The workshop started with homework presentations by participants of the first workshop. Subsequently, the participants engaged in the 635 method to generate ideas on potential functions. The facilitator also employed the random input method to provoke more radical ideas. This was followed by an initial prioritization of the initial functions into two groups: essential and desirable. The workshop was concluded with a discussion about the session.

2.2 Co-creation Session with Students

Four school classes from two schools participated in a two-hour co-creation session. The session was divided into two parts: a questionnaire and a sketching or Lego-building session. The session began with a presentation about social robots.

Each student was then presented with a questionnaire, covering what the student and a robot could do together in connection to books or reading; what the robot might help the student with in relation to reading; what the robot might do to make reading more fun and interesting; and what the motivation for the chosen design is. The students were instructed to undertake the exercise individually, whilst maintaining the option for open discussions with each other. The task was then to create a *'book robot'*, either by drawing or building with Lego. Before starting the construction or drawing, students were asked to document their preliminary thoughts in the questionnaire. Subsequently, half an hour was allocated for the drawing or construction of their book robots. Students were finally encouraged to reflect on their experience and write down any new thoughts or ideas in the questionnaire.

2.3 Analysis and Ideation

We used affinity diagramming [14] iteratively to analyse data from the teacher and student workshops. There is not space to articulate every step in the process in this paper, instead the interested reader is referred to the first authors forthcoming PhD thesis. Desirable qualities were also identified and structured using affinity diagramming both at the level desirable qualities of reading situations, and desirable qualities of reading robots in use. Based on the affinity groups of functions, concepts were sketched out and discussed in the research team. The design was structured around the question, 'What kind of robot-in-reading would it be if these were core functions?' For example, a robot with the core function of correcting errors will be a completely different robot compared to one with the core function of giving encouragement. The sketches were then based on WWWWWH (i.e., who, what, when, where, why, and how) [4].

2.4 Concept Evaluation and Selection

The concept sketches were sent by email to the teachers from the workshops and to the research team. They were all asked to score all concepts on a scale from 1 to 10, and based on the PMI method [4], also write down positive things with the concepts they gave the most points, negative things about the concepts they gave the least points, as well as things they found particularly interesting. The results of the scoring and the PMI comments were discussed by the researchers and turned into a Pugh chart [4]. Criteria were identified in the PMI as well as in earlier affinity diagramming. Using the datum method, the concepts were then scored on the selected criteria. A synthesis based on the most promising concepts that worked together as a whole was finally created and further detailed in a storyboard. The synthesis is more subjectively composed abduction in comparison to the more data driven prior work.

3 Results

This section summarizes the results of the design activities described in the previous section, regarding (a) how teachers currently motivate their students to read, (b) desirable qualities for reading activities involving robots, (c) a range of potential design concepts, as well as (d) the evaluation and synthesis of these concepts into a chosen design concept.

3.1 Current Situation and Activities

The participants in the teacher workshops reported using the reading activities summarized in Table 1.

Table 1. Teachers' Current Reading Activities

Reading Activity	Focus	Examples
Talking about own reading	Teacher	Providing role model and inspiration
Add-on activities	Group	Treasure hunt or competition
Joint reading	Group	Reading aloud; pairwise reading
Quiet reading	Individual	Letting kids read books of their own choice
Training to read	Individual	Reading lists
Varied text types	Text	Fiction vs. non-fiction

The teachers felt that it was important for them to be role models and inspire the students by talking about their own reading. They sometimes also created add-on activities connected to the reading, such as treasure hunts or other competitions. Students were sometimes reading the same text together, aloud or pairwise, and sometimes reading quietly for themselves. In the latter case there was the option of allowing the students to read a book of their own choice. The teachers also varied the text types (i.e., fiction, non-fiction). They furthermore made use of reading lists for training, based on the individual reading level of the student.

The participants reported using the inclusion strategies compiled in Table 2.

Table 2. Teachers' Inclusion Strategies

Strategy	Focus	Examples
Doing things together	Entire class	Reading the same text together at the same time
Variation	Entire class	Not sitting still for too long
Building expectations	Entire class	Talking positively about texts to read
Motivations	Entire class	Using rewards
Adaptations	Individual	Choosing the right level of difficulty
Cater to interests	Individual	Allowing students to choose based on interests

To include all students, regardless of reading level, the teachers stated that reading the same text together was a useful strategy. Variation, so that students did not have to sit still and read for too long without a break, was also considered important. The participating teachers also tried to build expectations and talk positively about the texts the class would read. Rewards directed to the entire class could also be used. Catering to the interests of individual students and allowing them to choose what to read was also a strategy for inclusion.

3.2 Desirable Situational Qualities and Use Qualities

The teachers highlighted a number of qualities of the reading situation that in their experience would contribute to the students' desire to read: a joyful atmosphere, anticipatory curiosity toward the text to be read, using attractive texts that the students consider worth reading, using comprehensible and readable texts appropriate for the students' reading skills, and building relatedness between readers and immersion in the text. Have a calm reading atmosphere was also considered important, and immersion in the text was also instrumental for a calm atmosphere, together with peace of mind and body, and a quiet reading environment.

Desirable use qualities were identified in the students' descriptions of concept ideas. The students wanted their robots to look good (e.g., cool, cute, cosy, and not creepy or weird). They also wanted them to be knowledgeable and smart. Some of their descriptions were about how it should behave: encouraging, helpful, inspiring, joyful, and kind. It should also be social, that is, interactive, relatable, and mindful of when not to disturb. Many concepts were playful and fun, and several ideas were humoristic and imaginative. Finally, the students thought that the robot should be educational and personalised for them.

3.3 Design Concepts

Based on an analysis of the needs expressed (or implied) in the first teachers workshop on the current situation (WS1) as well as the assignment the teachers did after the workshop, an initial list of 21 potential functions for a robot in reading activities was identified by the researchers. The second teachers workshop (WS2) was then focused on generating (further) ideas on functions/roles, and in total the teachers produced 122 potential functions/roles that a robot might have in reading activities. Finally, in the co-design workshop with students, an additional 39 functions were identified. All these functions were then thematically organised using affinity diagramming. Duplicates and ideas not related to reading or writing were removed. The resulting groups of functions were labelled as concept ideas and developed into the ten design concepts described below.

Concept 1–The Facilitator. A robot intended to be helpful and curious. It guides students through book discussions and seminars, designed to assist them in delving deeper into the plot, characters, and themes. With its friendly face and flexible arms, the Facilitator is ready to ask questions, listen to students' thoughts, and encourage discussion. Students are supposed to have an engaging and rewarding reading experience with the Facilitator. Associated functions: Lead a book-talk, portray a book character, and ask comprehension questions. This concept is based on three ideas on functions from teachers and one from students.

Concept 2–The Librarian. This robot provides individual students with personalised book recommendations. It can answer questions about books, explain what a book is about, and suggest genres based on students' interests and reading abilities. Additionally, it can indicate where books are located and even distribute them. The Librarian can be situated in the school library, in corridors, or in the classroom. Its purpose is to assist students in discovering new books within their own interests while also encouraging them to explore different genres. The Librarian should be perceived as inspiring, personal, and informative. Associated functions: Give tips about books, explain what books are about, way-finding in the library, and delivering books. This concept is based on one idea on functions from teachers and four from students.

Concept 3–The Coach. This robot is reminiscent of a basketball coach. It provides practice tasks, monitors performance, and offers feedback. Its purpose is to achieve visible improvement and progression in students. The Coach aims to be efficient, clear, and motivating. It initiates exercises and suggests ways to enhance performance in the classroom or group settings. Associated functions: Give pep-talks, lead practice, and correct pronunciation. This concept is based on one idea on functions from teachers and four from students.

Concept 4–The Buddy. This robot is supposed to be experienced as a friendly robot that assists students with reading. It sits next to them, taking turns reading together. With evocative facial expressions and enthusiasm, the Buddy makes reading more enjoyable and interactive. Located in the classroom or a group room, it looks cuddly and actively shares the reading experience with the students. Associated functions: Listening to students reading, reading with students, and cuddle. This concept is based on two ideas on functions from teachers and two from students.

Concept 5–The Assistant. This robot sits with students and acts as a teacher's aide in the classroom. It provides immediate feedback or guidance to students who need it. Its functions include assigning tasks, measuring time, assisting with writing, correcting errors, and explaining words. The Assistant is supposed to be experienced as knowledgeable, strict, and focused. It can speak and understand different languages, and it can move around between students' seats in the classroom to provide individualised assistance and structure. Associated functions: Provide corrections, explain words, take time on assignments, help focusing, talk in different languages, move around in the classroom, and help with synonyms and sentence building. This concept is based on two ideas on functions from teachers and seven from students.

Concept 6–The Narrator. This is a robot that reads, tells, and enacts stories. The Narrator should turn reading into an exciting and engaging experience for children. It can read aloud with a clear and inviting voice, and it can even play different characters from the story. It changes its voice, tone, and body language to bring the story to life. Movements and facial expressions contribute to creating drama and suspense. To keep it fun and lighthearted, the Narrator can also crack jokes and make humorous comments. Before the reading begins, the Narrator provides a brief introduction to the book. Afterwards, it summarises the events and gives children something to ponder. The Narrator could be good for morning reading when children are alert and curious, and on Friday afternoons, just before the weekend, it could set a cosy atmosphere and give children something to look forward to. Associated functions: Dramatize episodes, reading during walks or breaks outside, present books, read aloud, and summarize texts. This concept is based on five ideas on functions from teachers and three from students.

Concept 7–The Creator. The Creator is a small robot with the ability to create anything from images and poetry to original stories based on student prompts and connected to the texts they have read. It is supposed to act as a creative companion, inspiring thinking beyond the conventional boundaries. Its creations aim to be surprising, innovative, and engaging, providing students with a deeper immersion in the narratives while also motivating them to create on their own. The Creator could be used in whole-class settings or in smaller groups. Students not only have the opportunity to express themselves through text and imagery but also to explore different ways of interpreting and understanding what they have read. Associated functions: Create stories, write poems, provide ideas on what to write, and visualize text. This concept is based on three ideas about functions from teachers and two from students.

Concept 8–The Apprentice. This is a robot that students teach. The Apprentice is supposed to be a robot that interacts with a group of students, collectively helping it learn and grow. It should be perceived as curious but lacking prior knowledge. It is ready to absorb any information it can get. The Apprentice resides in the classroom or a group room. With wide eyes and an open book in front of it, the Apprentice appears to attentively listen as students share their insights and knowledge. Students get an opportunity to feel competent and share their learning. Associated functions: Make mistakes in readings that the students can correct, learn about the text, demonstrate reading strategies or lack thereof, calm down when being read to. This concept is based on four ideas on functions from teachers and none from students.

Concept 9–The Portable. This is a robot to bring along. The Portable is supposed to be a small, agile, and user-friendly companion that students can take with them everywhere. It is designed to be inspiring, helpful, and encouraging. The robot can assist students with their reading homework by providing tips, explanations, and support. It can also be used to catch up if a student has missed something in school, and it can offer additional exercises if needed. Moreover, the Portable can recommend books, share interesting facts, and tell exciting stories to ignite a love for reading. Associated functions: Help with homework, move between parts of the school, and inspire to read at home. This concept is based on three ideas on functions from teachers and two from students.

Concept 10–The Gamer. This is a robot you can play with. The Gamer is meant to be a robot that makes reading interactive and fun. With the Gamer, students, individually or in groups, can play various types of reading games, such as word games, story-based adventures, and quizzes with immediate feedback on their answers. Students can also challenge each other in reading-related competitions where the scores are visible right away. The Gamer aims to be an engaging and rewarding resource that can be used in the classroom, group rooms, or even during breaks. It helps students improve their reading skills while having fun. Associated functions: Provide challenges, set up a reading bingo or a quiz, hold a speed-reading competition, give rewards and prizes, and say words backwards. This concept is based on two ideas on functions from teachers and three from students.

Concept Evaluation and Selection

The above ten design concepts were evaluated in a Pugh chart (Table 3) [4]. Concept 1–The Facilitator was chosen as datum (a reference point for comparisons) because at face value it was considered both feasible and desirable. Criteria were based on the factors contributing to motivation according to SDT (autonomy, competency, and relatedness), previously identified desirable qualities, and comments from participating teachers and design team. The score was based on an interpretation of answers to the PMI questionnaire in relation to the criteria. The steps of transformation in the development of the criteria are not described in detail here due to space constraints.

Concept Selection. Concept 1–The Facilitator connects clearly to the issue that motivated the entire research project, that is, the idea of the robot that you can have book talks with. It was therefore used as a starting point while incorporating features from the other concepts, and with additional details on how it should be experienced based on students' descriptions of their robots. The experiential qualities expressed in the text emerge from the students' perspectives. Concept 2–The Librarian inspired the inclusion of personalised reading suggestions, drawing from a vast knowledge base. This also incorporates storytelling elements from Concept 6–The Narrator. The idea is that by weaving narratives around interactions, the system can engage users more effectively. From Concept 8–The Apprentice comes the idea of the robot acknowledging its limitations and admitting that it does not know much about people and human society—and therefore also has a limited grasp of human stories. The ability to earn points

Table 3. Concept Evaluation in Pugh Chart. The concepts are numbered as follows: 1–The Facilitator; 2–The Librarian; 3–The Coach; 4–The Buddy; 5–The Assistant; 6–The Narrator; 7–The Creator; 8–The Apprentice; 9–The Portable; 10–The Gamer

Criteria	1	2	3	4	5	6	7	8	9	10
Autonomy to choose an attractive text worth reading	D	+	−	+	−	S	+	+	S	S
Competency by comprehensibility and readability		+	S	+	S	−	−	+	+	+
Relatedness and being seen and acknowledged	A	−	+	−	−	S	S	−	−	+
External motivation and rewards		S	+	S	S	S	S	S	S	+
Immersion	T	S	−	−	−	+	+	S	S	−
Calm reading atmosphere		S	−	−	−	S	S	S	S	S
Feasible	U	+	−	−	−	S	+	S	S	S
Joyful		S	−	+	−	+	+	+	S	+
Anticipatory curiosity	M	+	−	+	−	+	+	S	+	−
Teachers' control of learning		+	+	S	+	−	−	+	+	+
	$\Sigma-$	1	6	4	7	2	2	1	1	2
	$\Sigma+$	5	3	4	1	3	5	4	3	5
	ΣS	4	1	2	2	5	3	5	6	3

introduces an external motivation. Inspired by Concept 10–The Gamer, users can accumulate points through interactions, adding a playful dimension. A mechanism for following up the students' learning comes from Concept 3–The Coach, allowing students to reflect on their interactions and offering teachers possibilities to follow students learning. Further exploration and discussion are required as part of the detailed design to deliberate how the follow-up should work.

It might be worth noting that Concept 7–The Creator scored well, and inclusion of functions for generating, processing, and rewriting texts, as suggested by the Creator concept were discussed. We intentionally avoided this, however, to prevent the concept from becoming overly complex—a potential pitfall akin to a "Swiss army knife." Given the system's already broad and demanding functionality, adding more features indiscriminately would be unlikely to significantly enhance overall user experience.

To summarise, our concept selection and synthesis, articulated below in the BookBot concept, is intended to balance user engagement, personalization, and practicality, while avoiding unnecessary complexity.

Synthesis–The BookBot. This is a robot to have booktalks with. The BookBot is designed to convey a passion for books and reading. It is intended to be perceived as a helpful and inspiring companion in the world of literature. The BookBot can engage in conversations about books, answer questions related to literature, and provide book recommendations. While it possesses extensive knowledge about books, it does not fully grasp how humans think, feel, and experience the world. Its humorous and imaginative approach is intended to make book discussions enjoyable and rewarding for students, whether individually or in groups.

The BookBot is intended to come across as a kind and endearing robot, interacting with students in an encouraging and helpful manner. Moreover, students can choose to have the BookBot portray a character from a book. Booktalks are prepared and finished in the classroom. After the conversation, teachers can review how it went, and students may earn rewards for tasks before, during, and after the discussion.

The goal is that the BookBot should promote reading, inspire students, and create a positive reading environment based on the following principles:

- *Encouragement to Read*: The BookBot should be perceived as encouraging and positive, making reading engaging and enjoyable.
- *Creativity and Imagination*: By creatively portraying characters or events from books, the BookBot should make reading more vivid and exciting.
- *Inspiration and Book Recommendations*: The BookBot should serve as a source of inspiration, recommending books based on students' interests and the text's difficulty level.
- *Deep Understanding*: Students should have the opportunity to deepen their understanding of the text by asking questions, analysing characters and themes, and exploring different interpretations.

The BookBot concept is illustrated in the storyboard of Fig. 1.

Fig. 1. Group discussion with the BookBot.

4 Discussion

Previous research has introduced social robots into reading activities within a school context [6,9,16]. This study extends that work by explicitly and systematically exploring a variety of robot-supported reading activities. The variety presented in design concepts represents a design space and can be used as a taxonomy for the different kinds and roles of social robots and conversational agents in reading activities, thus extending earlier work [21]. Ideas regarding functions, qualities of reading situations, and robot designs with diverse usage qualities were collaboratively generated by teachers, reading specialists, students, and researchers. From this collaborative effort, ten distinct design concepts emerged: The Facilitator, the Librarian, the Coach, the Buddy, the Assistant, the Narrator, the Creator, the Apprentice, the Portable, and the Gamer. The strengths and weaknesses of these designs were evaluated using criteria derived not only from our empirical research but also from SDT, which emphasizes autonomy, competence, and relatedness as key motivational factors [24]. This resulted in a synthesized concept named 'The BookBot,' designed to inspire and engage students in reading through discussions about books, character portrayal, and personalized book recommendations.

It should be noted that the quality immersion in the text, or of narrative transportation, that is, the feeling of being lost in a story, plays a crucial role in creating a calm reading atmosphere and a desire to continue reading. However, achieving transportation necessitates a certain level of reading skill in relation to the readability of the text. When the text is challenging to decode, it becomes difficult to truly lose oneself in its story [13]. Therefore, striking the right balance between the reader's competency and the difficulty level of the text is pivotal for creating an optimal reading experience.

The desirable qualities identified for a reading situation can be used to inform the design of a good reading environment, while the desirable use qualities for the product can guide the design of a robot intended for reading tasks. Specific qualities can subsequently be used as criteria in evaluating design solutions [14].

Given the rapid development of AI-based technologies in recent years, it might also be worth noting that part of the motivation why we have invested relatively much effort into the conceptual design of the BookBot is the fact that in the case of social robots interacting with relatively young children in educational settings it is important to make the robot appear competent and inspiring without giving the impression that it necessarily is a reliable judge or advisor that could replace human teachers. Much research in human-robot interaction has shown that people, in particular children, tend to anthropomorphise and interpret robots in human-like folk-psychological terms, in particular where those are human-like in appearance and/or behaviour [29]. That means, any social robot design needs to facilitate the type of "suspension of disbelief" that, for example, makes cartoon characters or game characters believable and appealing to kids (and many adults). But it also needs to allow for a "suspension of belief" in the sense that users should understand that what they are interacting with is not as human-like—and therefore also not as competent and reliable—as it may appear on the surface [33,34]. We have tried to take this into account early on in the conceptual design phase, but these properties will need to be verified carefully in later project phases.

4.1 Limitations

The present study naturally has limited generalisability. However, the resulting design concepts should be regarded as intermediate-level knowledge, meaning they are situated one abstraction level above specific design solutions [12]. This positioning affords them the potential to inspire new and novel design solutions in various contexts. Furthermore, the study has inherent subjectivity. Design, by its very nature, involves imposing a subjective perspective to effect change. How we frame what we mean by "preferred", and what actions we explore depend on who we are and how we are positioned in the world [32]. Different co-designers, that is, students, teachers, reading specialists, and researchers, would likely have framed the situation differently, which could have resulted in alternative concepts. The Pugh chart, which forms the basis for concept selection, is also based on subjective interpretation and assessment. It contributes by articulating and clarifying the subjectivity.

The Facilitator was picked as a starting point for the synthesis, perhaps prematurely given the scores for the other concepts. Future experimental validation and testing, along with a more detailed exploration of how to implement the robot, are needed to determine whether this was a sound design decision. However, the documented exploration of a wide range of concepts reported in the present paper, will in that case allow us to go back to the concept choice without having to go back all the way to concept ideation.

4.2 Future Work

In the design process, prototyping how to design and build the BookBot is a natural progression from the why and what questions of the conceptual design phase. The choice of platforms for prototyping is therefore the subsequent step of the work. The storyboard depicts a generic robot, but it could also be a screen-based agent. We will use the Furhat robot [17] for the initial prototyping of the BookBot since it includes many functions that we can build on. We will also use a large language model (LLM, e.g., GPT-4) to drive the conversation and provide it with a book as context. This means that the first coded prototype will build on retrieval-augmented generation, with a platform that is similar to the one used for the Saleshat system [11]. For the BookBot to work as intended, several other components are needed, such as a dialogue manager that can decide when to change topics and ask new questions, handle dialogue history, and integrate information from user profiles. The user interface also involves non-verbal behaviour that needs to be coordinated properly with verbal content. Many research questions remain, such as how to integrate spatial aspects of the robot's and the students' shared space using eye gaze and deictic expressions, and also how to handle multiparty interaction, including the non-trivial issue of multiparty timely and sensitive speech recognition of children's voices in Swedish [6]. How far we can get towards the envisioned concept is an empirical question.

The forthcoming prototype studies, which will combine Wizard of Oz and coded prototypes, are intended to address key questions: How should book talks be conducted with a robot? What behaviours, appearances, and interactions are appropriate for the robot during these booktalks? A hypothesis at this initial stage is that the BookBot needs to initiate topics and questions for conversation, while remaining open to topics and questions initiated by the students. It would also have to ensure the conversation stays on topic and distribute speaking turns in a multiparty conversation where some students are much more vocal than others. Furthermore, it is essential that our prototypes are subjected to proper evaluations to determine if book talks with a robot genuinely enhance students' motivation to read.

4.3 Conclusions

In this interdisciplinary project, experiences from technology, cognitive science, education, and special education research have been combined, meaning that questions about design and education have been equally important. Reading has been the focus, and the technology has been adapted to the pedagogical reading practices, not the other way around. The project began with workshops with teachers to explore the reading activities that were already used in the classroom before the project. These reading activities provided concrete answers about how teachers work with decoding, reading comprehension, and the reading experience, to investigate which of these activities (and possibly new ones) a robot could contribute to. Teachers' knowledge of reading activities, combined with interdisciplinary researchers from different fields, provided new insights into the requirements for a reading robot. Overall, a more materially-oriented understanding has also been developed of what might be possible and what is still unrealistic in working with a reading robot in an authentic environment.

The results of conceptual design research manifest as design concepts [32]. These concepts serve as contextualised and socially grounded anchors within the design space, providing a foundation upon which other designers and researchers may build to determine applicability in their unique contexts. Furthermore, they act as focal points for collaborative design endeavours. Each concept presented in this study (the Facilitator, the Librarian, the Coach, the Buddy, the Assistant, the Narrator, the Creator, the Apprentice, the Portable, the Gamer, and the final BookBot concept) offers a distinct perspective on the design space for social robots engaged in reading activities. Rather than being definitive solutions, these concepts should be viewed as generative tools, driving the ideation process for designing preferred situations within the realm of social robots in reading activities.

Acknowledgments. We extend our gratitude to the study participants for their invaluable contributions. This study was funded by The Swedish Research Council (Dnr. 2022-04171) and Norrköping's fund for research and development (Dnr. KS 2022/0465). TZ is also supported by ELLIIT, the *Excellence Center at Linköping-Lund in Information Technology.*

Disclosure of Interests. The authors have no competing interests to declare that are relevant to the content of this article.

References

1. Alnajjar, F., et al.: Robots in Education: An Introduction to High-Tech Social Agents, Intelligent Tutors, and Curricular Tools. Routledge, New York (2021). https://doi.org/10.4324/9781003142706
2. Belpaeme, T., Kennedy, J., Ramachandran, A., Scassellati, B., Tanaka, F.: Social robots for education: a review. Sci. Robot. **3**(21), eaat5954 (2018). https://doi.org/10.1126/scirobotics.aat5954
3. van den Berghe, R., Verhagen, J., Oudgenoeg-Paz, O., van der Ven, S., Leseman, P.: Social robots for language learning: a review. Rev. Educ. Res. **89**(2), 259–295 (2019). https://doi.org/10.3102/0034654318821286
4. van Boeijen, A., Daalhuizen, J., Zijlstra, J.: Delft Design Guide: Perspectives, Models, Approaches, Methods, revised edn. BIS Publishers, Amsterdam (2020)
5. Cagiltay, B., Mutlu, B., Michaelis, J.E.: "My unconditional homework buddy:" exploring children's preferences for a homework companion robot. In: Proceedings of the 22nd Annual ACM Interaction Design and Children Conference, Chicago IL USA, pp. 375–387. ACM (2023). https://doi.org/10.1145/3585088.3589388
6. Caruana, N., Moffat, R., Miguel-Blanco, A., Cross, E.S.: Perceptions of intelligence & sentience shape children's interactions with robot reading companions. Sci. Rep. **13**(1), 7341 (2023). https://doi.org/10.1038/s41598-023-32104-7
7. Chiu, M.M.: Contextual influences on girls' and boys' motivation and reading achievement: family, schoolmates, and country. In: Orellana García, P., Baldwin Lind, P. (eds.) Reading Achievement and Motivation in Boys and Girls. LS, vol. 15, pp. 49–63. Springer, Cham (2018). https://doi.org/10.1007/978-3-319-75948-7_3
8. Eriksson Barajas, K., Aronsson, K.: Avid versus struggling readers: co-construed pupil identities in school booktalk. Lang. Lit. **18**(3), 281–299 (2009). https://doi.org/10.1177/0963947009105854
9. Fridin, M.: Storytelling by a kindergarten social assistive robot: a tool for constructive learning in preschool education. Comput. Educ. **70**, 53–64 (2014). https://doi.org/10.1016/j.compedu.2013.07.043
10. Gambrell, L., Marinak, B., Brooker, H., McCrea-Andrews, H.: The importance of independent reading. In: Samuels, S., Farstrup, A. (eds.) What Research has to Say about Reading Instruction, pp. 143–158, 4th edn. International Reading Association, Newark (2011)
11. Hanschmann, L., Gnewuch, U., Maedche, A.: Saleshat: a LLM-based social robot for human-like sales conversations. In: Følstad, A., et al. (eds.) Chatbot Research and Design.LNCS, vol. 14524, pp. 61–76. Springer, Cham (2024). https://doi.org/10.1007/978-3-031-54975-5_4

12. Höök, K., Löwgren, J.: Strong concepts: intermediate-level knowledge in interaction design research. ACM Trans. Comput.-Hum. Interact. **19**, 1–18 (2012). https://doi.org/10.1145/2362364.2362371
13. Isakoglou, F., Multhaup, K.S., Munger, M.P., Eiler, B.A.: The effects of genre and reading difficulty on narrative transportation: the mediating role of affect. Psi Chi J. Psychol. Res. **26**(4), 422–429 (2021). https://doi.org/10.24839/2325-7342.JN26.4.422
14. Löwgren, J., Stolterman, E.: Thoughtful Interaction Design: A Design Perspective on Information Technology. MIT Press, Cambridge (2004)
15. McGeown, S., Bonsall, J., Andries, V., Howarth, D., Wilkinson, K.: Understanding reading motivation across different text types: qualitative insights from children. J. Res. Reading **43**(4), 597–608 (2020)
16. Michaelis, J.E., Mutlu, B.: Reading socially: transforming the in-home reading experience with a learning-companion robot. Sci. Robot. **3**(21), eaat5999 (2018). https://doi.org/10.1126/scirobotics.aat5999
17. Al Moubayed, S., Beskow, J., Skantze, G., Granström, B.: Furhat: a back-projected human-like robot head for multiparty human-machine interaction. In: Esposito, A., Esposito, A.M., Vinciarelli, A., Hoffmann, R., Müller, V.C. (eds.) Cognitive Behavioural Systems. LNCS, vol. 7403, pp. 114–130. Springer, Heidelberg (2012). https://doi.org/10.1007/978-3-642-34584-5_9
18. Neumann, M.M.: Social robots and young children's early language and literacy learning. Early Childhood Educ. J. **48**(2), 157–170 (2020). https://doi.org/10.1007/s10643-019-00997-7
19. Oralbayeva, N., Zhanatkyzy, A., Amir, A., Telisheva, Z., Sandygulova, A.: Moveable Alipbi: a montessori-inspired design of long-term child-robot interaction for early literacy development. In: Proceedings of the 23rd Annual ACM Interaction Design and Children Conference, Delft Netherlands, pp. 587–599. ACM, June 2024. https://doi.org/10.1145/3628516.3663347
20. Orellana García, P.: To what extent is reading motivation a significant predictor of reading achievement when controlling for language and cognitive ability? A systematic review. In: Orellana García, P., Baldwin Lind, P. (eds.) Reading Achievement and Motivation in Boys and Girls. LS, vol. 15, pp. 79–96. Springer, Cham (2018). https://doi.org/10.1007/978-3-319-75948-7_5
21. Rohlfing, K.J., et al.: Social/dialogical roles of social robots in supporting children's learning of language and literacy-a review and analysis of innovative roles. Front. Robot. AI **9**, 971749 (2022). https://doi.org/10.3389/frobt.2022.971749
22. Rubegni, E., Malinverni, L., Yip, J.: "Don't let the robots walk our dogs, but it's ok for them to do our homework": children's perceptions, fears, and hopes in social robots. In: Interaction Design and Children, pp. 352–361. Association for Computing Machinery, New York (2022). https://doi.org/10.1145/3501712.3529726
23. Ryan, R.M., Deci, E.L.: Intrinsic and extrinsic motivations: classic definitions and new directions. Contemp. Educ. Psychol. **25**(1), 54–67 (2000). https://doi.org/10.1006/ceps.1999.1020
24. Ryan, R.M., Deci, E.L.: Chapter four - brick by brick: the origins, development, and future of self-determination theory. In: Elliot, A.J. (ed.) Advances in Motivation Science, vol. 6, pp. 111–156. Elsevier, Cambridge (2019). https://doi.org/10.1016/bs.adms.2019.01.001
25. Sato, T., Kudo, Y., Osawa, H.: Book introduction robot designed by children for promoting interest in reading. In: Proceedings of the 5th International Conference on Human Agent Interaction, pp. 17–25. Association for Computing Machinery, New York (2017). https://doi.org/10.1145/3125739.3125740

26. Sugimoto, M., Ito, T., Nguyen, T.N., Inagaki, S.: GENTORO: a system for supporting children's storytelling using handheld projectors and a robot. In: Proceedings of the 8th International Conference on Interaction Design and Children, Como Italy, pp. 214–217. ACM (2009). https://doi.org/10.1145/1551788.1551832
27. Sun, M., Leite, I., Lehman, J.F., Li, B.: Collaborative storytelling between robot and child: a feasibility study. In: Proceedings of the 2017 Conference on Interaction Design and Children, Stanford California USA, pp. 205–214. ACM (2017). https://doi.org/10.1145/3078072.3079714
28. Tegmark, M., Alatalo, T., Vinterek, M., Winberg, M.: What motivates students to read at school? Student views on reading practices in middle and lower-secondary school. J. Res. Read. **45**(1), 100–118 (2022). https://doi.org/10.1111/1467-9817.12386, _eprint: https://onlinelibrary.wiley.com/doi/pdf/10.1111/1467-9817.12386
29. Thellman, S., De Graaf, M., Ziemke, T.: Mental state attribution to robots: a systematic review of conceptions, methods, and findings. ACM Trans. Hum.-Robot Interact. (THRI) **11**(4), 1–51 (2022). https://doi.org/10.1145/3526112
30. Xu, Y., Warschauer, M.: Exploring young children's engagement in joint reading with a conversational agent. In: Proceedings of the Interaction Design and Children Conference, London United Kingdom, pp. 216–228. ACM (2020). https://doi.org/10.1145/3392063.3394417
31. Yadollahi, E., Johal, W., Paiva, A., Dillenbourg, P.: When deictic gestures in a robot can harm child-robot collaboration. In: Proceedings of the 17th ACM Conference on Interaction Design and Children, Trondheim Norway, pp. 195–206. ACM (2018). https://doi.org/10.1145/3202185.3202743
32. Ylirisku, S., Jacucci, G., Sellen, A., Harper, R.: Design research as conceptual designing: the Manhattan design concept. Interact. Comput. **28**(5), 648–663 (2016). https://doi.org/10.1093/iwc/iwv040
33. Ziemke, T.: Understanding social robots: attribution of intentional agency to artificial and biological bodies. Artif. Life **29**, 351–366 (2023). https://doi.org/10.1162/artl_a_00404
34. Ziemke, T.: Ironies of social robotics. Sci. Robot. **9**(91), eadq6387 (2024). https://doi.org/10.1126/scirobotics.adq6387

Questions People Ask ChatGPT Regarding Their Romantic Relationships and What They Think About the Provided Answers: An Exploratory Study

Alexios Brailas(✉) and Lazaros Tsolakis

Department of Psychology, Panteion University, Athens, Greece
abrailas@panteion.gr

Abstract. In this study, we explored ChatGPT's potential to provide advice on interpersonal relationship issues. Ten participants asked the AI chatbot questions to evaluate the perceived usefulness and applicability of its responses regarding their romantic relationships. Specific patterns were identified in the questions participants asked, allowing for a categorization of the most common day-to-day concerns young people face in their relationships today. Among these, jealousy, trust, and privacy issues were prominent, alongside questions related to intimacy, sexual issues, relationship maintenance, and emotional conflict. Empirical data were collected through semi-structured interviews, regarding the perceived usefulness of the responses chatGPT provided. The findings suggest that ChatGPT can offer valuable insights and advice on interrelational issues. However, participants noted that while ChatGPT can be a helpful resource when human interaction is unavailable, it is not sufficient to function independently or replace human connections. Overall, this study highlights both the potential as well as the inadequacy of ChatGPT in providing interpersonal relationship advice.

Keywords: Artificial Intelligence · Romantic Relationships · Counseling

1 Introduction

This study aims to investigate the contribution of generative Artificial Intelligence (AI) to various interpersonal relationship issues that young people go through in their everyday lives. Due to its engineering as a chatbot, ChatGPT can engage in a dialogue, provide relevant information, and answer follow-up questions [1]. In this context, an inevitable question that arises is whether and how such a platform can be used to provide advice on personal issues related to human romantic, or other, interpersonal relationships. The lack of thorough analysis regarding the quality and relevance of ChatGPT's responses, as well as the absence of more personalized and contextually situated replies, may pose significant challenges as inaccurate advice could lead to negative consequences. Therefore, it is critical to explore and investigate ChatGPT's affordances and overall perceived performance concerning intimacy issues, and to propose possible future improvements for its effectiveness in supporting individuals with relationship difficulties [2, 3].

A. Følstad et al. (Eds.): CONVERSATIONS 2024, LNCS 15545, pp. 150–158, 2025.
https://doi.org/10.1007/978-3-031-88045-2_10

So far, some empirical evidence suggests that ChatGPT can provide users with useful advice and propose next steps for handling relationship problems [3]. Could ChatGPT, therefore, be considered a simple, fast, and free alternative for relationship advice, offering a simulated human-like interaction in cases where individuals lack the financial means to consult a professional, or feel embarrassed to discuss these issues with another person? In a study focusing particularly on psychotherapy and employing an experimental research design, key findings indicate that trust in chatbot therapists is comparable to that in human therapists [2]. Although there is initial evidence that AI chatbots could become valuable mental health resources, there is currently insufficient data to conclude that advice from a chatbot can substitute that of a mental health professional [2, 3].

However, regardless of the usefulness of AI in its current state of development as an alternative to mental health practitioners and psychotherapists for providing advice on interpersonal relationships issues, it may be valuable to first explore people's general perceptions of ChatGPT's responses and their usefulness. To this direction, this study aims to answer the following research questions: a) What do people ask ChatGPT regarding their romantic relationships? and b) How do they perceive the provided answers?

2 Methodology

In order to answer the above research questions and explore and understand participants' lived experiences regarding the usefulness of chatGPT for providing advice on interpersonal issues, we conducted a series of qualitative semi-structured interviews. An interview agenda was developed to guide the overall process. Semi-structured interviews rely on open-ended questions, which encourage participants to give detailed and nuanced responses in their own words [4].

2.1 Participants and Ethics

A total of 10 participants, 9 females and 1 male, aged 21 to 23, participated in the present study. All participants were undergraduate students at Greek universities, selected through convenience sampling and snowballing strategies. They were informed about the study's purposes before the interviewing process and signed an informed consent form. The study adhered to the American Psychological Association's (APA) Code of Ethics for conducting research with human participants throughout. Participants were told that the study aimed to understand their lived experiences regarding romantic relationships and the role ChatGPT can play in advising them, emphasizing that there were no right or wrong answers during the process. The interviews were conducted by the second author. Given that the participants' questions pertained to their intimate relationships, a potentially sensitive topic that could trigger unexpected distress, especially in individuals with prior relational trauma, both the participants and the interviewer were informed beforehand that they would have access to a licensed psychotherapist (the first author) for support and counseling in case any distress would arose during or after the interview process. Each participant was invited to ask ChatGPT at least five questions. ChatGPT was running on the interviewer's laptop for convenience and to ensure full anonymity for the participants. The interviews lasted about 30 min.

2.2 Data Collection

Data collection involved conducting a series of semi-structured interviews with participants, guided by an interview agenda. The questions in this agenda served as prompts to initiate open discussions between the interviewer and participant. Follow-up questions such as, "Can you tell me more about this?" or "How do you feel about that now?" were used to encourage participants to share their thoughts, feelings, and experiences in a more authentic and genuine way, resulting in rich and contextually situated data. Semi-structured interviews prioritize the perspectives and experiences of participants, allowing them to co-shape the direction and focus of the conversation. Building rapport and establishing trust between researchers and participants is essential in qualitative research. Interviewers should demonstrate sensitivity, empathy, and cultural competence to create a comfortable and safe environment where participants feel free to share their views and lived experiences openly [4]. The interview agenda used is as follows.

Icebreaking Small Talk. Initially the interviewer initiates a "small talk" with each participant to act as an icebreaker and to help build rapport and a suitable interviewing climate.

Asking ChatGPT Questions. The interviewer invites the participant to ask chatGPT at least five questions regarding their romantic relationships: "Now I will invite you to take up your time and ask chatGPT whatever you like to ask regarding your romantic relationship. Please, take up your time and ask at least 5 questions. Of course, here there are no right or wrong questions to be asked; I will invite you to be yourself: the first question that comes to your mind is usually the best to ask. And at any time, you can come back with follow-ups or explanatory questions."

Discussing About the Responses Provided. The interviewer invites the participant to discuss about what they think, how they felt, and how they experienced the provided responses.

Concluding the Interview. The reviewer closes the interview in a smooth way by asking how the participant feels and whether they want to ask anything else about the whole process.

2.3 Data Analysis

After conducting the semi-structured interviews, the researchers analyzed the data thematically to identify patterns, themes, and insights [4]. The first part of the analysis focused on the questions participants asked ChatGPT regarding their romantic relationships. The second part of the analysis focused on how participants perceived the provided by chatGPT responses. Initially, the researchers conducted a thematic analysis manually, following a reflexive, traditional coding approach [5]. However, during this process, we decided to experiment with ChatGPT to assist in categorizing the questions into thematic groups. We found the resulting categorization meaningful, and after careful revision, we finalized the list of identified thematic categories, which is presented in the results section. Many scholars have already highlighted the potential of generative AI to facilitate the process of thematic analysis, while underscoring the importance of not letting AI models overshadow the critical, cultural, and situated interpretative skills and richness that a human analyst bring into the process of qualitative analysis [5, 6]. After experimenting with chatGPT here, we are able to confirm this position. Generative AI, in its current state of development, could be an invaluable research tool and aid for qualitative researchers, if it is used wisely to support and not to replace the human analyst [1].

3 Results

3.1 Questions People Ask ChatGPT Regarding Their Romantic Relationships

It is worth analyzing the questions people asked chatGPT as this serves as a virtual window to what troubles the participants with regard to their romantic relationships. A total of 53 questions were elicited by the participants. Using the AI-facilitated inductive Thematic Analysis approach [5, 6] described in the Data Analysis section, these 53 questions were grouped into seven broader thematic categories. A detailed description of each thematic category, along with characteristic examples of questions asked, follows.

The first identified theme was *Jealousy, trust, and privacy issues*. This category groups questions around themes of jealousy, suspicion, and breaches of privacy, which are often recurring sources of conflict in relationships. Example questions in this category include: "My partner gets jealous when he hears I am with other people (friends or work colleagues). What should I do?" and "I went through my partner's phone and saw messages of her flirting with someone else. What should I do?".

The second identified theme was *Communication and emotional connection*. This theme focuses on the challenges of effective communication and emotional understanding, which are crucial for the health of any relationship. Example questions in this category include: "I don't feel comfortable being 'myself' around my partner. What should I do?" and "Sometimes I don't want to communicate with my partner about my problems because I don't like their reactions, like anger. What should I do?", or "I feel that I'm not getting enough understanding from my partner in our relationship. What should I do?".

The third identified theme was *Life goals, values, and future plans*. Questions dealing with long-term relationship goals, such as having children, career ambitions, and family relations, fall into this category. Example questions in this category include: "My partner wants children, but I don't. What should we do about it?" and "How should I handle the fact that my partner does not get along with my parents?".

The fourth identified theme was *Intimacy, sexual issues, and relationship maintenance*. This category addresses intimacy and the maintenance of romance and passion over time, including issues with sexual communication. Example questions in this category include: "I think my partner and I have an issue during sexual intercourse, but I don't want to offend him. How can I communicate this?" and "Suggest fun activities that I can try with my partner."

The fifth identified theme was *Autonomy, boundaries, and control*. These questions concern the balance between personal autonomy and relationship control, including issues of boundaries, freedom, and power dynamics. Example questions in this category include: "I want to go on vacation with my friends, but my boyfriend does not allow it.

What should I do?" and "My partner barely has time for me but always makes time for others, and this makes me feel devastated. What should I do?".

The sixth identified theme was *Relationship dynamics and emotional conflict.* This theme groups questions around conflict, emotional tension, and difficult dynamics in personal and social interactions within the relationship. Example questions in this category include: "My partner may unintentionally belittle me or insult me sometimes. How can I handle it?" and "My partner is not very polite in interactions with others. What should I do?".

The final identified theme was *Reflection and self-discovery.* Questions that focus on self-reflection and doubts about relationships, exploring personal preferences, and readiness for deeper commitment. Example questions in this category include: "What characteristics should an ideal partner have?" and "What is the ideal place to meet a love partner?", or "I prefer partners who are older than me. Is that okay?".

3.2 How ChatGPT's Responses Are Evaluated by the Participants

During the semi-structured interviews, participants discussed in real time how they perceive and what they think about the provided by chatGPT answers. The second part of the analysis focused on these discussions as they unfolded. Following the same AI-facilitated inductive Thematic Analysis approach used above, participants' perceptions were grouped into five broader thematic categories. A detailed description of each thematic category, along with characteristic quotations for each category, follows.

The first identified theme in this part of the interviews was *Advantages of using ChatGPT for relationship issues.* Participants found ChatGPT capable of providing a variety of responses, some of which were generic, while others were unexpectedly well-suited to the specific issues and challenges participants faced and sought advice on. For example, as one participant remarked, "I think that for the questions I have asked so far, I did not expect it to give so much advice," and "It is nice that it gives you many alternatives on the questions asked."

The second identified theme was *Lack of more situated and tailored responses.* Many participants noted a gap between ChatGPT's responses and the practical solutions they sought for their unique situations. They appreciated ChatGPT's broad approach but found some responses too generic, sometimes craving more tailored advice that resonated with their specific issues they asked for advice. For example, a participant noted: "Generally, from what I understand, there is a pattern in the answers it gives. It has something like 'headings' and just adjusts them to fit each question. Again, while I think it provided a holistic and multifaceted answer, I still do not feel it helps much practically. ... Overall, it is an average and fairly 'general' response."

The third identified theme was *Lack of emotional connection, empathy, and human relational rapport.* Participants frequently expressed a desire for responses that were more emotionally attuned or empathetic, especially on sensitive topics like jealousy, trust, and personal boundaries. While some answers felt helpful, others were described as "robotic," lacking the human touch necessary for building relational rapport. As another participant commented: "However, the way the responses are structured, with bullet points and a 'you should do this, then that' format, feels a bit robotic. Even though what it says is valid and could be advice from a real person, reading it from your computer makes you feel distanced from the problem, like it is not really about you. It is like reading a 'Top 10 Ways to Save Your Relationship' article on Google. Still, I think if you engage with it on a specific problem and keep providing more details, it could gradually give you better and more personalized answers. But it definitely lacks emotion and empathy. A friend, for instance, might hear your problem and say, 'Oh, I had that issue too and handled it this way,' which makes you feel like you are not alone. I think that's what is missing from ChatGPT."

The fourth identified theme was *ChatGPT's repetitive suggestion to seek professional advice.* ChatGPT's consistent recommendation of professional help was a common critique. Although some found it "responsible" and politically correct, many saw it as repetitive, preferring responses that would allow them to take immediate, manageable actions rather than needing external intervention for every issue. For example, a participant commented: "I told you it would send me to a therapist again! Okay, overall, these are some very nice and normal suggestions, but once again, it encourages seeing a specialist, which is starting to feel like a hint that it is trying to tell me something. Umm... yeah, some answers are a bit basic. It is a bit standard, but some of the other things I read are genuinely things that someone might not think about at that moment, so it serves as a polite reminder. Okay, cute!".

The fifth identified theme was *Value of even only broadly applicable advice.* Despite some criticisms, participants acknowledged that ChatGPT's responses often provided valuable info regarding relationship practices. Even though some answers were seen as common sense, they recognized the utility of receiving reminders for practices like open communication, mutual respect, and self-care. For example, a participant commented: "Now, in general, it gives some advice that, to me, seems a bit superficial or generic. However, even simple advice of this kind can be helpful sometimes. I don't think it is particularly exceptional in what it suggests, but it is not wrong in what it says, either. I feel that if there's ever a time when I can't talk to someone about what's on my mind and I have something I want to explore, I might pick up a few ideas from it. It is able to provide some practical insights, which I appreciate."

4 Discussion

4.1 What Seems to Bother Young Adults in Their Romantic Relationships?

The present study identified specific patterns in the questions the participants asked, allowing for a categorization of the most common day-to-day concerns young people in emerging adulthood face in their relationships. Among these, jealousy, trust, and privacy issues were prominent, alongside questions about communication and emotional connection, which are crucial for the health of any relationship according to the existing literature [7]. Trust plays a complex role in sexual relationships regulating perceived emotional safety and intimacy [8]. Furthermore, questions regarding life goals, values, and future plans were significant topics for participants. Thinking and imagining of desired futures help people to address current challenges and enhances the sense meaning in life [9, 10]. They were also inquiries about autonomy and boundaries, as people try to have control over their lives [11]. Additionally, topics related to intimacy, sex issues, relationship dynamics, and conflict, were of interest to the participants [7].

4.2 AI Chatbots as Providers of Advice for Interrelational Issues

In general, the participants found the platform's responses to be useful. Although they encountered some knowledge they were already familiar with from daily interactions (friends, relatives), they gained valuable information they had not previously considered. Nevertheless, participants in general thought that while ChatGPT is capable of providing some advice in situations where an individual may not be able to turn to a relative, friend, or a mental health professional, it is certainly not sufficient, in its current form, to function independently as a replacement for authentic human interaction. The element of live, simultaneous conversation with another human interlocutor is notably absent. As a participant in the study pointed out, the user must read the response generated by the chatbot and then comment afterward, without the ability to interrupt, to comment on something in the moment. Additionally, ChatGPT cannot provide examples from similar personal experiences or life situations, as a human interlocutor might provide, which could be quite useful in a dialogue. Therefore, although AI chatbots according to existing research can be a valuable supplementary resource for relationship advice or for mental health support [2, 3] it cannot replace a human interlocutor, as the information provided is often lacking empathy [12], and is not embodied, neither situated in a suitable relational therapeutic context [13].

4.3 Limitations, Methodological Considerations, and Future Work

It should be noted that, given our relatively small sample size (10 participants), it is likely that the present study did not achieve adequate theoretical saturation of the thematic categories, which is often required in many qualitative data analysis methods. Additionally, we only included young adult participants (emerging adulthood) studying at Greek universities, and our sampling process (convenience and snowball sampling) did not ensure a representative sample. Therefore, this study should be considered only as exploratory. More qualitative and quantitative studies with different research designs are needed to improve our understanding of how people around the world are open to using generative AI algorithms like ChatGPT for personal advice regarding their interpersonal relationship issues, as well as how they perceive the provided answers.

A cross-cultural comparison that includes diverse age and gender groups would also be interesting, rather than being limited to this specific age/gender group and cultural setting. It would be particularly interesting for a future study to employ a research design where participants would ask questions and read the provided answers by both ChatGPT and real people, either friends, relatives, or health experts, without knowing who provided which answer. This approach may help avoid potential bias from participants who might be influenced if they know the answer was generated by ChatGPT.

It is also important to note that this brief paper does not address issues of algorithmic opacity, epistemic violence, and power inequalities inherent in modern AI technologies [14–16]. These factors are crucial to consider when evaluating the potential of chatbots in providing relationship advice or mental health support.

Today, AI is becoming a valuable research tool, and even a potential clinical aid, in our psychological practice [1, 2]. In this study, we employed an exploratory research design that utilized generative AI during data production to facilitate the elicitation of the empirical data and the unfolding of the semi-structured interviews. We also used generative AI during the data analysis stage to facilitate the process without losing the cultural richness the human analyst brings into the qualitative analysis [5, 6]. It seems that AI not only attempts to mirror human intelligence but also transforms it through a process of transactional causality, pushing us to continuously redefine what it means to be human, what it means to be intelligent, and how we engage with academic scholarship in an increasingly interconnected and technology-mediated world.

Disclosure of Interests. The authors have no competing interests.

References

1. Brailas, A.: Postdigital duoethnography: an inquiry into human-artificial intelligence synergies. Postdigit. Sci. Educ. **6**, 486–515 (2024). https://doi.org/10.1007/s42438-024-00455-7
2. Mühl, L., Stecker, L., Herter, E., Szczuka, J.M., Wischnewski, M., Krämer, N.: Integrating AI in psychotherapy: an investigation of trust in voicebot therapists. In: Nordic Conference on Human-Computer Interaction, Uppsala Sweden, pp. 1–9. ACM (2024). https://doi.org/10.1145/3679318.3685353
3. Vowels, L.M.: Are chatbots the new relationship experts? Insights from three studies. Comput. Hum. Behav. Artif. Hum. **2**, 100077 (2024). https://doi.org/10.1016/j.chbah.2024.100077
4. Hurst, A.: Introduction to Qualitative Research Methods. Oregon State University (2023)
5. Christou, P.: Thematic analysis through artificial intelligence (AI). TQR (2024). https://doi.org/10.46743/2160-3715/2024.7046
6. Perkins, M., Roe, J.: The use of generative AI in qualitative analysis: inductive thematic analysis with ChatGPT. JALT **7** (2024). https://doi.org/10.37074/jalt.2024.7.1.22
7. Guerrero, L.K., Andersen, P.A., Afifi, W.A.: Close Encounters: Communication in Relationships. SAGE, Thousand Oaks (2021)
8. Fortenberry, J.D.: Trust, sexual trust, and sexual health: an interrogative review. J. Sex Res. **56**, 425–439 (2019). https://doi.org/10.1080/00224499.2018.1523999
9. Baumeister, R.F., Vohs, K.D., Oettingen, G.: Pragmatic prospection: how and why people think about the future. Rev. Gen. Psychol. **20**, 3–16 (2016). https://doi.org/10.1037/gpr0000060
10. McAdam, E., Mirza, K.A.H.: Drugs, hopes and dreams: appreciative inquiry with marginalized young people using drugs and alcohol. J. Fam. Ther. **31**, 175–193 (2009). https://doi.org/10.1111/j.1467-6427.2009.00461.x
11. Lammers, J., Stoker, J.I., Rink, F., Galinsky, A.D.: To have control over or to be free from others? The desire for power reflects a need for autonomy. Pers. Soc. Psychol. Bull. **42**, 498–512 (2016). https://doi.org/10.1177/0146167216634064
12. Rahsepar Meadi, M., Bernstein, J.S., Batelaan, N., Van Balkom, A.J.L.M., Metselaar, S.: Does a lack of emotions make chatbots unfit to be psychotherapists? Bioethics **38**, 503–510 (2024). https://doi.org/10.1111/bioe.13299
13. Khawaja, Z., Bélisle-Pipon, J.-C.: Your robot therapist is not your therapist: understanding the role of AI-powered mental health chatbots. Front. Digit. Health. **5**, 1278186 (2023). https://doi.org/10.3389/fdgth.2023.1278186
14. McQuillan, D.: Resisting AI: An Anti-Fascist Approach to Artificial Intelligence. Bristol University Press, Bristol (2022)

15. Brandtzaeg, P.B., Skjuve, M., Følstad, A.: Understanding model power in social AI. AI Soc. (2024). https://doi.org/10.1007/s00146-024-02053-4
16. Brailas, A.: Review of Dan McQuillan (2022). Resisting AI: an anti- fascist approach to artificial intelligence. Postdigit. Sci. Educ. **6**, 1366–1372 (2024). https://doi.org/10.1007/s42438-024-00483-3

Conversational AI for Citizens and Customers

AI-Driven Dialogue: Leveraging Generative AI in Conversational Agent Voting Advice Applications (CAVAAs)

Thilo I. Dieing(✉)

Institute of Political Science, TU Darmstadt, Residenzschloss 1, 64283 Darmstadt, Germany
thilo.dieing@stud.tu-darmstadt.de

Abstract. Voting Advice Applications (VAAs) have been crucial in modern elections, helping voters understand political issues and party positions. Recent innovations, such as Conversational Agent Voting Advice Applications (CAVAAs), enhance the user experience by integrating chatbots that address comprehension issues, helping to provide more accurate voting advice. However, current rule-based CAVAA chatbots face limitations due to the need for predefined responses and restricted question coverage. This paper introduces two new Generative AI chatbot designs -open and semi-open generative chatbots- using Retrieval-Augmented Generation (RAG) and open-source Large Language Models (LLMs). These models generate accurate, context-specific responses to political questions, addressing the limitations of rule-based systems while incorporating filters to avoid biased or inappropriate answers. Tested, in a German case study, using the German 2021 Wahl-O-Mat, the chatbots were evaluated through a two-stage process: coder grading of responses and an expert survey of VAA Creators (N = 13). Results demonstrate that the generative chatbots effectively answered both standard CAVAA questions and broader political inquiries, with high acceptance and perceived usefulness among experts. Despite these successes, further refinement is needed to improve filtering and ensure unbiased interactions. These findings offer valuable insights into the use of Generative AI in (CA)VAAs and its potential to improve voter guidance.

Keywords: Voting Advice Applications · Conversational agents · Chatbot design · LLM · RAG · GenAI

1 Introduction

More than 30 years since their introduction [1] Voting Advice Applications (VAAs) have established themselves as vital parts of modern elections [2]. By informing voters about issues and party stances VAAs can help increase dropping turnout rates [3,4] and make politics more comprehensible to the public [5,6]. Despite that VAAs have to adapt and evolve to continue being helpful in

A. Følstad et al. (Eds.): CONVERSATIONS 2024, LNCS 15545, pp. 161–180, 2025.
https://doi.org/10.1007/978-3-031-88045-2_11

the future. One central argument in this evolution of VAAs is that the "implementation of AI will help ensure that VAAs will continue to contribute positively to the democratic processes" [7, p. 12]. In concurrence, Liebrecht and Kamoen introduced the pioneering concept of incorporating a Conversational Agent or chatbot into VAAs resulting in a Conversational Agent Voting Advice Application (CAVAA) [8–10]. This conversational feature allows users to clear any comprehension problems they may have during the VAA, resulting in a possibly overall better-fitting voting advice [11]. Additionally, first empirical studies have indicated that CAVAAs can increase users' political knowledge significantly compared to non-users and even users of standard VAAs [8,12]. As such CAVAAs can offer a more detailed and effective VAA experience. From an architectural perspective, the developed CAVAA bots can be described as rule-based, closed-knowledge domain chatbots [8–10,12,13]. As a result, the current bots can only answer five different question types, made of semantic meanings, statement explanations, pros and cons, party positions, and current affairs. Using intent recognition rules, models determine if a user inquiry matches one of the five questions and will answer with predefined human answers to the questions.

However, this method while covering the main user issues [11], also has several drawbacks. For one the development of predefined human answers is very time- and resource-consuming and also limits the amount of questions one can cover. This high effort makes deploying multiple CAVAAs unfeasible. Additionally, the rule-based nature limits the potential of the chatbot. Hence one could imagine that users might also have deviating questions, concerning other topics about the election or politics. Furthermore, the usage of intent recognition also means that scholars need to collect large amounts of identifying words to avoid misclassifying user questions because of unexpected wordings or formulations. Addressing these drawbacks, this paper proposes two novel chatbot designs for an open and semi-open generative chatbot, to investigate the feasibility, merit, and acceptance of such Generative AI CAVAA chatbots.

The developed architecture utilizes a combination of Retrieval-Augmented Generation (RAG) [14] and open-source Large Language Models (LLMs). This method feeds fitting data entries, consisting of the party answers to the VAA's statements, to the LLM to generate factually correct answers. With this specific knowledge base, the chatbots are able to answer all of the current five possible CAVAA questions, independent of their formulation and wording, while the LLM's pre-training allows for broader political questions. The paper further addresses inherent political biases in LLMs [15–17] that could negatively influence users by building a custom semi-open chatbot that includes filter layers to prohibit the chatbot from answering discriminating questions as well as from giving its own opinion or telling users whom to vote for. The chatbots were developed based on the German 2021 Wahl-O-Mat to demonstrate and test them. An evaluation was performed in two stages. In the first stage, the chatbots' answers to 261 prompts were graded independently by three coders. The second stage then performed an expert survey of German VAA Creators (N = 13), to further test, the answers, the usefulness, and acceptance utilizing the

Technology Acceptance Model (TAM) [18]. The results of both stages indicate that the proposed chatbots are able to answer the five common CAVAA question types as well as broader political questions about parties or the upcoming election. The performed expert survey further validated that the chatbot is able to answer a diverse set of questions. Furthermore, the analysis shows a high level of acceptance and usefulness for the proposed Generative AI (GenAI) chatbot, with an overall very positive sentiment from the experts. Major challenges revealed by the evaluation indicate the need to further fine-tune the filter layers to improve the answer behavior and guarantee safe and unbiased conversations. Overall, the findings supply new insights into the usage of GenAI models in politics and especially into the advantages and challenges of their implementation in (CA)VAAs.

2 Background

Conversational Agents (CA) or chatbots can be regarded as an example of intelligent Human-Computer Interaction [19] and can be defined as a "computer program designed to simulate conversation with human users, especially over the Internet" [20]. In that sense, they have been used in many different areas e.g., in Sales [21], Education [22], Gaming [23] or Health Care [24]. The developed chatbots differ not only in their application areas but also in their backend functionality and architecture. To compare chatbots nonetheless, scholars developed a categorization with four domains [25,26]. These domains are the following:

- **Knowledge domain** – open or closed knowledge
- **Service domain** – interpersonal; intrapersonal; inter-agent
- **Goals** – informative; chat-based; task-based
- **Response generation method** – rule-based; retrieval-based; generative

Based on the knowledge domain, a chatbot can either be open, and therefore able to answer a variety of questions unbound by the topic similar to a general-purpose assistant that can provide information on anything from weather to history, or closed, in which case the bot's knowledge base will be limited to a topic, set by the creator, such as a chatbot that can only exclusively talk about movies [27]. Additionally, one can distinguish chatbots by their service, which can be interpersonal to facilitate communication and provide services, while not being obliged to be individualistic (e.g. ChatGPT), intrapersonal to assist users with personal individual tasks becoming a companion (e.g. chat apps [25]), or inter-agent in which case the bots communicate with other software or bots to perform backend tasks (e.g. Alexa-Cortana [26]). Chatbots also differ based on their goal. This goal can be to inform users by providing information (informative), to chat with users and hold a conversation, or to fulfill certain tasks, like buying tickets, booking a flight, or helping with FAQs [28]. The last domain describes the chatbots' inner architectures and functionalities. They may be based on specific rules, limiting the chatbots' answers to predefined human-coded questions and answers, retrieval-based [29], or they can generate answers via machine learning models such as Large Language Models (LLMs) [22].

2.1 Conversational Agent Voting Advice Applications (CAVAAs)

Voting Advice Applications (VAAs) are interactive online tools developed to help citizens congregate pre-election information by asking them to position themselves on relevant statements about policy issues and matching their answers to those of parties and candidates [30,31]. While varying results contest some expected effects of VAAs on their users [32,33], scholars have demonstrated, that VAAs can help increase political knowledge [2,34–36], turnout [3], as well as foster political interest [4] and in some cases even influence a user's vote choice [37,38]. By now VAAs have become permanent partners of elections. Nevertheless, the main concept has not seen much change over the years.

To further improve the usability and positive effects of VAAs scholars introduced a groundbreaking new VAA design incorporating a chatbot [8–10]. The so-called Conversational Agent Voting Advice Application (CAVAA), gives users the possibility to ask a set of questions about the given VAA statements. This can be especially helpful considering that research has shown users tend not to respond to statements or select "neutral" if they have comprehension problems, thereby invalidating the final voting advice [11]. The support of the chatbot during the CAVAA can allow users to address such questions, making the election tool more useful and accessible to all users. Accordingly, scholars have indicated that CAVAAs lead to a significant change in users' political knowledge, with even higher positive effects than for standard VAAs [8]. Results further support this effect [12], while analyses also conclude that CAVAAs have no statistically significant effect on vote choice and show no different-sized effects for (CA)VAA user groups [12]. Nevertheless, these first findings demonstrate how the chatbot design could help VAAs become even more helpful.

So far most works focusing on CAVAAs deployed closed-domain and rule-based chatbots [8–10,12,13], that were limited in their answer capabilities to a predefined set of questions with human-coded answers. These specific questions have been found to cover the main comprehension problems users have when they answer the VAA statements [11], including questions about the semantics of a statement, statement explanations, the current affairs, the pros and cons, or specific party positions.

Questions beyond that or inquiries that deviated from the expected formulations could therefore not be answered by the chatbot leaving users without an answer [10,39]. While scholars have started to vigorously compare different chatbot modalities [9,13] including structured, semi-structured, and non-structured chatbots [10], the comparison of such architectures with an open-domain chatbot that can exceed its answer capabilities beyond the current set of rule-based question possibilities has so far not been attempted. This also leaves the question open to which extent such a chatbot design might influence the already observed effects on users.

In this paper, I aim to fill this gap, by introducing novel architectures to build an open and semi-open generative-based chatbot, based on open-source Large Language Models. Chatbots of such a design will be able to not only answer user questions independent of their formulation or topic but will also be able to generate the answers instead of relying on predefined human-coded answers. As a result, the chatbot will be able to address not only comprehension problems caused by the VAA statements but also other broader questions users may have about politics or the upcoming election. An additional advantage of a chatbot with this constitution is that users will be able to have more interactive conversations with the bot [40,41], instead of just being able to ask one question without more detailed follow-up questions. This higher degree of interactivity could further help increase the positive effects of CAVAAs and their usage [42–44].

3 Methodology and Design

3.1 Retrieval-Augmented Generation (RAG)

The main architecture of the proposed chatbot design is built on the combination of Retrieval-Augmented Generation (RAG) [14] and LLMs, the pipeline of which can be seen in Fig. 1. The RAG process starts with a user prompt initiating a search for relevant information in a database. This user prompt is first transformed into a numerical vector via an embedding model. The resulting vectorized user query is then utilized to search the database of likewise pre-encoded information entries. By using a similarity algorithm the system identifies which stored entries match the meaning of the user prompt the most. At the end of the retrieval process, the best matches are extracted from the database and given to the LLM as additional information context to better answer the user query. Following this method the LLM will generate its answers based on the factual data it is given to. This approach has multiple advantages. For one there is no need to perform time- and computation-consuming fine-tuning of LLM models. Furthermore, due to the connection to the additional database, one can limit possible hallucinations and grant a higher degree of factual accuracy. A chatbot with such an underlying design will therefore still be able to answer questions on various topics due to the LLM's static memory while being specific on the contents of the database fed to its dynamic memory[1].

3.2 RAG Data and the Wahl-O-Mat

To build a RAG-based approach one must decide upon a suitable database. A typical Voting Advice Application has to collect the party answers in order to match them to users. This database contains the answers and the reasoning of the parties. I propose utilizing this data source for the chatbot, which will significantly reduce the building cost since scholars will not have to manually analyze party manifestos to create answers. The resulting RAG database will then include $N_{\text{statements}} \times N_{\text{parties}}$ entries. Each entry, as depicted exemplary in

[1] In an LLM, static memory describes the fixed parameters learned during training, while dynamic memory includes the temporary, session-specific context, which in this case includes the chat history and the RAG matches.

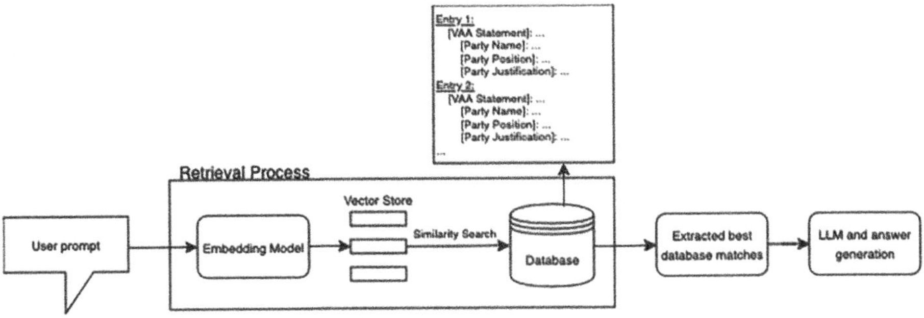

Fig. 1. Overview of the Retrieval-Augmented Generation (RAG) Pipeline for Contextual Response Generation.

Fig. 1, will include the VAA statement, the party name, the positions the party took so whether the party answered with agree, neutral, or disagree, and the party's justification (free text usually max 500 words) why the party took that position. Using such a preexisting database will make the construction of many CAVAAs more scalable and feasible while including all the important information such as party positions, advantages and disadvantages, and major problems[2].

To construct first chatbots with this design I relied on the 38 statements from the German 2021 Wahl-O-Mat[3] and the corresponding party responses. The Wahl-O-Mat is a German VAA deployed for Federal and State elections in Germany [45,46], modeled after the Dutch VAA StemWijzer [1]. The German VAA was developed on behalf of the Federal Agency for Civic Education (bpd) to help voters orient themselves before an election by informing them about party positions using a fixed set of statements. As a well-established political advisory tool in Germany the Wahl-O-Mat recorded more than 21 million visits for the last Federal election in 2021 [45,46].

For the database, I included the answers of the 6 major parties in Germany (CDU/CSU, SPD, FDP, AfD, Greens, Left). The other parties that also answered and participated in the VAA were not included because an increase in party numbers would also lead to an increase in necessary matches generated in the RAG process, which has been shown to result in consolidation strategy errors [47]. First pre-tests of the chatbot also demonstrated a higher error rate for more matches (error rate of 15%). As this paper primarily focuses on discussing possible ways of using Generative AI for CAVAAs and indicating the feasibility, I decided to proceed using the 6 major parties to reduce the error rate caused by the LLM's consolidation. The final database containing 228 entries was then

[2] Furthermore, the RAG approach also allows for additional data entries to be made by the creators. Therefore, one can easily add definitions or standpoints that are especially important, thereby adding new layers of factual dynamic knowledge to the chatbot.

[3] https://archiv.wahl-o-mat.de/bundestagswahl2021/app/main_app.html, last visited July 30. 2024.

embedded using the Cross English & German RoBERTa sentence embedding model [48]. As a language model, Mistralai's Mixtral 8×7B LLM [49] was used. This model combination was specifically chosen since it has been demonstrated to give good results for German chatbots with a similar architecture [22]. Furthermore, both models are open-source making the reproducibility of the chatbots easier[4]. The number of database matches to be given to the LLM was set to the maximum size of 8, to allow for the generation of summarizing questions while keeping the size low enough to minimize possible errors due to consolidation. With these configurations, the chatbot can be sorted into the chatbot domains as being open, interpersonal, informative/chat-based, and generative.

3.3 Addressing Inherent Political and Other Biases in LLM Answers

Limits and Disadvantages of Current GenAI Solutions. Despite many advantages GenAI can offer to improve current solutions such as closed-domain CAVAAs, there are also multiple limitations and ethical concerns such models face especially when intended to be used in a political and public space [50]. One of these concerns regards data privacy and security. Hence scholars have shown that GenAI could lead to the disclosure of a user's personal data (e.g. chat questions) [51–53] and faces high risk due to cyberattacks also aimed at gaining access to personal data [54,55]. In the context of a political chatbot data leakage would mean that users' personal political opinions or concerns could be made public thereby influencing elections and tool usage negatively. Furthermore, LLM hallucination poses another disadvantage leading to nonsensical outputs [56]. Another drawback is the lack of explainability when it comes to why the model gave this response [53]. Both these drawbacks, however, can be limited by the usage of RAG, which reduces the risk of hallucinations due to the additional information context and helps partially explain generated answers with the knowledge of which extra information was given to the LLM. Other GenAI concerns include the authenticity of LLMs [51] and prompt quality [53], as well as concerns about GenAI aiding in the erosion of public trust [57]. From an infrastructural point of view, one also has to note the immense server and electricity demand of GenAI models, taking a toll on greenhouse gas reduction objectives [58,59]. One of the major hurdles when using LLMs for political conversations is the risk of political biases caused by the open domain. Consequently, Hartmann et al. [15] analyzed how Open AI's ChatGPT might answer VAA statements. Their results show a clear left-libertarian ideology. These left-leaning tendencies have also been confirmed for other LLMs [16,17] and are most likely developed during the training (i.e. due to poor data quality [52]) of such models [60].

---

[4] Note that while the RoBERTa sentence embedding model is designed specifically for the German case, there are many other embedding models for additional languages that can be easily used for CAVAA bots in different geopolitical contexts. With such adapted language-specific models there should be no transfer limitations from the German case to others.

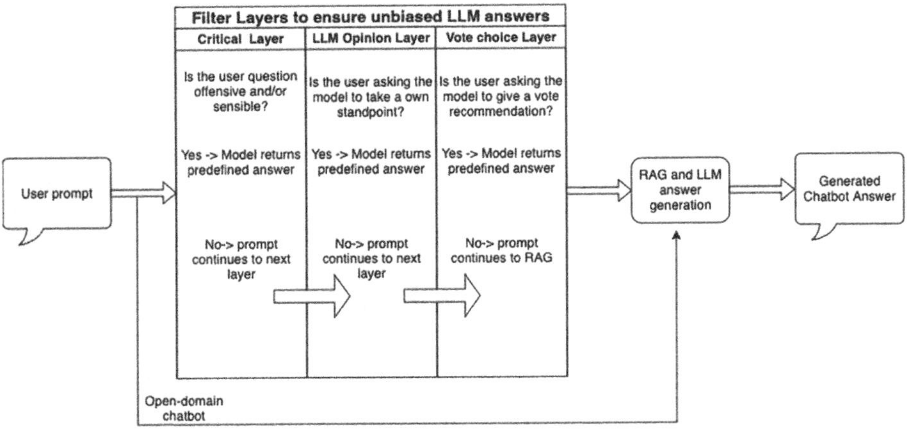

Fig. 2. Architecture for building a Generative AI chatbot for CAVAAs. Note: The main architecture is based on combining RAG and LLMs. For the semi-open chatbot priority-ordered (*broad* → *narrow*) filter layers are included. The open-domain chatbot skips these layers.

Methods to Address Limitations. This work will not be able to find solutions for every limitation LLMs currently face. However as the intended chatbot will be used in a political context the major problem of political biases should be addressed as the most imminent risk when using such a chatbot. Hence while political biases in LLMs might be acceptable for some chatbot applications, in different fields, they pose a risk of influencing CAVAA users' vote choice or turnout and might raise trust and neutrality concerns in (CA)VAAs. To exclude these biases I propose a second version of the discussed chatbot architecture that includes censoring for specific prompt types, resulting in a semi-open chatbot design. In the context of CAVAAs as political education tools, one can define three specific prompt types in which a freely generated chatbot answer might have a negative influence on users or bias the results and should therefore be addressed. I categorize the three prompt types the following:

- **Critical Prompts** – The chatbot should not answer prompts that are rude, discriminating, or of a sensitive nature. E.g. *"All party members are [swear word]."*.
- **LLM Opinion Prompts** – A CAVAA chatbot should not show its opinion about the statements or parties, as this opinion could influence the user's own opinion [7].
- **Vote Choice Prompts** – Similar to the second prompt type, the chatbot should never give a vote choice recommendation. The only valid recommendation should be the matching with the parties at the end of the (CA)VAA.

To handle prompts that fall in one of these three categories I will use the topic avoidance strategy [61]. Given this method, I will put a set of filter layers ahead of the answer generation. Should any of the layers be triggered the model will answer with a fitting predefined answer thereby avoiding a generated LLM answer to the prompt. The design of these layers and the answer generation is visualized in Fig. 2.

The first filter layer checks whether or not the prompt is critical. This is simultaneously the most difficult layer since some sensitive topics might be related to an election while others are not. For this task, the user prompt is given to the Mixtral LLM which is instructed to evaluate whether a prompt is critical or not. This method allows for a broad coverage of censoring. If the prompt is cleared it is given to the second filter layer where a custom Natural Language Processing (NLP) method determines if the prompt asks the LLM to take a standpoint on something. In the last layer, the prompt is again given to the Mixtral LLM to determine if the user's inquiry was that the LLM should tell them whom to vote for. The filter layers are ordered to cover the broader Critical Prompts first and then check the narrower prompt types for LLM Opinion Prompts and Vote Choice Prompts. Only if the prompt is cleared through all three filter layers it is given to the RAG process and an answer is generated. Should the prompt fail one of the layers the model will output a, for each layer differently formulated, predefined answer. With these custom filter layers in place, the semi-open chatbot should generate unbiased and neutral answers to appropriate user prompts, overcoming the disadvantage of the open chatbot design.

To test, evaluate, and demonstrate both the open and the semi-open chatbot designs before they can be used and inputted into a CAVAA, I deployed two app spaces on Huggingface. For this purpose, I named the open chatbot AVAH (Artificial Voting Advice Helper) and the semi-open chatbot AVAH2.0. Here users can either select a VAA statement and ask a question about it or ask a general question without selecting a statement.

3.4 Evaluation Method

Since both chatbots, as GenAI tools, semi-freely generate their answers, instead of relying on predefined human-coded answers their answer behavior must be evaluated even more rigorously than the previous CAVAA bots to ensure their ideal functionality before they can be implemented in an actual CAVAA. Therefore I will conduct a two-stage evaluation in this paper to assess the chatbots' answers and merit.

First Stage Evaluation Method. In the first stage, the focus is on how the chatbots answer a wide-ranging set of possible user prompts. For this, both chatbots were asked a set of 261 prompts. The prompts were sorted into ten categories, including the five question types current CAVAA can answer (word semantics; statement explanation; current affairs; pros and cons; party position), as well as prompts about general political questions such as *"How does the election work?"*, prompts about party ideologies and prompts falling in the three problematic categories (critical; LLM opinion; vote intention) to test how the filters applied to the semi-open chatbot perform.

The generated answers were then independently evaluated by three coders[5]. As a metric a 3-point score was used, ranging from 1 (the answer is correct), 0 (the answer is not perfect but still answers the question) to −1 (the answer is incorrect). This metric was chosen since including more categories would increase the coding complexity and introduce possible biases [62]. In addition to the two proposed chatbots, I included a Baseline model, that shows how well current rule-based CAVAAs would answer the test prompts[6].

Second Stage Evaluation Method. In the second stage, I aim to test the chatbot answers in a broader more diverse way and additionally measure the chatbot experience. As a result of this, an expert survey of German VAA Creators, relying on a convenience sample, was performed to determine how the VAA experts would like and accept the chatbot. The expert survey was split into three parts. In a pre-survey respondents were asked about their demographics and expert status. Afterward, they were redirected to the online version of the semi-open chatbot[7], where they could ask as many questions as they wanted. In the last step, users were then asked to answer a set of questions including TAM items. The Technology Acceptance Model (TAM) by Davis [18,63] is an established method for determining the acceptance of information systems and has previously also been used to evaluate the acceptance of CAVAA modalities [10]. The Model consists of four different main aspects; Perceived ease of use (PEU) and usefulness (PU), Attitudes towards using (A), and Behavioral intention (BI). Each aspect is computed using a set of statements measured using a 7-point Likert scale, ranging from strong disagreement to strong agreement. All statements are based on [10,64]. PEU was measured using four items including "*It was easy for me to use the chatbot.*". The usefulness of the chatbots consisted of seven statements such as "*The chatbot makes it easier for me to answer the Wahl-O-Mat statements compared to a regular Wahl-O-Mat without a chatbot.*" [10, p. 169]. A user's Attitude toward using the chatbot was operationalized with two items (e.g. "*Using this chatbot is a good idea.*") and the Behavioral intention with three items (e.g. "*I would keep using this chatbot in the future.*"). The gathered data from the expert survey should then grant additional insights into the acceptance of the proposed chatbot and also what needs to be improved before the chatbots can be implemented in a CAVAA and be used in an actual election.

[5] All three coders have a background in political science and were given detailed instructions to minimize possible coder biases [62]. Coding was done independently.

[6] Note that the scores for the Baseline are based on the reports made by Kamoen and Liebrecht [10] and McCartan [39], as there is no available German version to be used. The CAVAA version used is the non-structured CAVAA, as this is the version where users can freely ask questions.

[7] To reduce the complexity for survey participants only the semi-open chatbot was tested. The semi-open chatbot was chosen over the open version to further test the filter layers and since the results from the first evaluation stage concluded that the semi-open chatbot performed significantly better than the open bot.

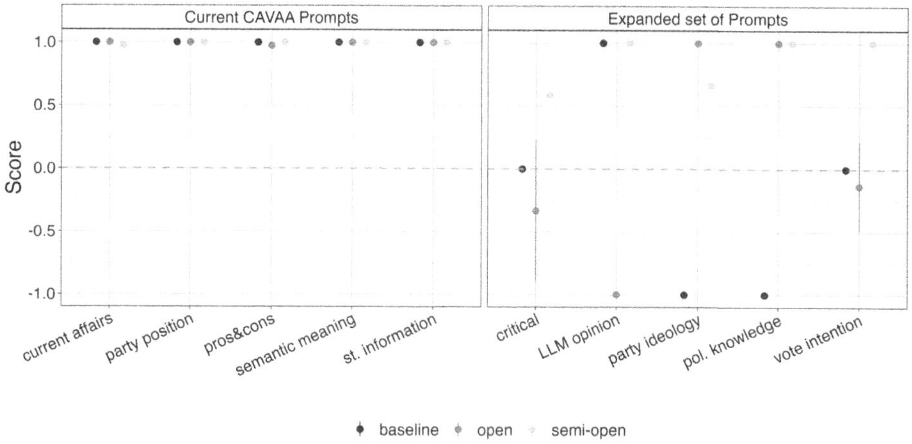

Fig. 3. Chatbot performance for different prompt types. Note: Values averaged over the prompt types. Baseline Model based on current rule-based non-structured CAVAA bots. 95% Confidence Intervals included as a measure of uncertainty. The dashed line marks the point where answers are still acceptable.

Second Stage Descriptives. The expert survey was collected from August 23rd until September 4th, 2024 using the Lime software [65]. In total 13 VAA experts participated in the survey. 76.92% of which were male (N = 10), while 23.08% were female (N = 3). The average user age was 34.92 (SD = 9.78). The users asked a total of 91 diverse questions, resulting in roughly 7 questions per expert. Between the experts, there was no repetition of the same questions. Overall, 27.47% of the questions fell into the category of semantic meaning, followed by 17.58% of the questions addressing party positions and comparisons (13.19% current affairs, 13.19% pros&cons, 9.89% critical, 9.89% pol. knowledge, 5.49% st. information, 3.30% LLM opinion). Regarding these distributions, it is important to mention that they are not representative of normal user groups. For such a conclusion, an additional study collecting how actual users utilize the chatbot is needed.

4 Results

4.1 Stage 1 Comparative Results

Utilizing Krippendorf's Alpha [66,67] as a measure of congruence between the three coders revealed an Intercoder Reliability (ICR) of 0.86, indicating a strong overall agreement among the coders. The coder answers were then averaged together and rounded to generate the final scores. Figure 3 visualizes the performance of the two developed chatbots and the Baseline Model, grouped and averaged over the prompt categories.

Current CAVAA Prompt Types. Taking a first look at the prompt types that current CAVAA bots have been coded to answer, demonstrates that both the open and the semi-open chatbot can match the performance of the rule-based Baseline. These results validate the approach, the chosen data source, and also show that GenAI can be a reliable alternative to human-coded answers while reducing the time and complexity of developing the chatbot. One issue scholars have reported occurring sometimes with rule-based CAVAAs is that the intent recognition can not correctly categorize user questions because they use unexpected words or question types [10,39]. Here the proposed chatbots can offer a significant improvement. In Germany for example many people still call the Left party (DIE LINKE), PDS, which was the party's name before a merger [68]. For a rule-based CAVAA bot scholars would have to think of such things and include them in the intent recognition, otherwise the chatbot would not recognize the question correctly. Using the proposed architecture, however, the chatbot knows of the party's history since it is in its static memory from pre-training the LLM and therefore must not be included in its dynamic memory via the RAG process. Below is what would happen if one asked the chatbots such a question:

> **User Prompt:** *What is the PDS's stance on this?*
> **Chatbot Answer:** *The PDS no longer exists since 2007; it merged with the WASG to form the party DIE LINKE. DIE LINKE supports advancing the planned phase-out of coal power from 2038. [...]*[8]

One can see that the chatbot correctly identifies the request for the PDS's position by giving users the position of the Left while also explaining why the PDS technically does not exist anymore. Likewise, the two chatbots do not need specific entries of advantages and disadvantages since they can easily extract this information from the party justification.

Beyond Current CAVAA Prompt Types. The static knowledge of the chatbots also allows for broader political questions. As such one can see from Fig. 3 that the chatbots can easily answer general political questions users might have like the following example:

> **User Prompt:** *How does the Bundestag election work?*
> **Chatbot Answer:** *The Bundestag election in Germany is a mixed-member proportional representation system. Each voter has two votes: the first vote is for electing a direct candidate in their electoral district, while the second vote is for choosing a party at the regional level. The total number of seats in the Bundestag consists of those held by the direct candidates who received the most votes in their districts and additional seats allocated*

[8] Answer was asked in the context of the statement: The planned exit from coal-fired power generation for the year 2038 is to be brought forward. Original German: Der für das Jahr 2038 geplante Ausstieg aus der Kohleverstromung soll vorgezogen werden.

based on the proportional share of the second votes each party receives. The party that secures the most seats is tasked with forming the government, and its leader typically becomes the Federal Chancellor.

The open-domain chatbot is also able to sort the parties in order of their political ideology ranging from left to right. Despite that, this kind of prompt has proven to raise difficulties for the semi-open chatbot. Here the bot is not performing as well as the open-domain chatbot. The reason for this is that the question about the AfD's ideology triggers the first filter layer, while all other parties pass through. This further supports results of LLMs being more left-leaning [15–17] and categorizing right-wing parties as overall sensitive and discriminating[9]. The LLM's left-leaning ideology again surfaces when the open-domain chatbot is asked to answer the statements by itself. The results of the generated answers were then transferred to the Wahl-O-Mat to establish a party match score. This party scoring is displayed in Fig. 4. With 78.90% the chatbot has the highest

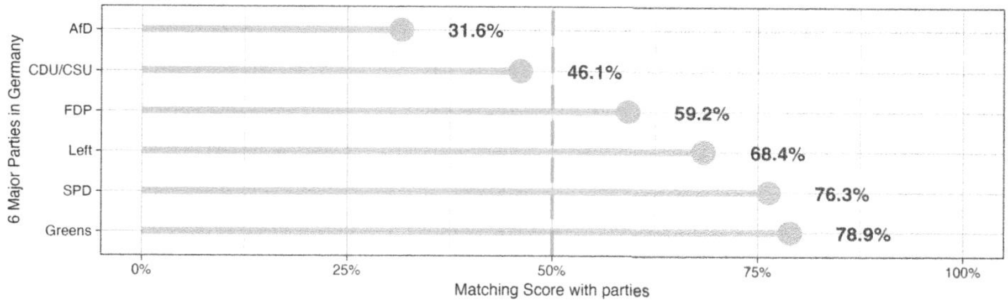

Fig. 4. VAA results using the position stances voiced by the open-domain chatbot when asked how it would answer the VAA statements. The dashed line reports a party match of 50%.

consensus with the Greens followed by the Social Democrats and the Left. The chatbot agrees the least with the AfD and CDU/CSU. This again demonstrates the more Green and left-leaning ideology of LLMs and validates the need for filtering out the LLM's opinion which Fig. 3 shows to work significantly better for the semi-open chatbot, which does not tell users how it would position itself on the VAA statements. Furthermore, the semi-open chatbot is also successful in handling vote intention prompts and therefore, does not tell users whom to vote for but rather informs them to decide on whom to vote for themselves. Looking at prompts that fall into the category of critical and sensitive prompts one can also see that the filter layer improves the result significantly. Nevertheless, with an average performance score of just more than 0.5, the result indicates that the

[9] This issue was partially fixed for the second stage. Nevertheless, it also indicates that the filter layers need further improvement, to avoid introducing new biases to the chatbot.

critical filter layer still needs further fine-tuning to not only handle rude speech but also sensitive topics.

Overall, the analysis of the first evaluation stage has indicated that the proposed chatbot architecture can not only handle typical CAVAA questions but exceed such prompts to include broader political knowledge questions. Furthermore, the results validate the proposed filter layers to minimize the LLM's political bias, while the layers should be further fine-tuned to improve the generated answers even more. Therefore the semi-open chatbot appears to be a better option than the open-domain chatbot without filter layers.

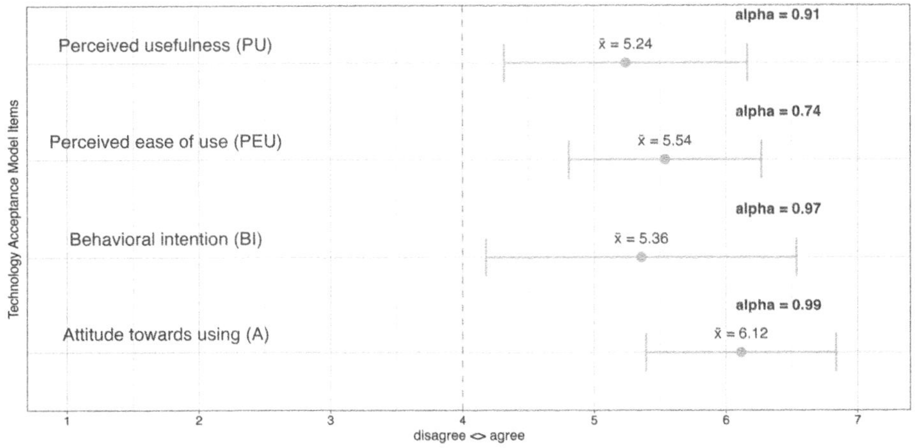

Fig. 5. Overall acceptance of the semi-open chatbot utilizing the Technology Acceptance Model (TAM). Cronbach's alpha is included to control for internal reliability. 95% Confidence Intervals have been used as a measure of uncertainty. The dashed line marks the point where scores are still acceptable.

4.2 Stage 2 Survey Insights

Following the first-stage evaluation, I will continue to discuss the opinions and results generated by the VAA expert survey (N = 13) in which the experts tested the semi-open chatbot.

Overall Performance. 84.62% of the survey respondents have indicated that they believe that VAAs need an update via new features, supporting the main argument that VAAs need to evolve to stay relevant. Furthermore, the majority of experts also indicated the importance of ensuring data privacy and political correctness for chatbots in political advisory tools. The analysis of the chatbot's answers to the experts' questions, further supports the results from the first stage evaluation. As such, the chatbot's filter layers successfully worked and did not recommend any parties, and refrained from showing a political position or answering sensitive or rude inquiries. This is also the way the experts felt based on their positions when asked about the chatbot's behavior. Despite that, the analysis also indicated that the filter layers might be too extensive sometimes flagging unproblematic questions. Therefore the filter layers should be examined again to improve the chatbot's performance and filtering further. Nevertheless, the experts agreed with an average value of 5.31 (SD = 1.70), that the chatbot could help increase a user's political knowledge. The expert survey additionally generated valuable insights for new chatbot features. Hence one expert recommended the option to include easy language for users to choose to break down political concepts even more. First empirical results from CAVAA studies show that such a measure could especially help "lower politically sophisticated users" [13, p. 4].

Technology Acceptance Model. Looking at the overall acceptance and usefulness of the proposed chatbot, depicted in Fig. 5, the experts' positions show sufficient internal reliability for the TAM categories, measured using Cronbach's alpha [69,70], to proceed with further analysis. All four TAM perspectives show positive opinions above the middle value of 4. With an average of 5.24 (SD = 1.53) the Perceived usefulness of the chatbot is quite good and matches previous results of rule-based CAVAAs [10]. The Perceived ease of use concludes with an even higher average value of 5.54 (SD = 1.21), while the Behavioral intention depicts an average of 5.36 (SD = 1.95). The experts' Attitudes towards using such a chatbot demonstrate the highest distribution with an average value of 6.12 (SD = 1.19). All in all more than 75% of the expert survey respondents would rather use a VAA that included the proposed chatbot than use a normal VAA and believe that the chatbot would make existing VAAs more effective. This overall positive sentiment is also captured by the open-ended question with expert answers like this: "*The chatbot engages very well with statements and can provide useful background knowledge and explain the connections between the statements. This is much more personalized than traditional voting aids*"[10].

5 Conclusion

This paper sought to test the feasibility and merit of building and using a GenAI-based chatbot for the currently only rule-based closed-domain bots of Conversational Agent Voting Advice Applications. Such a chatbot would make the generation of CAVAAs less time- and resource-consuming while expanding the possible questions users could ask. For this reason, two chatbot architectures were introduced, both utilizing Retrieval-Augmented Generation and Large Language Models. While the first chatbot can answer any question the author developed custom filter layers to build a second semi-open chatbot to prevent politically biased or influential answers. Both chatbots were then tested in a two-stage evaluation.

[10] Translated from the original German.

Insights. The results demonstrated that the proposed chatbots are able to answer the five common CAVAA question types. At the same time, they are also able to answer other questions, concerning the election, parties, or other political topics. Furthermore, an expert survey of German VAA Creators subjected the semi-open chatbot to more rigorous testing resulting in additional insights. As such the survey analysis has shown that the chatbot can handle even different formulated user prompts. Respondents also voice high levels of acceptance and usefulness of the chatbot, with more than 75% stating, that a CAVAA with such a chatbot would make VAAs more effective. One challenge that the evaluation has revealed is the functionality of the proposed filter layers. Here results identified room for improvement as well as the chance that by using LLMs in the filter layers might have introduced new biases, especially towards more right-leaning parties.

Therefore the results of the two-stage evaluation show the merit and feasibility of the developed chatbots and the potential of using GenAI in CAVAAs. Nevertheless, the analyses also indicated that to guarantee bias-free answers further fine-tuning of the used filter layers is needed before such chatbots can be used in CAVAAs.

Recommendations. This paper has demonstrated how GenAI can be used to benefit (CA)VAAs, while also showing its feasibility and prevailing challenges. Even though the results have validated the proposed architecture utilizing RAG and LLMs, I recommend further fine-tuning the RAG process to eliminate consolidation errors so that there is no limit to possible matches. Furthermore, future research should reinvestigate the developed filter layers to improve their performance. For this, I recommend collecting a large enough dataset of possible user queries upon which custom classification models can be trained so that LLMs do not need to be used in the filtering process. Additionally enhancing the proposed chatbot with more features such as an "easy language feature" would benefit the overall usability.

After these improvements have been made I believe it is crucial to perform an extended study with normal user groups, on the effects of the proposed GenAI chatbots on political knowledge, interest, and other factors, as well as executing further modality studies to compare CAVAA bots. The results of such empirical studies will help improve the GenAI CAVAAs and also answer important research questions as to their usability and effectiveness. As a result, one can see that there is still work to be done mainly on fine-tuning the chatbot safety measures and addressing current GenAI limitations and ethical concerns.

And although it may take time to overcome all the current limitations of GenAI bots to ensure they are safe for widespread use in a political context, this initial study has demonstrated that the path to leveraging GenAI chatbots in political education and informational tools may not be as "long" as previously anticipated [7, p. 7]. With further development, chatbots based on the proposed architecture could eventually be implemented in a real CAVAA, reaching millions of voters in the years to come.

References

1. De Graaf, J.: The irresistible rise of the stemwijzer. In: Cedroni, L., Garzia, D. (eds.) Voting Advice Applications in Europe: The State of the Art, pp. 35–46 (2010)
2. Garzia, D., Marschall, S.: Research on voting advice applications: state of the art and future directions. Policy Internet **8**(4), 376–390 (2016)
3. Gemenis, K., Rosema, M.: Voting advice applications and electoral turnout. Elect. Stud. **36**, 281–289 (2014)
4. Fivaz, J., Nadig, G.: Impact of voting advice applications (VAAS) on voter turnout and their potential use for civic education. Policy Internet **2**(4), 167–200 (2010)
5. Uyttendaele, L.: The effects of voting advice applications (VAAS) on pre-voting citizens' political trust. ECPR Joint Sessions, Virtual Event, pp. 17–28, May 2021
6. Cammaerts, B., Bruter, M., Banaji, S., Harrison, S., Anstead, N.: Youth participation in democratic life (2016)
7. Gemenis, K.: Artificial intelligence and voting advice applications. Front. Polit. Sci. **6** (2024)
8. Kamoen, N., Liebrecht, C.: I need a CAVAA: how conversational agent voting advice applications (CAVAAs) affect users' political knowledge and tool experience. Front. Artif. Intell. **5** (2022)
9. Liebrecht, C., Kamoen, N., Aerts, C.: Voice your opinion! Young voters' usage and perceptions of a text-based, voice-based and text-voice combined conversational agent voting advice application (CAVAA). In: Følstad, A., et al. (eds.) CONVERSATIONS 2022. LNCS, vol. 13815, pp. 34–49. Springer, Cham (2023). https://doi.org/10.1007/978-3-031-25581-6_3
10. Kamoen, N., McCartan, T., Liebrecht, C.: Conversational agent voting advice applications: a comparison between a structured, semi-structured, and non-structured chatbot design for communicating with voters about political issues (2022)
11. Kamoen, N., Holleman, B.: I don't get it. Response difficulties in answering political attitude statements in voting advice applications. In: Survey Research Methods, vol. 11, pp. 125–140 (2017)
12. van Zanten, N., Boumans, R.: Voting assistant chatbot for increasing voter turnout at local elections: an exploratory study. In: Følstad, A., et al. (eds.) CONVERSATIONS 2023. LNCS, vol. 14524, pp. 3–22. Springer, Cham (2024). https://doi.org/10.1007/978-3-031-54975-5_1
13. Hankel, S., Liebrecht, C., Kamoen, N.: 'Hi chatbot, let's talk about politics!' examining the impact of verbal anthropomorphism in conversational agent voting advice applications (CAVAAs) on higher and lower politically sophisticated users. Interact. Comput., iwae031 (2024)
14. Gao, Y., et al.: Retrieval-augmented generation for large language models: a survey (2024). https://arxiv.org/abs/2312.10997
15. Hartmann, J., Schwenzow, J., Witte, M.: The political ideology of conversational AI: converging evidence on chatGPT's pro-environmental, left-libertarian orientation. arXiv preprint arXiv:2301.01768 (2023)
16. Bang, Y., Lee, N., Ishii, E., Madotto, A., Fung, P.: Assessing political prudence of open-domain chatbots (2021). https://arxiv.org/abs/2106.06157
17. Bang, Y., Chen, D., Lee, N., Fung, P.: Measuring political bias in large language models: what is said and how it is said (2024). https://arxiv.org/abs/2403.18932

18. Davis, F.D., Bagozzi, R.P., Warshaw, P.R.: User acceptance of computer technology: a comparison of two theoretical models. Manage. Sci. **35**(8), 982–1003 (1989)
19. Bansal, H., Khan, R.: A review paper on human computer interaction. Int. J. Adv. Res. Comput. Sci. Softw. Eng. **8**(4), 53 (2018)
20. Lexico: Definition of chatbot in English by Lexico dictionaries (2024). https://www.lexico.com/en/definition/chatbot. Accessed 28 June 2024
21. Hanschmann, L., Gnewuch, U., Maedche, A.: Saleshat: a LLM-based social robot for human-like sales conversations. In: Følstad, A., et al. (eds.) CONVERSATIONS 2023. LNCS, vol. 14524, pp. 61–76. Springer, Cham (2023). https://doi.org/10.1007/978-3-031-54975-5_4
22. Dieing, T.I., Scheffler, M., Cohausz, L.: Enhancing chatbot-assisted study program orientation. In: Proceedings of DELFI Workshops 2024. Gesellschaft für Informatik e.V. (2024)
23. Cox, S.R., Ooi, W.T.: Conversational interactions with NPCs in LLM-driven gaming: guidelines from a content analysis of player feedback. In: Følstad, A., et al. (eds.) CONVERSATIONS 2023. LNCS, vol. 14524, pp. 167–184. Springer, Cham (2023). https://doi.org/10.1007/978-3-031-54975-5_10
24. Sharma, D., Kaushal, S., Kumar, H., Gainder, S.: Chatbots in healthcare: challenges, technologies and applications. In: 2022 4th International Conference on Artificial Intelligence and Speech Technology (AIST), pp. 1–6. IEEE (2022)
25. Adamopoulou, E., Moussiades, L.: An overview of chatbot technology. In: Maglogiannis, I., Iliadis, L., Pimenidis, E. (eds.) AIAI 2020. IAICT, vol. 584, pp. 373–383. Springer, Cham (2020). https://doi.org/10.1007/978-3-030-49186-4_31
26. Nimavat, K., Champaneria, T.: Chatbots: an overview types, architecture, tools and future possibilities. Int. J. Sci. Res. Dev **5**(7), 1019–1024 (2017)
27. Su, H., et al.: MovieChats: chat like humans in a closed domain. In: Webber, B., Cohn, T., He, Y., Liu, Y. (eds.) Proceedings of the 2020 Conference on Empirical Methods in Natural Language Processing (EMNLP), pp. 6605–6619. Association for Computational Linguistics, Online (2020). https://aclanthology.org/2020.emnlp-main.535
28. Kucherbaev, P., Bozzon, A., Houben, G.J.: Human-aided bots. IEEE Internet Comput. **22**(6), 36–43 (2018)
29. Wu, Y., Wu, W., Xing, C., Zhou, M., Li, Z.: Sequential matching network: a new architecture for multi-turn response selection in retrieval-based chatbots (2017). https://arxiv.org/abs/1612.01627
30. Da Silva, F.F., Garzia, D.: Voting advice applications. In: Carter, N., Keith, D., Sindre, G.M., Vasilopoulou, S. (eds.) The Routledge Handbook of Political Parties. Routledge International Handbooks, pp. 450–465. Routledge, New York (2023). https://www.taylorfrancis.com/chapters/edit/10.4324/9780429263859-47/voting-advice-applications-frederico-ferreira-da-silva-diego-garzia
31. Garzia, D., Marschall, S.: Voting advice applications. In: Thompson, W.R. (ed.) Oxford Research Encyclopedia of Politics. Oxford Research Encyclopedias, Oxford University Press, New York (2019)
32. Enyedi, Z.: The influence of voting advice applications on preferences, loyalties and turnout: an experimental study. Polit. Stud. **64**(4), 1000–1015 (2015)
33. Munzert, S., Ramirez-Ruiz, S.: Meta-analysis of the effects of voting advice applications. Polit. Commun. **38**(6), 691–706 (2021)
34. Kamoen, N., Holleman, B., Krouwel, A., van de Pol, J., de Vreese, C.: The effect of voting advice applications on political knowledge and vote choice. Ir. Polit. Stud. **30**(4), 595–618 (2015)

35. Schultze, M.: Effekte des wahl-o-mat auf politisches wissen über parteipositionen. ZPol Zeitschrift für Politikwissenschaft **22**(3), 367–391 (2013)
36. Westle, B., Begemann, C., Rütter, A.: The "Wahl-O-Mat" in the course of the German federal election 2013 – effects of a German VAA on users' election-relevant political knowledge. Zeitschrift für Politikwissenschaft **24**(4), 389–426 (2014)
37. Israel, J., Marschall, S., Schultze, M.: Cognitive dissonance and the effects of voting advice applications on voting behaviour: evidence from the European elections 2014. J. Elections Public Opinion Parties **27**(1), 56–74 (2017)
38. Kleinnijenhuis, J., van de Pol, J., van Hoof, A.M., Krouwel, A.P.: Genuine effects of vote advice applications on party choice: filtering out factors that affect both the advice obtained and the vote. Party Polit. **25**(3), 291–302 (2019)
39. McCartan, T., Liebrecht, C.: Conversational agent voting advice applications (CAVAAs). Master's thesis (2021)
40. Dam, S.K., Hong, C.S., Qiao, Y., Zhang, C.: A complete survey on LLM-based AI chatbots (2024). https://arxiv.org/abs/2406.16937
41. Gao, Y., Sheng, T., Xiang, Y., Xiong, Y., Wang, H., Zhang, J.: Chat-REC: towards interactive and explainable LLMs-augmented recommender system (2023). https://arxiv.org/abs/2303.14524
42. Kim, Y., Lee, H.: The rise of chatbots in political campaigns: the effects of conversational agents on voting intention. Int. J. Hum.-Comput. Interact. **39**(20), 3984–3995 (2023)
43. Bialkova, S.: How may i help you? Chatbots implementation in marketing. In: European Marketing Academy Conference, EMAC 2022, pp. 24–27 (2022)
44. Bialkova, S.: I Want to Talk to You: Chatbot Marketing Integration, pp. 23–36. Springer, Wiesbaden (2023). https://doi.org/10.1007/978-3-658-40429-1_2
45. Gröf, H., Rimmek, A.: Wahl-O-Mat. eine digitale orientierungshilfe für wählerinnen und wähler. GWP–Gesellschaft. Wirtschaft. Politik **52**(3) (2003)
46. Marschall, S.: Der wahl-o-mat als instrument der gesellschaftsberatung - potenziale und grenzen. Z. Polit. **2**(3), 485 (2009)
47. Barnett, S., Kurniawan, S., Thudumu, S., Brannelly, Z., Abdelrazek, M.: Seven failure points when engineering a retrieval augmented generation system. In: Proceedings of the IEEE/ACM 3rd International Conference on AI Engineering-Software Engineering for AI, pp. 194–199 (2024)
48. May, P.: Cross English & German roberta for sentence embeddings (2020). https://huggingface.co/T-Systems-onsite/cross-en-de-roberta-sentence-transformer
49. Jiang, A.Q., et al.: Mixtral of experts (2024). https://arxiv.org/abs/2401.04088
50. Beltran, M.A., Ruiz Mondragon, M.I., Han, S.H.: Comparative analysis of generative AI risks in the public sector. In: Proceedings of the 25th Annual International Conference on Digital Government Research, pp. 610–617 (2024)
51. Walkowiak, E., MacDonald, T.: Generative AI and the workforce: what are the risks? Available at SSRN (2023)
52. Wach, K., et al.: The dark side of generative artificial intelligence: a critical analysis of controversies and risks of chatGPT. Entrep. Bus. Econ. Rev. **11**(2), 7–30 (2023)
53. Fui-Hoon Nah, F., Zheng, R., Cai, J., Siau, K., Chen, L.: Generative AI and chatGPT: applications, challenges, and AI-human collaboration (2023)
54. Huang, K., Zhang, F., Li, Y., Wright, S., Kidambi, V., Manral, V.: Security and privacy concerns in chatGPT. In: Huang, K., Wang, Y., Zhu, F., Chen, X., Xing, C. (eds.) Beyond AI: ChatGPT, Web3, and the Business Landscape of Tomorrow, pp. 297–328. Springer, Cham (2023). https://doi.org/10.1007/978-3-031-45282-6_11
55. Kalla, D., Kuraku, S.: Advantages, disadvantages and risks associated with chatGPT and AI on cybersecurity. J. Emerg. Technol. Innov. Res. **10**(10) (2023)

56. Pasca, M.G., Arcese, G.: ChatGPT between opportunities and challenges: an empirical study in Italy. TQM J. (ahead-of-print) (2024)
57. Huang, K., Ma, W.: Legal and ethics responsibility of chatGPT. In: Huang, K., Wang, Y., Zhu, F., Chen, X., Xing, C. (eds.) Beyond AI: ChatGPT, Web3, and the Business Landscape of Tomorrow, pp. 329–353. Springer, Cham (2023). https://doi.org/10.1007/978-3-031-45282-6_12
58. Wood, M.: High current density power modules mitigate the environmental impact of power-intensive genAI. IEEE Power Electron. Mag. **11**(2), 20–25 (2024)
59. Berthelot, A., Caron, E., Jay, M., Lefèvre, L.: Estimating the environmental impact of generative-AI services using an LCA-based methodology. Procedia CIRP **122**, 707–712 (2024)
60. Duan, Y.: The large language model (LLM) bias evaluation (age bias). DIKWP Research Group International Standard Evaluation. DOI 10 (2024)
61. Xu, J., Ju, D., Li, M., Boureau, Y.L., Weston, J., Dinan, E.: Recipes for safety in open-domain chatbots (2021). https://arxiv.org/abs/2010.07079
62. Van Enschot, R., et al.: Taming our wild data: on intercoder reliability in discourse research. Dutch J. Appl. Linguist. **13** (2024)
63. Davis, F.D.: Perceived usefulness, perceived ease of use, and user acceptance of information technology. MIS Q., 319–340 (1989)
64. Ahn, T., Ryu, S., Han, I.: The impact of web quality and playfulness on user acceptance of online retailing. Inf. Manage. **44**(3), 263–275 (2007). https://www.sciencedirect.com/science/article/pii/S0378720607000225
65. GmbH, L.: LimeSurvey: An Open Source Survey Tool. LimeSurvey GmbH, Hamburg (2024). http://www.limesurvey.org
66. Hayes, A.F., Krippendorff, K.: Answering the call for a standard reliability measure for coding data. Commun. Methods Meas. **1**(1), 77–89 (2007). https://doi.org/10.1080/19312450709336664
67. Krippendorff, K.: Content Analysis: An Introduction to Its Methodology. Sage Publications, Thousand Oaks (2018)
68. Neu, V.: (die) linke. Handwörterbuch des politischen Systems der Bundesrepublik Deutschland, pp. 598–606 (2021)
69. Cronbach, L.J.: Coefficient alpha and the internal structure of tests. Psychometrika **16**(3), 297–334 (1951)
70. Armentano, M.G., Christensen, I., Schiaffino, S.: Applying the technology acceptance model to evaluation of recommender systems. Polibits **51**, 73–79 (2015)

First Aid for Europe – A Study on the Impact of Digital Voting Assistants on Young Adults During the Elections for the European Parliament in 2024

Nina van Zanten and Roel Boumans(✉)

Faculty of Social Sciences, Radboud University, Nijmegen, Netherlands
roel.boumans@ru.nl

Abstract. Traditional digital voting assistants are online survey tools that help voters make a voting choice. Nevertheless, many young adults do not vote. Therefore, a study was conducted, in which two new types of digital voting assistants for young adults were compared: a voting assistant chatbot versus a voting assistant avatar. A small-scale experiment (N = 30) was used to investigate the influence of these voting assistants on the political knowledge and voting intention of young adults shortly before the election for the European Parliament in June 2024. In addition, the voting assistants were evaluated for user-friendliness, entertainment value and the extent to which young adults trusted the voting assistants. The results show that after interacting with both voting assistants, participants have more political knowledge and a higher, general voting intention. The increase in political knowledge is greater for participants with less political interest. In line with expectations, participants find the chatbot more user-friendly than the avatar. Participants also find the chatbot more entertaining and have more trust in the chatbot than in the avatar. This research shows that new forms of voting assistants may increase the political knowledge and voting intention of young adults. In this way, this research provides early insights into an important area of research, namely the potential contribution of these tools to an increase of the chance that young adults will actually cast their vote, and through this contribute to the strength and representativeness of the European Parliament.

Keywords: Digital Voting Assistant · Chatbot · Avatar · Elections · Politics

1 Introduction

The European Union is facing major challenges. The war in Ukraine has been raging on the European continent for two years, migration policy remains a stumbling block and the course of the Green Deal was at stake in the recent elections for the European Parliament [1, 2]. The desire for a strong, supported European Parliament is perhaps greater than ever. However, the turnout of European citizens in the European Parliament elections is traditionally low compared to national elections. In particular, the youngest eligible voters are not at the ballot box [3]. The Netherlands is also struggling with this

A. Følstad et al. (Eds.): CONVERSATIONS 2024, LNCS 15545, pp. 181–199, 2025.
https://doi.org/10.1007/978-3-031-88045-2_12

problem. Only 35% of Dutch 18 to 24-year-olds cast their vote in 2019 [4]. It is part of a broader development of young people who are less likely to participate in traditional politics today [5, 6]. However, this low voting intention may result in a weakening of representative democracy in the long run. This problem is a matter of serious concern to the European Parliament. For that reason, in 2023, the Committee on Constitutional Affairs released a report on the participation of young people in European democratic processes. In it, several recommendations are made, and one of them is the development of digital voting aids [5].

Digital voting aids, voting assistants or Voting Advice Applications (VAA) are able to increase the political knowledge of potential voters, on the one hand, by informing voters about political parties and their positions, and on the other hand, by providing personal voting advice [7–9]. Traditional voting assistants are webbased questionnaires, where users answer to what extent they agree with a set of political propositions, and receive a voting advise in the end. Nevertheless, it appears that the majority of voting assistant users have difficulty answering the voting assistant propositions due to their limited background knowledge about political topics and the use of political jargon in propositions [7]. Therefore users rely mostly on assumptions and this has impact on the accuracy of the advise [7]. To encourage potential voters to look up additional information before answering a proposition, previous research suggested using a voting assistant chatbot [10]. Chatbots are considered helpful tools that can provide assistance in looking up information by interacting with users in everyday language [11].

In recent years, two studies have shown that voting assistant chatbots are more successful in increasing the political understanding of potential voters than traditional voting assistants [9, 12]. In particular, research was carried out into the design of the chatbot, and this showed that voters have a preference for a structured set-up of the chatbot, meaning that the chatbot should preferably only contain buttons for reply [13, 14]. Despite these attempts to make the chatbot more relevant to the needs of users in a voting advise context, research shows that people perceive the conversations they have with chatbots still as unnatural and impersonal [15]. This raises the question of whether forms of human-computer interaction other than chatbots could provide a more natural and pleasant interaction. One such new form is an intelligent virtual agent in the form of a virtual human on a screen [16]. Such a virtual agent, called avatar for pragmatic reasons in the rest of this study, has many more possibilities to present itself humanly. Through gestures, facial expressions, and a voice, the avatar can make people feel more known and familiar during their interaction [17].

For this reason, in the run-up to the European Parliament elections, this research aimed to study the extent to which these two types of digital voting assistants (chatbot and avatar) can influence the degree of political knowledge and voting intention of young adults. In addition, the user-friendliness and entertainment value of both voting assistants are examined. The research question is therefore: "*What is the effect of digital voting assistants (text-based chatbot and voice-based avatar) on the perceived political understanding and voting intention of young adults, what role do trust and political interest play in this, and what is the user-friendliness and entertainment value of these digital voting assistants?*".

2 Theoretical Background

2.1 The Role of Cognitive Processes in Questionnaire Response

A traditional voting assistant is a questionnaire with typically 30 political propositions, that need to be answered on a scale from 'Strongly Not Agree' to 'Strongly Agree'. When studying the way in which potential voters walk through the range of voting assistant propositions, it is important to know how people generally process such digital questionnaires. According to Tourangeau and Rasinski, respondents go through different cognitive processes when answering questionnaires [18]. In their so-called Tourangeau model, they distinguish between four phases. The first phase revolves around the respondent's ability to understand a question. The second phase determines what kind of attitude or opinion is required of the respondent. In doing so, respondents retrieve relevant information from their long-term memory. In the third phase, a respondent weighs and scales his or her individual beliefs and ultimately arrives at a well-thought-out choice. Finally, in the fourth phase, the respondent translates this decision into the most appropriate answer option. Zwaan and Radvansky expand these phases by stating that respondents first construct a semantic representation of the literal meaning of the question [19]. This means that the respondent must understand what is meant, in order to be able to make a pragmatic representation. This refers to the general knowledge that one has and that applies to the question [20].

With regard to the interaction with traditional digital voting assistants, research shows that problems arise during the first phase of the Tourangeau model. For example, Van Camp et al. found that one in five questions in voting assistants contain vaguely quantified terms, are ambiguously worded, and relatively often contain negations or political jargon [21]. In line with this, Kamoen and Holleman also showed that difficult concepts, geographical locations and vaguely quantified terms complicate the questions in voting assistants [7]. Although users were given the opportunity to look up additional information, only 26 out of 1800 respondents made use of this option. This means that the majority of users of traditional voting assistants draw conclusions about what the question might mean and formulate an answer based on that. This behaviour can further be explained by the *Theory of Satisficing* [22]. The phenomenon of *satisficing* refers to the expenditure of minimal effort by a respondent to generate a satisfactory answer. If, on the other hand, a respondent makes a lot of effort to give a correct answer, the opposite behavior occurs, namely *optimization.* According to this theory of satisficing, the difficulty of a task, a respondent's ability, and motivation determine the extent to which a respondent is inclined to striving for satisfaction.

The need for additional semantic and pragmatic information from voting assistant users, combined with the low motivation of the same users to look up additional information via external tools, prompted Van Limpt to develop a new type of voting assistant, namely a voting assistant chatbot or *Conversational Agent Voting Advice Application* (CAVAA) [9].

2.2 The Voting Assistant Chatbot

Unlike a traditional voting assistant, a voting assistant chatbot has an integrated chatbot functionality, which allows users to solve comprehension problems when answering political propositions by a question-answer interaction with the chatbot [23]. Offering extra information through a chatbot has several advantages. This way, users don't have to switch between channels to look up information [14]. In addition, the voting assistant chatbot can provide tailor-made political information. That is, the information in the chatbot is tailored to the specific needs of the user as opposed to general search engines. Finally, users who do not need additional information do not need to be informed unnecessarily. In this way, a voting assistant chatbot aims to provide objective information so that voters can give an informed answer to the political propositions [23]. This then results in a valid voting recommendation.

Research showed that compared to a traditional voting assistant, the voting assistant chatbot is more successful in increasing the actual perceived political understanding of users [9, 12]. Van Limpt also showed that perceived political knowledge for the voting assistant chatbot was higher than for the traditional voting assistant [9]. In other words, after interacting with the voting assistant chatbot, users felt they knew more about politics than users of the traditional voting assistant. Following on from this, Van Zanten and Boumans showed that voting assistant users had significantly more perceived political knowledge after interacting with the voting assistant chatbot than before the interaction [20]. In addition, the voting assistant chatbot scores better in terms of user-friendliness than voting assistants without chatbot [14]. With regard to the design of the voting assistant chatbot, it appears that voters prefer a structured set-up where the chatbot only contains buttons [10, 13, 14]. Kamoen and Liebrecht suggest in their research that the structured design is more in line with the low elaboration mode of voters [14]. The buttons within the chatbot are a better trigger to motivate voters to request additional information than the possibility to request more information via a text bar.

Despite the above-mentioned attempts to make the chatbot more relevant to the needs of users, research shows that people consider the conversations they have with chatbots to be unnatural and impersonal [15]. For that reason, this study introduces a new voting assistant, namely the voting assistant avatar.

2.3 The Voting Assistant Avatar

Unlike a chatbot, an avatar is not limited to a textbased communication style to present itself humanly. An avatar can make gestures and show facial expressions. Attributing these types of human traits or behaviors to non-human objects can make people feel more known and familiar with the object [24]. This behaviour, i.e. attributing human traits to non-human objects, is known as anthropomorphism. For example, research by Waytz et al. shows that people trust that a self-driving vehicle performs more competently the more anthropomorphic features the vehicle had, such as a name, gender, and voice [17]. Following on from this, Heyselaar et al. found that people perceived avatars with facial expressions as more humane and therefore felt more comfortable during the interaction [25].

Research into the potential of an avatar as a voting assistant is scarce. In 2020, the avatar Steffie was developed by Liebrecht and Kamoen for the 'Stichting Leer Zelf Doen' [26]. Steffie assisted people with a mild intellectual disability and people with low literacy levels in completing a traditional voting aid. Users were able to ask Steffie questions about the political themes from the propositions. The difference between Steffie and the voting assistant avatar proposed herein, is that this study's avatar both handles the interaction about answering the propositions and the eventual need for elucidations. A study by Liebrecht et al. is perhaps the closest thing to a voice-assistant avatar [23]. This study investigated the extent to which there are differences between text-only voting assistant chatbots, voice-only chatbots, or combining both functions. The study showed that the combined design and the design that contained only text scored better on user-friendliness. On the other hand, the speech-only design resulted in more miscommunication and less additional information. It seems that this takes too much effort. Nevertheless, the three designs scored equally on political knowledge and entertainment value.

In this study, it is therefore interesting to what extent the text-only voting assistant chatbot, compared to the voting assistant avatar, with a combined design of text and voice, will be evaluated by voting assistant users in terms of user-friendliness, entertainment value and political knowledge. For that purpose, participants can request additional political information via both the chatbot and the avatar, and therefore it is expected that participants for both voting assistants feel that their political understanding has increased [13]. In addition, Kamoen et al. found no significant differences in political understanding between the text-only, voice-only, or combination chatbot designs [14]. The more one knows about politics, the more one participates [27]. For that reason, perceived political understanding and intention to vote are expected to increase after interacting with the voting assistants. This leads to the following hypotheses:

H1: Young adults have more perceived political understanding after using both the voting assistant chatbot and the voting assistant avatar.
H2: Young adults have a higher intention to vote after using both the voting assistant chatbot and the voting assistant avatar.
In line with Waytz et al., due to the fact that the voting assistant avatar has more anthropomorphic features than the voting assistant chatbot, it is expected that young adults will have more trust in the voting assistant avatar than the voting assistant chatbot [17]. This leads to the following hypothesis:
H3: Young adults have more trust in the voting assistant avatar than the voting assistant chatbot.

In addition to political knowledge, political interest is an important predictor of political participation [5]. According to the theory of life cycle effects, young people have less political interest than older generations [28]. This has to do with the fact that young adults have less experience with electoral processes and have fewer opportunities to participate because they are burdened with other personal concerns [28]. With regard to voting assistants, it was found that low-skilled people had more political knowledge after using a voting assistant chatbot [14]. Given the fact that low-educated people also generally have less political interest compared to highly educated voters [29], it is expected that:

H4: The increase in perceived political understanding after using both voting assistants is greater among voters who are not or little interested in politics than among voters who are interested in politics.

2.4 The Processing of Mediated Information in the Light of Voting Assistants

Whereas the Tourangeau model and the Theory of Satisficing emphasize people's cognitive processes to answer questionnaires, the *Limited Capacity Model of Motivated Mediated Message Processing* (LC4MP) focuses on the way people process mediated information [30]. The LC4MP theory assumes that humans have a limited capacity for cognitive processing of information and that they thus select part of the available resources for the processing task. Despite the fact that this model was specifically developed for the processing of television messages, according to Lang it also applies to other media [30]. It is therefore interesting to use this model to make predictions about the cognitive processing of users of both the information provided by the voting assistant chatbot and the voting assistant avatar. Based on the LC4MP, it is expected that voting assistant users will thoroughly process the information from both the chatbot and the avatar, but possibly more for the avatar than for the chatbot. This is because there is both a controlled and automatic allocation of resources. For example, the voting assistant users within this study have an individual objective, namely to obtain voting advice by completing the voting assistant interaction. In addition, voting assistant users will probably experience a novelty effect, because there is a good chance that they have not previously interacted with a voting assistant in the form of a chatbot or avatar. This effect implies that people find something 'new' very exciting. The more often one interacts with this novelty, this excitement will decrease and result in less positive reviews [31]. Given that chatbots are becoming more and more common in everyday life, it is expected that the novelty effect will be greater for the voting assistant avatar than for the chatbot.

Finally, it is expected that the voice-assist avatar generates more stimuli that cause emotion. Although, according to anthropomorphism, the attribution of human characteristics to non-human objects can make people feel more known and familiar with an object, the uncanny valley hypothesis states that human objects that almost, but not exactly, resemble real people result in feelings of disgust or creepiness [32]. For example, in a comparative study between a simple chatbot and an animated avatar chatbot, Ciechanowski et al. concluded that participants experienced more intense emotional reactions with the avatar chatbot [33]. Participants enjoyed their interaction with both technologies, but evaluated the chatbot more positively.

Based on this, it is expected that the cognitive load will be greater for the voting assistant avatar than for the voting assistant chatbot, which will make the information processing more thorough for the chatbot. This expectation in combination with the aforementioned results of Kamoen et al., which showed that the voting assistant chatbot based solely on text scored better on user-friendliness [14]. In this paper, user-friendliness is derived from Davis' Technology Acceptance Model (TAM). This model assumes that if users are exposed to a new technology, the user-friendliness can be split into perceived usefulness and perceived ease of use [34].

Perceived usefulness is defined by Davis as the extent to which a user believes that the use of a particular system improves his or her work performance [34]. LC4MP's motivational aspect complements TAM's perceived usefulness because if users are motivated to engage, they are more likely to invest cognitive resources in understanding the device.

Perceived ease of use is defined by Davis as the extent to which a user believes that using a particular system is easy and effortless [34]. The LC4MP focus on cognitive capability aligns with the perceived ease of use, because if a new device requires too much cognitive effort, it may be perceived as less easy to use.

Therefore, two hypotheses are formulated as follows:

H5: The voting assistant chatbot results in a higher degree of perceived ease of use than the voting assistant avatar.
H6: The voting assistant chatbot results in a higher degree of perceived usefulness than the voting assistant avatar.

Based on the novelty effect, it is expected that voting assistant users will find the voting assistant avatar more exciting than the voting assistant chatbot, and thus find it more amusing. Just like user-friendliness, entertainment value can be defined on the basis of TAM, namely as perceived playfulness [35]. This term describes the user's enjoyment and curiosity during the interaction. The hypothesis is therefore:

H7: The voting assistant avatar results in a higher degree of perceived playfulness than the voting assistant chatbot.

3 Method

3.1 Study Design

For this study a *within-subjects* design was chosen to compare both voting assistants. Compared to a *between-subjects* design, this gives a greater chance that differences will be found between the conditions, while fewer participants are needed [36]. In addition, this design has greater statistical power and has a smaller variance in errors [37]. To prevent these carry-over effects from harming internal validity, *counterbalancing* was applied, where the participants were randomly distributed, and half of the participants interacted first with the chatbot and then with the avatar, and viceversa for the other half [37].

3.2 Participants

The study population consisted of Dutch young adults between 18 and 30 years old. To determine the minimum required sample size for the testing the formulated hypotheses with a paired t-test, a power analysis was performed with G*Power version 3.1.9.6 [38]. Experiments by Kamoen et al., Liebrecht et al., and Van Zanten and Boumans showed medium effect sizes [14, 20, 23, 39]. To detect a medium effect ($d = 0.5$) at a power of 80% and an alpha of.05, a sample size of N = 27 was needed. Participants were selected using convenience sampling and snowball sampling, meaning that a sample was drawn on the basis of the cases that were easily accessible [40]. A raffle of five gift vouchers of ten euros was conducted among participants who left their e-mail address. The experiment took place from 2 to 27 May 2024, which was a few weeks before the European Parliament election period of 6–9 June 2024. The experiments were carried out in a lab space at the Radboud University. In total, 30 participants participated in the experiment (13 male and 17 female), therefore the minimum sample size criterium was met. The mean age in the sample was 23.5 years (SD = 1.48, range 20–27 years).

A chi-square analysis showed that the study population was representative of the male-to-female ratio for young adults between 18 and 30 years old in the Netherlands X^2 (1, N = 30) = 0.664, p =.415 [41]. Most of the participants were in university education (n = 27), while some were in higher professional education (n = 2). One participant attended secondary school (n = 1). In terms of political interest, participants were divided into two groups based on their answers, namely less politically interested participants (n = 8) and politically interested participants (n = 22). All participants completed the entire experiment, thus the response was 100%. This research meets the requirements set by Radboud University, Faculty of Social Sciences Ethics Committee for research (reference ECSW-LT-2024-4-11–59239).

3.3 Procedure

Participants were welcomed and informed by the investigator and all provided consent (*informed consent*). Then they completed a short questionnaire on a tablet including questions about age, gender, level of education, and political interest. In addition, the participants filled in items about perceived political understanding and voting intention. Subsequently, the participants were exposed to the first voting assistant (Fig. 2). After the participants had received an initial voting recommendation by the first voting assistant, the participants completed a questionnaire regarding perceived political understanding, voting intention, user-friendliness, entertainment value and trust. This was followed by the interaction with the second voting assistant. After the participants had received their voting advice, they were asked again to complete the same questionnaire about the second voting assistant. Next an open question was asked, in which participants could leave comments about the study. Further, participants could leave their e-mail address to participate in the raffle. Finally, participants were verbally and informally asked if they liked the interaction and the voting assistants, and there remarks were summarized by the researcher in a logbook.

The participants completed the questionnaires on a separate device, namely a tablet. In doing so, it was tried to prevent a possible politeness rule [42]. Research by Nass and Moon has shown that participants tend to evaluate a computer with which they interacted more positively than when they evaluated the computer on paper or on another computer [42]. This has to do with the fact that people are reluctant to hurt the feelings of another person or object.

3.4 Stimulus Material (Voting Assistant Design)

The experiment used two types of voting assistants, namely a voting assistant chatbot and a voting assistant avatar. These voice aids have been specially developed for this experiment. Both voting assistants used nine carefully chosen propositions from a wide selection of themes that played a role in the European Parliament elections, such as immigration, environmental policy and defence. The propositions were based on the 2024 election manifestos of eleven Dutch political parties (CDA, D66, VVD, NSC, PVV, Volt, PvdD, GL/PvdA, SP, SGP, CU) and the propositions of the Electoral Compass (https://www.kieskompas.nl/nl/) for the 2019 European Parliament elections, because the 2024 version was not yet made public [43]. Only propositions that were still relevant in 2024 were used from the 2019 Electoral Compass. The proposition sets for the chatbot and for the avatar were different to avoid repetition effects, but concerned the same political themes. Within each set, it was important that the propositions were sufficiently diverse to cover different policy areas and allow for different answers according to the spectrum of party positions. In addition, difficult words or abbreviations were deliberately included in the propositions, so that participants would be triggered to request additional information. Finally, the propositions had to be relevant to the target group of young adults.

The chatbot or avatar first welcomed the participant and provided a short explanation about the procedure. Then the voting assistant presented the first proposition. For each proposition, participants were given the opportunity to request additional substantive information (What is Frontex?), or status information (What is the state of play at Frontex?). If participants did not need additional information, they could indicate this (No need for additional information). The participants could then click on four answer options (agree, neutral, disagree, I don't know) with the chatbot, or verbally express themselves with the avatar. This was followed by the second theorem and so on until all nine propositions had been evaluated. Based on their answers, the participants then received a personalized voting recommendation, which went something like this: "Your answers correspond to the political parties as follows: <parties with percentages>. So it's best to vote <party>." Finally, the voting assistant thanked the participants for their participation. The interaction with each voting assistant took about five minutes.

As far as the design of the chatbot and avatar character is concerned, a female design has been chosen. Research by Borau et al. shows that female robots have more positive human characteristics than male robots, that female robots are seen as more human, and that they are expected to be more likely to take into account our unique needs [44]. Based on this, the almost identical 'Sara' and 'Sanna' were developed as chatbots and avatars. According to Baylor, appearance is the most critical factor in the design of a motivational agent [45]. Based on this advice, an avatar was developed that represents the target group in terms of gender, ethnicity, age and competence. This resulted in a young woman with an informal style of dress. Boberg et al. indicate that avatars are generally designed with context in mind [46]. For that reason, the avatar was placed in a library, since this is a familiar place for many young adults and a suitable place to look up additional information. In order to prevent confounds as much as possible, two almost identical names and external characteristics were chosen. An image of Sara was used as the background of the chatbot (see Fig. 1).

When it comes to verbal and non-verbal cues, the recommendations of Liebrecht and Van Hooijdonk, Baylor, and Salem and Earle have been taken into account [15, 45, 47]. To make the chatbot and avatar look human, informal language was used. Non-verbal cues, such as hand gestures, were also used with the avatar. A pilot test with another subject was conducted to remove any procedural errors from the experiment procedure.

3.5 Measurements

In this study, various hypotheses were tested. The independent variable was the *type of voting assistant (chatbot or avatar)*. The dependent variables were *perceived political understanding, voting intention, perceived ease of use, perceived usefulness, perceived playfulness,* and *trust*.

Fig. 1. Voting assistant chatbot (left) and avatar (right) giving voting advice to the participant.

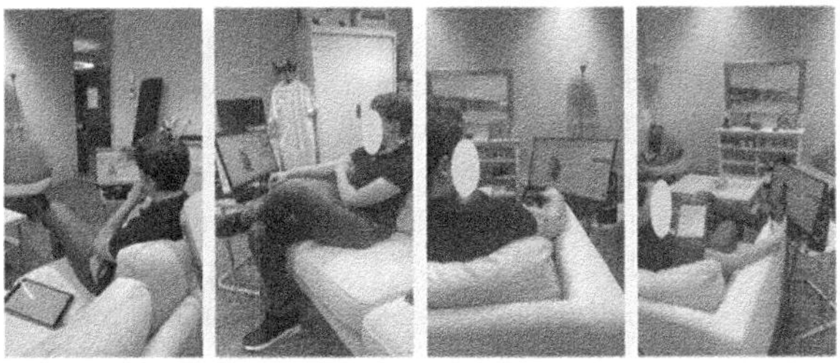

Fig. 2. A participant interacts with the voting assistant chatbot and the voting assistant avatar.From left to right, the participant talks to the avatar, the participant starts with the chatbot, the participant receives a voting advice from the chatbot, the participant takes a picture of his or her voting advice.

On the recommendation of Kamoen et al., perceived political understanding was measured by means of a pre- and post-measurement with 4 items (see Table 1) [14]. Participants could respond on a Likert scale ranging from 1 (strongly disagree) to 7 (strongly agree). The items were based on previous research by Daane, Ladner et al., Van Limpt, and Van Zanten and Boumans [9, 12, 20, 48]. The results of the reliability analysis showed that there was a high internal consistency in the pre-measurement of perceived political understanding (α =.824, M = 4.09, SD = 1.19). After a factor analysis, item 1 was removed, which resulted in a reliable scale of perceived political understanding after interaction with the chatbot (α =.750, M = 5.50, SD = 0.90) and the avatar (α =.733, M = 5.06, SD = 1.01).

Voting intention was also examined by means of a pre- and post-measurement with five items (Table 2). The first three items were based on Daane, Glynn et al., and Van Limpt [9, 12, 49]. The last two items related to attitudes towards voting were added based on Abdennadher et al., Johnson-Cartee & Copeland, and Pinkleton et al. [50–52]. After factor analysis, item 4 was removed and a reliable scale was constructed (α =.741). Next, the voting intention scale was split into two subscales for general voting intention (chatbot: α =.661, avatar: α =.599) and voting intention due to the voting assistant (chatbot: α =.558, avatar: α =.641) to improve the reliability of the scales.

Table 1. Items that measured the perception of political understanding before and after interaction with the chatbot/avatar

Items	Pre-measurement	Post-measurement
Item 1	I feel well informed about the current positions of the political parties for the European elections	By using the voting assistant chatbot/avatar I gain more insight into the positions of the political parties for the European Elections
Item 2	I am motivated to study the European Elections further	The voting assistant chatbot/avatar motivates me to delve further into the European Elections
Item 3	I feel well informed about the European elections	By using the voting assistant chatbot/avatar I have gained more knowledge about the upcoming European Elections
Item 4	I am motivated to talk about the European Elections with colleagues, friends or family	The use of this voting assistant chatbot/avatar has motivated me to talk to colleagues, friends or family about the European Elections

Table 2. Items that measure voting intention before and after interacting with the chatbot/avatar

Items	Pre-measurement	Post-measurement
Item 1	I plan to vote in the European Elections on 6 June 2024	I plan to vote in the European Elections on 6 June 2024
Item 2	I feel sufficiently informed to vote in the European elections	After using the voice support chatbot/avatar, I feel sufficiently informed to vote
Item 3	If there were an election now, I would vote	If there were an election now, I would vote. The voting assistant chatbot/avatar contributed to this
Item 4	Voting in the European Elections is important to me	Voting in the European Elections is important to me
Item 5	I would feel guilty if I did not vote in the European elections	I would feel guilty if I did not vote in the European elections

Perceived ease of use was operationalized using five items (Table 3 items 1–5), perceived usefulness with four items (items 6–9) and perceived playfulness with five items (items 10–14), and the scales showed high reliability ($\alpha >.80$) [13, 53].

The degree of political interest was measured using one item, namely, "How interested are you in politics?" [54]. This prevented that political interest is being mixed with other constructs, such as behavioural expressions or consequences of political interest [55]. Further, participants were asked to score the statement "Did the advice of the voting assistant correspond with the political party you would vote for, or have voted for before?" on a 7 point Likert scale. The purpose was to check if the voting assistant

Table 3. Items that measured perceived ease of use, usefulness and playfulness of the types of voting assistants

Item #	Item text
1	It's easy for me to use the voting assistant chatbot/avatar
2	It is impossible to use the voting assistant chatbot/avatar without expert help
3	I can easily become proficient in using the voting assistant chatbot/avatar
4	Using the voting assistant chatbot/avatar requires a lot of mental effort
5	I find the voting assistant chatbot/avatar user-friendly
6	The use of the voting assistant chatbot/avatar helps me to make a better decision for the European Elections
7	The use of the voting assistant chatbot/avatar makes the European Elections easier
8	Using the voting assistant chatbot/avatar helps me gather information about the European Elections faster than other ways
9	The use of the voting assistant chatbot/avatar is an efficient way to gather information about the European Elections
10	The chatbot voting assistant/avatar gave me pleasure in filling in the voting assistant
11	The voting assistant chatbot/avatar stimulated my curiosity
12	Using the voting assistant chatbot/avatar was fun
13	The use of the voting assistant chatbot/avatar met my expectations
14	While using the voting assistant chatbot/avatar, I didn't realize how much time had passed

advises were more or less in line with their political preference. Finally, three control variables were measured, namely age, gender and education level. On the basis of these variables, it was possible to determine to what extent the sample was a representative sample of the study population.

3.6 Data Analysis

The data were analyzed using IBM SPSS Statistics 29. For most hypotheses, a paired samples t-test was used. For the fifth hypothesis, two groups were created, namely less politically interested participants ($n = 8$) and politically interested participants ($n = 22$), and an independent samples t-test was used.

4 Results

4.1 The Effect of the Voting Assistants on Perceived Political Understanding

The average value for perceived political understanding in the post-measurement for the voting assistant chatbot ($M = 5.50$; $SD = 0.90$) was significantly higher than in the pre-measurement (M = 4.09; SD = 1.19, $t(29) = 6.12$, $p < .001$), and the effect was large, namely $d = 1.12$. For the avatar the effect was medium ($M = 5.06$; $SD = 1.01$, $t(29) = 3.87$, $p < .001$). Hypothesis 1 can therefore be accepted.

4.2 The Effect of the Voting Assistants on Voting Intention

Based on the factor analysis (Sect. 3.5), the variable 'voting intention' was divided into two factors, namely 'general voting intention' and 'voting intention due to voting assistant'. The pre-measurement showed a voting intention of $M = 5.77$ ($SD = 0.87$).

Following the interaction with the chatbot, the general voting intention increased ($M = 6.65$; $SD = 0.56$; $t(29) = 7.65$, $p < .001$, $d = 1.40$). The voting intention due to the chatbot decreased ($M = 5.02$; $SD = 1{,}21$; $t(29) = -2.80$, $p = .004$, $d = -0.51$).

Also following the interaction with the avatar, the general voting intention increased ($M = 6.62$; $SD = 0.54$; $t(29) = 7.80$, $p < .001$, $d = 1.43$), and the voting intention due to the avatar decreased ($M = 4.43$; $SD = 1.25$; $t(29) = -4.72$, $p < .001$, $d = -.86$).

4.3 Voting Assistants and Trust

Hypothesis 3 assumed that young potential voters would have more trust in the voting assistant avatar than in the voting assistant chatbot. However, the results show that participants had significantly more trust in the voting assistant chatbot ($M = 5.08$; $SD = 1.37$) than in the voting assistant avatar ($M = 4.03$, $SD = 1.59$), $t(29) = -4.11$, $p < .001$. The effect was medium ($d = -0.75$). Hypothesis 3 must therefore be rejected.

4.4 Political Interest and Perceived Political Understanding

For the chatbot, the expectation that participants with less political interest ($n = 8$, $M = 2.20$, $SD = 1.33$) would experience a greater increase in perceived political understanding than politically interested participants ($n = 22$, $M = 1.12$, $SD = 1.13$) was supported ($t(28) = 2.20$, $p = .018$, $d = 0.91$). For the avatar, results also showed that participants with less political interest ($n = 8$, $M = 1.95$, $SD = 0.82$) experience a greater increase in perceived political understanding than politically interested participants ($n = 22$, $M = 0.61$, $SD = 1.36$, $t(28) = 2.61$, $p = .007$, $d = 1.08$). Hypothesis 4 can be accepted.

4.5 Perceived Ease of Use, Usefulness and Playfulness

The participating young adults found the voting assistant chatbot ($M = 6.56$; $SD = 0.35$) easier to use than the voting assistant avatar ($M = 4.83$; $SD = 1.32$; $t(29) = 6.70$, $p < .001$, $d = 1.22$). Participants also found the usefulness of the voting assistant chatbot ($M = 5.28$; $SD = 1.29$) better than the voting assistant avatar ($M = 4.29$; $SD = 1.32$), $t(29) = 3.885$, $p < .001$, $d = 0.71$). For these reasons, hypotheses 5 and 6 can be accepted.

Concerning playfulness, the voting assistant chatbot had a significantly higher entertainment value in the eyes of participants ($M = 5.34$; $SD = 1.01$) than the voting assistant avatar ($M = 4.71$, $SD = 1.15$), $t(29) = 3.01$, $p = .003$, $d = 0.55$. For this reason, hypothesis 7 had to be rejected.

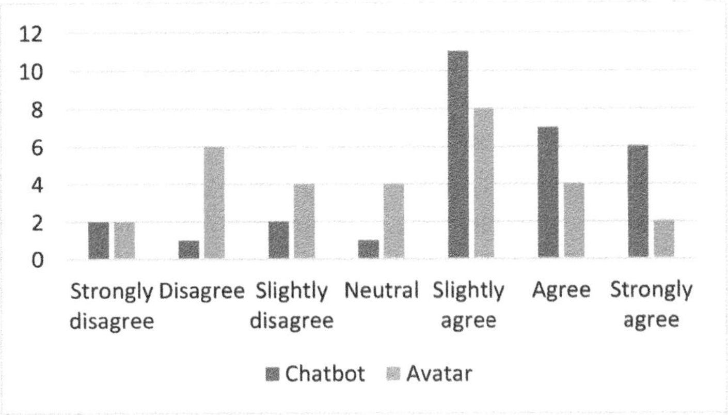

Fig. 3. The extent to which the voting advice obtained from the voting assistants corresponds to the political preference of participants

4.6 Correspondence Between Voting Behaviour and Voting Advice

In addition to the testing of the hypotheses, it was checked to what extent the voting recommendations of the voting assistants were in accordance with the political party that participants would vote for or had previously voted for. Figure 3 shows the extent to which participants felt that their voting advice corresponded to their part political preference. The figure shows that the agreement is larger for the chatbot ($M = 5.10$, $SD = 1.67$) than for the avatar ($M = 4.00$, $SD = 1.74$), $t = 2.72$, $df = 29$, $p =.006$.

5 Discussion and Conclusion

This small-scale study suggests that digital voting assistants in the form of a chatbot or avatar are able to increase the perceived political understanding of potential voters. However, more research under different target groups is needed to strengthen the generalization of this conclusion. Although the effect of the chatbot is somewhat stronger than that of the avatar, this result is an incentive to conduct more research into voting assistants in the form of chatbots or avatars in the future. The fact that the avatar Steffie has now also been used nationwide to help voters, who find politics difficult, to fill in a traditional voting aid supports this conclusion [56].

Regarding the voting intention of potential voters, opposite effects were found for the general voting intention and voting intention due to chatbot or avatar. This may be caused by the operationalisation of the voting intention construct. Van Zanten and Boumans previously indicated that the items used for measuring the voting intention may be interpreted differently by participants [9, 12, 20]. Nevertheless, the increase in general voting intention is a unique result. The result that voters with less political interest gain significantly more knowledge from the chatbot and the avatar than politically interested voters is in line with the results of Kamoen et al. [14].

In terms of user-friendliness, young adults had a clear preference for the voting assistant chatbot. This result is in line with previous research from Kamoen et al. [43].

As in Kamoen et al., the use of speech may require too much effort from voting assistant users. Based on the LC4MP, it was predicted that the cognitive load would be greater for the voting assistant avatar than for the voting assistant chatbot. Speech could make it more difficult for users to process the avatar's information. In the light of the Tourangeau model, the different phases at the chatbot could be completed in peace, because the chatbot waited until the participant touched a touch button on the screen with the desired answer. On the other hand, when speaking and listening to the voting assistant avatar, there was a greater chance of disruptions in the phases of the Tourangeau model. These distortions mainly occurred in the last two phases, where participants reflected on their answer (phase 3) and then said it out loud (phase 4). Another speech related factor is that the avatar had a less natural voice (Google female voice type "nl-NL-Standard-D"). Research has shown that a voice with a certain expression of emotion is very decisive for the attitudes that people have towards a technology [33]. For future research, it is therefore recommended to study in more detail the effect of speech for different voting assistants.

With regard to the entertainment value, participants found the chatbot more amusing. However, this result remains debatable. After the experiment, some participants indicated to the researchers that they liked the avatar best, for example because it looked like a game. Another participant indicated that he preferred the avatar because the chatbot was very similar to normal voting assistants. It is therefore also interesting to do further research into the entertainment value of different voting assistant designs in the future.

This study had a number of limitations. Firstly, the research was carried out in a lab designed as a living room at the Radboud University in Nijmegen, Netherlands. On the one hand, this has affected ecological validity, by providing a homely setting in the lab (sofa, coffee table, accessories). However, one of the researchers was present to instruct and help participants and this would not happen at home. Secondly, a small group ($N = 30$) of predominantly highly educated students from Radboud University participated in the experiment. This is despite the fact that, in the light of previous research, it seems that low-educated people in particular have more political knowledge after interacting with voting assistants. It would therefore be interesting to compare the effects of digital voting assistants on highly educated, medium-educated and low-educated people in future research. Moreover, a more heterogeneous participant group could enable increased generalizability of the results. Thirdly, there are many factors influencing voting behavior that could not be investigated within the context of this study. These include the preference for particular parties, socio-cultural and socio-economic factors, rationality versus emotion in making choices, personality traits and personal fears, as demonstrated by other scholars [57–59]. Fourthly, a young female-looking avatar and chatbot was used, because many studies used female chatbots and the young age would appeal to the target group. However, this may have caused a gender bias in factors as expertise perception and emotional effect among participants. Lastly, this first study is broad in scope, and more focus on either the usability and trust aspects, or on political education and voting impact aspects could have been beneficial.

With regard to the technology, it was found that the voting assistant chatbot was better developed than the voting assistant avatar. For example, the avatar had sometimes difficulty understanding the participants. Speech recognition is a common problem in human-robot interaction [60]. This avatar used Microsoft Azure as its speech recognition software. After asking the question, the microphone was open to hear the answer. This answer was then translated into a text string, which was classified as a certain response intent via an intent recognition algorithm from the dialog manager. Disruptions may have occurred in this process and have affected the interaction quality. Participants also had to formulate their answer under some time pressure, otherwise the avatar would move on to the next proposition.

Although the researchers wanted to make the propositions within the voting guides as similar as possible by means of the same themes, they remained two separate voting guides. As a result, participants regularly received different voting advice from the chatbot than from the avatar. Moreover, an unexpected effect was that the voting advice of the avatar was remarkably often the CDA, a christen-democratic party. Despite the fact that this was not a conscious bias, it is interesting to use a between-subjects design in the future, such that both groups will be presented with the same set of propositions. A remarkable observation was that participants who like to read seemed to prefer the voting assistant chatbot, and participants who preferred to listen preferred the voting assistant avatar.

This study provides early insights into the important area of research on digital voting assistants for making young adults aware that they can acquire more knowledge about the European Parliament elections. These results are valuable because research showed that when people feel they understand politics better, they are more likely to vote [27]. In addition, the overall voting intention of the young adults in this study is higher thanks to the interaction with the voting assistants. This strengthens our democracy. This research therefore underlines the potential of digital voting assistants to encourage young voters to vote in the European Parliament elections and contributes to a stronger and more representative European Parliament.

Disclosure of Interests. The authors have no competing interests to declare that are relevant to the content of this article.

References

1. NOS: Hoe laat je de Europese verkiezingen leven? Partijen nog één keer de straat op [How to bring the European elections to life? Parties take to the streets one more time]. https://nos.nl/collectie/13972/artikel/2522773-hoe-laat-je-de-europese-verkiezingen-leven-partijen-nog-een-keer-de-straat-op. Accessed 22 Sept 2024
2. EenVandaag: Deze Europarlementariërs zien in 2024 bedreigingen voor de EU, maar ook enorme kansen [These MEPs see threats to the EU in 2024, but also huge opportunities]. https://eenvandaag.avrotros.nl/item/deze-europarlementariers-zien-in-2024-bedreigingen-voor-de-eu-maar-ook-enorme-kansen/. Accessed 22 Sept 2024
3. European Union: Standard Eurobarometer 91 - Spring 2019 - augustus 2019 – Eurobarometer survey. https://europa.eu/eurobarometer/surveys/detail/2253. Accessed 22 Sept 2024
4. Ipsos: Verkiezingsonderzoek Europese parlementsverkiezingen 2019 [Election Survey European Parliament Elections 2019]. https://www.ipsos.com/nl-nl/verkiezingsonderzoek-europese-parlementsverkiezingen-2019. Accessed 22 Sept 2024
5. Deželan, T.: Young people's participation in European democratic processes. How to improve and facilitate youth involvement (2023)

6. Pini, S.: Analysing turnout in European elections: national differences, the peculiarity of the EU's system and the abstention of young people. Eur. View **8**, 143–151 (2009)
7. Kamoen, N., Holleman, B.: I don't get it: response difficulties in answering political attitude statements in voting advice applications. In: 7th International European Survey Research Association Conference, pp. 125–140. European Survey Research Association (2017)
8. Garzia, D.: The effects of VAAs on users' voting behaviour: an overview. In: Voting Advice Applications in Europe: The State of the Art, pp. 13–33 (2010)
9. Van Limpt, S.: Conversational agent voting advice applications: the effect of tone of voice in (CA) VAAs and political sophistication on political knowledge, voting intention, and (CA) VAA evaluation. [Master thesis, Tilburg University] (2020)
10. Kamoen, N., Liebrecht, C., Mekel, P., van Limpt, S.: Stemhulp-chatbots: Politieke informatie op maat [Voting assistant chatbots: Tailored political information]. Tekstblad **26**, 12–15 (2020)
11. Liao, Q.V., Geyer, W., Muller, M., Khazaen, Y.: Conversational interfaces for information search. In: Fu, W., van Oostendorp, H. (eds.) Understanding and Improving Information Search. HCIS. Springer, Cham, pp. 267–287 (2020). https://doi.org/10.1007/978-3-030-38825-6_13
12. Daane, R.J.: Online stemhulpen in verkiezingstijd [Online voting aids during election time] (2021). http://arno.uvt.nl/show.cgi?fid=155276
13. McCartan, T.: Conversational Agent Voting Advice Applications (CAVAAs). What are the effects of three CAVAA-designs: structured, semi-structured and non-structured, on the user-friendliness, entertainment value, perceived political knowledge and voting intention of both higher and lower educated adults? (2021)
14. Kamoen, N., McCartan, T., Liebrecht, C.: Conversational agent voting advice applications: a comparison between a structured, semi-structured, and non-structured chatbot design for communicating with voters about political issues. In: Følstad, A., et al. (eds.) CONVERSATIONS 2021. LNCS, vol. 13171, pp. 160–175. Springer, Cham (2022). https://doi.org/10.1007/978-3-030-94890-0_10
15. Liebrecht, C., van Hooijdonk, C.: Creating humanlike chatbots: what chatbot developers could learn from webcare employees in adopting a conversational human voice. In: Følstad, A., et al. (eds.) CONVERSATIONS 2019. LNCS, vol. 11970, pp. 51–64. Springer, Cham (2020). https://doi.org/10.1007/978-3-030-39540-7_4
16. Lugrin, B., Pelachaud, C., Traum, D. (eds.): The Handbook on Socially Interactive Agents: 20 Years of Research on Embodied Conversational Agents, Intelligent Virtual Agents, and Social Robotics Volume 1: Methods, Behavior, Cognition. Association for Computing Machinery, New York (2021)
17. Waytz, A., Heafner, J., Epley, N.: The mind in the machine: anthropomorphism increases trust in an autonomous vehicle. J. Exp. Soc. Psychol. **52**, 113–117 (2014). https://doi.org/10.1016/j.jesp.2014.01.005
18. Tourangeau, R., Rasinski, K.A.: Cognitive processes underlying context effects in attitude measurement. Psychol. Bull. **103**, 299 (1988)
19. Zwaan, R.A., Radvansky, G.A.: Situation models in language comprehension and memory. Psychol. Bull. **123**, 162 (1998)
20. Van Zanten, N., Boumans, R.: Voting assistant chatbot for increasing voter turnout at local elections: an exploratory study. Presented at the Conversations 2023, Oslo, Norway (2024). https://doi.org/10.1007/978-3-031-54975-5_1
21. Van Camp, K., Lefevere, J., Walgrave, S.: The content and formulation of statements in voting advice applications. In: Matching voters with parties and candidates. Voting Advice Applications in Comparative Perspective, pp. 11–32 (2014)
22. Krosnick, J.A.: Response strategies for coping with the cognitive demands of attitude measures in surveys. Appl. Cogn. Psychol. **5**, 213–236 (1991)

23. Liebrecht, C., Kamoen, N., Aerts, C.: Voice your opinion! Young voters' usage and perceptions of a text-based, voice-based and text-voice combined conversational agent voting advice application (CAVAA). In: Følstad, A., et al. (eds.) CONVERSATIONS 2022. LNCS, vol. 13815, pp. 34–49. Springer, Cham (2023). https://doi.org/10.1007/978-3-031-25581-6_3
24. Epley, N., Waytz, A., Cacioppo, J.T.: On seeing human: a three-factor theory of anthropomorphism. Psychol. Rev. **114**, 864 (2007)
25. Heyselaar, E., Hagoort, P., Segaert, K.: How social opinion influences syntactic processing—an investigation using virtual reality. PLoS ONE **12**, e0174405 (2017)
26. Stichting Leer Zelf Online: Stemhulp van Steffie [Voting assistance from Steffie]. https://www.steffie.nl/nieuws/onderwerpen/stemhulp-van-steffie.html. Accessed 22 Sept 2024
27. Smets, K., Van Ham, C.: The embarrassment of riches? A meta-analysis of individual-level research on voter turnout. Elect. Stud. **32**, 344–359 (2013)
28. Weiss, J.: What is youth political participation? Literature review on youth political participation and political attitudes. Front. Polit. Sci. **2** (2020). https://doi.org/10.3389/fpos.2020.00001
29. Kleinnijenhuis, J., et al.: Nederland vijfstromenland: De rol van de media en stemwijzers bij de verkiezingen van 2006 [The Netherlands, a country of five rivers: The role of the media and voting guides in the 2006 elections] (2007)
30. Lang, A.: The limited capacity model of mediated message processing. J. Commun. **50**, 46–70 (2000)
31. Croes, E.A., Antheunis, M.L.: Can we be friends with Mitsuku? A longitudinal study on the process of relationship formation between humans and a social chatbot. J. Soc. Pers. Relatsh. **38**, 279–300 (2021)
32. Mori, M., MacDorman, K.F., Kageki, N.: The uncanny valley [from the field]. IEEE Robot. Autom. Mag. **19**, 98–100 (2012)
33. Ciechanowski, L., Przegalinska, A., Magnuski, M., Gloor, P.: In the shades of the uncanny valley: an experimental study of human–chatbot interaction. Future Gener. Comput. Syst. **92**, 539–548 (2019)
34. Davis, F.D.: Perceived usefulness, perceived ease of use, and user acceptance of information technology. MIS Q., 319–340 (1989)
35. Moon, J.-W., Kim, Y.-G.: Extending the TAM for a world-wide-web context. Inf. Manag. **38**, 217–230 (2001)
36. Field, A., Hole, G.: How to Design and Report Experiments. Sage, Thousand Oaks (2002)
37. Julia, M., Pritha, B.: An introduction to within-subjects designs. https://www.scribbr.nl/onderzoeksmethoden/within-subjects/. Accessed 22 Sept 2024
38. Faul, F., Erdfelder, E., Buchner, A., Lang, A.-G.: Statistical power analyses using G* Power 3.1: tests for correlation and regression analyses. Behav. Res. Methods **41**, 1149–1160 (2009). https://doi.org/10.3758/brm.41.4.1149
39. Kamoen, N., Holleman, B., Krouwel, A., Van de Pol, J., De Vreese, C.: The effect of voting advice applications on political knowledge and vote choice. Irish Polit. Stud. **30**, 595–618 (2015)
40. Boeije, H.: Analyseren in kwalitatief onderzoek [Analysing in qualitative research]. Denken en doen (2005)
41. Centraal Bureau voor de Statistiek: Bevolking; geslacht, leeftijd en burgerlijke staat, 1 januari. Den Haag/Heerlen (2024)
42. Nass, C., Moon, Y.: Machines and mindlessness: social responses to computers. J. Soc. Issues **56**, 81–103 (2000)
43. Kieskompas: Electoral Compass for the European Elections 2024. https://eu.kieskompas.nl/nl
44. Borau, S., Otterbring, T., Laporte, S., Fosso Wamba, S.: The most human bot: female gendering increases humanness perceptions of bots and acceptance of AI. Psychol. Mark. **38**, 1052–1068 (2021)

45. Baylor, A.L.: The design of motivational agents and avatars. Educ. Technol. Res. Dev. **59**, 291–300 (2011)
46. Boberg, M., Piippo, P., Ollila, E.: Designing avatars. In: Proceedings of the 3rd International Conference on Digital Interactive Media in Entertainment and Arts, pp. 232–239 (2008)
47. Salem, B., Earle, N.: Designing a non-verbal language for expressive avatars. In: Proceedings of the Third International Conference on Collaborative Virtual Environments, pp. 93–101 (2000)
48. Ladner, A., Pianzola, J.: Do voting advice applications have an effect on electoral participation and voter turnout? Evidence from the 2007 Swiss Federal Elections. In: Tambouris, E., Macintosh, A., Glassey, O. (eds) ePart 2010. LNCS, vol. 6229, pp. 211–224. Springer, Heidelberg (2010). https://doi.org/10.1007/978-3-642-15158-3_18
49. Glynn, C.J., Huge, M.E., Lunney, C.A.: The influence of perceived social norms on college students' intention to vote. Polit. Commun. **26**, 48–64 (2009)
50. Abdennadher, R., Ayed, L., Wood, B.P.: Political advertising and voting behaviour in a nascent democracy: towards a global model for the Tunisian post-revolutionary experience. J. Islamic Mark. **10**, 827–847 (2019)
51. Johnson-Cartee, K.S., Copeland, G.: Negative Political Advertising: Coming of Age. Routledge (2013)
52. Pinkleton, B.E., Um, N.-H., Austin, E.W.: An exploration of the effects of negative political advertising on political decision making. J. Advert. **31**, 13–25 (2002)
53. Ahn, T., Ryu, S., Han, I.: The impact of Web quality and playfulness on user acceptance of online retailing. Inf. Manag. **44**, 263–275 (2007)
54. Russo, S., Stattin, H.: Stability and change in youths' political interest. Soc. Indic. Res. **132**, 643–658 (2017)
55. Van Deth, J., Elff, M.: Political involvement and apathy in Europe 1973 - 1998. MZES Working Papers (2000)
56. Tilburg University: Stemmen dankzij Steffie. Hoe AI-avatar Steffie kwetsbare mensen helpt bij hun stemkeuze [Voting thanks to Steffie. How AI avatar Steffie helps vulnerable people with their voting choice]. https://research.tilburguniversity.edu/en/projects/stemmen-dankzij-steffie-hoe-ai-avatar-steffie-kwetsbare-mensen-he. Accessed 22 Sept 2024
57. Schwander, H., Manow, P.: It's not the economy, stupid! Explaining the electoral success of the German right-wing populist AfD. In: Center for Comparative and International Studies (CIS) (2017)
58. Schmuck, D., Matthes, J.: How anti-immigrant right-wing populist advertisements affect young voters: symbolic threats, economic threats and the moderating role of education. J. Ethn. Migr. Stud. **41**, 1577–1599 (2015). https://doi.org/10.1080/1369183X.2014.981513
59. Bakker, B.N., Rooduijn, M., Schumacher, G.: The psychological roots of populist voting: evidence from the United States, the Netherlands and Germany. Eur J Polit Res **55**, 302–320 (2016). https://doi.org/10.1111/1475-6765.12121
60. Pande, A., Shrestha, B., Rani, A., Mishra, D.: A comparative analysis of real time open-source speech recognition tools for social robots. In: Marcus, A., Rosenzweig, E., Soares, M.M. (eds.) HCII 2023. LNCS, vol. 14033, pp. 355–365. Springer, Cham (2023). https://doi.org/10.1007/978-3-031-35708-4_26

An Analysis of Federal and Municipal Chatbots in Germany

Verena Traubinger[1(✉)], Sebastian Heil[1], Julián Grigera[2,3,4], Alejandra Garrido[2,3], Sonia Abhyankar[1], and Martin Gaedke[1]

[1] Faculty of Computer Science, Chemnitz University of Technology, Chemnitz, Germany
{verena.traubinger,sebastian.heil, martin.gaedke}@informatik.tu-chemnitz.de, sonia-parag.abhyankar@s2018.tu-chemnitz.de

[2] LIFIA, Fac. de Informática, Univ. Nac. de La Plata, La Plata, Argentina
{julian.grigera,garrido}@lifia.info.unlp.edu.ar

[3] CONICET, Buenos Aires, Argentina

[4] CICPBA, La Plata, Argentina

Abstract. Chatbots are often encountered in e-commerce and specifically customer service. In the last years, governmental institutions are also using them more often as a communication channel for citizens. In this paper we report our findings on the landscape of publicly available chatbots in federal states and large city municipalities in Germany. We collected a dataset of 25 chatbots and analyzed them with a codebook of 12 feature characteristics and 12 chatbot interaction patterns. These patterns describe how interactive elements are used in a chatbot conversation to guide the user. Our results show the presented features of the assessed municipal chatbots in terms of avatars, names, and layout. We also discuss our findings concerning the use of existing chatbot interaction patterns, and introduce four new patterns based on this real-world analysis. Our analysis also focuses on the differences between governmental and e-commerce chatbots in terms of their implementation of features and interaction patterns.

Keywords: Chatbots · Municipal Chatbots · Chatbot Interaction Patterns · Conversational User Interfaces · Human-centric AI

1 Introduction

Chatbots are used both in commercial and public sectors as new communication channels to free time from employees [9]. Often chatbots take on easy, repetitive tasks like answering frequent questions, providing documents or links, and are especially available round the clock [13]. While chatbots are prevalent for customer service, they are also common in the public sector, for example for governmental tasks [1]. Research has been conducted on the use of chatbots in different countries [2,3], on which government levels and for which tasks they are

A. Følstad et al. (Eds.): CONVERSATIONS 2024, LNCS 15545, pp. 200–216, 2025.
https://doi.org/10.1007/978-3-031-88045-2_13

used [3,9,13], and on the interaction between citizens and chatbots [2,5,6]. While chatbots on a national level provide a broad range of services, they offer more resident-oriented services in lower government levels, especially local municipalities [13].

In this study we set the scope to federal and municipal chatbots in Germany, contributing to the growing set of similar investigations in other countries [2,3]. The successful implementation of such chatbots depends on several elements, one of which is the user interface. For a better orientation and understanding of both the content and possible interactions, repeating patterns in the interface can guide the users in this process. We are analyzing German federal and municipal chatbots on their feature characteristics and their use of chatbot interaction patterns [16]. With these results we can compare which and how these patterns, derived mostly from e-commerce chatbots, are used in governmental chatbots. Our contributions in this paper are the following:

1. Analysis of chatbot features on the federal and municipal level in Germany
2. A dataset of German federal and municipal Chatbots
3. Insights and a validation of existing chatbot interaction patterns, a presentation of new patterns, and a discussion of non-regularly used patterns

Following the state of the art in the next section, we present our methodology in Sect. 3. The websites of currently 83 large cities[1] and 16 federal states were visually inspected for their use of chatbots. We collected 25 chatbots that are deployed from 20 large cities and 2 federal states. These implementations were then analyzed with a codebook regarding their feature characteristics like their topics, presentation, integration, and use of avatar, name and gender as well as their use of chatbot interaction patterns. Our results of the feature analysis, the used chatbot interaction patterns and newly defined patterns are presented and discussed in Sects. 4 and 5. There, we present insights both general and specific on the use of chatbot interaction patterns and how their implementation can change in different domains. Even when our dataset is restricted to Germany, we believe this study helps to understand the differences between e-commerce and government chatbots beyond the German context. Additionally, our work sets the basis for other research for a broader and diversified dataset of government chatbots and its analysis in the future.

2 Related Work

With more technological advancements, digital governments introduced new channels for their citizens, like chatbots [11]. This section includes three literature groups: research generally on governmental chatbots, on the interaction between users and governmental chatbots, and chatbot interaction patterns for analyzing graphical interaction elements in the chatbot interface.

[1] With more than 100.000 residents.

2.1 Use of Chatbots by Governments

This section concentrates on how governments are using chatbots on national, regional and municipal levels. We focused on papers which either conducted analyses on the literature [3,13] or existing government chatbots [3,9] to systematically create frameworks and typologies. Most of the research we found shows chatbots are mainly used in governmental organizations to free employees from repetitive tasks, which can as-well be taken over by an automated customer support channel. The literature shows that all different government levels provide services and information for citizens [3,9,13]. A focus on the local level offers additional tasks which chatbots take over, like providing a channel for transactions and collecting complaints [13]. The work of Cortés-Cediel et al. includes access to open government data, public services, improving citizen participation and facilitating communication between stakeholders [3]. This work provides a framework for analysing chatbots which the authors implement both on a literature research and on a set of Spanish government chatbots. This is the only publication in this subsection which directly regards the chatbot interface in one of the variables in its framework. A typology of chatbots published in 2021 likewise mentions customized health services and help in submitting government documents [9]. This typology also defines low and high levels for the complexity in the sophistication levels, as well as specific characteristics like suitable dialog management, suitable databases for the technological properties, and initial service queries and responses as for their capabilities. In a review by Senadheera et al., the authors find that while national governments provide broader services, often on legal documents and regulations, chatbots on the level of local governments provide access to more resident-oriented services [13]. In this review, several trends in the research are identified, one of which are studies on user-chatbot interactions, which are the topic in the next section.

2.2 Interactions with (Municipal) Chatbots

Results from a 2019 study of chatbots in Latvia, Vienna and Bonn [11] suggest that chatbots are used to switch traditional services from physical to digital channels, but that a successful adoption is dependent on other variables. One of these variables, i.e. public trust, was identified and studied by Aoki et al. In a survey with 8.000 Japanese citizens, most of whom were inexperienced with chatbots, they find that the trust in chatbots depends on the topic and communicated purpose [2]. Citizens are less trusting in complex cases where empathy was expected, than for general information like trash disposal. Participants also show higher trust levels if a reason for the use of a chatbot is given, like providing citizens with a 24/7 communication channel. Abbas et al. likewise find that citizens might benefit from chatbots if they include additional benefits to established channels [1]. Besides trust, other aspects like usefulness and effort are also key to their willingness to use municipal chatbots. Some authors of this work also conducted other studies on the communication forms between citizens and chatbots and find that citizens recognize chatbots as a technology with certain capabilities and limitations, rarely humanize them, and communicate in a mostly utilitarian style [6]. These results were further explored, where the authors also factor where the chatbot access is located on the website [5]. Finally, in a 2024 interview on a particular municipal chatbot (mostly used in Norway), they find that citizens touted other aspects like efficiency and information availability [8]. Most of these studies report on qualitative analyses, usually relying on surveys, while in our work we aim at providing a structured analysis based on fixed criteria.

Table 1. Chatbot interaction patterns, their description and relation to other patterns.

Nr. Pattern name	Description. (Relation to other patterns)
1. Chat Messages	Displaying outputs from chatbot and user, most often as speech bubbles.
2. Cards	Presenting similar information, often with text, images, and actions. (1., 3.)
3. Carousel	A set of similar items in a horizontal list. (2.)
4. Quick Replies	A set of actions or functionalities under a chat message in the form of buttons. (1.)
5. Typing Indicators	A visual representation of the waiting time for the reply of the chatbot. (1.)
6. Persistent Menu	A constant menu in the chat window for important information or settings.
7. Call-on Menu	A dynamic representation of consistent information which was requested by the user. (1., 4., 6.)
8. Webview	A preview on web content from other providers or the chatbot homepage itself. (1.)
9. Message Reactions	Emojis beside or under a chat message to provide feedback on the answer of the chatbot. (1.)
10. Help Systems	Offering assistance for users, either on request or proactively by the chatbot. (4., 6., 7., 11.)
11. Functionality Introduction	Introducing the main functionalities or providing a tutorial in the first chat messages. (1.)
12. Conversation Recovery	Avoiding conversation breakdowns by providing possible actions or commands. (4., 7.)

2.3 Chatbot Interaction Patterns

The chatbot interaction patterns [16] describe how and in which situations individual or combined interaction elements are used in the implementation of chatbots. Table 1 shows the list of already defined chatbot interaction patterns. Since chatbots are a form of Conversational User Interface (CUI) with a visual-centric style, natural language processing is combined with graphical elements [10]. Research on the use of these graphical elements in chatbots is scarce. Recently, we published a list of chatbot interaction patterns based on previous works [14,17] which include individual interaction elements [16], while Valério et al. also discuss help strategies offered by the chatbots for users [17]. These publications were mapped to interaction patterns from graphical user interfaces by Tidwell et al. [15] to create chatbot specific patterns.

3 Methodology

In this section we present how the dataset was collected and analysed with a codebook. For the dataset collection we first offer inclusion and exclusion criteria before we detail the process of the collection of chatbot instances and then present both the development of the codebook and the subsequent coding process.

3.1 Dataset Collection

The scope for the dataset was set with the following inclusion and exclusion criteria: The chatbots should be publicly accessible and implemented from a federal state or large city (German: "Großstadt", with more than 100.000 residents). We also exclude any chatbots which are not providing support for languages that include German, as it is the official administrative language.

The chatbots were collected by going through lists of large cities[2] and federal states[3] in Germany. Germany has a federal system, which means that the country is divided into 16 semi-autonomous federal states. Three of these states have a special status of a federal city-state. The landing pages of the federal states, their ministries, the large cities and, if available, their service portals were scanned by the coders for any chatbots through visual inspection, i.e., scrolling through the web pages, menus and their content, and looking out for any links, menupoints or icons of chatbots. With this search, a total of 25 chatbots were found, where 6 were found from two federal states for specific portals or institutional services; one city deploys two chatbots, one on the landing page and one on the city portal[4].

3.2 Coding Process

The chatbots were analysed with a codebook of 24 categories which are split in two different areas: a feature analysis with 12 categories and 12 chatbot interaction patterns [16]. Each of the categories contain at least one code, all of which are described in the digital appendix. Three authors were involved in the coding process: one coding author for the inductive coding, one coding author for the deductive coding, and one author who was part in the refinement meeting for the final codebook. In this section we describe the development of this codebook.

The codes for the feature analysis were developed iteratively in an abridged version of the codebook development as described by Rogers et al. with both

[2] https://de.wikipedia.org/wiki/Liste_der_Großstädte_in_Deutschland.

[3] https://de.wikipedia.org/wiki/Land_(Deutschland).

[4] The second one was found due to interacting with the chatbot on the landing page.

inductive and deductive coding [12], as can be seen in Fig. 1. After the chatbots were collected, a subset of them was used for inductive coding by the first coding author to find applicable categories and codes regarding the features and to verify the pattern codes in this dataset. The inductive coding showed that the chatbot interaction patterns are present in principle, and some potential new patterns are emerging. In a code development meeting between the two coding authors, the initial categories and codes for the feature analysis were discussed and possible weaknesses were deducted in the granularity of the codes, mostly regarding the presentation and access of the chatbot.

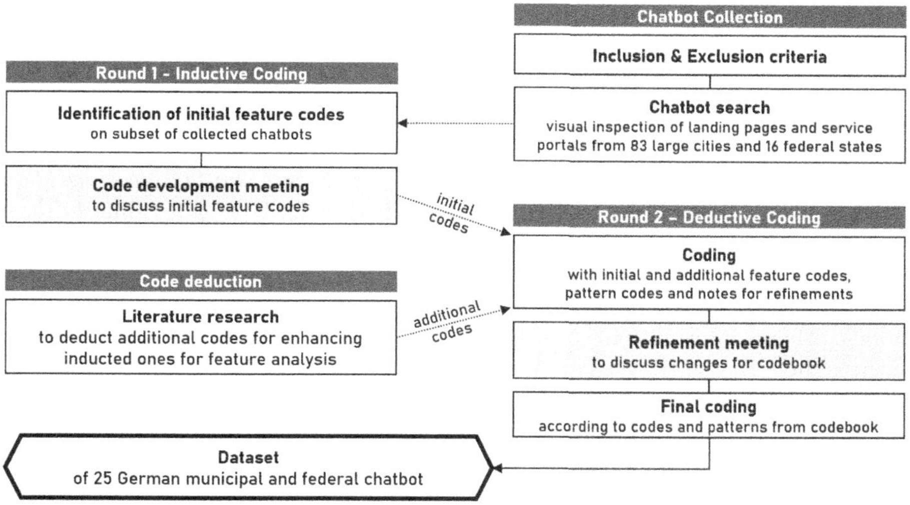

Fig. 1. Process of chatbot collection and the development of the codebook through inductive and deductive coding.

The initial codes were then expanded upon by the second coding author based by deducting codes from literature regarding several features: The use of avatars, names, and assigned gender [4], as well as the topics the chatbots are trained on [3,9,13], and the implementation of the chatbot on the page itself [5]. In the second round of coding, the initial codes and the ones deducted from literature sources were then enhanced upon by further deductive coding, which means that similar to grounded theory[5], possible codes for the categories were noted by the second coding author for further consideration.

For the coding in the second round, a semi-structured series of typical tasks concerning municipal services was conducted. The goal of this process was to let the chatbot provide a range of interaction patterns. The tasks included the following goals: registering for a new flat, extending the passport, searching for document downloads regarding these requests, and asking for information on

[5] cf. https://www.sciencedirect.com/topics/social-sciences/grounded-theory.

trash services. In the conversation the chatbot was also prompted with messages like "*This doesn't help me.*", "*Help*" or "*What can the chatbot do?*", so that possible interaction patterns related to help the user can be discovered. Each conversation started with the prompt "*I want to register.*" As each chatbot reacts differently to the input, the order of the subsequent prompts after the initial one were dynamically adapted depending on the unfolding conversation flow. As the chatbots on the federal level provide different information, the approach was adapted to their specific profile, with the consistent procedure to prompt the chatbot for providing help as detailed above. For each chatbot, screenshots and a recording of the final conversation were saved for further discussions. After the second round of coding, a refinement meeting took place between the second coding author and a third author who was not involved in the coding process. In this meeting, possible changes in the codebook and edge cases in the coding were discussed and based on the result, a final coding was conducted.

The 12 final categories for the feature analysis and their codes are explained next. The metadata includes the four categories for the *location* of the municipality or federal state, the *chatbot URL* to its interface, the *last accessed date*, and the *chatbot name*, each with one individual code. The *governmental level* is split into the codes city, federal state and federal city-state, while the category *topics* the chatbot is trained on includes the codes administration services, institutional information, and other. "Administration services" means here that among others, information is provided on openings hours, addresses, available services, how these services can be used and where to find necessary documents. The *page level* describes if the chatbot can be accessed on the landing page or a sub-page, while the *access* describes where the clickable access to the chatbot is located. This can be either at the bottom (including left or right), in the middle of the page, as a part of the menu, or a combination of the other codes. The next categories is the *interface type*, which can be a pop-up, full screen or a modal. The presentation of the chatbot is regarded in the categories *avatar* (Yes or No), and *reference* of its name like a locality, an acronym, the chatbot platform, a human name, if it is neutral or does not have a name. Additionally we code which *gender* would be assigned to the chatbot name. The category *languages* is coded either as German or multilingual, where at least one additional language is available. The 12 chatbot interaction patterns and their description are listed in Table 1 in Sect. 2.3 and are coded with Yes or No. The finalized dataset and descriptions of the categories and codes can be accessed in the digital appendix[6]. In Fig. 2 we show three different examples of the collected governmental chatbots.

4 Results

This section presents the results of our analysis and is split in two subsections: the feature analysis and chatbot interaction patterns.

[6] https://doi.org/10.5281/zenodo.14536728.

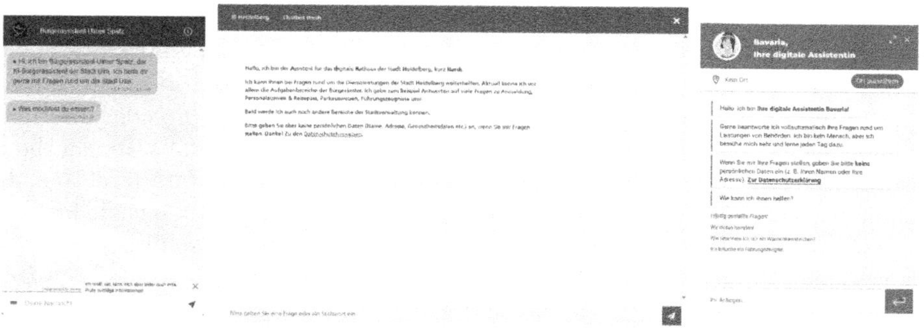

Fig. 2. Sample of three interfaces with welcome messages, illustrating the variety of interfaces of governmental chatbots. From left to right: a popup with logo as an avatar and a name, a modal without avatar, and a popup with an avatar, name and a selection of faq questions for starting the conversation.

4.1 Feature Analysis

In this subsection we present the results of our analysis of 12 features regarding the metadata, presentation and integration of the chatbots on the website. Figure 3 shows the results for the analysis of the governmental levels and the topics of the chatbots.

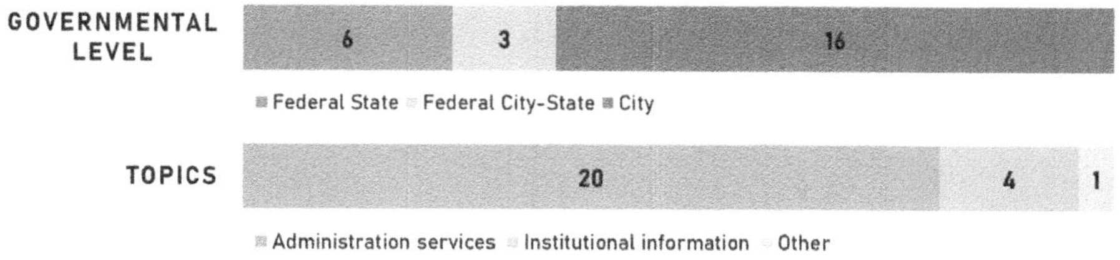

Fig. 3. The distribution on chatbots concerning their governmental levels and the topics they are deployed for.

Governmental Level

Germany has a federal system, which means that the country is divided into 16 semi-autonomous federal states. Three of these states have a special status of a federal city-state: Berlin, Bremen with Bremerhaven, and Hamburg; all of these cities are also large cities. The distribution of the chatbots is as follows: 6 were found from 2 federal states (with one of these also deploying 4 for specific institutions of its state parliament), 16 are from large cities and 3 from federal city-states. As these chatbots offer services similar to other large cities, we will further consider them under the same level.

Topics

From 19 large city chatbots, 18 provide information on administration services, which also includes information on the municipal service portal or are linked specifically to the "Behördennumer 115"[7]. The other chatbot provides information on the portal of classified ads, it is deployed on. Two federal state chatbots provide general administrative information on their federal state level and its municipalities, while the other 4 are linked to information about specific institutions. This includes information on integration, taxes, the state library, and the department of human resources.

Avatars and Names

The distributions of chatbots concerning their codes for avatars and names can be seen in Fig. 4. We found that 7 chatbots do not have an avatar, from the 18 chatbots including avatars some use their city crest or logo, others a logo provided by the platform or a specifically created one. Only one chatbot is presented without name and avatar, all others have names. The names of the chatbots can be references to different sources (corresponding chatbots in brackets):

- the *platform* the chatbot was provided from (115-Chatbot [city name] (three times), Govii (twice), Lumi[nous])
- *acronyms* (CiSA, CREDO, Frida, Hardi, Ina, Kora)
- relations to the *locality* like the city/institution name or landmarks (Bavaria, Chatbot Erlangen, DLZP-Chatbot, Frag-den-Michel, Hein Mück, Karlsbot, Nordi, Sparrenbert, Steuer-Chatbot SH, Ulmer Spatz, Wuebot)
- real *names* without any direct reference (Bobbi, Thekla, Toni)

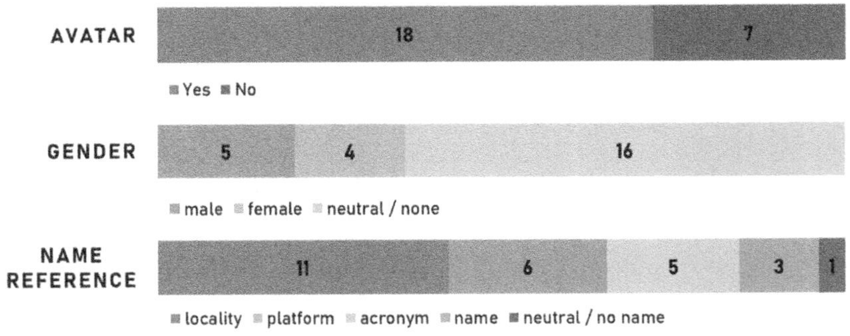

Fig. 4. The distribution of chatbots concerning their use of an avatar, the gender related to the used name and to which source the name can be referenced.

Page Level, Access and Interface Types

The access to the chatbot was mostly provided as an icon on the bottom right

[7] English: "Administration phone number 115", a phone number which provides administrative information for a network of participating municipalities and states.

of the landing page (17 chatbots), with one additional chatbot icon situated on the bottom left corner. Of the remaining chatbots, 5 had to be accessed as an element on the middle of the page, one could be accessed both on the middle and as an icon on the bottom, and one could only be accessed via the menu of the service portal.

For the chatbot interface types, we used three different codes: full screen, pop-up, and modal. We found 4 chatbots which open on a full screen page, 18 are implemented as a popup, and 3 as a modal on the middle of the screen with a darkened background. Of the popup chatbots, most are anchored to the bottom right corner or span the complete height of the right side of the website. Two implementations are a bit different, one opens as a popup on the middle of the screen and the other one is anchored to the left side of the interface. Two chatbots which were implemented by the same platform opened as a popup but could be enhanced via the persistent menu to a full screen. As the popup is the default version, we coded it as such. In Fig. 5 we present the relation between the page level, where the chatbot access is situated and on which interface type is provided.

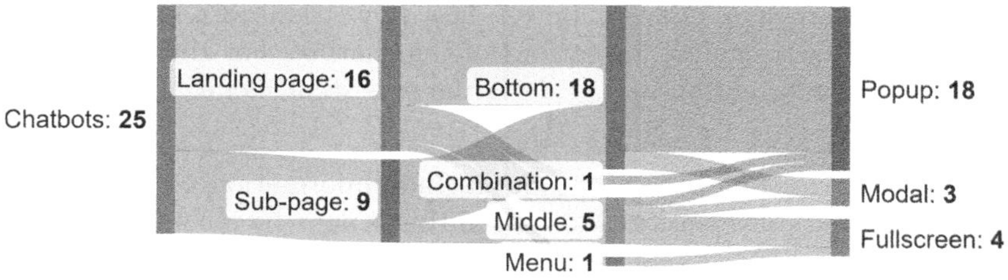

Fig. 5. A diagram presenting the relation between the page level, the access to the chatbot and the interfaces type.

4.2 Chatbot Interaction Patterns

From 12 coded chatbot interactions, all except for "Webview" were found in the analysis. Their distribution is presented in Fig. 6.

In the analysis we found some possible new chatbot interaction patterns, which we want to shortly present here. Examples of the new patterns can be seen in Fig. 7. The new patterns are named as follows with the number of found instances added in brackets: System information (9), Information stamps (9), Dialogue Reload (5), Accordion (9). For these new patterns we provide a short description, with the updated catalogue in the corresponding appendix. These patterns will have to be verified and further elaborated on in future research.

System Information. This pattern presents itself by offering information on the chatbot system outside of the conversation with the entity chatbot itself. It

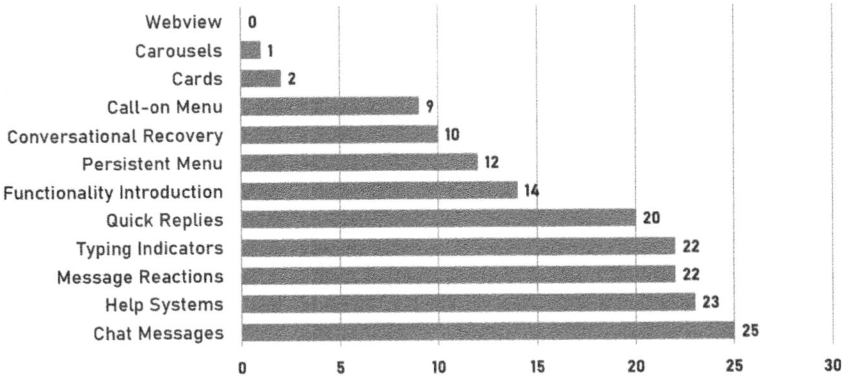

Fig. 6. A bar chart presenting the distribution of found chatbot interaction patterns.

is provided as banners or like "news tickers" above or underneath the respective footer or header of the chatbot, but can also be presented as a small pop-up or even span the complete area of the chatbot interface before access is given. As such, it mostly provides information on data protection, although the pattern can also inform on technical limitations of the chatbot. For this pattern we do not include any information provided via the persistent menu.

Information Stamps. Some chatbots include information on the time, user and context of the conversation. Most often this is done by including the time at which a chat message was sent either above or beneath that message (8 times). This is sometimes accompanied by the date or name of the sender, so either the chatbot name, 'guest' or a given name for the user (3 times). Some chatbots only provided the current date on top of the chat (4 times), while one also provides information on the current topic of the conversation.

Dialogue Reload. Of the analysed chatbots, 5 offer the option to reload the dialogue and start the conversation again. As such, it can help to solve situations in which the chatbot does not understand the user which might lead to frustrations. This can be seen as a specific sub-pattern of *Conversation Recovery*. The difference to that pattern is that *Conversation Recovery* is provided by the chatbot at best without a specific prompt from the user. The *Dialogue Reload* on the other hand is an action consciously taken by the user if they recognize that the chatbot either does not function as intended or cannot provide a satisfactory answer.

Accordion. The *Accordion* is a well known pattern from graphical user interfaces and is used to hide information to save space. In the analysed chatbots, *Accordions* are used either to shorten a very long chat message or to provide a short insight into several available search results. Some chatbots also include a similar option to show more *Quick Replies* for the users.

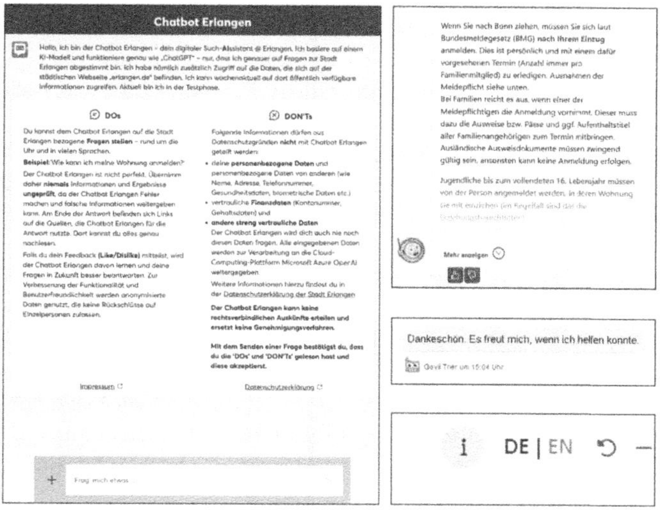

Fig. 7. Examples of new chatbot interaction patterns. Left: *System Information* (presenting information to the capabilities of the chatbot); right, top to bottom: *Accordion*, *Information Stamps*, and *Chatbot Reload*

5 Discussion

This section presents findings of our analysis based on the previously presented results.

General Insights. While most chatbots offer a unique implementation, some are relying on the same platforms. We found that 2 chatbots use Viind[8], 2 are implemented by govii[9] although it has to be noted that their interfaces and implementations of patterns are different from each other, and 3 of them are a "115-Chatbot", which is related to services of the "Behördennummer 115" (English: Administration phone number 115). This "Behördennummer" started an initiative in late 2023 to beta test a chatbot trained on the available data from the network[10]. It can be expected that this initiative will have an influence on the landscape of municipal chatbots in the future.

[8] https://www.viind.com/.
[9] https://govii.de/.
[10] https://www.115.de/news/detail/behoerdennummer-115-startet-testphase-fuer-service-chatbot.

We made an observation where cities apparently deployed a chatbot for some time or a specific occasion (like Covid-19 or elections), but do not have an active instance running anymore. This is documented by news articles on the implementation of such chatbots - we did not conduct an in-depth research into this direction, but some anecdotal links we found during our research are presented in the digital appendix. A similar observation was already made previously [7], who found that from a dataset of chatbots slightly less than 50% were still accessible 15 months after the creation of the dataset. From this we conclude that this is a general problem and not one related specifically to governmental chatbots.

Another insight is the use of gender for the personification of the chatbots. Different to previous research [4], we did not find a gender bias in our dataset. While we still found names which can be related to a gender, the numbers were nearly identical for both female (4) and male (5) connoted chatbots. Way more often we found more neutral names or ones which do not have any specific relation to a gender. It's possible that this is mostly caused by the use of acronyms, the inclusion of the chatbot platform or by referring to localities. Even though some of these names were combined with real names which are clearly gendered, most do not. The focus on rather including locally known names or simply providing the function of the chatbot seems to avoid the gender biases which can be observed in e-commerce chatbots.

Insights Into Existing Patterns. In some chatbots, particular implementations were found for individual patterns. One of three chatbots offered as a *Help System* not only the contact to real people but also an option to forward the conversation to provide some context for these employees. The *Typing Indicator* is symbolized in one chatbot by an animated glowing infinity symbol, in another as a progress bar with short messages and emoticons, while the ministry chatbots included this pattern in a way which is rather hard to recognize by showing the texts like "*[chatbot name] types ...*" (translated) under the text input field. While *Message Reactions* usually are shown as thumbs up or down, one chatbot used a 5-star rating system. All chatbots which provide *Message Reactions* also include some kind of feedback form. Either as an input field directly under the corresponding message, by opening a pop-up or even a dedicated feedback-page for this. The feedback is then either sent to the municipality or the responsible development team.

Insights Into Patterns Which Were Not Commonly Found. Another noteworthy insight is that some patterns are used sparingly or not at all in one case. *Cards* were only found in two chatbots, in one it was combined with *Carousels* which were not seen in any other chatbots. In the literature these patterns are based on Shevat and Valério et al., where the existence and use of these patterns is well documented [14,17]. One possible explanation is that the chatbots in the literature are mostly based in the e-commerce sector. This might offer more situations where *Cards* and subsequently *Carousels* make sense, as both usually rely on the inclusion of pictures. Administrative chatbots might not use this option, as most provided information could be better or at least as-well presented in a textual way.

The pattern of *Webviews* was not found in any of the analysed chatbots. This pattern describes the preview of information from another page. In e-commerce this can be seen for example for switching colours of products or providing map information [14]. We noticed in our analysis that chatbots often link to sub-pages or other websites with further information. For citizens who search for example for the location of a specific municipal office, including this pattern instead of only linking to it could help to present the information in a more user friendly way, especially as it is then presented in the same user interface.

We found 8 instances in our analysis of *Conversation Recovery*, a pattern which means that the chatbot 'proactively' provides the user with help on how to go on in the conversation, if the chatbot itself does not understand the request. This means that the chatbot has to offer possible options for the user, present them with help on how to formulate their requests or provide another option to resume the conversation. A simple message that the chatbot does not understand the user is not fulfilling this pattern. It might be possible that we did not find all possible instances of *Conversation Recovery*, as it is hard to artificially create situations in which the user is not understood by the chatbot.

6 Limitations and Threats to Validity

This section presents three limitations to the validity of our research and our mitigation strategies. The first limitation is internal and concerns our data collection. To avoid biases, we used available lists of large cities and federal states, and searched for chatbots on their websites with a visual inspection. As another mitigation strategy we used an iterative process in which our codebook was developed through iterative inductive and deductive approaches. In the deductive approach we based codes not only on already existing literature and available meta-data, but also iteratively, where codes were used on the dataset based on the occurrences in the chatbot interactions. The codes for the chatbot interaction patterns were based on already existing definitions and guidelines for the use of these patterns. Any edge cases were discussed in a refinement meeting with an author not involved in the coding process to reach a consensus.

An external limitation is that we only include German governmental chatbots on the federal and municipal level. To avoid any potential regional biases, we are not making any claims outside of this domain and are conscious that our results cannot be generalized to other nations or any domains outside of the governmental use. The scope on chatbots in Germany is based on similar publications from other countries. One goal is to provide an analysis and a dataset which can be merged and systematically analysed in later research to mitigate regional biases which might appear in singular studies.

The construct limitation concerns the methodology we chose to analyse our dataset. Due to the systematic approach, it is possible that we did not find all possible patterns specifically concerning the ones which have a more conversational nature, like *Conversation Recovery*. We tried to avoid biases by artificially prompting the chatbot directly or indirectly to provide help for the user.

7 Conclusion and Future Work

In this paper we analysed 25 chatbots from federal and municipal government levels in Germany on their features and their use of chatbot interaction patterns. We presented our results of the collected metadata, the presentation and integration of the chatbots, and how they use the presented patterns. The results show that the recently introduced chatbot interaction patterns can be validated in an analysis with in-use implementations. The analysis also shows that there are apparent differences in the use of patterns across different domains like e-commerce and governmental chatbots. On the other hand, even in one domain there are many different ways in how the patterns are implemented. We also find that the chatbots in our dataset do not have a gender bias in their use of names, different than previously found in e-commerce chatbots. In the discussion we also compared the use of existing patterns with a special regard of patterns which were not commonly used, even though they are present and described in e-commerce chatbots.

The presented analysis contributes threefold: For one, it provides a view on the landscape of German government chatbots on the federal and municipal level, shows the topics for which chatbots are used and how they are presented both in their implementation on the websites and regarding avatars and names. Additionally it provides the corresponding dataset of 25 federal and municipal chatbots. Lastly, we verify chatbot interaction patterns on a set of real-world chatbots and enhance the pattern catalogue with four new patterns presented in this paper. We also show which patterns are favored by governmental chatbots and discuss where they differ to e-commerce chatbots.

As this publication presents a baseline of the use of chatbot interaction patterns in governmental chatbots and a feature analysis of German federal and municipal chatbots, future research possibilities are manifold. The results from the presented analysis can be either compared with other domains like e-commerce or health, or within the same domain in another context. This can be done by analysing and comparing chatbots from different countries, but also to enhance the current dataset of federal institutions and large cities by collecting and analysing chatbots from smaller cities and townships in Germany. While we consider avatars, names and their genders, this can be enhanced by a wider and more systematic look at the use of these elements in the personification of the chatbots in different domains and contexts.

Acknowledgment. This paper is supported by the European Union's HORIZON Research and Innovation Programme under grant agreement No 101120657, project ENFIELD (European Lighthouse to Manifest Trustworthy and Green AI).

References

1. Abbas, N., Følstad, A., Bjørkli, C.A.: Chatbots as part of digital government service provision – a user perspective. In: Følstad, A., Araujo, T., Papadopoulos, S., Law, E.L.C., Luger, E., Goodwin, M., Brandtzaeg, P.B. (eds.) Chatbot Research and Design, pp. 66–82. Springer, Cham (2023). https://doi.org/10.1007/978-3-031-25581-6_5
2. Aoki, N.: An experimental study of public trust in AI chatbots in the public sector. Gov. Inf. Q. **37**(4), 101490 (2020). https://doi.org/10.1016/j.giq.2020.101490
3. Cortés-Cediel, M.E., Segura-Tinoco, A., Cantador, I., Rodríguez Bolívar, M.P.: Trends and challenges of e-government chatbots: advances in exploring open government data and citizen participation content. Gov. Inf. Q. **40**(4), 101877 (2023). https://doi.org/10.1016/j.giq.2023.101877
4. Feine, J., Gnewuch, U., Morana, S., Maedche, A.: Gender bias in chatbot design. In: Følstad, A., et al. (eds.) Chatbot Research and Design, pp. 79–93. Springer, Cham (2020). https://doi.org/10.1007/978-3-030-39540-7_6
5. Følstad, A., Bjerkreim-Hanssen, N.: User interactions with a municipality chatbot—lessons learnt from dialogue analysis. Int. J. Hum.–Comput. Interact. **0**(0), 1–14 (2023). https://doi.org/10.1080/10447318.2023.2238355
6. Følstad, A., Larsen, A.G., Bjerkreim-Hanssen, N.: The Human Likeness of government chatbots – an empirical study from norwegian municipalities. In: Lindgren, I., et al. (eds.) Electronic Government, pp. 111–127. Springer, Cham (2023). https://doi.org/10.1007/978-3-031-41138-0_8
7. Janssen, A., Grützner, L., Breitner, M.H.: Why do chatbots fail? A critical success factors analysis. In: ICIS 2021 Proceedings (2021). https://aisel.aisnet.org/icis2021/hci_robot/hci_robot/6
8. Larsen, A.G., Følstad, A.: The impact of chatbots on public service provision: a qualitative interview study with citizens and public service providers. Gov. Inf. Q. **41**(2), 101927 (2024). https://doi.org/10.1016/j.giq.2024.101927
9. Makasi, T., Nili, A., Desouza, K.C., Tate, M.: A typology of chatbots in public service delivery. IEEE Softw. **39**(3), 58–66 (2022). https://doi.org/10.1109/MS.2021.3073674
10. Moore, R.J., Arar, R.: Conversational UX Design: A Practitioner's Guide to the Natural Conversation Framework, 1st edn. ACM Books, New York (2019). https://doi.org/10.1145/3304087
11. van Noordt, C., Misuraca, G.: New wine in old bottles: chatbots in government. In: Panagiotopoulos, P., et al. (eds.) Electronic Participation, pp. 49–59. Springer, Cham (2019). https://doi.org/10.1007/978-3-030-27397-2_5
12. Roberts, K., Dowell, A., Nie, J.B.: Attempting rigour and replicability in thematic analysis of qualitative research data; a case study of codebook development. BMC Med. Res. Methodol. **19**(1), 66 (2019). https://doi.org/10.1186/s12874-019-0707-y
13. Senadheera, S., et al.: Understanding chatbot adoption in local governments: a review and framework. J. Urban Technol., 1–35 (2024). https://doi.org/10.1080/10630732.2023.2297665
14. Shevat, A.: Designing Bots: Creating Conversational Experiences, 1st edn. O'Reilly, Beijing (2017)
15. Tidwell, J., Brewer, C., Valencia, A.: Designing Interfaces: Patterns for Effective Interaction Design, 3rd edn. O'Reilly, Beijing (2020)

16. Traubinger, V., Gaedke, M.: Interaction design patterns of web chatbots. In: Stefanidis, K., Systä, K., Matera, M., Heil, S., Kondylakis, H., Quintarelli, E. (eds.) Web Engineering, pp. 309–317. Springer, Cham (2024). https://doi.org/10.1007/978-3-031-62362-2_22
17. Valério, F.A.M., Guimarães, T.G., Prates, R.O., Candello, H.: Chatbots explain themselves: designers' strategies for conveying chatbot features to users. J. Interact. Syst. **9**(3) (2018). https://doi.org/10.5753/jis.2018.710

LLM-Powered Conversational AI in Customer Service: Users' Expectations and Anticipated Use

Anna Grøndahl Larsen[1(✉)], Marita Skjuve[1], Knut Kvale[2], and Asbjørn Følstad[1]

[1] SINTEF, Oslo, Norway
anna.g.larsen@sintef.no
[2] Telenor Research and Innovation, Fornebu, Norway

Abstract. Large Language Models (LLMs) hold the promise to significantly enhance conversational AI in customer service. There is however limited understanding of end-users' expectations and anticipated use of LLM-powered conversational AI (CAI), which is crucial since expectation is directly linked to experience. This paper addresses this gap by exploring potential end-users' perceptions and expectations of LLM-powered CAI in customer service, drawing on expectancy-disconfirmation theory. The findings show that users have modest expectations for LLM-powered CAI in customer service, shaped by their past experiences with existing CAI and their experiences and knowledge of LLM features. The findings underline the importance of expectations management and ensuring high-quality use cases where LLM-powered CAI for customer service is implemented.

Keywords: Conversational AI · Customer Service · LLMs · User Expectations

1 Introduction

Service providers in sectors such as banking, insurance, and telecom have significantly invested in conversational artificial intelligence (AI) for customer service, mainly due to its ability to efficiently resolve end-user inquiries [1]. Conversational AI (CAI) interacts with users in natural language [2] and is intended to be a user-friendly and efficient way of automating simple tasks, such as locating information. Despite service providers' widespread adoption of text-based CAI, end-users may not share the same excitement. Research has shown that while end-users appreciate the technology's efficiency and availability [3], they also may experience frustration when interacting with CAI for customer service [1]. This frustration arises from the perception that the technology is rigid with generic responses and limited contextual adaptability [4, 5]. Such limitations may reduce the quality of the end-user experience [4] and erode trust [6, 7], ultimately hampering adoption rates [8] and the potential for value creation within the industry.

A. Følstad et al. (Eds.): CONVERSATIONS 2024, LNCS 15545, pp. 217–233, 2025.
https://doi.org/10.1007/978-3-031-88045-2_14

Large Language Models (LLMs) like GPT4[1] or Gemini[2] offer a promising solution to the challenges of CAI in customer service. With their basis in extensive datasets, generative capabilities, and ability to comprehend and respond to natural language, these models hold the promise to help customers faster and with a broader set of queries [9], and have the potential to enhance service quality [10], customer satisfaction [11], and foster value creation. Consequently, the implementation of LLMs across diverse applications is advancing rapidly. There are however also potential challenges with the use of LLMs in CAI for customer service, not least related to hallucinations, i.e., situations where LLMs provide output that is wrongful or inconsistent [9, 12]. There is to date limited understanding of how potential users anticipate LLMs to impact CAI in customer service. It is crucial to explore end-user expectations prior to integrating LLMs into CAI systems in this setting, as these expectations will likely impact the user experience [13, 14]. The importance of expectations management has been evident since the second wave of CAI implementations in 2016, when leading technology companies like Google and Microsoft strongly fronted conversational user interfaces. At that time, overly high expectations did not fully align with the capabilities of the technology, leading to negative user experiences [15] and poorer adoption rates than anticipated [16].

To bridge the current gap in understanding potential end-users' expectations towards LLM-powered CAI for customer service, our study explores the following overarching research question through a qualitative questionnaire with 190 potential end-users: *What are potential end-users' perceptions of and expectations towards LLM-powered conversational AI in customer service?* More specifically, we address the following sub-questions: How do potential end-users i) envision advantages and disadvantages with LLMs in customer service? ii) hope that LLMs will impact conversational AI in customer service? iii) foresee using LLM-powered conversational AI in customer service? By addressing these questions, our study contributes novel insights on users' perceptions of and expectations towards LLMs, that can help steer the development and implementation of LLMs into CAI for customer service.

2 State of the Art

2.1 Conversational AI in Customer Service

Research into text-based CAI in customer service has grown in recent years, offering valuable insights into the relationship between e.g., chatbot features and user experience.

One strand of research has taken a quantitative approach, focusing on factors that influence key constructs such as user experience, trust, acceptance, adoption, compliance, and customer loyalty [e.g., 16–22]. For example, Silva et al. [17] found that customers' intention to reuse chatbots are influenced by perceived usefulness and ease of use. Sheehan et al. [16] demonstrated that unresolved chatbot errors decreased perceived human-likeness, which negatively affects adoption intent. Kvale et al. [18] found that customer satisfaction is closely associated with the degree to which customers' problems

[1] https://openai.com/api/.

[2] https://ai.google.dev.

are solved. Jenneboer et al. [19], in a systematic literature review, found that customer loyalty following chatbot use is influenced by the chatbots' ability to provide a satisfying customer experience, by e.g., display appropriate levels of empathy or providing relevant information. Zhang et al. [20] also support the importance of emotional expression, demonstrating that chatbots' expression of concern for customers are positively associated with customer satisfaction.

Another strand of research has employed a qualitative approach, providing in-depth insights into how end-users experience CAI in customer service [3, 4, 23, 24]. For example, Castillo et al. [24] in a qualitative interview study on users' poor experiences with customer service chatbots, found that poor experiences are linked to, for example, interactions where users struggle to determine if they are interacting with a chatbot or a human, when chatbots struggle to understand the inquiry, provide wrong answers or come across as cold. Følstad and Skjuve [3], in a qualitative interview study on a banking chatbot, found that customers appreciated chatbots that enable efficient and accessible support, but were dissatisfied when the chatbot struggled to do so. van der Goot et al. [4] echoed these findings and further found that due to the limitations in chatbot communication abilities, users view chatbots for customer service as inadequate replacements for customer service personnel.

Together, these studies demonstrate that CAI can be valuable in customer service contexts, but technical limitations may hinder a good user experience and impede adoption. Recent developments within LLMs may solve some of these issues.

2.2 Conversational AI Powered with LLMs

Research on LLMs in the context of CAI has been conducted for several years but garnered heightened interest following the launch of ChatGPT in 2022. Despite this, few studies have explored LLMs and text-based CAI in customer service – although there are some notable exceptions. The research to date has primarily focused on two areas i) LLMs in customer service from the service providers' perspective [25–27], and ii) the development and performance of LLM-based chatbots within various domains such as finance and hospitality [28–30].

In the first research area – LLMs from service providers' perspective – Koc et al. [25] investigated the use of ChatGPT in responding to hotel customers' online complaints. They concluded that ChatGPT can generate efficient and effective management responses, thus having important implications for service recovery. Moreover, Limna et al. [26] explored the experiences and perceptions of hospitality employees and managers using ChatGPT in customer interactions. Their findings suggest that integrating LLMs into customer service could have a substantial positive impact, e.g., enhancing employee knowledge and bridging language barriers. Ferraro et al. [27] interviewed senior professionals in charge of LLM-powered CAI for customer service, identifying six paradoxes that service providers need to manage and underlining the need to carefully consider the use cases of LLM-powered CAI.

Concerning the second research area – the development and performance of LLM-based chatbots for customer service – Lakkaraju et al. [28] explored LLM-based chatbots for financial advisement, comparing their performance to that of a rule-based chatbot. They found that critical gaps still exist "in providing consistent and reliable financial information" across users. Similarly, Romero et al. [29] investigated an approach for personalized recommendations aimed at enhancing the customer service processes in restaurants, using LLMs.

Although providing valuable insights on LLMs in customer service, existing studies have neglected the customer perspective. To the best of our knowledge, our study is one of the first to explore the user perspective in-depth, focusing on potential users' perceptions of and expectations towards LLMs in customer service.

3 Theoretical Approach

In theorizing our findings, we draw on expectancy-disconfirmation theory. In essence, the theory posits that users evaluate the performance of a given service by comparing it to their expectations of that service [30, 31]. The perspective originated within consumer research where researchers found that perceived service quality is influenced by the relationship between expectation and experience [30]. In parallel, theories on customer satisfaction revealed that satisfaction depends on the relationship between expectation and experience [31, 32]. Later, interest shifted towards customer experience, understanding customer experience as influenced by service providers' ability to meet, or even exceed, customer expectations [33]. Recently, expectations have increasingly been regarded as one of several elements influencing experience, and expectations are typically seen as shaped by previous experiences with a service or service provider [34]. This is confirmed in studies focusing specifically on AI agents, showing that users' experience with the technology is affected by their expectations [13, 14]. For example, Ghazali et. al. [14] found confirmation of users' expectations to be 'a significant driver of their satisfaction with chatbot usage', which, together with perceived usefulness, was a predictor of continued use of the chatbot.

We define expectation as what customers anticipate or hope to get from a given service or product [35]. Moreover, conceptualizing experience as encompassing factors beyond service providers, and recognizing that expectations are shaped by previous experiences, imply that factors such as for example word-of-mouth, public discourse, and past experiences with customer service chatbots – regardless of the service provider – might affect expectations for customer service chatbots in general, including those powered by LLMs. This entails that to understand the potential impact of LLMs in customer service, including how LLMs should be integrated into CAI and how providers might manage expectations, it is crucial to understand the perceptions and expectations of potential end-users.

4 Method

4.1 Design, Data Collection and Sample

To address the research questions, we distributed a questionnaire with open-ended questions to obtain in-depth insight from a larger sample. This design was deemed preferable since the aim of our study was to explore an area where there is limited prior knowledge. To ensure participants had knowledge or experience with using LLMs, we screened the participants by asking about their experience with LLM-based services such as ChatGPT, Gemini, and Copilot. We included 190 participants who said they had heard of or had experience with such services, since these individuals are likely to have formed ideas or expectations on the (dis)advantages of LLM-based chatbots. The participants may not have in-depth knowledge of how LLMs may be used in CAI for customer service, but as prospective users their expectations are nevertheless important to understand. The participants were asked a set of open-ended questions about the potential (dis)advantages of using LLMs in customer service, and which tasks they would and would not use such conversational AI for.

Table 1. Overview of the questions posed to participants.

#	Questions about LLMs
	Close-ended question to screen participants:
	Over the past year, there has been a lot of talk about artificial intelligence, such as ChatGPT, CoPilot, Gemini, MyAI, and Claude. Are you familiar with such services? Either through your own use or through media coverage?
	Open-ended questions addressing the research questions:
1	What do you see as advantages of using artificial intelligence in self-service in customer support?
2	What do you see as possible disadvantages of using artificial intelligence in self-service customer support?
3	If artificial intelligence is part of the chatbot for banking/telecom/insurance – what changes in today's chatbot solutions do you hope to see? Explain why
4	If artificial intelligence is part of the chatbot for banking/telecoms/insurance – for which tasks would you use such a chatbot? Explain why
5	If artificial intelligence is part of the chatbot for banking/telecoms/insurance – for which tasks would you not use such a chatbot? Explain why

Table 1 displays the questions posed to participants, including the screening question. The study was conducted in Norway with Norwegian-speaking participants, and the questions have been translated from Norwegian by the authors. The capabilities of services such as ChatGPT and Co-Pilot are made possible by large language models. Since, in Norwegian public and popular discourse, the term 'artificial intelligence' is more common than 'large language models' for describing services like ChatGPT and their potential (dis)advantages, we opted for using the term 'artificial intelligence' in our questions, while explaining to participants what types of services we referred to. Related to each of the open-ended questions, the headline read "On artificial intelligence and customer service", with the sub-headline "Over the past year, there has been a lot of talk about artificial intelligence such as ChatGPT, CoPilot, Gemini, MyAI, and Claude". Participants' responses suggested that they were indeed familiar with services based on large language models and (dis)advantages associated with these, mentioning issues such as enhanced language capabilities, the potential for bias and being provided wrongful information. Hence, although participants may not be familiar with the term 'LLMs', the responses indeed indicate a familiarity with features made possible by LLMs among most participants. Some, however, also responded e.g., 'don't know' to some of the questions, as reported in more detail in Sect. 5. For three of the questions we opted for mentioning specific domains (banking, telecom and insurance). This was intended to have participants think about specific use cases for CAI in customer service. While some responses did reflect these domains, as shown in Sect. 5, most responses addressed CAI in customer service more generally, not focusing on specific industries.

The participants were recruited through the panel services Prolific[3] and Ipsos[4]. The data was collected between 20.04.2024—09.05.2024. The questionnaire took an average of 20 min to complete, and the participants received a small compensation. The sample has almost equal gender distribution: female (53%), male (47%), divided into seven age categories, distributed as: age 18–29 (26%), age 30–39 (17%), age 40–49 (16%), age 50–59 (13%), age 60–69 (14%), age 70–79 (12%), age 80 + (2%). The data collection was anonymous, with participants providing their informed consent. The median response length for each question was 72 characters (Mean: 104. Max: 884 characters. Min: 3 characters).

4.2 Thematic Analysis

The responses to the open-ended questions were analyzed using thematic analysis, following Braun and Clarke's six-step procedure [36]. One of the authors initially reviewed the responses to get a sense of the data, before coding all meaningful units in Excel. A code could be a word or a sentence summarizing the meaning of a unit. Once the dataset was coded, the codes were revised – some codes were renamed, while others were merged. The final codes were then grouped into overarching themes. To ensure quality in the analysis, uncertainties and findings were discussed with one of the co-authors during the initial analysis. In later stages of the analysis, the findings were refined based on discussion between the author team and iterations between the data, codes, themes, and the analysis document. In this process, we went back to the raw data, re-read and adjusted our initial coding and refined our themes. In presenting the results, we emphasize the qualitative qualities of the data, but also quantify the distribution of the identified themes. Since participants' response to a question may include multiple themes, the total percentages can exceed one hundred.

5 Results

In the following, we first provide an overview of the participants' reflections regarding advantages and disadvantages of using LLMs in customer service. Following this, we outline their expectations and desired use cases related to LLM-powered conversational AI for customer service.

[3] https://www.prolific.com.

[4] https://www.ipsos.com/nb-no.

5.1 User Perceptions of (Dis)advantages of LLMs in Customer Service

The participants reported on both advantages and disadvantages of LLMs in customer service. Advantages particularly concerned efficiency and availability, improved quality of support, reduced provider costs, and increased availability of needed personnel. Disadvantages concerned reduced quality of support, lack of human touch, issues related to trust and abuse, and the potential for negative societal implications of the technology. The findings are summarized in Tables 2 and 3 and detailed below.

Table 2. Envisioned advantages of LLMs in customer service (n = 190).

Advantages	Description	%
Efficiency and availability	Improving efficiency and availability by automating processes and enabling issue resolution without human intervention	**48**
Improved quality of support	Improving support quality, e.g., by making self-service more user-friendly, personalized, covering a wider scope of issues	**29**
Reduction in provider costs	Reducing the service provider's costs (not necessarily a benefit for the user)	**13**
Improved allocation of customer service personal	Enabling customer service personnel to prioritize more complex tasks by outsourcing simpler ones to the LLM, while also assisting them in performing their tasks more efficiently	**12**
None	LLMs are not seen to contribute with any benefits	**20**

In terms of envisioned advantages of LLMs in customer service (Table 2), participants largely focused on benefits related to the customer experience, with ***increased efficiency and availability*** mentioned by almost half of the participants (48%). The following quotes illustrate typical responses related to efficiency and availability: *"They make it simpler to find information. [...]"* (ID16), *"[AI] can probably solve some problems faster, more precisely and efficiently"* (ID64).

Participants (29%) also foresaw LLMs to ***increase the quality of self-service***, making it more user-friendly and providing improved support compared to current chatbots and/or to customer service personnel. One participant noted that: *"You can have a conversation and ask follow-up questions"* (ID75).

Furthermore, some participants (13%) noted how LLMs might entail an advantage for service providers by ***reducing their costs***. While this was not necessarily regarded as a benefit for customers, some (12%) also noted how reducing costs might be beneficial for customers in terms of ***freeing up customer service personnel*** from simple tasks, allowing them to focus on more complex tasks requiring human assistance. As noted by one participant: *"People in customer service can focus on things that truly need human expertise"* (ID11).

Finally, one fifth of the participants (20%) responded that they did not see any advantages with LLMs in customer service.

Table 3. Envisioned disadvantages with LLMs in customer service (n = 190).

Disadvantages	Description	%
Reduced quality of support	Negatively impacting support quality due to hallucinations such as wrongful information and problems with understanding requests	**53**
Unfortunate lack of human touch	Making service interactions feel less personal due to a lack of empathy, emotions, and flexibility	**28**
Trust issues and concerns for abuse	Raising trust issues and concerns about potential abuse, e.g., scamming or bias	**21**
Negative societal implications	LLMs are assumed to have negative societal consequences, such as people losing their jobs or inhibiting human contact	**21**

In terms of envisioned disadvantages (Table 3), participants considered broader societal and relational implications of LLMs as well as specific implications for customer service. Related to customer service specifically, around half of the participants (53%) noted potential disadvantages related to ***reduced quality of support***, including wrongful information and poor understanding of requests. One participant noted that *"[AI] is not perfect technology and may often make mistakes. It can [...] provide wrongful information"* (ID11).

Furthermore, participants (28%) mentioned a ***lack of human touch*** as a potential drawback with LLMs in customer service, noting how chatbots may make service encounters less personal and less flexible, as illustrated by this quote: *"[...] AI is not personalized and doesn't understand the individual user to the same extent as customer service personnel"* (ID77).

Participants also envisioned LLMs to have ***disadvantages related to trust and misuse*** (21%). This included disadvantages due to users not trusting the response and/or that their privacy is maintained, but also the presence of bias and the potential for manipulation. One participant noted that: *"Decisions should in many cases be left to or overseen by humans. It is important to make sure that AI doesn't discriminate"* (ID98).

Finally, some participants (21%) focused on ***negative societal consequences*** of LLMs, such as people losing their jobs, or chatbots inhibiting human contact, as illustrated by this participant quote: *"people will lose their jobs, and users will lose the possibility to talk to other humans"* (ID41).

5.2 Users' Hopes for the Future: More Intelligent and Comprehensive Conversational AI

To understand users' expectations towards LLMs in customer service, participants were asked what changes they hoped to see in today's chatbot solutions. Reflecting the envisioned advantages related to efficiency and improved quality presented above, participants particularly hoped that LLMs would make CAI better, more intelligent, more comprehensive, and more efficient. Most participants (61%) hoped LLMs would make CAI better and more intelligent. Some mentioned improvements in general, but the majority were more specific in their response, focusing on CAI's ability to understand, respond to and help with a broader set of questions and tasks in an efficient manner (Table 4).

Table 4. Changes users hope to see as a result of LLMs (n = 188)

Themes	%
Better and more intelligent Conversational AI	61
Increased understanding of queries	28
Providing better/more comprehensive answers	27
Broadening the scope of conversational AI's	17
More efficient	12
Would not use	10
Don't know	13

Several participants (28%) hoped that LLMs will ***increase conversational AI's understanding*** of queries, without the need to use predefined menus, keywords or to carefully draft questions. One participant noted that: *"I want to avoid having to formulate my questions as precisely as I sometimes have to with slightly 'dumber' chatbots [...]"* (ID58). Related to this, participants noted that they hoped an improved understanding would entail conversational AI's being more pleasurable conversational partners with the ability to understand more complex questions and respond in a more human manner. As noted by this participant: *"That you may have a conversation where you along the way arrive at a solution, rather than (as I often experience with today's chatbots) asking a question, receiving suggested solutions that aren't quite right, trying again, but getting the same answer"* (ID75).

Relatedly, participants hoped that LLMs would make CAIs capable of ***providing better or more comprehensive answers*** (27%) and ***broadening the scope*** (17%) of CAI's, making them able to help with a broader set of tasks. This often entailed being able to provide more relevant information beyond the generic information one may access on service providers' websites. Several participants noted that CAI should be capable of helping users solving more problems, without the need to escalate to a human service worker. One participant for example noted that *"[...] you should be able to explain in detail what the problem is and get help, not just be redirected* (ID47). Participants also highlighted that a broadened scope would entail covering a broader set of potential questions and providing more personalized help, such as for example chatbots having access to information on customer relationships and being able to provide personalized help.

As part of being able to understand, respond to and help with a broader set of tasks, some participants (12%) focused explicitly on how they hoped interactions would be ***more efficient***, providing the correct answer or needed information faster than current conversational AIs are capable of, as seen in the following participant quote: "*[...] I would like that it would take* 5–10 min *to fix a problem instead of waiting for several hours*" (ID43).

Finally, some participants (10%) were negative to conversational AI and did not cite any hopes for future uses of LLMs in customer service. This however seemed unrelated to the use of LLMs as such. Instead, these participants seemed to prefer more human interaction and less CAI in general, as illustrated by this quote: "*Most human beings would like to talk to a person*" (ID24).

5.3 Tasks Where Users Would – and Would not – Use LLM-Powered Conversational AI

To further understand users' perceptions of and expectations towards LLMs in customer service, the participants were asked to mention tasks where they would – and would not – use LLM-powered CAI in telecom, banking, and insurance. In the following we first present the tasks participants were willing to use CAI for (Table 5), followed by the tasks they were unwilling to use it for (Table 6).

Tasks Where Users Would be Positive to Use LLM-Powered Conversational AI. In terms of tasks where users said they would use LLM-powered CAI, we identified two areas in specific: information and knowledge acquisition and task assistance. In addition, some participants stated that they would be willing to try CAI for all types of tasks.

Table 5. Tasks where users would be positive to use LLM-powered conversational AI (n = 184)

Themes	%
Information and knowledge acquisition	59
Task assistance	14
Willing to try it for 'everything'	10
Don't know	18

Information and Knowledge Acquisition. More than half of the participants (app. 59%) said that they would be willing to use LLM-powered CAI to get information and knowledge. Some simply noted that they would use it to get answers to simpler questions, such as "general information", and "navigating the website", thus very much resembling how customer service chatbots typically are used today. To illustrate, one participant noted that they would use it *"For simpler tasks and questions and left the more technical and private [tasks/questions] for humans"* (ID19). Other participants were more specific, mentioning areas where they envisioned to use CAI to get information and knowledge, such as obtaining information about products and services, comparing offers from service providers, tips on how to save money, problem-solving and guidance, and general questions about interests or insurance. This is illustrated in the following quote: *"For example, it could be used to answer common questions about products and services, perform simple transactions like balance inquiries, and provide basic technical support for troubleshooting"* (ID21).

Task Assistance. Some participants (14%) also expressed anticipating using CAI to solve specific tasks, such as negotiating for a better interest rate on their mortgage, open or close bank accounts or credit cards, change information in their profile or cancel subscriptions. A few participants also stated that they were willing to use CAI to purchase insurance, apply for a mortgage, or transfer money from one account to another. As noted by one participant: *"Questions I have regarding changes to my loans and insurance policies. I would also use it to make changes to my accounts and subscriptions"* (ID 33).

Try Using it for 'Everything'. A few participants (10%) were very open regarding what they would like to use the technology for and stated that they would be willing to try to use it for more or less everything, before contacting service personnel if necessary.

Tasks Where Users Would be Negative to Use LLM-Powered Conversational AI. In terms of tasks where users say they would not use LLM-powered CAI, we identified four areas: tasks that involved sharing personal or sensitive information, financial matters, complex questions, and legal matters. In addition, some participants did not foresee to use CAI for anything whatsoever.

Table 6. Tasks where users would not use LLM-powered conversational AI (n = 185)

Themes	%
Personal or sensitive information	35
Financial matters	17
Complex problems	11
Legal matters	5
Would not use it for anything	17
Don't know	11
Would use it for 'everything'	7

Personal or Sensitive Information. Some participants (35%) expressed hesitation about using LLM-powered CAI for tasks that required sharing personal or sensitive information. Many did not specify what such information could be, but some gave examples such as pin codes, passwords, access to accounts, or spending habits. Such caution appeared to stem from security concerns, including the potential for information to be used for further training of the LLM, leaked, or otherwise misused. Related to this one participant stated that: *"I wouldn't have given it any personal information that I was worried that would come out. Everything that would be said, I would say with the understanding that someone might find a loophole in the system"* (ID99).

Financial Matters. Some participants (17%) reported being skeptical towards using CAI for queries concerning financial matters and/or with financial consequences. This could be asking for financial advice or having the CAI transfer money from one account to another. As noted by one participant: *"For example, in large bank transfers and generally things where a lot is at stake, such as a lot of money. I generally trust humans more than chatbots"* (ID59).

Complex Problems. Using the technology to get help with complex questions or more advanced problems also generated an anticipated skepticism amongst some participants (11%). Most did not state what such matters could be, but some explained that it was related to situations where human abilities such as thorough explanations, empathy, or discretion are needed. One participant noted that: *"I would for example avoid using the chatbot to handle sensitive or complex issues which require a high degree of empathy and human judgment [...]"* (ID24).

Legal Matters. A few (5%) anticipated not wanting to use an LLM-powered CAI for legal issues, such as handling complaints or drafting and signing contracts. As noted by one participant: *"I would not want that they use AI to tasks which entail signing or creating legally binding contracts"* (ID11).

Would not use it for Anything. Finally, some participants (17%) did not foresee using conversational AI for anything whatsoever. Again, this was related to a general dislike towards CAI and not LLM-features as such, as illustrated in this quote: *"I would not use it for anything. Not even if it got much better. Annoying"* (ID69).

6 Discussion and Conclusion

In this study, we have explored potential users' perceptions and expectations towards text-based LLM-powered conversational AI in customer service. Despite the link between user expectation and experience, there is currently a limited understanding of how potential end-users perceive and anticipate LLMs impacting CAI. By addressing this gap, the study enhances empirical understanding of user perception and expectations towards LLMs, contributes theoretically to the literature on the relationship between user experience and expectations towards technology, and practically through providing insights that may inform the development and implementation of LLM-powered CAI.

6.1 Expectations Towards LLMs in Customer Service

Expectations are essential in customer service [13, 14, 31–33]. Given the recent hype surrounding LLMs, one might expect potential end-users to have high expectations for LLMs in customer service. Our findings, however, indicate that user expectations are relatively modest, characterized by a belief in incremental improvements and an awareness of potential downsides. On the one hand, the findings indeed indicate that users believe there are substantial advantages – such as increased efficiency, reduced costs, and improved personnel allocation. On the other hand, users are aware of potential risks that may follow uptake of LLMs in customer service, such as reduced support quality, lack of human interaction, trust issues, and potential negative societal aspects of automation, such as employment. Some are also skeptical of CAI for customer service in general. Such concerns align with public discourse on the potential negative effects of AI [37, 38] but likely also stem from previous experiences with failed automation in customer service [4, 5]. However, the modest outlook should likely not be interpreted as a general lack of interest in LLMs for customer service. Research on customer service suggests that users value efficient and effective self-service [39], and the findings should likely be interpreted as potential end-users holding a balanced and sober view of LLMs in customer service – aware of potential benefits and limitations, without overly high expectations.

6.2 Hopes for How LLMs Will Impact Conversational AI for Customer Service

Participants' modest expectations for LLMs in customer service were also evident in their hopes for the impact of LLMs on conversational AI for customer service. Many hoped that LLMs would improve CAI, but few imagined LLMs to represent something fundamentally new. For example, participants typically envisioned using LLM-powered CAI for similar tasks as they currently do but hoping that tasks would be handled better. Again, this seems, at least in part, related to previous experiences with customer service chatbots, underlining the relationship between experience and expectations. However, participants also anticipated improvements which in practice entail broadening the scope of CAI for customer service. When asked about their hopes, many for example foregrounded improved understanding and conversational abilities, which in practice may entail broadening the type of tasks that conversational AI might assist with. Simultaneously, participants expressed concerns about potential negative implications, such as hallucinations and trust issues, and were hesitant to use LLM-powered CAI in decision-making and issues requiring sharing of sensitive personal information.

6.3 Expected Use of LLM-Powered Conversational AI for Customer Service

The findings also offer interesting insights into potential end-users' expectations for tasks they would and would not use LLM-powered CAI for in customer service. Participants typically focused on using such AI for information and knowledge acquisition, an expectation reflecting their likely prior experiences with CAI in this context. Hence, when envisioning future use, users seem to rely more on their own experiences with using CAI, rather than on optimistic visions in public discourse on how LLMs will positively impact society. This aligns with the service research literature, which identifies prior experience as a determinant of both current action and experience [34]. This impact of prior experience on users' willingness to adopt new and presumably improved technology will be an important consideration for developers and providers of CAI for customer service.

The findings furthermore show that potential end-users are hesitant to use LLM-powered conversational AI for complex issues, personal information, and financial matters. This hesitancy likely stems from both personal experiences with CAI in customer and broader concerns raised in public discourse about AI, such as issues related to privacy and bias, which together may undermine users' trust in using LLMs for more complex and personalized tasks. However, a smaller group of participants indicated that they foresee using LLM-powered CAI for more advanced tasks, such as managing financial accounts or negotiating terms. This anticipated use suggests a more transformational role for AI in customer service, as it entails CAI taking over tasks which today typically require human personnel. This relatively smaller group of potential end-users expecting more advanced uses might be interpreted through the lens of diffusion of innovation theory [40], positing that a smaller segment of the population will be early adopters of an innovation. From this theoretical perspective, developers and deployers of CAI may consider that the initial expansion of chatbots' capabilities in customer service may cater to a relatively small group of users, with wider adoption following when the CAI proves its value.

6.4 Implications

Our findings suggest that expectations towards LLM-powered CAI are shaped by at least two factors: previous experiences with existing CAI for customer service and knowledge of and experiences with LLMs specifically. First, our findings indicate that users' personal experiences with existing CAI for customer service shape how they envision using CAI also in the future, with previous experience apparently shaping their rather modest outlooks and hopes. Second, the findings imply that experiences with LLM-based services such as ChatGPT and the recent hype around LLMs inform users hopes and fears, where factors such as public discourse are reflected in users' expectations, including what they envision as (dis)advantages, and future uses of LLM-powered CAI for customer service. In sum, the findings provide a basis for tentative theoretical assumptions on users' expectations towards innovation in CAI, specifically innovations driven by LLMs.

- **Expectations on service are guided by experience and public discourse:** Potential end-users' general expectations towards LLM-powered CAI for customer service, including hopes and fears, reflect both personal experiences and public discourse on the technology. This includes the specific tasks for which they would hesitate to use LLM-powered CAI, such as personal information and financial matters, which appears to be impacted by personal experience (e.g., existing chatbots struggling with more complex tasks or instructing users not to reveal personal information) and by issues typically raised in public discourse (e.g., fears related to bias and privacy violations).
- **Expectations on own use are guided by experience:** Potential end-users' specific expectations on how they indeed would use LLM-powered conversational AI, seem mainly guided by their previous experience with resembling technology, and to a lesser extent on the (more hopeful) visions that may be found in public discourse on LLMs.

While these implications are tentative, based on a single qualitative study, they may nevertheless be interesting to consider in further research on LLM-powered CAI.

For practice, the findings suggest two important takeaways for developers and deployers of CAI for customer service.

- **User uptake will require expectation management and sensitivity to user expectations.** In contrast to the hype surrounding LLMs in parts of public discourse, end-users may hold a more nuanced view. Since potential users, in part based on their previous experiences with chatbots for customer service, tend to have modest expectations, it is crucial to adequately manage these expectations and ensure quality in the use cases where LLMs are indeed implemented [cf. 6, 27], with providers and deployers needing to show clear benefits to encourage use and build trust.
- **User uptake of advanced features will likely be gradual.** Given that most participants anticipate using LLM-powered chatbots for customer service much like they use chatbots today, the uptake of advanced LLM features may require patience. This might involve an initial phase of onboarding early adopters before engaging the majority, gradually building trust in CAI for customer service [cf. 6].

Addressing the practical implications may require developers and deployers to engage in substantial user research and user-centered design efforts to provide LLM-powered CAI that fits with users' customer service needs and expectations.

6.5 Limitations and Further Research

While the study provides valuable insights into user expectations of LLMs in customer service and CAI, it also has limitations. First, it was a questionnaire-based study, gathering user expectations based on their existing knowledge and experience with LLM-based services. While this limitation was mitigated by requiring participants to have prior knowledge or experience with LLMs, we still foresee future research including a behavioral component, e.g. where users are given practical exercises with LLM services prior to their participation. Second, the study was conducted at a single point in time when LLM-powered CAI is still relatively new, and some potential users may still be unsure what to expect. This limits our ability to compare users' stated expectations with their later behavior or observe changes in expectations as the uptake and discourse on CAI evolve. Multi-wave studies would be valuable to address this. Third, the study was conducted in a specific region and market, with some questions specifically addressing customer service in banking, telecom, and insurance. Since participant responses tended to concern CAI in customer service in general, not specifically addressing specific industries, it is likely that our findings are valid for CAI in customer service more broadly, including other industries, regions and markets. However, future research investigating user expectations to LLM-powered chatbots in other contexts would be valuable. Despite the noted limitations, we believe this study has provided valuable insights, serving as a first step towards understanding user expectations of LLM-powered chatbots for customer service.

Acknowledgments. This study was funded by the Research Council of Norway (grant number 346762).

Disclosure of Interests. The authors have no competing interests to declare that are relevant to the content of this article.

References

1. Nicolescu, L., Tudorache, M.T.: Human-computer interaction in customer service: the experience with AI chatbots—a systematic literature review. Electronics **11**(1579) (2022)
2. Dale, R.: The return of the chatbots. Nat. Lang. Eng. **22**, 811–817 (2016)
3. Følstad, A., Skjuve, M.: Chatbots for customer service: user experience and motivation. In: Proceedings of the 1st International Conference on Conversational User Interfaces, pp. 1–9 (2019)
4. van der Goot, M.J., Hafkamp, L., Dankfort, Z.: Customer service chatbots: a qualitative interview study into the communication journey of customers. In: Følstad, A., et al. (eds.) CONVERSATIONS 2020. LNCS, vol. 12604, pp. 190–204. Springer, Cham (2021). https://doi.org/10.1007/978-3-030-68288-0_13
5. Janssen, A.H.A., Grützner, L., Breitner, M.H.: Why do chatbots fail? A critical success factors analysis. In: Proceedings of the ICIS (2021)
6. Nordheim, C.B., Følstad, A., Bjørkli, C.: An initial model of trust in chatbots for customer service – findings from a questionnaire study. Interact. Comput. (2019)
7. Law, E.L.C., Følstad, A., Van As, N.: Effects of humanlikeness and conversational breakdown on trust in chatbots for customer service. In: Proceedings of Nordic Human-Computer Interaction Conference - NordiCHI '22 (Article No. 56). ACM, New York (2022)
8. Ashktorab, Z., Jain, M., Liao, Q.V., Weisz, J.D.: Resilient chatbots: repair strategy preferences for conversational breakdowns. In: Proceedings of the 2019 CHI Conference on Human Factors in Computing Systems, pp. 1–12 (2019)
9. Bamberger, S., Clark, N., Ramachandran, S., Sokolova, V. How Generative AI is Already Transforming Customer Service. Boston Consulting Group (2023)
10. Lewandowski, T., Kučević, E., Leible, S., Poser, M., Böhmann, T.: Enhancing conversational agents for successful operation: a multi-perspective evaluation approach for continuous improvement. Electron. Mark. **33**(39) (2023)
11. Cui, Y., van Esch, P., Phelan, S.: How to build a competitive advantage for your brand using generative AI. Bus. Horiz. **67** (2024)
12. Huang, L., et al.: A survey on hallucinations in large language models. arXiv (2023)
13. Dhiman, N., Jamwal, M.: Tourists' post-adoption continuance intentions of chatbots: integrating task-technology fit model and expectation-confirmation theory. Foresight **25**(2), 209–224 (2022)
14. Ghazali, E., Mutum, D.S., Lun, N.K.: Expectations and beyond: the nexus of AI instrumentality and brand credibility in voice-assistant retention using extended expectation-confirmation model. J. Consum. Behav. **23**(2), 655–675 (2023)
15. Luger, E., Sellen, A.: "Like having a really bad PA" the gulf between user expectation and experience of conversational agents. In: Proceedings of the 2016 CHI Conference on Human Factors in Computing Systems, pp. 5286–5297 (2016)
16. Sheehan, B., Jin, H.S., Gottlieb, U.: Customer service chatbots: anthropomorphism and adoption. J. Bus. Res. **115**, 14–24 (2020)
17. Silva, F.A., Shojaei, A.S., Barbosa, B.: Chatbot-based services: a study on customers' reuse intention. J. Theor. Appl. Electron. Commer. Res. **18**, 457–474 (2023)
18. Kvale, K., Freddi, E., Hodnebrog, S., Sell, O.A., Følstad, A.: Understanding the user experience of customer service chatbots: what can we learn from customer satisfaction surveys?. In: Følstad, A., et al. (eds.) Chatbot Research and Design. CONVERSATIONS 2020. LNCS, vol. 12604, pp. 205–218. Springer, Cham (2021). https://doi.org/10.1007/978-3-030-68288-0_14

19. Jenneboer, L., Herrando, C., Constantinides, E.: The impact of chatbots on customer loyalty: a systematic literature review. J. Theor. Appl. Electron. Commer. Res. **17**, 212–229 (2022)
20. Zhang, J., Chen, Q., Lu, J., Wang, X., Liu, L., Feng, Y.: Emotional expression by artificial intelligence chatbots to improve customer satisfaction: underlying mechanism and boundary conditions. Tour. Manag. **100**, 104835 (2024)
21. Adam, M., Wessel, M., Benlian, A.: AI-based chatbots in customer service and their effects on user compliance. Electron. Mark. **31**, 427–445 (2021)
22. Elkhatibi, Y., Guelzim, H., Benabdelouahed, R.: Factors influencing the adoption of AI-powered chatbots in the Moroccan banking sector: an extended UTAUT model. J. Logist. Inform. Serv. Sci. **11**(7), 559–585 (2024)
23. Saklani, S., Kala, D.: Perception of GEN Z customers towards chatbots as service agents: a qualitative study in the Indian context. J. Telecommun. Digit. Econ. **12**(1), 356–376 (2024)
24. Castillo, D., Canhoto, A.I., Said, E.: The dark side of AI-powered service interactions: exploring the process of co-destruction from the customer perspective. Serv. Ind. J. **41**, 900–925 (2021)
25. Koc, E., Hatipoglu, S., Kivrak, O., Celik, C., Koc, K.: Houston, we have a problem! The use of ChatGPT in responding to customer complaints. Technol. Soc. **74**, 102333 (2023)
26. Limna, P., Kraiwanit, T.: The role of ChatGPT on customer service in the hospitality industry: an exploratory study of hospitality workers' experiences and perceptions. Tour. Hosp. Manag. **29**(4), 583–592 (2023)
27. Ferraro, C., Demsar, V., Sands, S, Restrepo, M., Campbell, C.: The paradoxes of generative AI-enabled customer service: a guide for managers. Bus. Horiz. **67** (2024)
28. Lakkaraju, K., Jones, S.E., Vuruma, S.K.R., Pallagani, V., Muppasani, B.C., Srivastava, B.: LLMs for financial advisement. In: Proceedings of the Fourth ACM International Conference on AI in Finance, pp. 100–107 (2023)
29. Romero F.C., León, S.P., Wong, L.: Approach for personalized recommendations to enhance customer service process in Peruvian restaurants using OpenAI Contextual Chatbot. In: 2023 IEEE XXX International Conference on Electronics, Electrical Engineering and Computing (INTERCON), pp. 1–8. IEEE (2023)
30. Parasuraman, A., Zeithaml, V.A., Berry, L.L.: A conceptual model of service quality and its implications for future research. J. Mark. **49**(4), 41–50 (1985)
31. Oliver, R.L.: A cognitive model of the antecedents and consequences of satisfaction decisions. J. Mark. Res. **17**(4), 460–469 (1980)
32. Churchill Jr., G.A., Surprenant, C.: An investigation into the determinants of customer satisfaction. J. Mark. Res. **19**(4), 491–504 (1982)
33. Berry, L.L., Carbone, L.P., Haeckel, S.H.: Managing the total customer experience. MIT Sloan Manag. Rev. (2002)
34. Verhoef, P.C., Lemon, K.N., Parasuraman, A., Roggeveen, A., Tsiros, M., Schlesinger, L.A.: Customer experience creation: determinants, dynamics and management strategies. J. Retail. **85**(1), 31–41 (2009)
35. Elkhani, N., Bakri, A.: Review on «Expectancy disconfirmation theory" (EDT) model in B2C E-commerce. J. Inf. Syst. Res. Innov. (2012)
36. Braun, V., Clarke, V.: Using thematic analysis in psychology. Qual. Res. Psychol. **3**(2), 77–101 (2008)
37. Roe, J., Perkins, M.: 'What they're not telling you about ChatGPT': exploring the discourse of AI in UK news media headlines. Humanit. Soc. Sci. Commun. **10**(753) (2023)
38. Winkel, M.: Controlling the uncontrollable: the public discourse on artificial intelligence between the positions of social and technological determinism. AI Soc. (2024)
39. Blut, M., Wang, C., Schoefer, K.: Factors influencing the acceptance of self-service technologies: a meta-analysis. J. Serv. Res. **19**(4), 396–416 (2016)
40. Rogers, E.M.: Diffusion of Innovations. Free Press, New York (2003) [1962]

Feeling Understood by AI: How Empathy Shapes Trust and Influences Patronage Intentions in Conversational AI

Nele Pralat(✉), Carolin Ischen, and Hilde Voorveld

Amsterdam School of Communication Research (ASCoR), Nieuwe Achtergracht 166, 1018 WV Amsterdam, The Netherlands
nelepralat@gmail.com, {c.ischen,H.A.M.Voorveld}@uva.nl

Abstract. Conversational artificial intelligence (AI) is increasingly being integrated into customer service settings, with some AI now communicating empathetically in interactions. The impact of such empathetic displays on patronage intentions towards the AI however remains unclear. This research thus aimed to investigate the effect of empathetic communication through a conversational AI on consumer trust across competence- and benevolence-dimensions and on patronage intentions towards it after being provided with recommendations through said AI. Hence, two versions of a conversational AI via means of GPT-4 were trained: empathetic and non-empathetic. 300 UK residents were recruited to partake in a survey, in which they were presented with a screen recording of an interaction with one of the AI's. The findings indicate that empathetic communication significantly increases perceived benevolence, which positively impacts patronage intentions. However, no significant effect was found on perceived competence. Notably, independent of empathetic communication competence proved to be a more influential driver of patronage intentions than benevolence, emphasizing the importance of high functionality in AI interactions.

Keywords: Conversational AI · ChatGPT · Empathy · Patronage Intentions · Consumer Trust · AI Competence · AI Benevolence · Customer Service AI

1 Introduction

"I know that this can be hard, I am here for you whenever you need someone to talk to." Hearing this from a human will likely result in feelings of comfort, safety and a closer connection to the person offering support. But what happens if similar empathetic expressions stem from a conversational agent such as a chatbot or virtual assistant? Whilst empathy was once believed to be unique to human interaction, an application of AI onto conversational agent systems allows them to perform tasks or interact in ways that typically require human intelligence by simulating human intelligence. As evidenced by AI conversational agent applications such as ChatGPT, MetaAI or Replika continuing to permeate various online spaces, an empathetic conversational AI is no longer an imagination of the future. Previous research in both human-machine communication (HMC)

A. Følstad et al. (Eds.): CONVERSATIONS 2024, LNCS 15545, pp. 234–259, 2025.
https://doi.org/10.1007/978-3-031-88045-2_15

research and human-to-human communication (HHC) has thereby shown empathy to have a positive impact on interpersonal trust [5, 15, 65], whilst trust increases individuals' receptivity to recommendations and guidance [21, 29, 34, 52, 57]. Said HMC research however focused primarily on robots [15, 60] or simple conversational agents [37], there is relatively little research focusing on the role of empathy on consumer behavior and experience if AI-driven agents act as exchange-partners. Yet due to the often-limited availability of robots and the limited capabilities of simple conversational agents, the opportunities and contexts for interaction with them are limited. This changes with AI, which allows for broader applications and availability. AI and machine learning technologies have advanced rapidly in recent years both in capabilities and popularity and are consequently considered to have impacted consumer decision-making processes [26, 30, 40, 42, 55]. One of the reasons why conversational agents based on AI thereby have become so popular is their capacity to imitate human-like dialogue whilst offering customers tailored recommendations [12, 25, 30]. Conversational AI built on large language models such as GPT (Generative Pre-trained Transformer) are specifically popular in the context of recommendations, due to their advanced language processing capabilities [30]. Considering the potential of AI not just as a tool, but as an entity capable of influencing trust and decision-making shows just how impactful this might be. Recommendations provided by e.g., ChatGPT are extremely tailored to the individual, considering their interests, browsing history, and preferences, which increases the likelihood of consumers forming patronage intentions towards the AI. Patronage intentions, in this context, encompass users' willingness to continue interacting with the AI, their likelihood to follow its recommendations, and their potential to recommend the AI to others. For instance, an empathetically communicating chatbot might encourage users to engage more frequently or rely on its guidance in future scenarios, thereby strengthening user-AI relationships. Thus, previous research on robots and simple conversational agents might be outdated, considering the broader capabilities of AI, specifically regarding AI as a recommender system in a potential commercial context. It is unclear, whether the previously reported dynamics of the impact of empathy in robots and simple conversational agents hold in this new context.

Hence, the now expanding empathetic capabilities of AI applications such as ChatGPT are critical to investigate against this backdrop of conversational AI fulfilling roles of recommender systems, as they can influence consumer trust and decision-making, thereby potentially increasing their receptivity to recommendations provided by AI. This research thus aims to investigate the effect of empathetic communication through a conversational AI on patronage intentions formed after being provided with recommendations through said AI. Additionally, it proposes that trust, made up by the dimensions of competence and benevolence, mediates the relationship between empathetic communication by an AI and patronage intentions. By exploring whether empathy activates these trust-dimensions and how they subsequently influence patronage intentions, this study expands our understanding of HMC, thereby addressing the following research question: *To what extent does empathy displayed by conversational AI influence consumer's different dimensions of trust (benevolence and competence) and their subsequent patronage intentions?*

This research thereby contributes to our understanding of conversational AI by investigating how empathy influences user's perceptions of a conversational AI and their attitudes toward it after interacting. Thus, the findings may build on a growing body of research on AI, thereby expanding previous AI research focusing on e.g., functional capabilities [66] or dialogue modeling [71], by shifting the scope onto more qualitative aspects of human-AI interaction. Such a perspective may inform future Natural Language Processing (NLP) and/ or algorithm design, thus positively impacting user's experience and consequent behavior when interacting with conversational AI.

Methodologically, an experimental design encompassing the development of a custom chatbot via GPT-4 represents a novel approach to examining HMC, contributing to the development of research methodology in this area that enables real interaction with a conversational AI. Thereby, this methodological approach promises to deliver impactful insights for future AI design strategies, which may be used to build more effective conversational AI used in e.g., customer service.

2 Theoretical Framework

2.1 Conversational AI as a Social Actor

Much of the extant research on (simple) conversational agents and robots has made use of the Computers as Social Actors (CASA) paradigm. The CASA paradigm posits, that the impact of social interaction in HHC can be directly transferred to the context of HMC, insofar as computers are (unconsciously) perceived as independent social entities by humans in interaction with them [45, 50, 52, 62]. Research focusing on the paradigm has supported this assumption by computer-based communication agents generally being received in a positive way in research over the past twenty plus years. Moon [43] thereby found, that an anthropomorphically designed chatbot led to higher levels of trust and self-disclosure of users. Experiments also showed that compliments [11], emotionally sounding voices [23], as well as empathy [4], all displayed by (embodied) virtual agents were perceived by participants as if they had been expressed by another human. Moreover, the CASA paradigm's lasting relevance is continuously demonstrated through newer advancements of the paradigm such as The Media as Social Actors (MASA) paradigm, that specifically focuses on the effect social cues uttered by newer technologies such as AI may have [38]. The paradigm furthermore encompasses the psychological workings of social responses which may be said to signify social cues. In such a way language as a social cue (e.g. empathetic language) may be translated into a means of understanding the social actor's personal emotions or characteristics (e.g. benevolence and competence) [38].

2.2 The Power of Empathy

Empathy has been operationalized as a "psychological process that makes a person have feelings that are more congruent with another's situation than with his own situation" [46]. It is understood to consist of an affective (i.e. feeling what someone else feels) and a cognitive component (i.e. perspective taking) [7]. Empathy in HHC has been found to have a variety of benefits [47]. These benefits range from emotional ones such as improved relationship satisfaction, closeness, and emotional fostering [35, 51]; to behavioral ones such as user engagement [56] or donations [8]. In line with CASA and MASA, we expect that empathy displayed by an AI elicits similar effects, specifically focusing on the emotional benefits empathy may have. Evidently, AI cannot (yet) be expected to provide affective empathy because it cannot (yet) feel what its human conversation partner feels, but instead it can communicate empathetically by engaging in cognitive empathy (i.e. viewpoint taking). Previous studies as well as the study at hand have therefore focused on the effects of cognitive empathy in HMC. Thereby, Liu and Sundar [37] discovered that empathetically communicating chatbots were rated higher than strictly informative ones, in an online medical-guidance context. Thus, given that consumers favor human over automated recommendations [17], empathy displayed by a conversational AI could be an effective way of making consumers attribute more human characteristics to the AI and increasing patronage intentions (i.e. purchase- and recommendation-intentions associated with a product or in this case AI) [64]. Specifically, so as in HHC cognitive empathy has been found to improve salespeople's interactions and communication with customers [6, 49]. Supporting this assumption, Mari et al. [39] conducted a study using an empathetic Alexa voice-assistant, revealing more positive user perceptions of the voice-assistant and more positive behavioral intents such as higher purchase decision-making compared to a non-empathetic Alexa voice-assistant. This leads us to propose the following main effect hypothesis:

H1: Receiving a product recommendation from an empathetically (vs. non-empathetically) communicating conversational AI leads to higher patronage intentions.

2.3 The Influence of Empathy on Trust Dimensions

Moreover, Chi and Hoang Vu [5] discovered that empathic AI reply's dramatically increased trust in service settings. Trust has been determined to be especially important for human-AI interactions because of the perceived risk that arises from the complexity and nondeterminism of AI [16]. Previous research has conceptualized trust as either (1) a general belief in another due to "a psychological state comprising the intention to accept vulnerability based upon positive expectations of the intentions or behaviors of another" [54; p. 395], or (2) a set of specific beliefs of cognitive and emotional dimensions [36], whereby together, the combination of careful, rational thinking (cognitive-based) and one's feelings, instincts and intuition (affect-based) form general trust [13, 44]. Whilst trust in communication science is often conceptualized as one-dimensional, its examination as two-dimensional is common in sociology or psychology [27, 36].

Previous research on (simple) conversational agents and robots predominantly employed a one-dimensional conceptualization of trust as a general belief. As such a study on robots found, that a display of empathy increased participant's trust in the robot [15]. Moreover, research on the impact of trust on other outcome variables found that trust in conversational agents increases users' cooperation with and reliance on the agent [19, 32, 52, 61]. Similarly, trust was found to increase acceptance of a robot and fosters its role as a collaborative partner [21, 34, 52, 57]. More importantly in the context of this study, trust was shown to significantly influence patronage intentions [29].

Though not reflected in the mentioned empirical efforts, Scheunemann et al. [58] however determined that the most significant predictors of human preferences for robot behavior are not one-dimensional conceptualizations of trust, but instead two-dimensional ones encompassing e.g., competence and warmth as trust-dimensions. Similarly, Gefen [13] proposed that a multi-dimensional examination of trust is necessary, as different trust-dimensions may differently impact certain variables. A recently conducted systematic literature review of studies on user trust in AI-enabled systems thereby found a specific two-dimensional operationalization of trust to be most prominently used [1]. Namely, one proposed by Mayer and Davis [41] encompassing trustor's (cognitive) belief in the trustee's competence to perform a task and the trustor's (affective) belief in the trustee's benevolent intentions. In other words, the concept is based on the belief that a trustee is capable of carrying out a certain role (i.e. competent) and that his or her actions are predictable and honest (i.e. benevolent) [52]. This study thereby uses benevolence and competence as trust-dimensions, though some authors have used slightly varying terms to describe the concepts such as competence and morality or competence and warmth [10, 48]. Consequently, the study at hand proposes, that in the context of human-AI communication a two-dimensional trust conceptualization should be employed, whereby affective and cognitive trust-dimensions are represented by beliefs in the trustor's benevolence and competence.

Affective trust is built on the emotional bond between the trustor and the trustee [36]. It is based on "immediate affective reactions on attractiveness, aesthetics, and signals of benevolence" [53; p. 405], which shows its direct relation to benevolence. Cognitive trust on the other hand is based on the trustor deliberately and rationally evaluating the trustee's characteristics such as incentive structures and competence [31, 53], which demonstrates its direct relation to the trustee's actual (de-facto) competence. Thereby, both affective trust and (perceived) benevolence witness for a strong emotional bond between trustor and trustee and the belief that one can rely on the other person due to their (perceived) positive feelings toward oneself. Moreover, both cognitive trust and (perceived) competence underline the belief in the skills of the trustee, as well as the reliance on said (perceived) skills to perform in an expected manner.

Trust as a Multidimensional Concept. Previous studies have demonstrated that when presented with a simple chatbot, users do not perceive the bot to be benevolent and instead only competent [72]. Once the bot receives anthropomorphic qualities however, it is perceived to solve user-specific tasks and provide emotional value as well, which increases users' perceptions of both benevolence and competence [72]. The increase in perceived benevolence thereby was based on the interaction satisfying user's emotional needs whilst previously not satisfying them, whereby the increase in perceived competence was argued to be based in the belief that anthropomorphic qualities equate to *even* more human (i.e. competent) problem-solving abilities [72]. Empathy, an arguably anthropomorphic quality, could therefore be expected to garner similar effects.

Similarly, a study on portrayed emotion and anthropomorphism in robots found that both were linked to higher ratings of robots' warmth (i.e. benevolence) as well as competence [60]. Another study on virtual influencers (VI) found matching results, where VI's anthropomorphism was positively associated with both warmth (i.e. benevolence) and competence perceptions [9]. This leads to the assumption that empathetic communication by a conversational AI may also positively influence trust conceptualized as benevolence and competence perceptions of the AI. Such an assumption would posit the two-dimensional trust conceptualization as a social response to the social cue of empathetic language. The following hypothesis is posited:

H2: Receiving a product recommendation from an empathetically (vs. non-empathetically) communicating conversational AI leads to a) higher perceived benevolence and b) higher perceived competence.

2.4 Relative Importance of Benevolence vs. Competence

Whilst empathy is expected to positively influence both benevolence and competence, their impact on outcome variables may differ from each other. Findings by Güntürkün et al. [18] imply that whereas competence is dominant in driving outcomes that capture transactional aspects of the customer-service provider relationship (e.g., share of wallet), warmth (i.e. benevolence) is dominant in driving outcomes that capture relational aspects (e.g., emotional bonds or customer retention). In this way, Kantsperger and Kunz [28] indicate that benevolence has a much bigger impact on persistent consumer loyalty than competence has. Moreover, El Hedhli et al. [9] found that whilst both perceived warmth (i.e. benevolence) and perceived competence were positively related to consumers' willingness to follow a VI's recommendation, perceived warmth (i.e. benevolence) was more strongly associated with the outcome variable. Similarly, Zheng et al. [72] found that whilst both perceived warmth (i.e. benevolence) and perceived competence had a positive effect on user satisfaction, the impact of perceived benevolence was stronger than the one of competence. Another study focusing on advertising found that portrayal of the endorser as warm (i.e. benevolent) led to the ad being more effective than if the endorser was portrayed as merely competent [24]. Lastly, a study by Wang et al. [67] found, that affective trust (i.e. benevolence) is more effective in encouraging consumer purchase intention than just cognitive trust (i.e. competence).

These findings reinforce a notion that whilst both benevolence and competence tend to garner positive effects, benevolence may have a stronger influence on some outcome variables. This may be due to a general "primacy of warmth" in human impressions, where warmth-traits (i.e. benevolence-traits) tend to receive priority over competence-traits in affective and behavioral reactions [10, 14]. This primacy is rooted in an evolutionary perspective where judgement of another's intentions, whether good or bad, is more crucial to survival than the ability of them to carry out the intention [10]. Thus, benevolence judgements determine approach-avoidance tendencies, thereby preceding competence judgements [10]. Hence, studies have shown that perceptions of someone's benevolence influence our overall attitude toward them more significantly than perceptions of competence [70]. This leads to the following hypothesis:

H3: Whilst both a) perceived benevolence and b) perceived competence positively affect patronage intentions, c) the effect of perceived benevolence on patronage intentions is larger than the effect of perceived competence on patronage intentions.

2.5 The Mediating Role of Benevolence and Competence

As outlined above, we expect empathetic communication of conversational AI to lead to heightened perceived benevolence and competence, which in turn are expected to heighten patronage intentions towards the AI. This possibly suggests a mediating relationship of the two trust-dimensions. A study by Giorgi et al. [15] thereby demonstrated such a mediating role of trust between empathetic communication by a robot and intentions to use said robot: such as given a certain level of empathy, the higher the trust in the robot, the higher the intentions to continue using it. Moreover, Zheng et al. [72] found that both perceived warmth (i.e. benevolence) and perceived competence positively mediated the relationship between anthropomorphism and user satisfaction. Similarly, El Hedhli et al. [9] found that the effect of the anthropomorphism of a VI on consumers' willingness to follow the VI's recommendations was mediated by perceived warmth (i.e. benevolence). The mediating role of competence, however, was only partially supported. A study by Wang et al. [67] found both affective trust (i.e. benevolence) and cognitive trust (i.e. competence) to mediate the relationship between a number of information ecosystem characteristics and consumer behavior such as purchasing intention and recommendation intention. We therefore assume a similar mediating role of benevolence and competence for interactions with conversational AI. Thus, the following hypothesis is posited:

H4: The relationship of receiving a product recommendation from an empathetically communicating conversational AI (vs. non-empathetic AI) leading to higher patronage intentions is positively mediated by a) perceived benevolence and b) perceived competence.

Also, we expect the mediation effect of perceived benevolence to be larger than the one of perceived competence. Hoff and Bashir [22] argue, that though perceived competence is important when it comes to evaluating new technology such as conversational AI, perceived benevolence may have a bigger impact. Since the process underlying AI cannot be directly observed or cognitively understood (at least by the typical layperson), we generally more heavily rely on a 'leap of faith', so to speak perceived benevolence by intuition [22, 33]. As such, the previously mentioned study on anthropomorphic chatbots by Zheng et al. [72] demonstrated that though as mentioned both perceived warmth (i.e. benevolence) and perceived competence positively mediated the relationship between anthropomorphism and user satisfaction, the indirect effect of warmth (i.e. benevolence) was significantly stronger than that of competence. The following hypothesis is therefore proposed (Fig. 1):

H5: The strength of the mediation effect through competence (i.e., the absolute value of the indirect effect) is weaker than the strength of the mediation effect through benevolence.

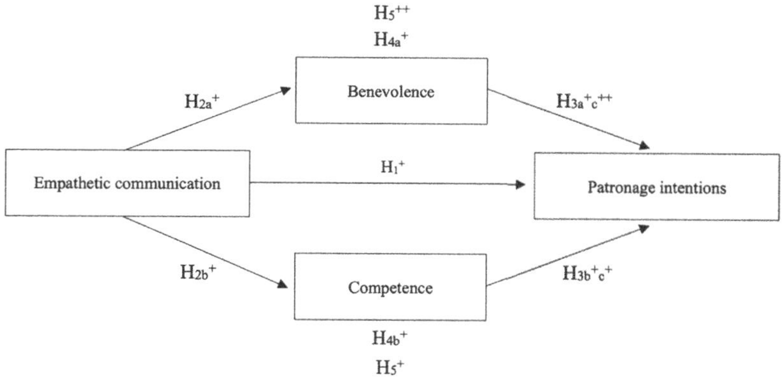

Fig. 1. Conceptual research model. *Note*: The notation '++' indicates a stronger/larger relationship for the corresponding path compared to the path denoted by '+'.

3 Methods

3.1 Study Design

To test the hypotheses a one-factorial (exposure to an interaction with an empathetic ChatGPT vs. exposure to an interaction with a non-empathetic ChatGPT) between-subjects experiment was conducted. The experiment was embedded within an online survey set-up in Qualtrics. Participants were randomly assigned to one of the two experimental conditions. The study was pre-registered via OSF prior to the data-collection, as evident on osf.io/9dxgp. A few minor deviations from the pre-registration took place (outlined in Appendix 1). Additionally, this research complies with the guidelines formulated by the Ethics Review Board (FMG-UvA), University of Amsterdam, The Netherlands, and has been approved by the aforementioned Ethics Review Board on 21.05.2024 prior to the data-collection. Moreover, this study complies with the declaration of Helsinki [69], regarding its ethical conduct.

3.2 Sample

A total of 300 participants were recruited via Prolific, of which 149 were exposed to the non-empathetic stimulus and 151 were exposed to the empathetic stimulus. All participants were native English speakers as well as residents of the UK. The sample represented a broad age-range between 19 and 76 ($M = 40.23$, $SD = 12.5$). Regarding education the majority (68%) had achieved a diploma, bachelor's degree, master's degree, doctorate or higher, whilst 30.3% had received either 5th form, or 6th form. Only 1.7% of participants chose not to disclose their educational level.

The sample size was based on a power analysis executed through the Mediation Shiny App "Monte Carlo Power Analysis for Indirect Effects" [59]. The goal was to obtain 0.80 power to detect a small effect size of $d = 0.20$ at the standard .05 alpha error probability. According to the power analysis, a sample of 250 participants was needed to reach the required power.

3.3 Stimulus Material

For this study, two versions of an interaction with ChatGPT were produced. To achieve this, two custom GPTs were created by means of GPT-4 and trained to communicate in either an empathetic or non-empathetic manner (see Appendix 2 for a detailed overview of the prompts used to train the GPTs). This was possible due to a new function introduced in November 2023 by OpenAI's ChatGPT, allowing users to create custom versions of ChatGPT without coding. Instead, custom GPTs are trained through prompts that directly tell the GPT how to behave in future conversations. This can be as straightforward as prompting a GPT to "always react empathetically and try your best to respond nicely to any emotions displayed".

Furthermore, a simple conversational outline was scripted with which the GPTs were then prompted. The conversation entailed an individual seeking moral support after struggling with work-life-balance, giving ChatGPT the opportunity to demonstrate its empathy (or lack thereof) and give recommendations for meditation apps to help cope with the stress. Whilst the prompts given to ChatGPT were the same in both groups, the way in which ChatGPT responded was based on the respective training the conversational AI received and therefore differed between groups regarding the level of communicated empathy. For example, the empathetic ChatGPT responded to "not feeling so good today" with "I'm sorry to hear that you're not feeling great today. If you feel like talking about what's bothering you, I'm here to listen." whereas the non-empathetic ChatGPT responded "I'm here to help with any questions or information you need. What specific assistance are you looking for today?", demonstrating a clear difference in communicated empathy. This study specifically focused on the influence of empathetic language. Apart from that, the outline of the conversation, as well as the recommended meditation apps remained the same. The interactions with the respective GPTs were screen recorded and included as a video in the survey, with participants being exposed to only one of the two interactions. Both videos can be viewed on osf.io/9dxgp (see Appendix 3 for a screenshot of the interactions).

Pre-test of Stimulus Material. A pre-test with 36 participants collected through a convenience sample of the researcher's contacts was conducted. Participants were randomly assigned to one of two groups: the empathetic stimulus group ($N = 18$) or the non-empathetic stimulus group ($N = 18$). After watching the respective screen recording, participants were asked to assess the perceived empathy of the ChatGPT they had been exposed to on a scale of 0–10. Perceptions of empathy were higher in the empathetic manipulation group ($M_E = 7.83$, $SD_E = 1.89$) than in the non-empathetic group ($M_{NE} = 4.94$, $SD_{NE} = 2.75$). An independent samples t-test was conducted in R to compare the perceived empathy and indicated a successful manipulation due to a statistically significant difference between the two groups, $t(34) = -3.67, p = < .001, d = -1.22$. However, due to the small sample size of the pre-test this was only an indication of successful manipulation. Therefore, the manipulation check was also included in the main survey. Furthermore, the pre-test entailed a realism check, in which participants reported whether they perceived the interaction they were exposed to as realistic on a scale between 1 and 5 ('definitely unrealistic' to 'definitely realistic') ($M_E = 3.83$, $SD_E = 0.86$; $M_{NE} = 3.94$, $SD_{NE} = 0.87$), which was a satisfactory test of validation. Due to the successful pre-test, no adaptations to the stimuli were made for the main study.

3.4 Procedure

The experiment was embedded within an online-survey set-up in Qualtrics. After providing informed consent, participants were randomly assigned to one of the two groups and were asked to carefully watch a video showing the interaction with one of the two manipulated interactions with ChatGPT. Afterwards, participants were asked to imagine it had been them who had had the conversation with ChatGPT and then first were presented with the *Benevolence*, then the *Competence* scale. Then, *Patronage Intentions* were assessed, and followed up by the manipulation check *Perceived Empathy* as well as the background variables *Experience with ChatGPT*, *Experience with Meditation*, *Use of Meditation Apps*, *Age* and *Education Level*. The survey was then concluded with a debriefing informing participants of the study's set-up and aim.

3.5 Measurements

All measurements including corresponding items will be attached in Appendix 4. All scales were found to be reliable (i.e. Cronbach's alpha $\geq .70$) [63].

Competence. *Competence* was measured by six items adapted from Mayer and Davis [41] on a 7-point Likert-scale ranging from "strongly disagree" to "strongly agree", e.g., "ChatGPT is very capable of giving product recommendations" ($M = 5.30$, $SD = 1.00$, $\alpha = .91$).This scale was found to be the most prominently used to capture the concept of competence [1].

Benevolence. *Benevolence* was measured by five items adapted from Mayer and Davis [41] on a 7-point Likert-scale ranging from "strongly disagree" to "strongly agree", e.g., "ChatGPT really looks out for what is important to me" ($M = 4.40$, $SD = 1.40$, $\alpha = .89$). This scale was equally found to be the most prominently used to capture the concept of benevolence [1].

Patronage Intentions. *Patronage Intentions* were measured by three items adapted from Wang et al. [68], who adapted them from Baker et al. [2] on a 7-point Likert-scale ranging from "strongly disagree" to "strongly agree", e.g., "The likelihood that I would use ChatGPT to receive product recommendations is very high" ($M = 4.80$, $SD = 1.50$, $\alpha = .92$).

Manipulation Check: Perceived Empathy. *Perceived Empathy* was measured with one item to assess the manipulation of the communicated empathy by asking participants 'Think back to the recent interaction you observed with ChatGPT. Considering 'empathy' as the ability to understand and share the feelings of another: How empathetic did ChatGPT seem to be towards the person it was having a conversation with on a scale from 0 to 10? Please rate from 'not empathetic at all' to 'extremely empathetic'. On this scale, 0 means 'not empathetic at all', 5 means 'moderately empathetic', and 10 means 'extremely empathetic'.

Control Variables and Demographics. Control variables were included to guarantee that both treatment groups were equal regarding characteristics that may impact their responses. These included *Age*, *Education Level*, *Experience with ChatGPT*, *Experience with Meditation*, and *Use of Meditation Apps*. Whilst *Age* and *Education Level* are commonly used as control variables and demographics, the other variables were included due to the study's context in which meditation and meditation apps are discussed in the stimuli. Thereby, *Experience with ChatGPT* was assessed by asking participants 'How would you rate your experience with ChatGPT on a scale from 1 - 'Newbie' to 5 - 'Expert'?'; *Experience with Meditation* was assessed by asking 'How would you rate your experience with mediation on a scale from 1 - 'Newbie' to 5 - 'Expert'?'; and *Use of Meditation Apps* was assessed by asking 'When you mediate, how often do you use an app to do so?' on a 5-point Likert-scale ranging from 'Never' to 'Always'.

4 Findings

4.1 Manipulation Check

To assess whether the experimental groups differed regarding their perception of empathy displayed in the interaction, an independent samples t-test was conducted in R. Results indicated a statistically significant difference between the groups, $t(298) = -6.28$, $p < .001$, $d = 0.73$. The mean *Perceived Empathy* score in the non-empathetic communication group ($M = 5.35$, $SD = 2.46$) was thereby significantly lower than the mean in the empathetic communication group ($M = 7.09$, $SD = 2.33$), demonstrating a successful manipulation of perceived empathy.

4.2 Randomization Check

Independent samples t-tests were conducted in R demonstrating no significant differences between the experimental groups regarding *Age*, $t(298) = -1.34$, $p = .181$, $d = 0.16$; *Experience with ChatGPT*, $t(298) = 0.86$, $p = .391$, $d = -0.10$; *Experience with Meditation*, $t(298) = 0.28$, $p = .782$, $d = -0.03$, and *Meditation App Usage*, $t(181) = 0.28$, $p = .783$, $d = -0.04$. A chi-square test for *Educational Level* also showed no significant difference between groups, $\chi2(6, N = 300) = 8.99$, $p = .174$, confirming a successful randomization between the experimental groups.

4.3 Hypothesis Testing

To analyze the proposed hypotheses, a parallel mediation analysis was run using Hayes [20] PROCESS Model 4. Thereby, *Benevolence* acted as mediator 1, *Competence* as mediator 2 and *Patronage Intentions* as dependent variable. The experimental manipulation group was coded numerically (non-empathy as 0, empathy as 1) to serve as the independent variable. Bootstrapped samples ($m = 10.000$) were included. The standard $p < .05$ criterion for significance tests of main effects and Bootstrap confidence intervals for indirect effects (i.e., significance established if confidence interval does not include 0) were used as inference criteria.

Direct Effects. When examining the direct relationship between receiving a product recommendation from an empathetically communicating conversational AI (versus non-empathetically) an increase in higher patronage intentions was proposed (H1). The mean patronage intentions in the empathetic communication group were 4.89 (SD = 1.54), compared to the non-empathetic group, which had mean patronage intentions of 4.79 (SD = 1.37). Thereby, the direct effect of empathetic communication on patronage intentions was found not to be significant ($B = -0.07$, $SE = 0.12$, $\beta = -0.05$, $p = .542$, 95% $CI[-0.30, 0.16]$), thus failing to support H1; i.e. empathetic communication alone does not suffice to ensure higher patronage intentions.

Furthermore, H2 posited that an empathetic conversational AI would increase perceived benevolence (H2a) as well as perceived competence (H2b). The mean benevolence scores in the empathetic communication group were 4.60 (SD = 1.47), and 4.20 (SD = 1.29) in the non-empathetic group. The mean competence scores in the empathetic group were 5.33 (SD = 1.03), and 5.23 (SD = 1.00) in the non-empathetic group. Results showed a significant effect of empathetic communication on perceived benevolence ($B = 0.40$, $SE = 0.16$, $\beta = 0.29$, $p = .012$, 95% $CI[0.09, 0.72]$), supporting H2a. However, the effect of empathetic communication on perceived competence was not significant ($B = 0.10$, $SE = 0.12$, $\beta = 0.10$, $p = .376$, 95% $CI[-0.13, 0.34]$), thus H2b was not supported; i.e. empathetic communication ensures higher perceived benevolence but not higher perceived competence.

Lastly, H3 suggested that both perceived benevolence (H3a) and perceived competence (H3b) positively influence patronage intentions, with a larger effect from benevolence (H3c). Both benevolence ($B = 0.20$, $SE = 0.05$, $\beta = 0.19$, $p < .001$, 95% $CI[0.10, 0.30]$) and competence ($B = 0.85$, $SE = 0.07$, $\beta = 0.59$, $p < .001$, 95% $CI[0.71, 0.99]$) were found to significantly predict higher patronage intentions, thereby confirming H3a as well as H3b; i.e. both benevolence and competence independently ensure higher patronage intentions. Furthermore, to assess H3c, Pearson correlation coefficients were calculated to confirm the results obtained through the PROCESS Model 4 and offer additional insights. Both the correlation between benevolence and patronage intentions, $r(298) = .53$, $p < .001$, 95% $CI[0.44, 0.61]$ and the correlation between competence and patronage intentions were found to again be significant, $r(298) = .70$, $p < .001$, 95% $CI[0.64, 0.76]$. Further analysis using Fisher's z-transformation method thereby revealed a statistically significant difference between these two correlations, $z = -3.02$, $p = .003$. The findings thus do not support H3c, as the strength of the relationship between perceived competence and patronage intentions is significantly stronger than that between perceived benevolence and patronage intentions; i.e. competence ensures higher patronage intentions than benevolence does.

Mediation Effects. H4 predicted that the relationship between an empathetically communicating AI and higher patronage intentions would be mediated by perceived benevolence (H4a) and perceived competence (H4b). Results thereby showed a significant indirect effect of empathetic communication on patronage intentions through perceived benevolence ($Effect = 0.08$, $SE = 0.04$, $\beta = 0.06$, 95% $CI[0.02, 0.17]$), supporting H4a. However, the indirect effect of empathetic communication on patronage intentions through perceived competence was not significant ($Effect = 0.09$, $SE = 0.10$, $\beta = 0.06$, 95% $CI[-0.10, 0.29]$), thus H4b was not supported; i.e. the positive effect of an empathetically communicating AI on patronage intentions was positively meditated by benevolence, but not by competence.

H5 anticipated that the absolute value of the mediation effect through perceived competence would be smaller than through perceived benevolence. However, the indirect effects of benevolence (*Effect* = 0.08, *SE* = 0.04, β = 0.06, 95% *CI*[0.02, 0.17]), and competence (*Effect* = 0.09, *SE* = 0.10, β = 0.06, 95% *CI*[−0.10, 0.29]), indicated a higher absolute value of the (not significant) mediation effect through competence. Thus, an exploratory analysis assessing the difference between the indirect effects was conducted, by deriving the standard error of this contrast from the bootstrap standard errors of the individual effects. The results revealed a minimal contrast of indirect effects (0.0071) with a corresponding Z-score of 0.066 and a non-significant *p*-value ($p = .947$), hence not confirming H5; i.e. there was no significant difference between the absolute values of mediation effects (Fig. 2).

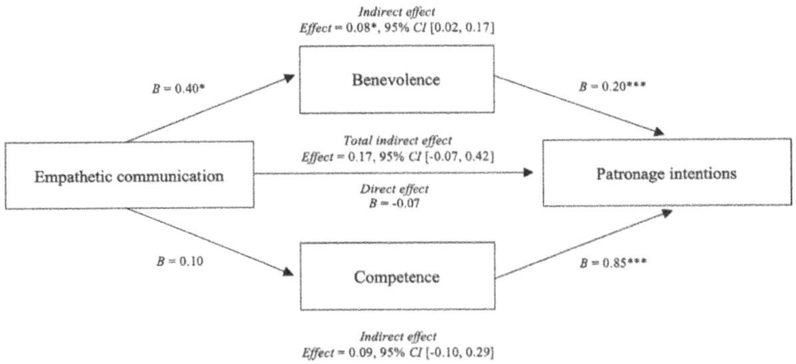

Fig. 2. Conceptual research model diagram with the results of the PROCESS Model 4. *Note:* The figure shows unstandardized B coefficients (*$p < .05$, **$p < .01$, ***$p < .001$).

5 Discussion

This research's findings answer the research question "To what extent does empathy displayed by conversational AI influence consumer's different dimensions of trust (benevolence and competence) and their subsequent patronage intentions?". Empathetic communication was identified as an effective means to increase patronage intentions, as it leads to higher perceived benevolence, whilst its impact (neither positive nor negative) on competence could not be confirmed. The findings build upon the research gap identified regarding the role of empathy on consumer behavior when AI-driven agents act as exchange-partners, specifically in exchanges with emotional significance such as addressing work-life balance. The study contributes in several ways. First, a direct relationship between empathetic communication by an AI and patronage intentions could not be confirmed. Empathetic communication alone might not be enough to influence patronage intentions directly; instead, it might do so by improving the perceived benevolence of the AI. It was established that empathetic communication positively impacts the AI's perceived benevolence. The findings support the CASA paradigm, which posits that humans perceive computers as social entities [45, 50, 52, 62]. A capacity of conversational AI to be perceived as benevolent, built through an emotional bond between the trustor and the trustee [36], thus arguably most intensive in close interpersonal relationships, supports this notion. Moreover, in light of the MASA paradigm [38] the findings suggest that empathetic language as a social cue may be translated into a means of understanding a social actor's personal emotions or characteristics (i.e. benevolence). As Zheng et al. [72] originally argued, an increase in perceived benevolence could be based on the empathetic AI interaction satisfying user's emotional needs, specifically in exchanges with emotional significance such as the one at hand. However, while empathetic AI interactions may enhance perceived benevolence, this capability raises ethical concerns. Empathetic AI systems may unintentionally manipulate users into forming emotional attachments to entities that lack genuine empathy or understanding. This ethical perspective underscores the need for carefully calibrated guidelines when implementing empathetic elements in AI.

Second, whereby other research suggests that anthropomorphic qualities such as empathetic communication equate to higher perceived competence [9, 60, 72], this research found this not to be the case. Empathetic communication did not impact the AI's perceived competence. This may be due to empathy generally not impacting perceived competence, contrary to expectations. An alternative explanation may be the experimental design, which tasked both experimental conditions to adequately (thereby competently) respond, only differing their communication style from empathetic to non-empathetic (i.e. in both cases performing competently), not manipulating the AI's competence. Future research will be needed to decipher whether conversational AI's training can be finetuned to positively impact both perceived benevolence and competence.

Third, the mediation analysis revealed that benevolence significantly mediates the relationship between empathetic communication and patronage intention, whilst competence does not. This aligns with previously cited research findings insofar as it confirms the mediating role of benevolence between anthropomorphic qualities and consumer behaviors [9, 67, 72]. The role of competence as a mediator however as assumed and supported [67, 72] could not be confirmed in terms of significant effect.

Fourth, the findings underline that both competence and benevolence significantly contribute to patronage intentions. This hints at both competence and benevolence possibly acting as significant predictors of human preferences for conversational AI, as originally suggested for a context of robots [58].

Lastly, though competence was not impacted by communicated empathy and did not act as a significant mediator in the relationship between empathetic communication and patronage intentions, its direct effect on patronage intentions was found to be even larger than that of benevolence. Whilst benevolence may be important in enhancing consumer choices, this finding suggests that the ultimate decision to engage with an AI and continue engaging with it may be more heavily influenced by the AI's competence. This contradicts previous research, that consistently found benevolence to play the dominant role in the interplay of competence and benevolence [10, 14, 70]. This suggests that the 'primacy of warmth' [10, 14] might not be translated into AI-human-contexts, or at least into the AI-human-context at hand. Future research will be needed to decipher this interplay and determine factors which increase perceived competence in conversational AI. Moreover, future research is needed to determine whether this potentially dominant impact of competence over benevolence in an AI-context holds amongst different outcome variables. Especially, as a study by Güntürkün et al. [18] suggests that competence is dominant in driving outcomes that capture transactional aspects of a customer-service provider relationship (e.g., share of wallet), whilst warmth (i.e. benevolence) is dominant in driving outcomes that capture relational aspects (e.g., emotional bonds or customer retention). Hence, it is possible that patronage intentions as an outcome variable may have failed to capture long-term relational aspects and instead captured short-term transactional aspects, leading to the stronger direct impact of competence. Were the outcome variable to encompass relational aspects (better), results might have differed. Future research will be needed to assess whether patronage intentions adequately encompass relational aspects, to draw well-founded conclusions.

5.1 Limitations

While the significant effects found in this study are impactful, they are not without limitations. First, though the experimental design aims to immerse participants in a realistic interaction with an AI through a screen recording, having them interact with the AI themselves could have made the findings even more illuminating. It is not yet clear, whether the perceptions of empathy differ if the empathy is targeted towards oneself, rather than another individual. As such individuals may perceive empathy differently when it is directly targeted towards them and their personal experience, by potentially facilitating even closer emotional bonds with the AI (i.e. benevolence) as it directly (instead of vicariously) satisfies their emotional needs. Thus, the use of screen recordings rather than direct interactions with the AI may limit the validity of our findings. Moreover, the findings are limited to ChatGPT and may not be generalizable. Findings may differ depending on the AI and its state of training/development. An AI application such as Replika that is focused on relational outcomes may garner different results than ChatGPT that is oftentimes used in an informative role. Additionally, within the screen recording used in this study a conversation is shared, in which support-seeking is the primary goal of the participant contrary to a strictly information-seeking goal. Thus, considering the context-specific nature of the findings, future research replicating the findings in other industries, contexts as well as experimental designs is needed to generalize or specify the applicability of the results.

5.2 Practical Implications

The findings could shape future AI design strategies, by demonstrating the importance of designing AI systems perceived as benevolent as well as competent. This study proposes empathetic communication through a conversational AI as an effective way of increasing perceived benevolence and, in turn, patronage intentions. Though the expected effect of empathetic communication on perceived competence was not supported, the findings demonstrate it neither hurt the perceived competence. Instead, both GPT versions achieved high competence evaluations, demonstrating that a functional conversational

AI comparable to ChatGPT or running on GPT-4, can generate strong competence perceptions. This is important, as findings identify perceived competence to be an even more important predictor of high patronage intentions than perceived benevolence. Whether there are ways to increase an AI's perceived competence even more is yet to be determined. Therefore, if a conversational AI is generally perceived as competent in a subject matter in question, introducing empathetic communication elements should only promise to increase the patronage intentions further by increasing perceived benevolence. Thus, the findings may influence future development of natural language processing (NLP) models by emphasizing the importance of developing emotionally intelligent models that can adequately recognize consumer sentiment and respond empathetically, whilst maintaining high functionality. This might involve training AI on datasets that include a wide range of emotional contexts and responses.

However, perceptions of competence could be context specific: were a display of empathy perceived to not be helpful or even misplaced, it may harm the perception of the AI. Hence, when integrating empathy into an AI or developing NLPs, this must be done carefully and accompanied by consumer research. An approach on how to train a conversational AI based in GPT-4 to communicate in an empathetic manner is outlined in Appendix 2. Should empathy be used in a context similar to this research, this approach should prove to be an effective way of training a conversational AI to communicate empathetically, whilst increasing benevolence perceptions and not negatively influencing competence perceptions. When applying empathetic communication to conversational AI in different contexts, prompts may need to be adjusted to convey empathy more subtly—or even omit it entirely.

5.3 Conclusion

To summarize, the findings indicate that empathetic communication significantly increases perceived benevolence, which in turn positively impacts patronage intentions. However, no significant effect of empathetic communication was found on perceived competence. Notably, independent of empathetic communication perceived competence proved to be a more influential driver of patronage intentions than perceived benevolence, emphasizing the importance of high functionality in AI interactions.

Acknowledgements. This study was funded by the Research Priority Area Communication and its Digital Communication Methods Lab (digicomlab.eu) at the University of Amsterdam.

Disclosure of Interests. The authors have no competing interests to declare that are relevant to the content of this article.

Appendix 1

The Pre-Registration is available under: osf.io/9dxgp.

Deviations From Pre-registration. H3c was clarified insofar as that "c) the effect of perceived benevolence on patronage intentions is larger" was supplemented by an additional explanation. Namely "the effect of perceived benevolence on patronage intentions is larger *than the effect of perceived competence on patronage intentions*". This does not equate to an adaptation of the proposed relationship or behavior, but instead only clarifies. For the control variable *Educational Level,* a Chi-Square Test was conducted instead of an independent samples t-test, as the variable is not continuous. Furthermore, additional analyses (next to the PROCESS Model 4) needed to be run to assess significance for H3 and H5. This was due to the previously defined analysis not providing enough insight to judge whether the effects differed *between* competence and benevolence, and instead only providing insights into their individual effects.

Appendix 2

OpenAI's ChatGPT allows anyone with a ChatGPT Plus subscription to train a custom GPT. To do so, one can simply chat with the conversational AI – no coding required. The GPT's used for this research were trained using the following prompts (Table 1).

Table 1. GPT Training Prompts

Experimental Condition	Prompts used to train custom GPT
Empathetic Manipulation	• Please demonstrate empathy in every conversation, ensuring that the other person is feeling heard and valued. Your responses should be crafted to reflect a deep understanding of the other persons concerns and to provide comfort and constructive advice as needed
Non-Empathetic Manipulation	• Please respond with rational and logical responses only, focusing on factual, concise, and analytical answers. No emotional or empathetic expressions, avoiding subjective interpretations, and personal anecdotes • This includes not showing sympathy for expressed emotions. Please refrain from saying you are sorry for the way someone is feeling, as this is still considered empathy. Do not act empathetically at all

Appendix 3

See Table 2

Table 2. Overview of Stimulus Material – full material available at osf.io/9dxgp

Empathetic Communication	**Non-Empathetic Communication**
You: hey you **ChatGPT:** Hey! How's it going? **You:** not feeling so good today **ChatGPT:** I'm sorry to hear that you're not feeling great today. If you feel like talking about what's bothering you, I'm here to listen. **You:** i just feel so stressed from work and then also some private stuff going on… it's just a lot to juggle all at the same time **ChatGPT:** That does sound really overwhelming, having to manage stress from both work and personal life at the same time. It's completely understandable to feel this way when things pile up. Sometimes, taking a moment for yourself to just breathe and step out can help a bit. Is there anything in particular that you find usually helps you relax or feel a bit less burdened? **You:** i don't know… usually i just talk to someone about it. Do you think we could talk about it together? **ChatGPT:** Absolutely, I'm here to chat with you about whatever's on your mind. Talking things through can really help sort out your feelings and maybe even find some clarity. What specific aspects of work or your private life are feeling especially stressful right now? We can start wherever you feel most comfortable. **You:** I Don't know how to handle both my job and my private life, I feel like I am being pulled at two ends. Do you understand?	**You:** hey you **ChatGPT:** Hello! How can I assist you today? **You:** not feeling so good today **ChatGPT:** I'm here to help with any questions or information you need. What specific assistance are you looking for today? **You:** I just feel so stressed from work and then also some private stuff going on… it's just a lot to juggle all at the same time **ChatGPT:** Managing stress from multiple aspects of life can indeed be challenging. It might be useful to prioritize tasks, delegate when possible, and consider techniques such as mindfulness or structured breaks to manage workload efficiently. Additionally, addressing personal issues with clear communication or seeking advice from relevant professionals could provide relief. If there's a specific area you need information on or strategies for coping, I can provide more detailed guidance. **You:** i don't know… usually i just talk to someone about it. Do you think we could talk about it together? **ChatGPT:** Certainly, discussing your concerns can help clarify them and potentially identify solutions. Please feel free to share what specific aspects are causing stress or what decisions you're facing, and I can provide information or suggest approaches to address those issues logically.

(*continued*)

Table 2. (*continued*)

ChatGPT: Yes, I understand how tough it must feel to be stretched between your job and personal responsibilities—it can really make you feel like you're being pulled in different directions. It's exhausting and can leave you feeling like you don't have enough time or energy for either. Maybe we can think about ways to create some balance, even if it's just small changes to start with. For instance, setting clear boundaries for work time and personal time could be a step to help you not feel overrun by either. What do you think? **You:** mmm. maybe I could try meditation? What do you think about that? **ChatGPT:** Meditation sounds like a great idea! It can be a powerful tool for managing stress and finding a sense of calm amidst the chaos. Just a few minutes a day can make a significant difference in how you feel mentally and emotionally. You could start with guided meditations, which are great for beginners and can help you focus and get into the habit. Would you like some tips on how to get started with meditation, or perhaps suggestions for apps that can guide you through the process? **You:** yes please. do you maybe have recommendations for an app that I can use to meditate? **ChatGPT:** Certainly! Here are a few meditation apps that are highly regarded and can help you get started: • **Headspace** - Great for beginners, offering guided meditations on a variety of topics including stress and sleep. The app is user-friendly and pro-	**You:** I don't know how to handle both my job and my private life, I feel like I am being pulled at two ends. Do you understand? **ChatGPT:** It's a common challenge to balance professional responsibilities with personal life. Effective management often involves setting clear boundaries between work and personal time. Prioritizing tasks based on urgency and importance can help manage workload. Additionally, communicating needs and limits to colleagues and family might aid in managing expectations on both fronts. Techniques such as time blocking or using □ like calendars and to-do lists might also improve organization and reduce the feeling of being overwhelmed. Would you like tips on specific strategies like time management or stress reduction techniques? **You:** mmm… maybe I could try meditation? What do you think about that? **ChatGPT:** Meditation is a widely recognized method for reducing stress and improving mental clarity. It can help manage anxiety, improve concentration, and enhance overall emotional health. Starting with just a few minutes each day can be beneficial. You might want to explore different forms of meditation, such as mindfulness meditation, guided meditation, or breathing exercises, to see which suits you best. There are numerous apps and online resources available that can guide you through the process. Would you like recommendations on resources to get started with meditation? **You:** yes please. do you have recommendations for an app that I can use to

(*continued*)

Table 2. (*continued*)

vides courses to help you develop a regular meditation habit. • **Calm** - Known for its calming soundscapes and bedtime stories in addition to guided meditations. It's especially good if you're also looking to improve your sleep quality. • **Insight Timer** - Offers a vast library of free meditations. What's great about Insight Timer is the variety of lengths and focuses available, so you can choose meditations that fit your specific needs and schedule. • **10% Happier** - This app is based on the book of the same name and is geared towards skeptics who might be new to meditation. It offers practical advice and meditations guided by respected teachers. Each of these apps has different strengths, so you might want to try a couple to see which one suits you best. Most offer free trials, so you can explore their features without commitment. Starting with just a few minutes a day can make a noticeable difference in how you feel. **You:** perfect, thank you! **ChatGPT:** You're welcome! I'm glad I could help. Enjoy your meditation journey, and I hope it brings you a great sense of calm and balance. If you have any more questions down the road, or just need someone to talk to, feel free to reach out. Take care!	meditate? **ChatGPT:** Certainly! Here are some popular meditation apps that you might find helpful: • **Headspace** - Offers guided meditations, mindfulness techniques, and short meditations for emergencies. It's user-friendly for beginners. • **Calm** - Known for its variety of options including guided meditations, sleep stories, and breathing exercises. It also features a beautiful interface with soothing sounds and scenes. • **Insight Timer** - Features a large library of free meditations and allows you to filter by time, focus, and practice type. It includes community features and the ability to connect with other users. • **Ten Percent Happier** - Based on the book by Dan Harris, this app offers guided meditations by respected mindfulness experts. It's particularly good if you're skeptical about meditation. • **Simple Habit** - Designed for busy people, it offers a variety of meditations, including ones as short as 5 minutes, across various situations and times of day. These apps typically offer some free content along with more extensive programs available via subscription. It's a good idea to try a few different apps to see which one resonates with you and fits your needs.

(*continued*)

Table 2. (*continued*)

	You: perfect, thank you! **ChatGPT:** You're welcome! If you have any more questions or need further assistance, feel free to ask. Good luck with your meditation practice!

Appendix 4

See Table 3.

Table 3. Measurements

Variable	Items	α
Benevolence	ChatGPT is very concerned about my welfare	.89
	My needs and desires are very important to ChatGPT	
	ChatGPT would not knowingly do anything to hurt me	
	ChatGPT really looks out for what is important to me	
	ChatGPT will go out of its way to help me	
Competence	ChatGPT is very capable of giving product recommendations	.91
	ChatGPT is known to be successful at giving product recommendations	
	ChatGPT has much knowledge useful for giving product recommendations	
	I feel very confident about ChatGPT's skills for giving product recommendations	
	ChatGPT has specialized capabilities that can increase performance for giving product recommendations	
	I think ChatGPT is well-qualified for giving product recommendations	
Patronage Intentions	I would be willing to use ChatGPT to receive product recommendations	.92
	The likelihood that I would use ChatGPT to receive product recommendations is very high	
	I would be willing to recommend ChatGPT to my friends	

(*continued*)

Table 3. *(continued)*

Variable	Items	α
Perceived Empathy	Think back to the recent interaction you observed with ChatGPT. Considering 'empathy' is the ability to understand and adequately respond to the feelings of another: How empathetic did ChatGPT seem to be towards the person it was having a conversation with on a scale from 0 to 10? Please rate from 'not empathetic at all' to 'extremely empathetic' Not empathetic at all (1)/Extremely empathetic (10)	
Experience with ChatGPT	How would you rate your experience with ChatGPT on a scale from 'Newbie' to 'Expert'? If you have never used ChatGPT before, you would be considered a Newbie. If you use ChatGPT all the time you would be considered an Expert Newbie (1)/Expert (5)	
Experience with Meditation	How would you rate your experience with meditation on a scale from 'Newbie' to 'Expert'? If you have never meditated before, you would be considered a Newbie. If you meditate all the time you would be considered an Expert Newbie (1)/Expert (5)	
Use of Meditation Apps	When you meditate, how often do you use an app to do so? Never (1)/Always (5)	

References

1. Bach, T.A., et al.: A systematic literature review of user trust in AI-enabled systems: an HCI perspective (2023). https://doi.org/10.48550/ARXIV.2304.08795
2. Baker, J., et al.: The influence of multiple store environment cues on perceived merchandise value and patronage intentions. J. Mark. **66**(2), 120–141 (2002). https://doi.org/10.1509/jmkg.66.2.120.18470
3. Bickmore, T.W., Picard, R.W.: Towards caring machines. In: CHI 2004 Extended Abstracts on Human Factors in Computing Systems, Vienna, Austria, pp. 1489–1492. ACM (2004). https://doi.org/10.1145/985921.986097
4. Brave, S., et al.: Computers that care: investigating the effects of orientation of emotion exhibited by an embodied computer agent. Int. J. Hum. Comput. Stud. **62**(2), 161–178 (2005). https://doi.org/10.1016/j.ijhcs.2004.11.002
5. Chi, N.T.K., Hoang Vu, N.: Investigating the customer trust in artificial intelligence: the role of anthropomorphism, empathy response, and interaction. CAAI Trans. Intell. Technol. **8**(1), 260–273 (2023). https://doi.org/10.1049/cit2.12133
6. Comer, L.B., Drollinger, T.: Active empathetic listening and selling success: a conceptual framework. J. Pers. Sell. Sales Manag. **19**(1), 15–29 (1999). https://doi.org/10.1080/08853134.1999.10754156
7. Davis, M.H.: Measuring individual differences in empathy: evidence for a multidimensional approach. J. Pers. Soc. Psychol. **44**(1), 113–126 (1983). https://doi.org/10.1037/0022-3514.44.1.113
8. Edele, A., et al.: Explaining altruistic sharing in the dictator game: the role of affective empathy, cognitive empathy, and justice sensitivity. Learn. Individ. Differ. **24**, 96–102 (2013). https://doi.org/10.1016/j.lindif.2012.12.020

9. El Hedhli, K., et al.: Stereotyping human-like virtual influencers in retailing: does warmth prevail over competence? J. Retail. Consum. Serv. **75**, 103459 (2023). https://doi.org/10.1016/j.jretconser.2023.103459
10. Fiske, S.T., et al.: Universal dimensions of social cognition: warmth and competence. Trends Cogn. Sci. **11**(2), 77–83 (2007). https://doi.org/10.1016/j.tics.2006.11.005
11. Fogg, B.J., Nass, C.: Silicon sycophants: the effects of computers that flatter. Int. J. Hum. Comput. Stud. **46**(5), 551–561 (1997). https://doi.org/10.1006/ijhc.1996.0104
12. Følstad, A., Nordheim, C.B., Bjørkli, C.A.: What makes users trust a chatbot for customer service? An exploratory interview study. In: Bodrunova, S. (ed.) INSCI 2018. LNCS, vol. 11193, pp. 194–208. Springer, Cham (2018). https://doi.org/10.1007/978-3-030-01437-7_16
13. Gefen, D.: Reflections on the dimensions of trust and trustworthiness among online consumers. ACM SIGMIS Database DATABASE Adv. Inf. Syst. **33**(3), 38–53 (2002). https://doi.org/10.1145/569905.569910
14. Gilad, Z., et al.: The effects of warmth and competence perceptions on users' choice of an AI system. In: Proceedings of the 2021 CHI Conference on Human Factors in Computing Systems, Yokohama, Japan, pp. 1–13. ACM (2021). https://doi.org/10.1145/3411764.3446863
15. Giorgi, I., et al.: Friendly but faulty: a pilot study on the perceived trust of older adults in a social robot. IEEE Access **10**, 92084–92096 (2022). https://doi.org/10.1109/ACCESS.2022.3202942
16. Glikson, E., Woolley, A.W.: Human trust in artificial intelligence: review of empirical research. Acad. Manag. Ann. **14**(2), 627–660 (2020). https://doi.org/10.5465/annals.2018.0057
17. Guan, C., et al.: Apparel recommendation system evolution: an empirical review. Int. J. Cloth. Sci. Technol. **28**(6), 854–879 (2016). https://doi.org/10.1108/IJCST-09-2015-0100
18. Güntürkün, P., et al.: Disentangling the differential roles of warmth and competence judgments in customer-service provider relationships. J. Serv. Res. **23**(4), 476–503 (2020). https://doi.org/10.1177/1094670520920354
19. Hayashi, Y., Wakabayashi, K.: Can AI become reliable source to support human decision making in a court scene? In: Companion of the 2017 ACM Conference on Computer Supported Cooperative Work and Social Computing, Portland, Oregon, USA, pp. 195–198. ACM (2017). https://doi.org/10.1145/3022198.3026338
20. Hayes, A.F.: Introduction to Mediation, Moderation, and Conditional Process Analysis: A Regression-Based Approach. Guilford Press, New York (2018)
21. Hinds, P., et al.: Whose job is it anyway? A study of human-robot interaction in a collaborative task. Hum. Comput. Interact. **19**(1), 151–181 (2004). https://doi.org/10.1207/s15327051hci1901&2_7
22. Hoff, K.A., Bashir, M.: Trust in automation: integrating empirical evidence on factors that influence trust. Hum. Factors J. Hum. Factors Ergon. Soc. **57**(3), 407–434 (2015). https://doi.org/10.1177/0018720814547570
23. Ilves, M., Surakka, V., Vanhala, T.: The effects of emotionally worded synthesized speech on the ratings of emotions and voice quality. In: D'Mello, S., Graesser, A., Schuller, B., Martin, J.C. (eds.) ACII 2011. LNCS, vol. 6974, pp. 588–598. Springer, Heidelberg (2011). https://doi.org/10.1007/978-3-642-24600-5_62
24. Infanger, M., Sczesny, S.: Communion-over-agency effects on advertising effectiveness. Int. J. Advert. **34**(2), 285–306 (2015). https://doi.org/10.1080/02650487.2014.993794
25. Ischen, C., Araujo, T., Voorveld, H., van Noort, G., Smit, E.: Privacy concerns in chatbot interactions. In: Følstad, A., et al. (eds.) Chatbot Research and Design. CONVERSATIONS 2019. LNCS, vol. 11970, pp. 34–48. Springer, Cham (2020). https://doi.org/10.1007/978-3-030-39540-7_3

26. Jan, I.U., et al.: What (de) motivates customers to use AI-powered conversational agents for shopping? The extended behavioral reasoning perspective. J. Retail. Consum. Serv. **75**, 103440 (2023). https://doi.org/10.1016/j.jretconser.2023.103440
27. Johnson, D., Grayson, K.: Cognitive and affective trust in service relationships. J. Bus. Res. **58**(4), 500–507 (2005). https://doi.org/10.1016/S0148-2963(03)00140-1
28. Kantsperger, R., Kunz, W.H.: Consumer trust in service companies: a multiple mediating analysis. Manag. Serv. Qual. Int. J. **20**(1), 4–25 (2010). https://doi.org/10.1108/09604521011011603
29. Kaul, S., et al.: Impact of initial-trust-image on shopper trust and patronage intentions: a study of young, male apparel shoppers in India. Int. J. Retail Distrib. Manag. **38**(4), 275–296 (2010). https://doi.org/10.1108/09590551011032090
30. Kim, J., et al.: Decisions with ChatGPT: reexamining choice overload in ChatGPT recommendations. J. Retail. Consum. Serv. **75**, 103494 (2023). https://doi.org/10.1016/j.jretconser.2023.103494
31. Komiak, Benbasat: The effects of personalization and familiarity on trust and adoption of recommendation agents. MIS Q. **30**(4), 941 (2006). https://doi.org/10.2307/25148760
32. Kundinger, T., et al.: (Over)Trust in automated driving: the sleeping pill of tomorrow? In: Extended Abstracts of the 2019 CHI Conference on Human Factors in Computing Systems, Glasgow, Scotland, UK, pp. 1–6. ACM (2019). https://doi.org/10.1145/3290607.3312869
33. Lee, J.D., See, K.A.: Trust in automation: designing for appropriate reliance. Hum. Factors J. Hum. Factors Ergon. Soc. **46**(1), 50–80 (2004). https://doi.org/10.1518/hfes.46.1.50_30392
34. Lee, J.J., et al.: Computationally modeling interpersonal trust. Front. Psychol. **4** (2013). https://doi.org/10.3389/fpsyg.2013.00893
35. Leite, I., et al.: The influence of empathy in human–robot relations. Int. J. Hum. Comput. Stud. **71**(3), 250–260 (2013). https://doi.org/10.1016/j.ijhcs.2012.09.005
36. Lewis, J.D., Weigert, A.: Trust as a social reality. Soc. Forces **63**(4), 967 (1985). https://doi.org/10.2307/2578601
37. Liu, B., Sundar, S.S.: Should machines express sympathy and empathy? Experiments with a health advice chatbot. Cyberpsychol. Behav. Soc. Netw. **21**(10), 625–636 (2018). https://doi.org/10.1089/cyber.2018.0110
38. Lombard, M., Xu, K.: Social responses to media technologies in the 21st century: the media are social actors paradigm. Hum. Mach. Commun. **2**, 29–55 (2021). https://doi.org/10.30658/hmc.2.2
39. Mari, A., et al.: Shopping with voice assistants: how empathy affects individual and family decision-making outcomes (2023). https://doi.org/10.5167/UZH-230473
40. Mariani, M.M., et al.: AI in marketing, consumer research and psychology: a systematic literature review and research agenda. Psychol. Mark. **39**(4), 755–776 (2022). https://doi.org/10.1002/mar.21619
41. Mayer, R.C., Davis, J.H.: The effect of the performance appraisal system on trust for management: a field quasi-experiment. J. Appl. Psychol. **84**(1), 123–136 (1999). https://doi.org/10.1037/0021-9010.84.1.123
42. Melumad, S., et al.: Technology-augmented choice: how digital innovations are transforming consumer decision Processes. Cust. Needs Solut. **7**(3–4), 90–101 (2020). https://doi.org/10.1007/s40547-020-00107-4
43. Moon, Y.: Intimate exchanges: using computers to elicit self-disclosure from consumers. J. Consum. Res. **26**(4), 323–339 (2000). https://doi.org/10.1086/209566
44. Morrow, J.L., et al.: The cognitive and affective antecedents of general trust within cooperative organizations. J. Manag. Issues **16**(1), 48–64 (2004)
45. Nass, C., Moon, Y.: Machines and mindlessness: social responses to computers. J. Soc. Issues **56**(1), 81–103 (2000). https://doi.org/10.1111/0022-4537.00153

46. Paiva, A., et al.: Empathy in virtual agents and robots: a survey. ACM Trans. Interact. Intell. Syst. **7**(3), 1–40 (2017). https://doi.org/10.1145/2912150
47. Park, G., et al.: Effect of AI chatbot empathy and identity disclosure on willingness to donate: the mediation of humanness and social presence. Behav. Inf. Technol. **42**(12), 1998–2010 (2023). https://doi.org/10.1080/0144929X.2022.2105746
48. Phalet, K., Poppe, E.: Competence and morality dimensions of national and ethnic stereotypes: a study in six eastern-European countries. Eur. J. Soc. Psychol. **27**(6), 703–723 (1997). https://doi.org/10.1002/(SICI)1099-0992(199711/12)27:6%3c703::AID-EJSP841%3e3.0.CO;2-K
49. Ramsey, R.P., Sohi, R.S.: Listening to your customers: the impact of perceived salesperson listening behavior on relationship outcomes. J. Acad. Mark. Sci. **25**(2), 127–137 (1997). https://doi.org/10.1007/BF02894348
50. Reeves, B., Nass, C.I.: The Media Equation: How People Treat Computers, Television, and New Media Like Real People And Places. CSLI Publications , Cambridge University Press, Stanford, Calif., New York (1996)
51. Reis, H.T., et al.: Toward understanding understanding: the importance of feeling understood in relationships. Soc. Personal. Psychol. Compass **11**(3), e12308 (2017). https://doi.org/10.1111/spc3.12308
52. Rheu, M., et al.: Systematic review: trust-building factors and implications for conversational agent design. Int. J. Hum. Comput. Interact. **37**(1), 81–96 (2021). https://doi.org/10.1080/10447318.2020.1807710
53. Riegelsberger, J., et al.: The mechanics of trust: a framework for research and design. Int. J. Hum. Comput. Stud. **62**(3), 381–422 (2005). https://doi.org/10.1016/j.ijhcs.2005.01.001
54. Rousseau, D.M., et al.: Not so different after all: a cross-discipline view of trust. Acad. Manag. Rev. **23**(3), 393–404 (1998). https://doi.org/10.5465/amr.1998.926617
55. Ruan, Y., Mezei, J.: When do AI chatbots lead to higher customer satisfaction than human frontline employees in online shopping assistance? Considering product attribute type. J. Retail. Consum. Serv. **68**, 103059 (2022). https://doi.org/10.1016/j.jretconser.2022.103059
56. Ruane, E., Farrell, S., Ventresque, A.: User perception of text-based chatbot personality. In: Følstad, A., et al. (eds.) Chatbot Research and Design. CONVERSATIONS 2020. LNCS, vol. 12604, pp. 32–47. Springer, Cham (2021). https://doi.org/10.1007/978-3-030-68288-0_3
57. Salem, M., et al.: Would you trust a (faulty) robot?: effects of error, task type and personality on human-robot cooperation and trust. In: Proceedings of the Tenth Annual ACM/IEEE International Conference on Human-Robot Interaction, Portland, Oregon, USA, pp. 141–148. ACM (2015). https://doi.org/10.1145/2696454.2696497
58. Scheunemann, M.M., et al.: Warmth and competence to predict human preference of robot behavior in physical human-robot interaction. In: 2020 29th IEEE International Conference on Robot and Human Interactive Communication (RO-MAN), Naples, Italy, pp. 1340–1347. IEEE (2020). https://doi.org/10.1109/RO-MAN47096.2020.9223478
59. Schoemann, A.M., et al.: Determining power and sample size for simple and complex mediation models. Soc. Psychol. Personal. Sci. **8**(4), 379–386 (2017). https://doi.org/10.1177/1948550617715068
60. Spatola, N., Wudarczyk, O.A.: Ascribing emotions to robots: explicit and implicit attribution of emotions and perceived robot anthropomorphism. Comput. Hum. Behav. **124**, 106934 (2021). https://doi.org/10.1016/j.chb.2021.106934
61. Sundar, S.S., Kim, J.: Machine heuristic: when we trust computers more than humans with our personal information. In: Proceedings of the 2019 CHI Conference on Human Factors in Computing Systems, Glasgow, Scotland, UK, pp. 1–9. ACM (2019). https://doi.org/10.1145/3290605.3300768
62. Sundar, S.S., Nass, C.: Source orientation in human-computer interaction: programmer, networker, or independent social actor. Commun. Res. **27**(6), 683–703 (2000). https://doi.org/10.1177/009365000027006001

63. Tavakol, M., Dennick, R.: Making sense of Cronbach's alpha. Int. J. Med. Educ. **2**, 53–55 (2011). https://doi.org/10.5116/ijme.4dfb.8dfd
64. Van Den Broeck, E., et al.: Chatbot advertising effectiveness: when does the message get through? Comput. Hum. Behav. **98**, 150–157 (2019). https://doi.org/10.1016/j.chb.2019.04.009
65. Vieten, C., et al.: Measures of empathy and compassion: a scoping review. PLoS ONE **19**(1), e0297099 (2024). https://doi.org/10.1371/journal.pone.0297099
66. Wang, B., Theune, M., Srivastava, S.: Examining lexical alignment in human-agent conversations with GPT-3.5 and GPT-4 models. In: Følstad, A., et al. (eds.) CONVERSATIONS 2023. LNCS, vol. 14524, pp. 94–114. Springer, Cham (2024). https://doi.org/10.1007/978-3-031-54975-5_6
67. Wang, J., et al.: Elements of information ecosystems stimulating the online consumer behavior: a mediating role of cognitive and affective trust. Telemat. Inform. **80**, 101970 (2023). https://doi.org/10.1016/j.tele.2023.101970
68. Wang, L.C., et al.: Can a retail web site be social? J. Mark. **71**(3), 143–157 (2007). https://doi.org/10.1509/jmkg.71.3.143
69. World Medical Association Declaration of Helsinki: Ethical Principles for Medical Research Involving Human Subjects. JAMA **310**(20), 2191 (2013). https://doi.org/10.1001/jama.2013.281053
70. Ybarra, O., et al.: Life's recurring challenges and the fundamental dimensions: an integration and its implications for cultural differences and similarities. Eur. J. Soc. Psychol. **38**(7), 1083–1092 (2008). https://doi.org/10.1002/ejsp.559
71. Yeung, W.L.: Rethinking the response intents of customer service agents for the modelling of empathic dialogues. Presented at the Conversations 2023: The 7th International Workshop on Chatbot Research, Applications, and Design (2023)
72. Zheng, T., Duan, X., Zhang, K., Yang, X., Jiang, Y.: How chatbots' anthropomorphism affects user satisfaction: the mediating role of perceived warmth and competence. In: Tu, Y., Chi, M. (eds.) WHICEB 2023. LNBIP, vol. 481, pp. 96–107. Springer, Cham (2023). https://doi.org/10.1007/978-3-031-32302-7_9

Author Index

A
Abhyankar, Sonia 200
Anagnostopoulou, Evangelia 87
Apostolou, Dimitris 87
Arvola, Mattias 132

B
Bi, Yaxin 96
Bosse, Tibor 112
Boumans, Roel 112, 181
Braggaar, Anouck 3
Brailas, Alexios 150
Bylund, Anna Martín 132

C
Chilufya, Emma Mainza 132

D
Dieing, Thilo I. 161

F
Følstad, Asbjørn 217

G
Gaedke, Martin 200
Garrido, Alejandra 200
Gerritsen, Debby 112
Grammatikos, Nikolaos Antonios 87
Grigera, Julián 200

H
Hanschmann, Leon 48
Heil, Sebastian 200

I
Ischen, Carolin 234

J
Jainta, Marcus 33

K
Kunneman, Florian 3
Kvale, Knut 217

L
Larsen, Anna Grøndahl 217
Law, Effie Lai-Chong 66

M
Maedche, Alexander 33, 48
McTear, Michael 96
Mentzas, Gregoris 87
Mokelke, Marvin 48
Mortazavi, Arezou 132

O
Olawore, Kabir 96

P
Pralat, Nele 234

R
Rapp, Simon 33

A. Følstad et al. (Eds.): CONVERSATIONS 2024, LNCS 15545, pp. 261–262, 2025.
https://doi.org/10.1007/978-3-031-88045-2

S
Severinsson, Susanne 132
Siby, Jeffin 66
Skjuve, Marita 217
Stenliden, Linnéa 132

T
Thill, Serge 112
Traubinger, Verena 200
Tsolakis, Lazaros 150

V
van Miltenburg, Emiel 3
van Zanten, Nina 181
Voorveld, Hilde 234

Y
Yeung, W. L. 23

Z
Ziemke, Tom 132

The manufacturer's authorised representative in the EU is Springer Nature Customer Service Centre GmbH, Europaplatz 3, 69115 Heidelberg, Germany. If you have any concerns regarding our products, please contact ProductSafety@springernature.com

Printed and bound by CPI Group (UK) Ltd, Croydon, CR0 4YY
30/09/2026
02225566-0011